MARS

ALSO AVAILABLE FROM **TOKYOPOP**®

MANGA

*INDICATES 100% AUTHENTIC MANGA (RIGHT-TO-LEFT FORMAT)

ANGELIC LAYER*
BABY BIRTH* (September 2003)
BATTLE ROYALE*
BRAIN POWERD* (June 2003)
BRIGADOON* (August 2003)
CARDCAPTOR SAKURA
CARDCAPTOR SAKURA: MASTER OF THE CLOW*
CLAMP SCHOOL DETECTIVES*
CHOBITS*
CHRONICLES OF THE CURSED SWORD (July 2003)
CLOVER
CONFIDENTIAL CONFESSIONS* (July 2003)
CORRECTOR YUI
COWBOY BEBOP*
COWBOY BEBOP: SHOOTING STAR* (June 2003)
DEMON DIARY (May 2003)
DIGIMON
DRAGON HUNTER (June 2003)
DRAGON KNIGHTS*
DUKLYON: CLAMP SCHOOL DEFENDERS* (September 2003)
ERICA SAKURAZAWA* (May 2003)
ESCAFLOWNE* (July 2003)
FAKE*(May 2003)
FLCL* (September 2003)
FORBIDDEN DANCE* (August 2003)
GATE KEEPERS*
G-GUNDAM* (June 2003)
GRAVITATION* (June 2003)
GTO*
GUNDAM WING
GUNDAM WING: ENDLESS WALTZ*
GUNDAM: THE LAST OUTPOST*
HAPPY MANIA*
HARLEM BEAT
INITIAL D*
I.N.V.U.
ISLAND
JING: KING OF BANDITS* (June 2003)
JULINE
KARE KANO*
KINDAICHI CASE FILES* (June 2003)
KING OF HELL (June 2003)

KODOCHA*
LOVE HINA*
LUPIN III*
MAGIC KNIGHT RAYEARTH* (August 2003)
MAGIC KNIGHT RAYEARTH II* (COMING SOON)
MAN OF MANY FACES* (May 2003)
MARMALADE BOY*
MARS*
MIRACLE GIRLS
MIYUKI-CHAN IN WONDERLAND* (October 2003)
MONSTERS, INC.
NIEA_7* (August 2003)
PARADISE KISS*
PARASYTE
PEACH GIRL
PEACH GIRL: CHANGE OF HEART*
PET SHOP OF HORRORS* (June 2003)
PLANET LADDER
PLANETS* (October 2003)
PRIEST
RAGNAROK
RAVE MASTER*
REAL BOUT HIGH SCHOOL*
REALITY CHECK
REBIRTH
REBOUND*
SABER MARIONETTE J* (July 2003)
SAILOR MOON
SAINT TAIL
SAMURAI DEEPER KYO* (June 2003)
SCRYED*
SHAOLIN SISTERS*
SHIRAHIME-SYO* (December 2003)
THE SKULL MAN*
SORCERER HUNTERS
TOKYO MEW MEW*
UNDER THE GLASS MOON (June 2003)
VAMPIRE GAME* (June 2003)
WILD ACT* (July 2003)
WISH*
X-DAY* (August 2003)
ZODIAC P.I.* (July 2003)

CINE-MANGA™

AKIRA*
CARDCAPTORS
JIMMY NEUTRON (COMING SOON)
KIM POSSIBLE
LIZZIE McGUIRE
SPONGEBOB SQUAREPANTS (COMING SOON)
SPY KIDS 2

NOVELS

SAILOR MOON
KARMA CLUB (COMING SOON)

TOKYOPOP KIDS

STRAY SHEEP (September 2003)

ART BOOKS

CARDCAPTOR SAKURA*
MAGIC KNIGHT RAYEARTH*

ANIME GUIDES

GUNDAM TECHNICAL MANUALS
COWBOY BEBOP
SAILOR MOON SCOUT GUIDES

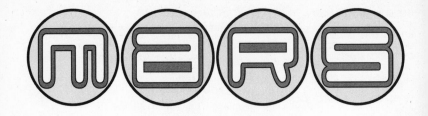

Volume 10
By Fuyumi Soryo

LOS ANGELES • TOKYO

Translator - Shirley Kubo
English Adaption - Elizabeth Hurchalla
Contributing Editor - Jodi Bryson
Retouch and Lettering - Joy Cha
Cover Layout - Anna Kernbaum

Editor - Julie Taylor
Managing Editor - Jill Freshney
Production Coordinator - Antonio DePietro
Production Manager - Jennifer Miller
Art Director - Matthew Alford
Director of Editorial - Jeremy Ross
VP of Production & Manufacturing - Ron Klamert
President & C.O.O. - John Parker
Publisher & C.E.O. - Stuart Levy

Email: editor@TOKYOPOP.com
Come visit us online at www.TOKYOPOP.com

A ⊙ TOKYOPOP® Manga

TOKYOPOP® is an imprint of Mixx Entertainment, Inc.
5900 Wilshire Blvd. Suite 2000, Los Angeles, CA 90036

ISBN: 1-59182-129-0

First TOKYOPOP® printing: May 2003

10 9 8 7 6 5 4 3 2 1

Printed in the USA

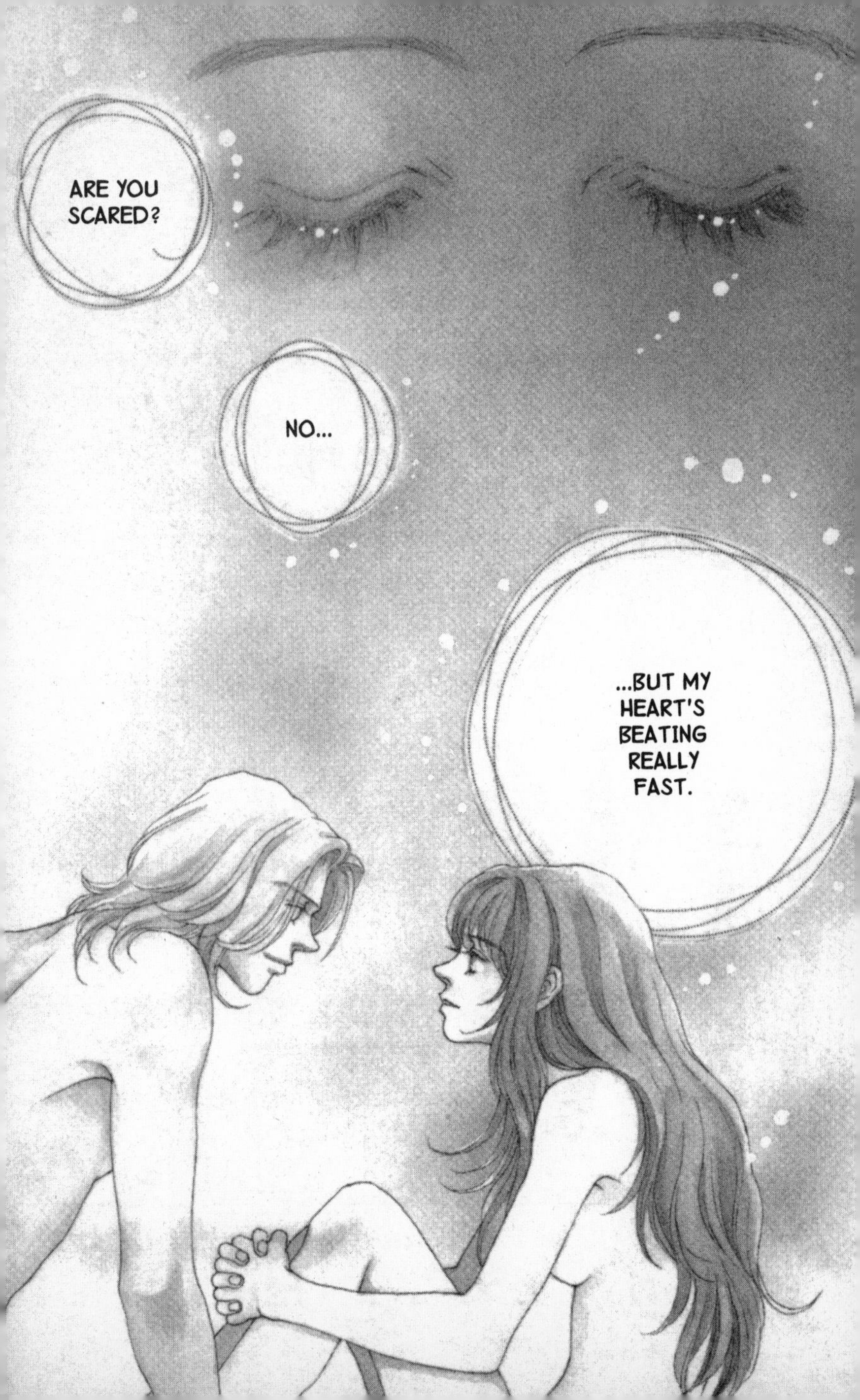
ARE YOU SCARED?
NO...
...BUT MY HEART'S BEATING REALLY FAST.

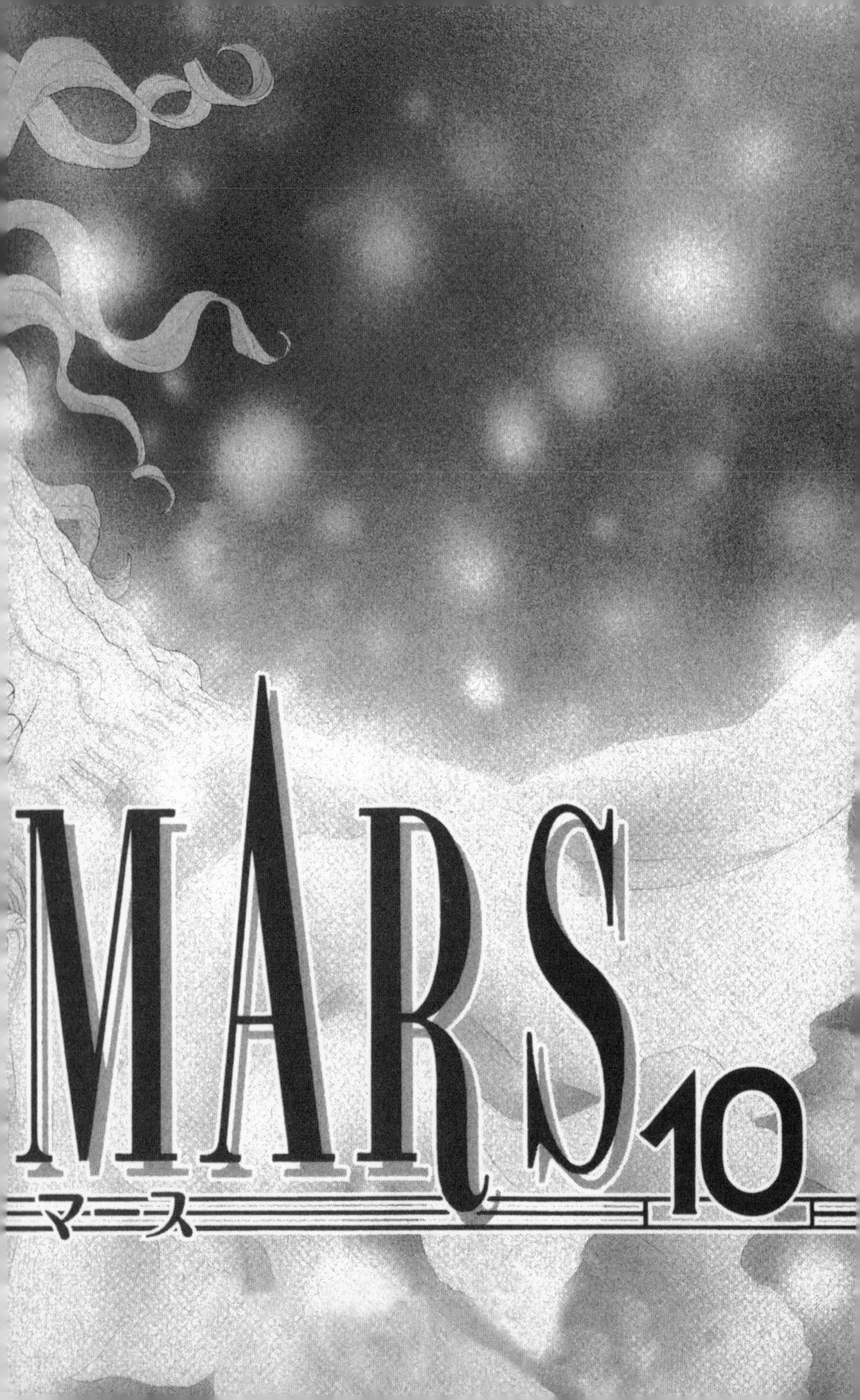
MARS
マース
10

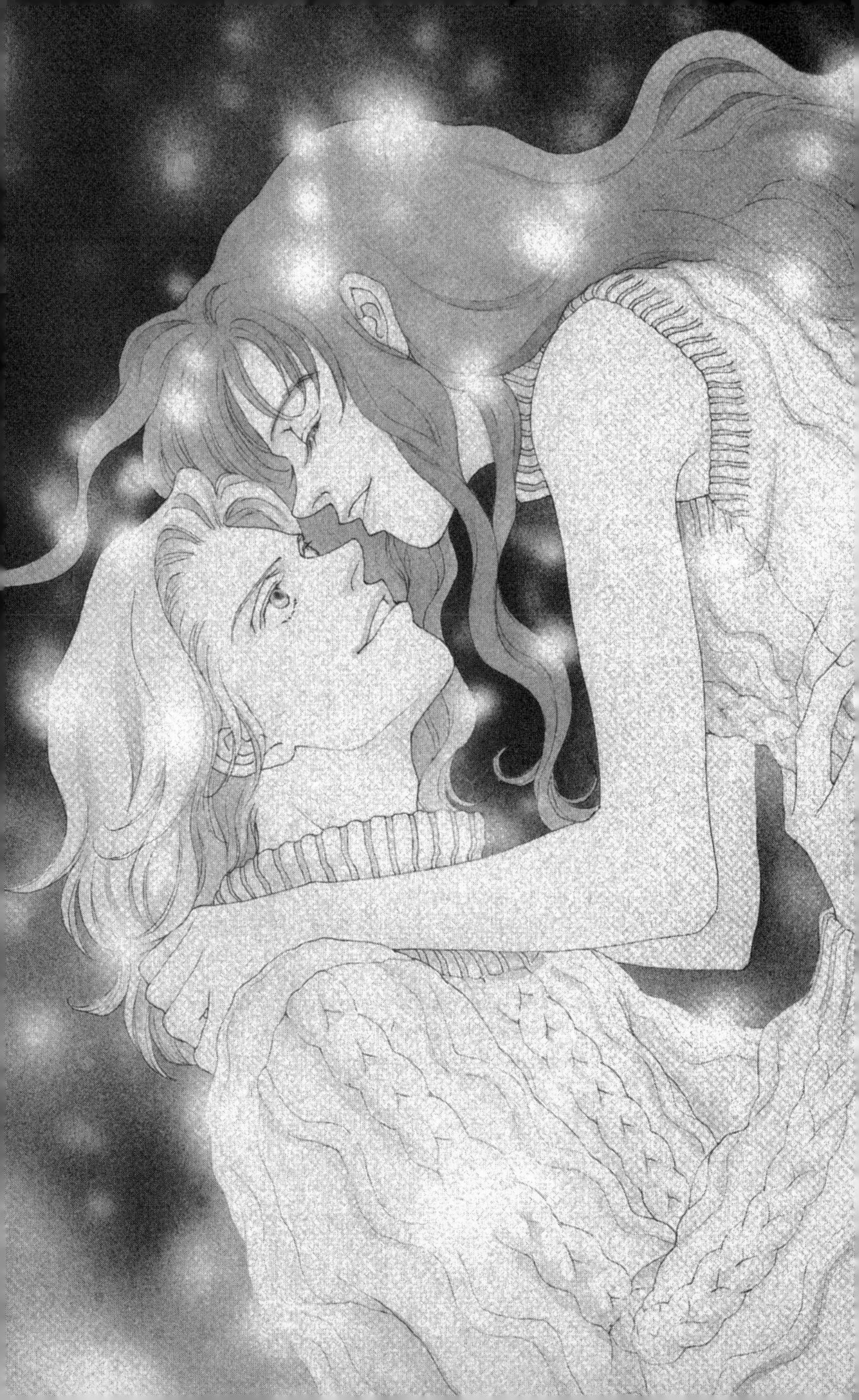

MARS

レジエンド オブ マース

LEGEND OF MARS

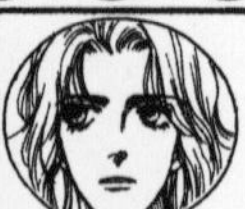

REI KASHINO: A HIGH SCHOOL STUDENT WHO RACES MOTORCYCLES AND LIKES KIRA'S PAINTINGS. HIS TWIN BROTHER SEI IS DEAD.

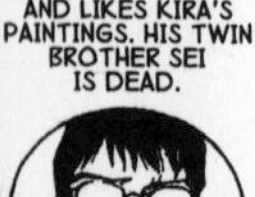

KIRA'S STEPFATHER: HE'S THE MAN WHO RAPED KIRA. HE'S NOW IN THE HOSPITAL WITH INJURIES.

THE STORY UNTIL NOW:

KIRA FALLS FOR REI WHEN SHE SPOTS HIM KISSING A STATUE OF MARS IN THE ART STUDIO. THEY BEGIN DATING, AND SOON THEY START GOING OUT. WHEN KIRA AND HER MOM MOVE BACK IN WITH THE MAN WHO RAPED KIRA IN JUNIOR HIGH, REI AND KIRA'S RELATIONSHIP IS TORN APART. HOWEVER, THEY SOON FIND THEY CAN'T STAY AWAY FROM EACH OTHER AND GET BACK TOGETHER. WHEN KIRA'S STEPFATHER STARTS GRILLING HER ABOUT HER RELATIONSHIP WITH REI, SHE HAS FLASHBACKS OF HER HORRIBLE PAST AND FEELS SUCH HATRED TOWARD HER STEPFATHER THAT SHE ENDS UP SERIOUSLY INJURING HIM. SHE RUNS AWAY FROM HOME AND MOVES IN WITH REI...AND DECIDES TO OFFER ALL OF HERSELF TO HIM. THEIR SOULS HAVE BECOME ONE...

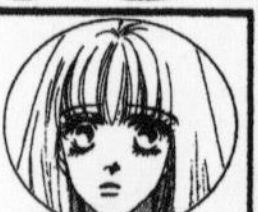

KIRA ASO: REI'S GIRLFRIEND. SHE JUST MOVED IN WITH HIM. HER STEPFATHER RAPED HER IN JUNIOR HIGH.

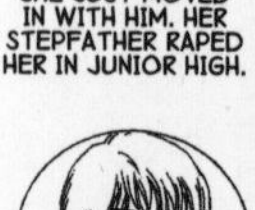

TATSUYA: REI'S FRIEND. HE'S WORRIED ABOUT REI AND KIRA'S RELATIONSHIP.

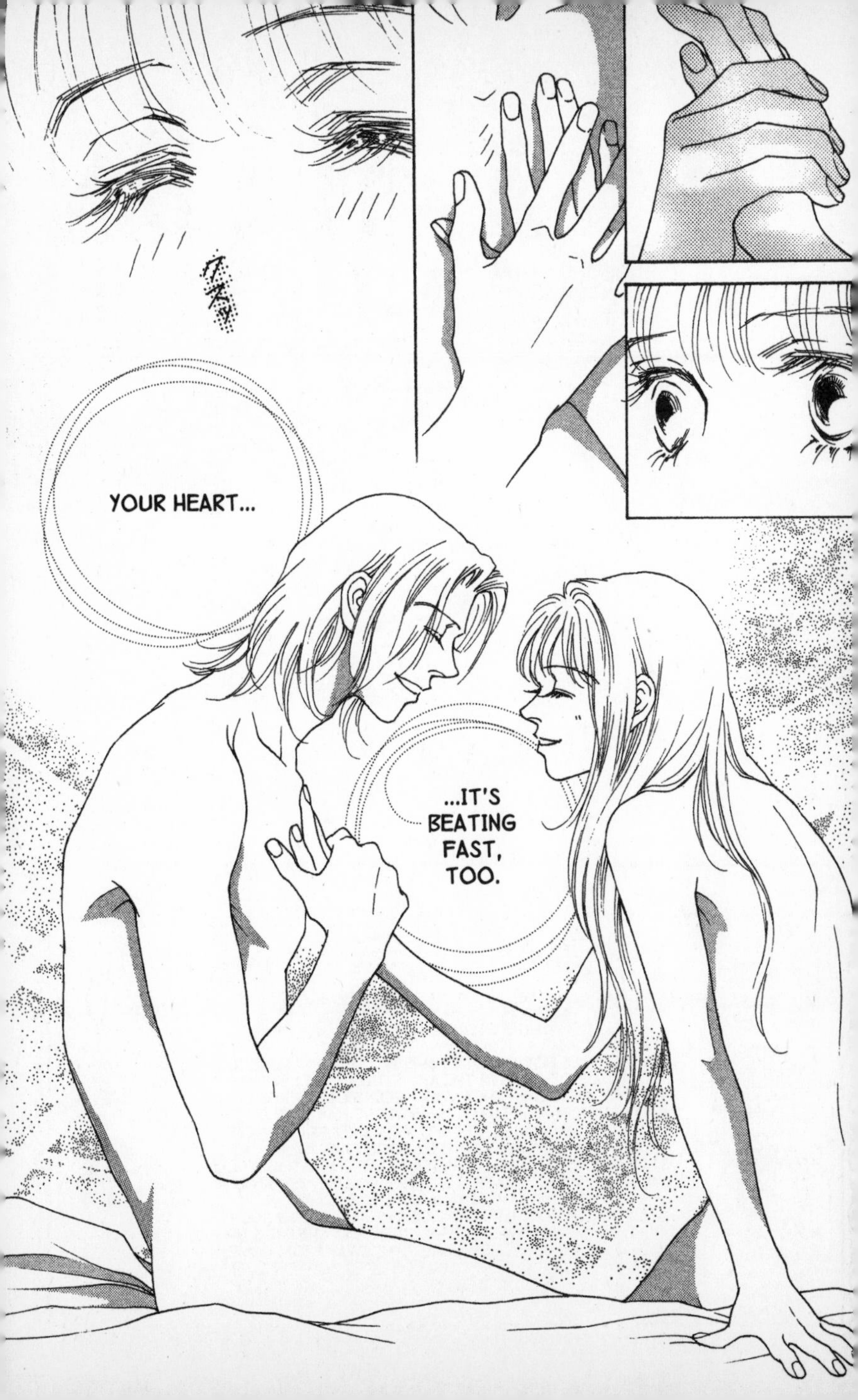
クスッ
YOUR HEART...
...IT'S BEATING FAST, TOO.

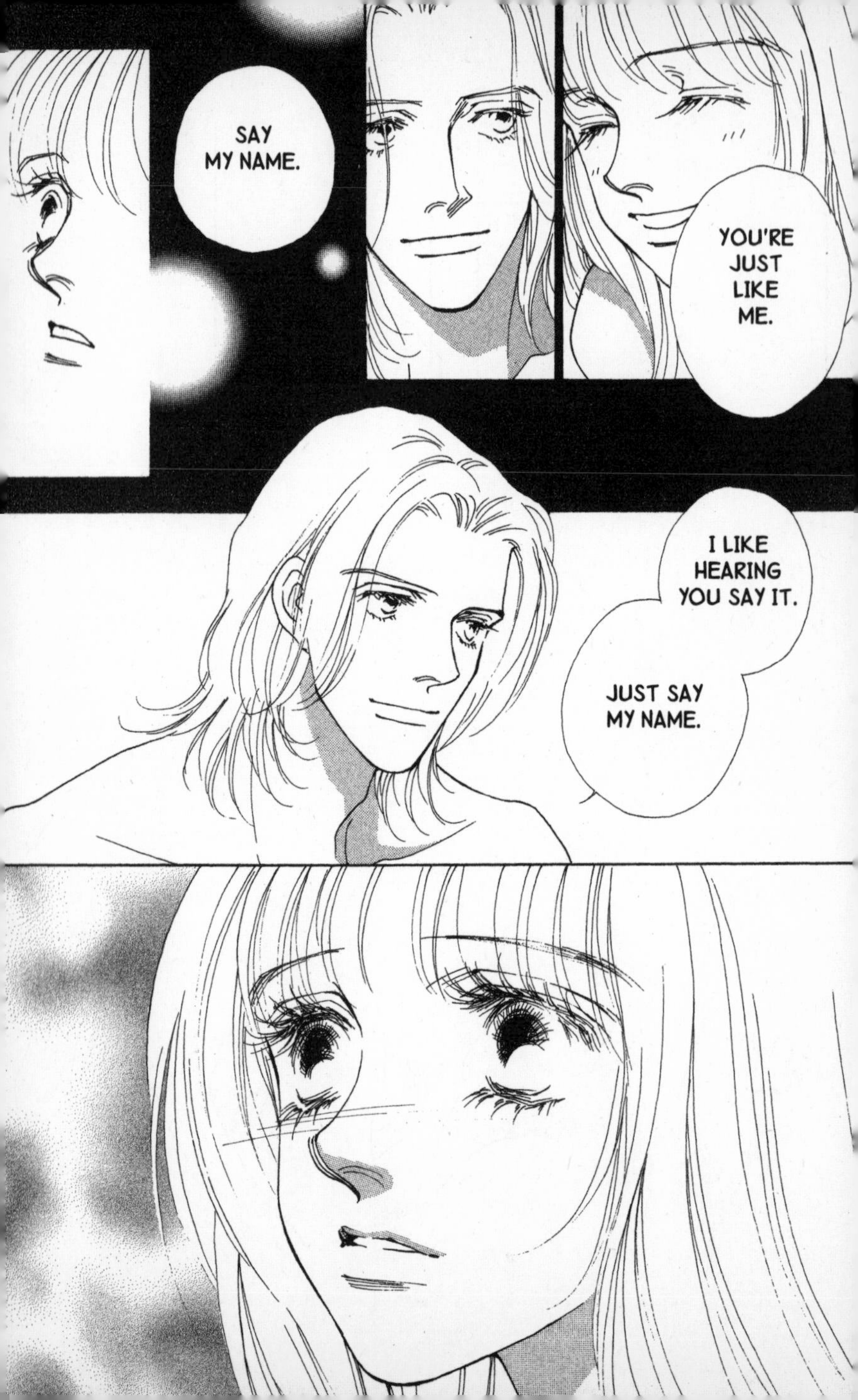
YOU'RE JUST LIKE ME.
SAY MY NAME.
I LIKE HEARING YOU SAY IT.
JUST SAY MY NAME.

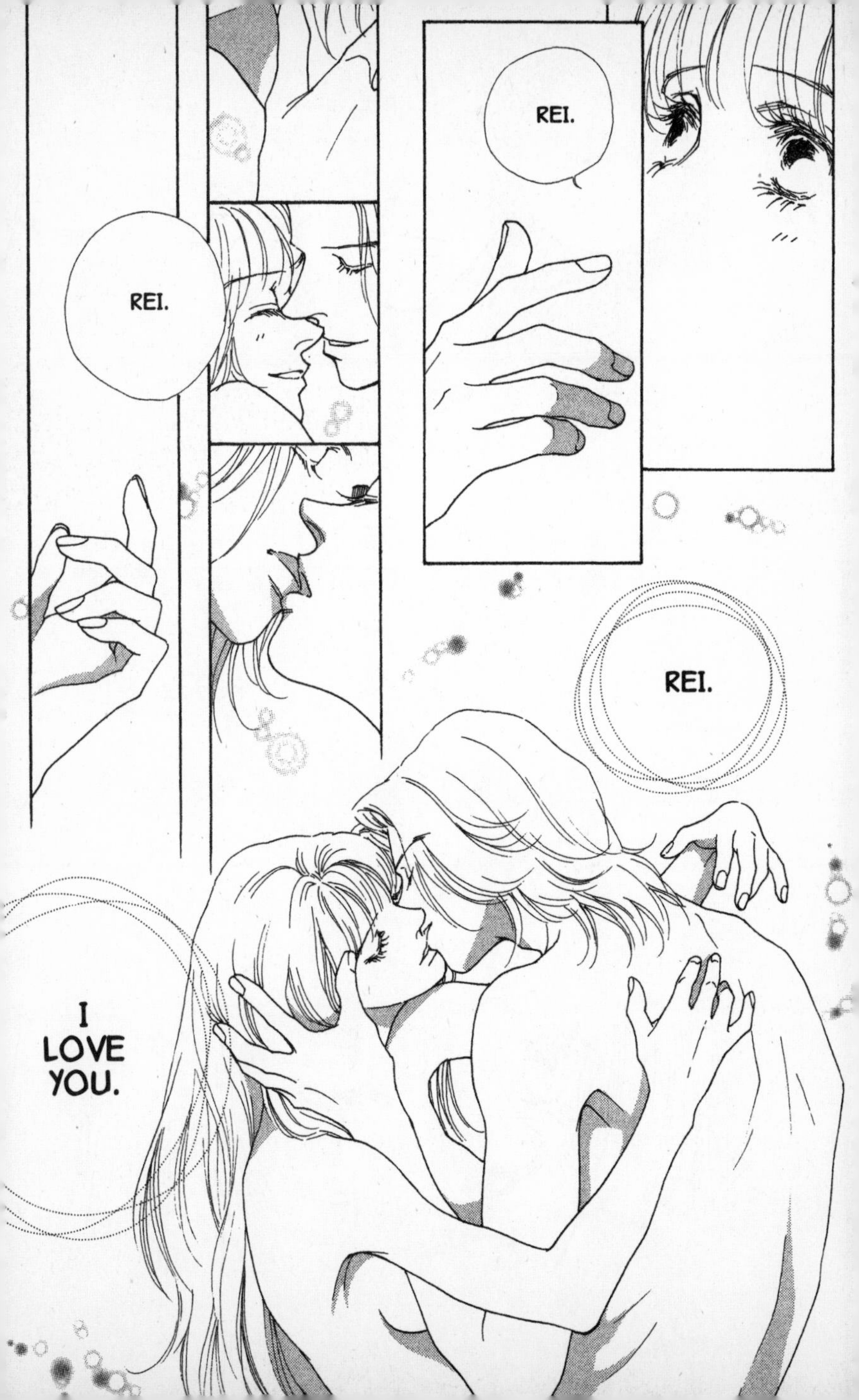
REI.
REI.
REI.
I LOVE YOU.

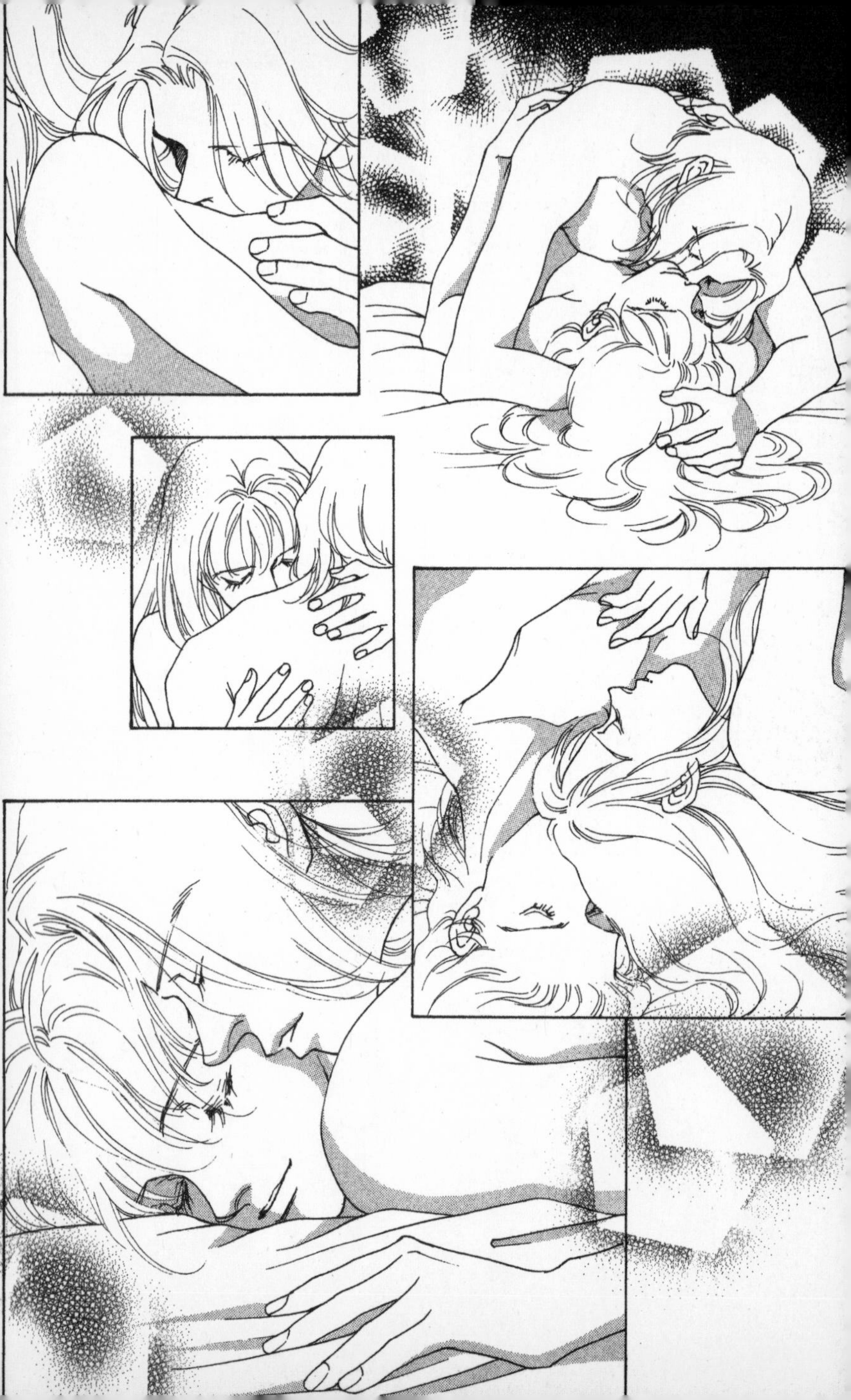

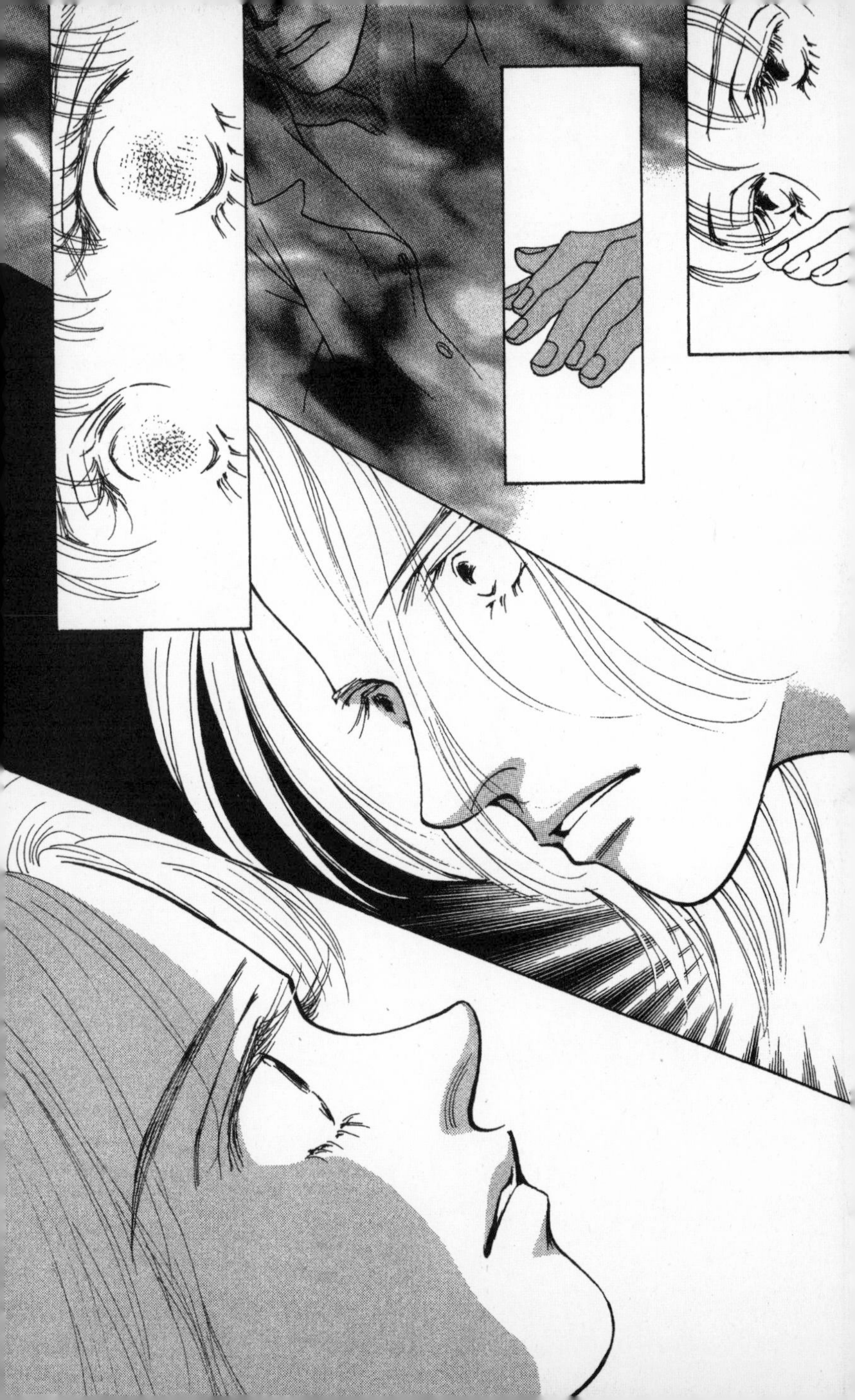

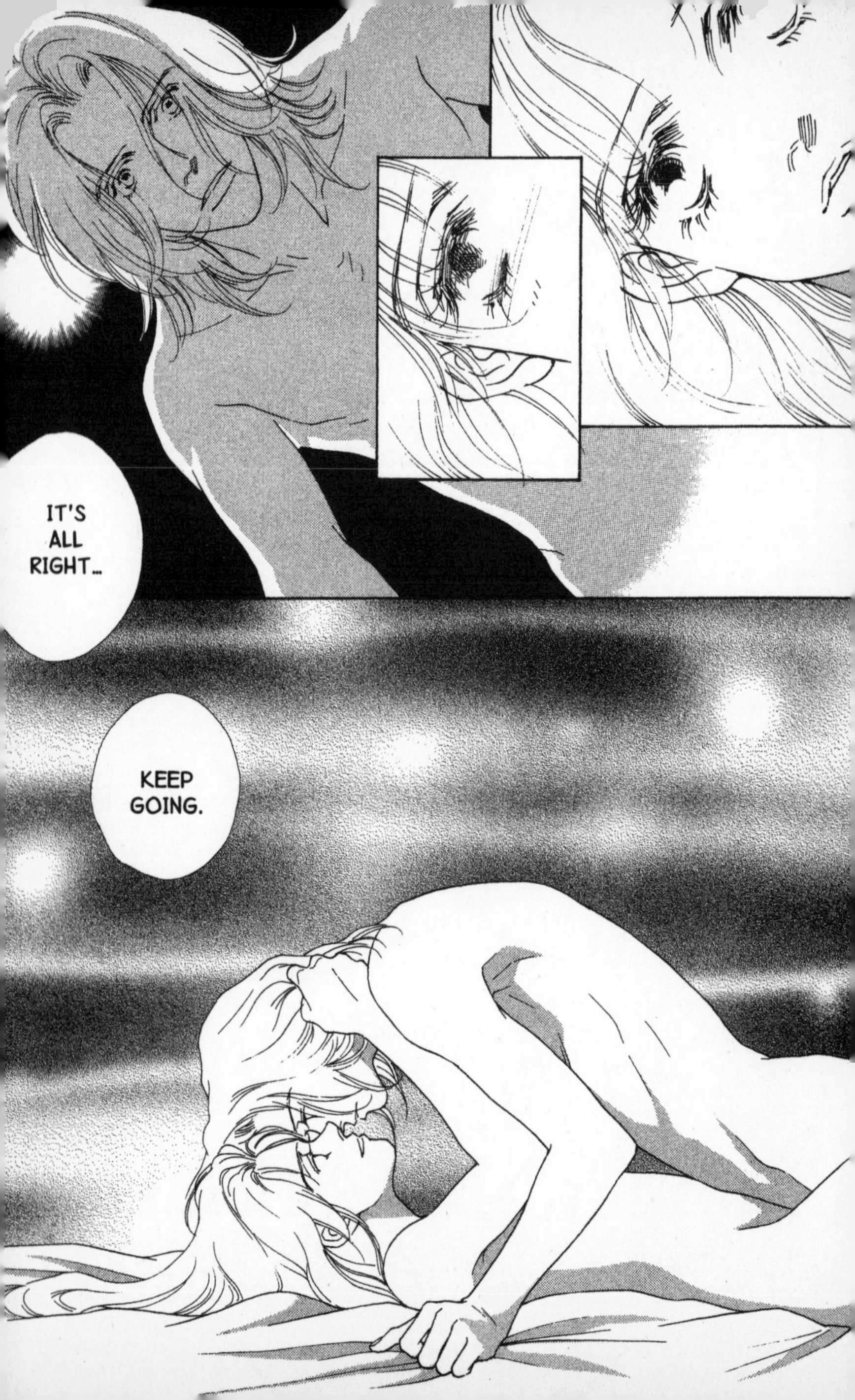
IT'S ALL RIGHT...
KEEP GOING.

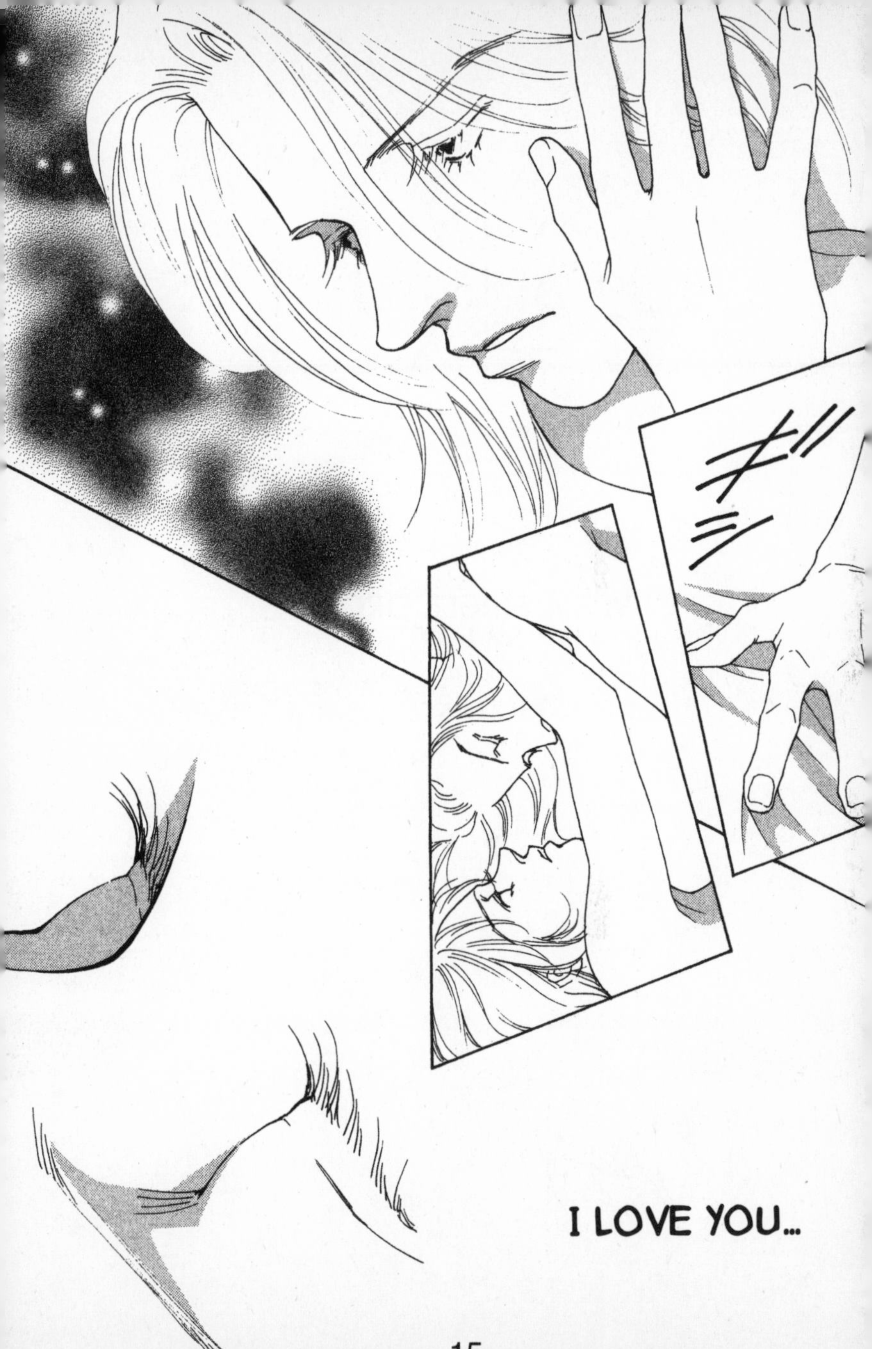
ギシ
I LOVE YOU...

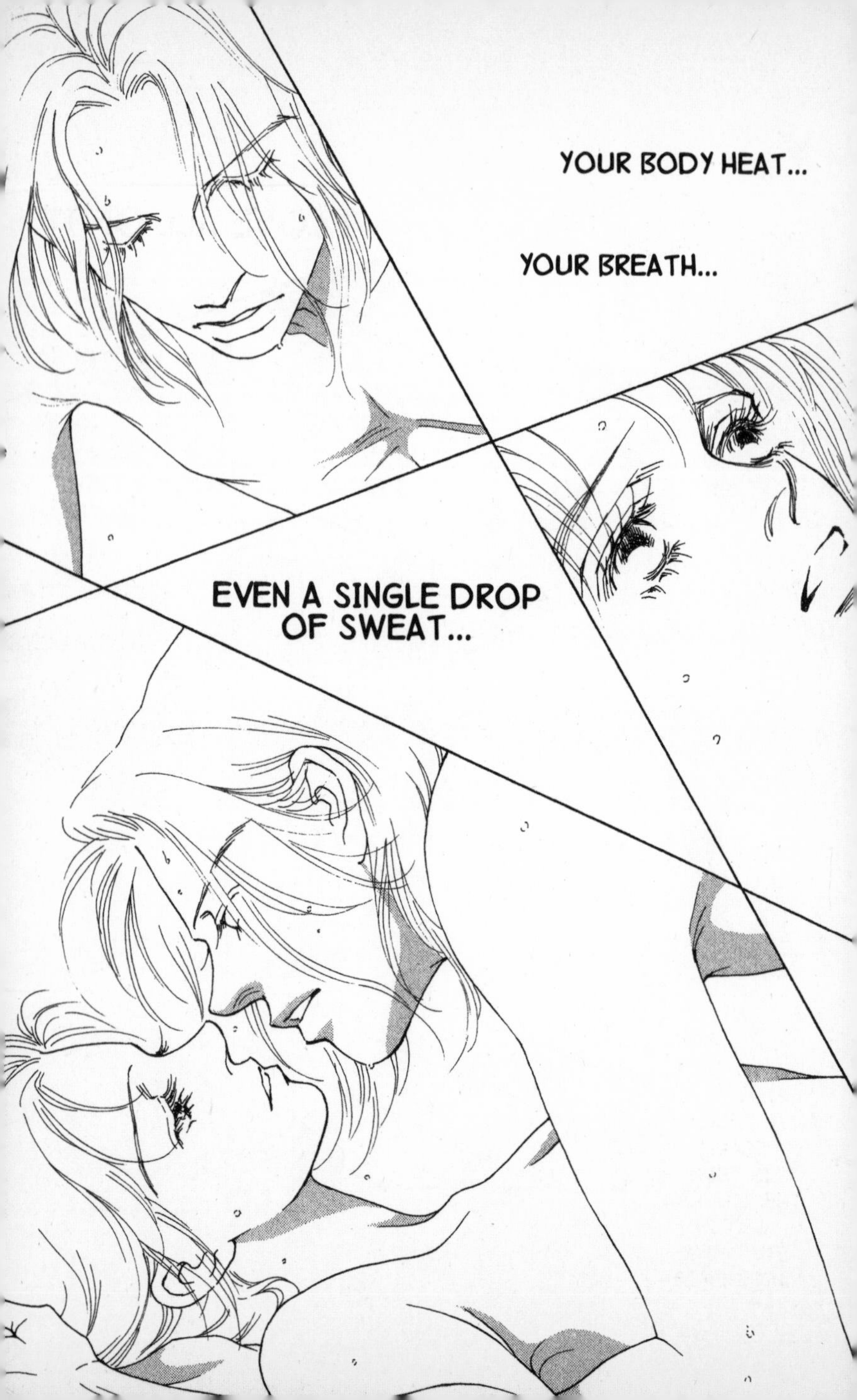
YOUR BODY HEAT...
YOUR BREATH...
EVEN A SINGLE DROP OF SWEAT...

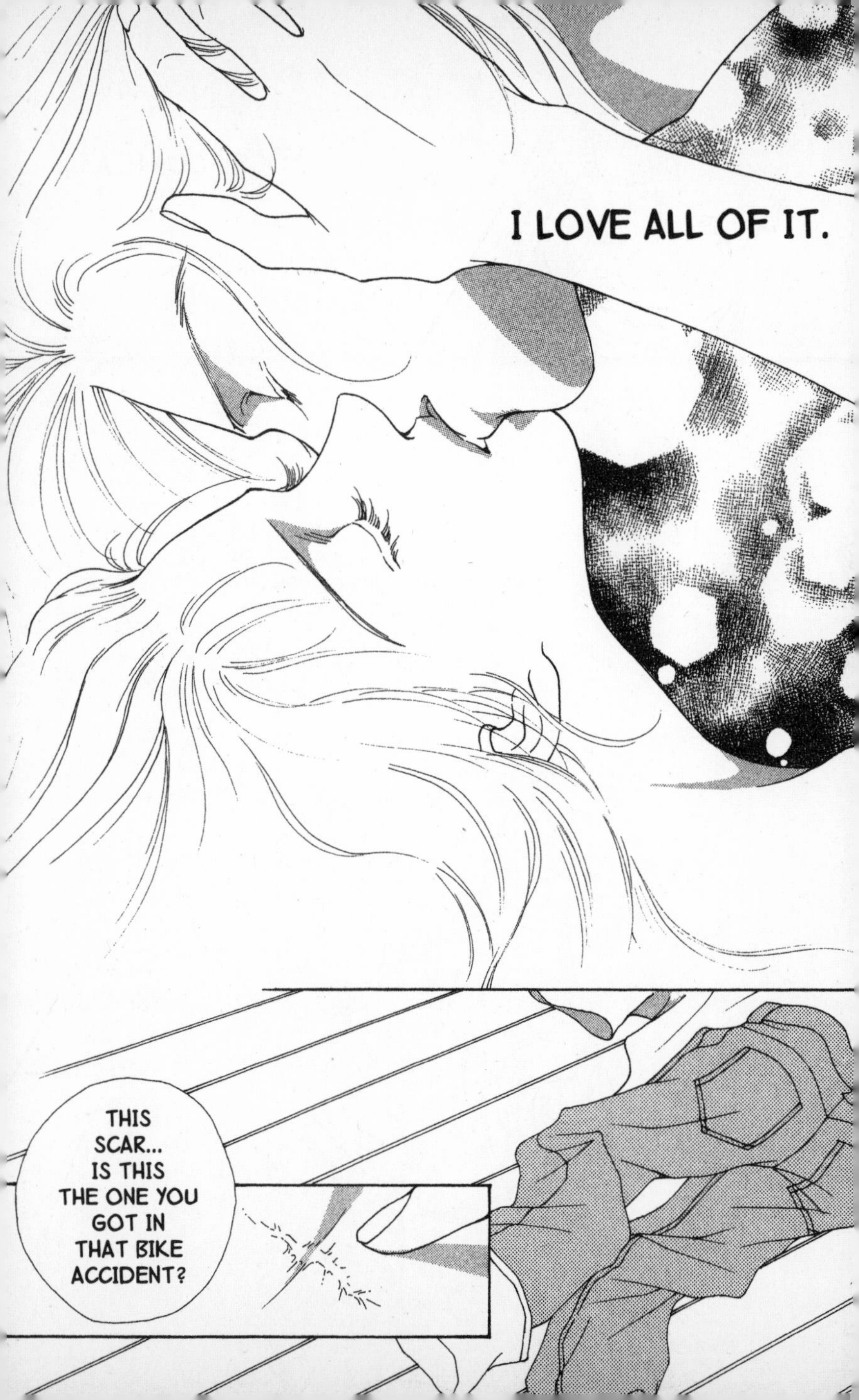
I LOVE ALL OF IT.
THIS SCAR... IS THIS THE ONE YOU GOT IN THAT BIKE ACCIDENT?

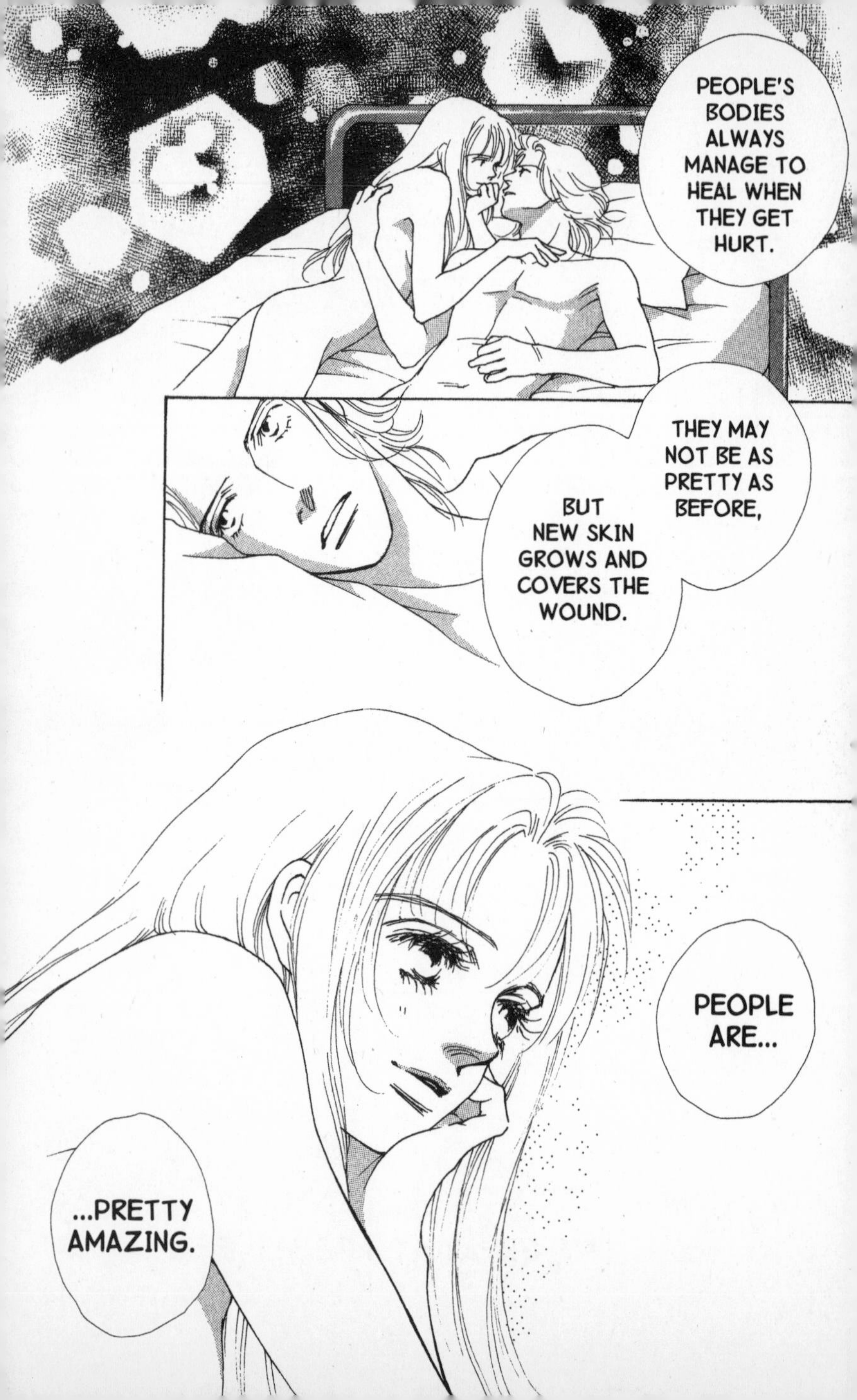
PEOPLE'S BODIES ALWAYS MANAGE TO HEAL WHEN THEY GET HURT.
THEY MAY NOT BE AS PRETTY AS BEFORE,
BUT NEW SKIN GROWS AND COVERS THE WOUND.
PEOPLE ARE...
...PRETTY AMAZING.

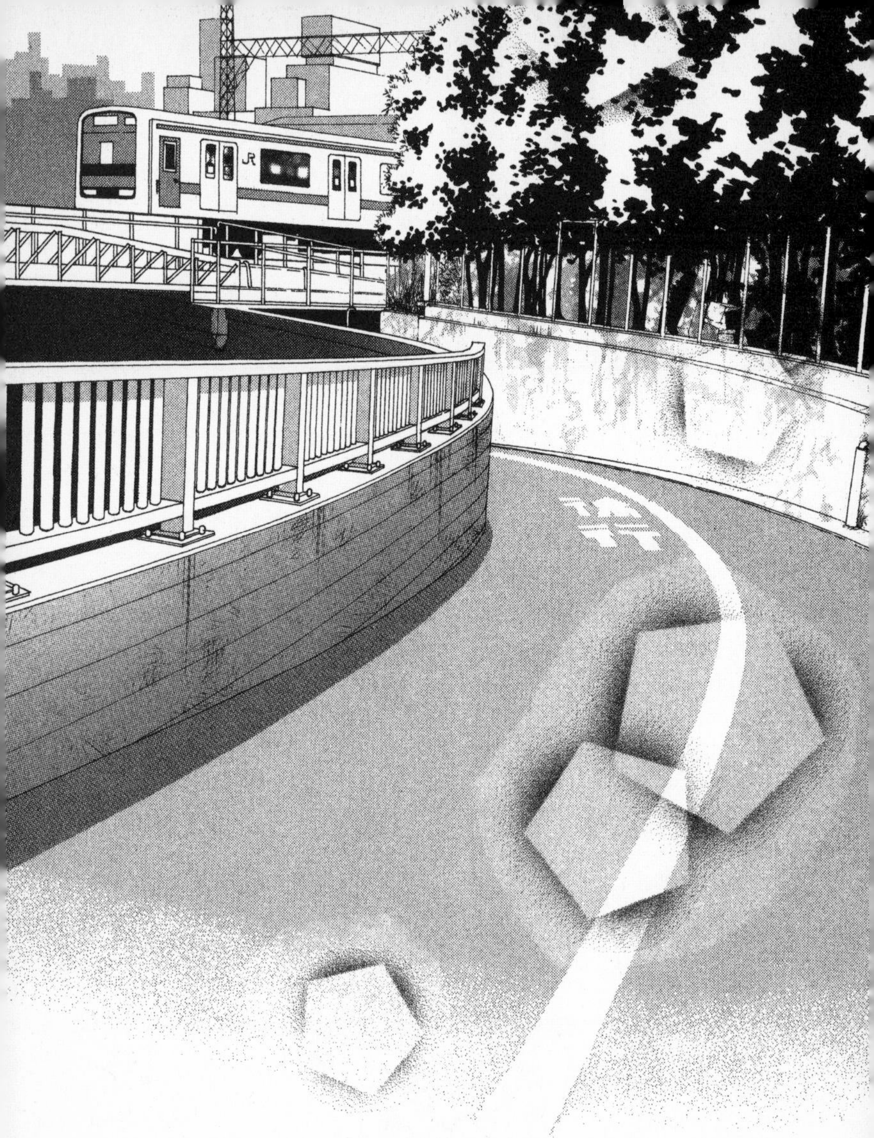

IT'S GREAT... TO BE ALIVE.

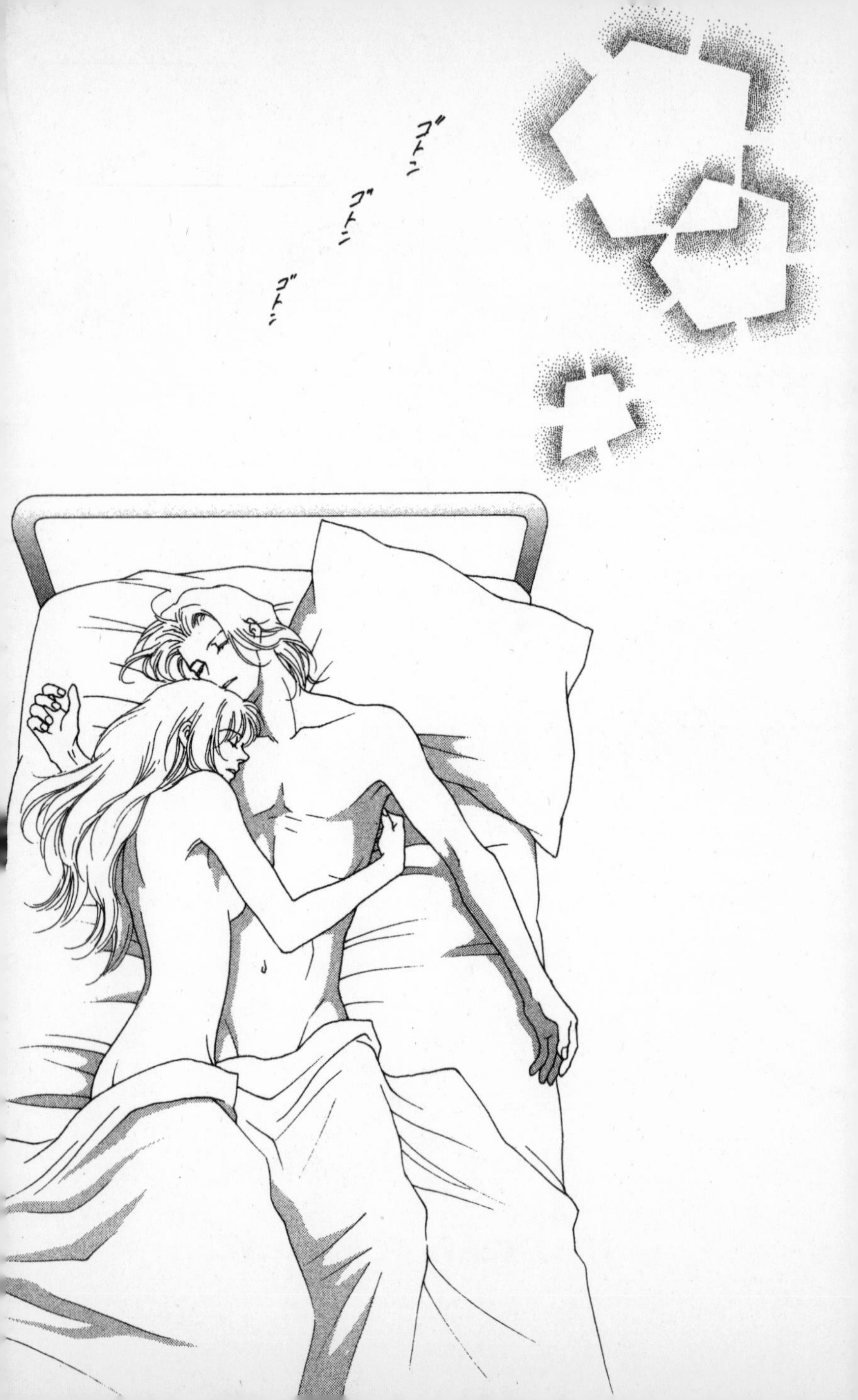
ゴトン
ゴトン
ゴトン

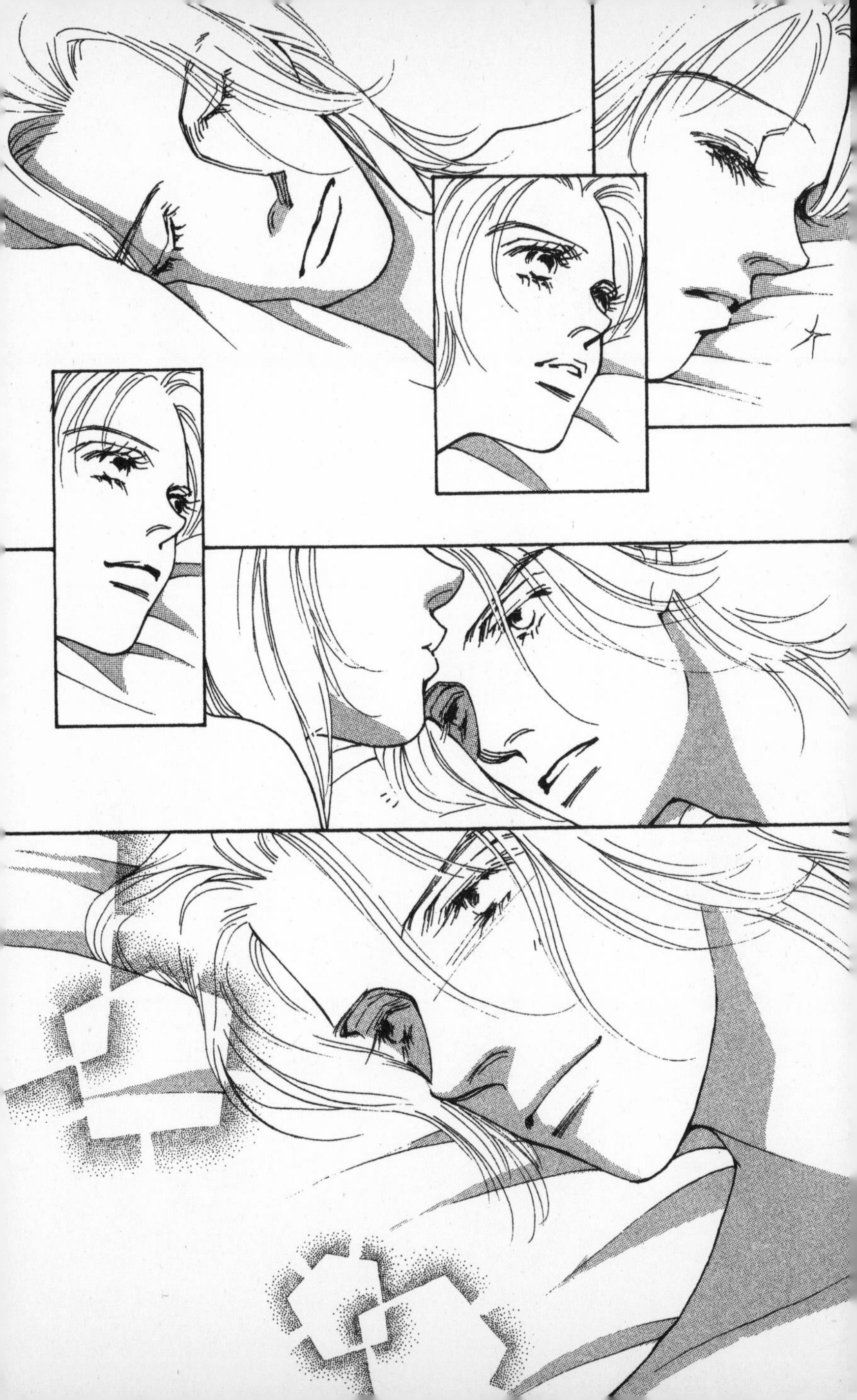

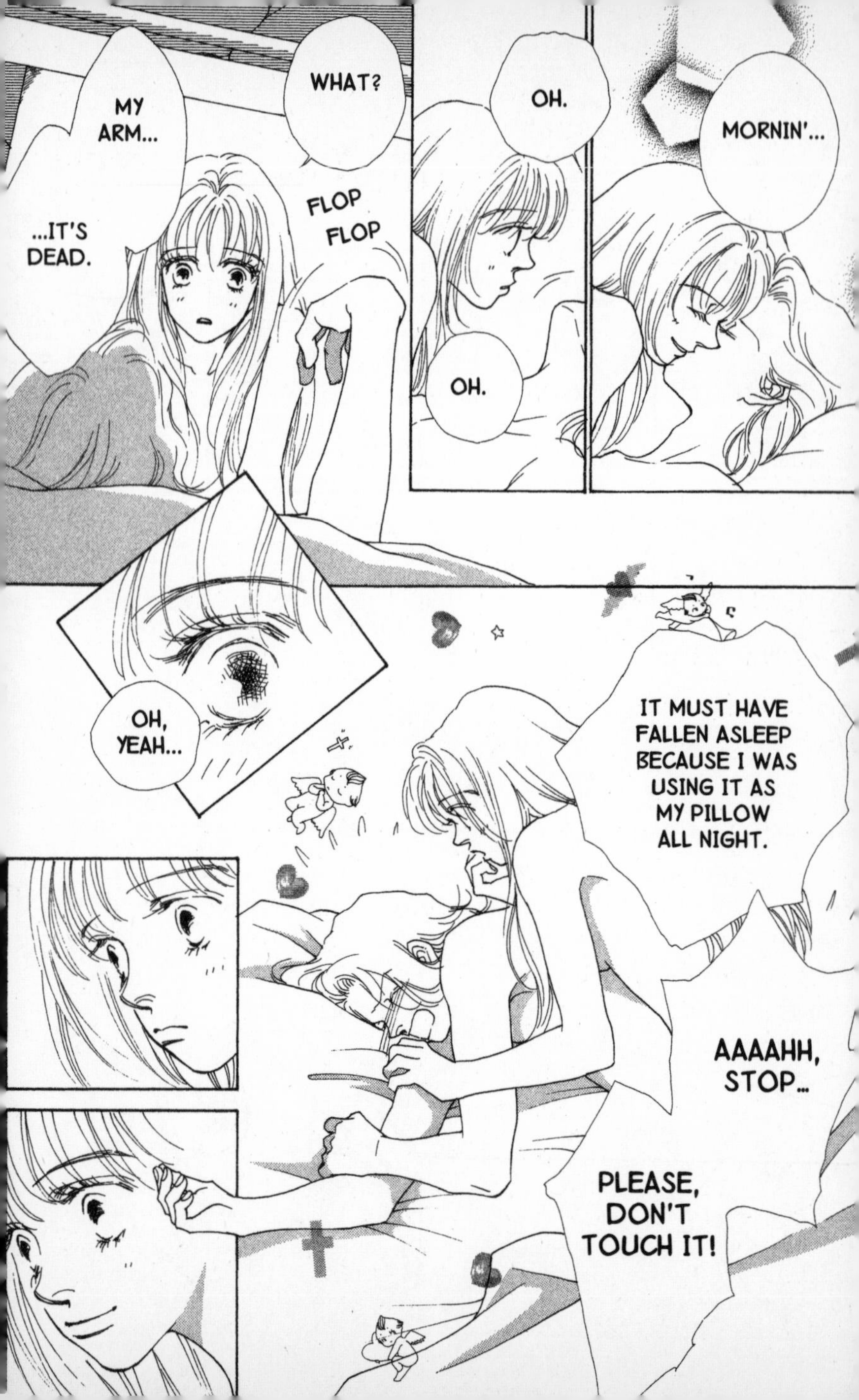
MORNIN'...
OH.
OH.
WHAT?
MY ARM...
FLOP FLOP
...IT'S DEAD.
OH, YEAH...
IT MUST HAVE FALLEN ASLEEP BECAUSE I WAS USING IT AS MY PILLOW ALL NIGHT.
AAAAHH, STOP...
PLEASE, DON'T TOUCH IT!

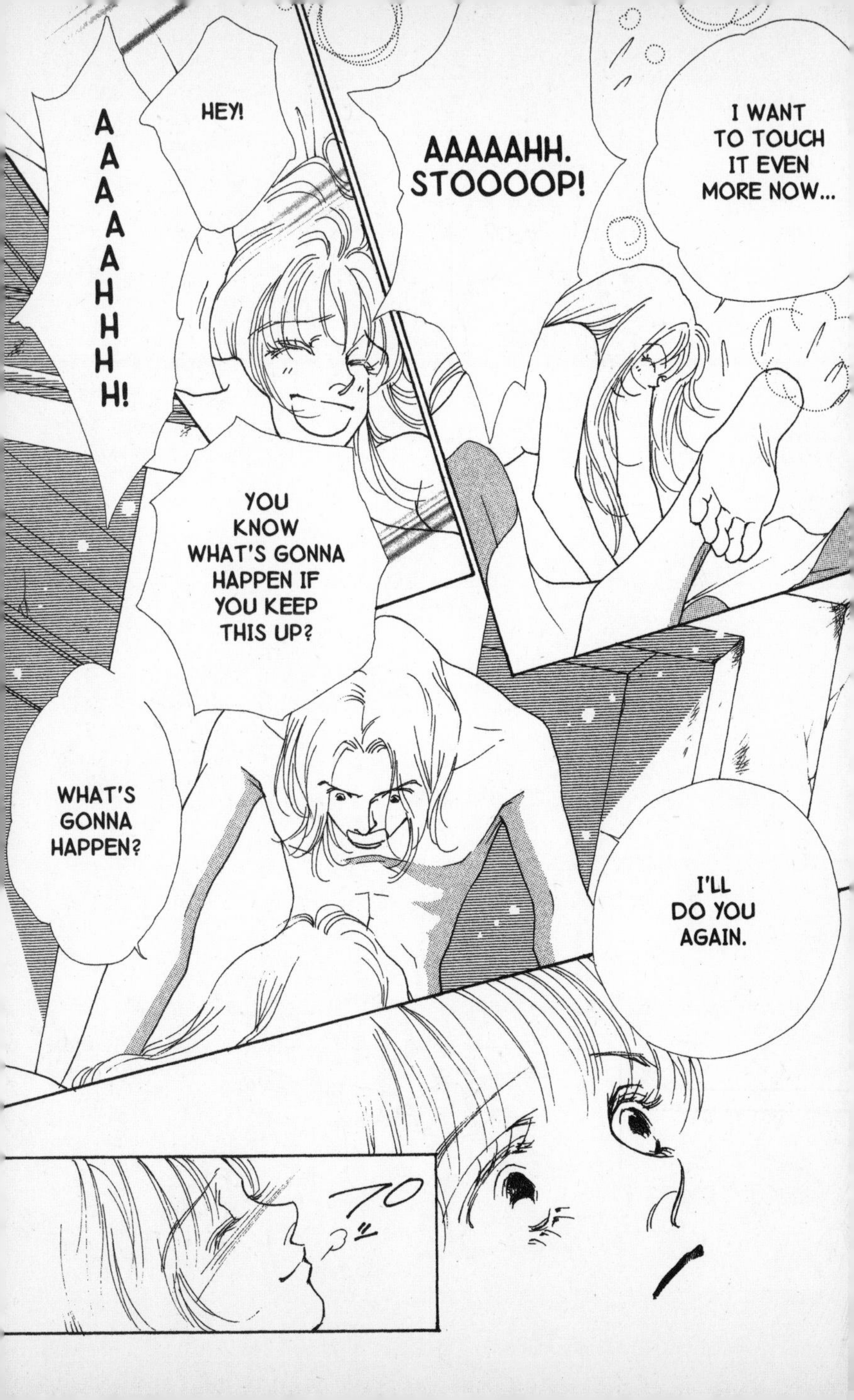

I WANT TO TOUCH IT EVEN MORE NOW...
AAAAAHH. STOOOOP!
HEY!
AAAAAHHHH!
YOU KNOW WHAT'S GONNA HAPPEN IF YOU KEEP THIS UP?
WHAT'S GONNA HAPPEN?
I'LL DO YOU AGAIN.

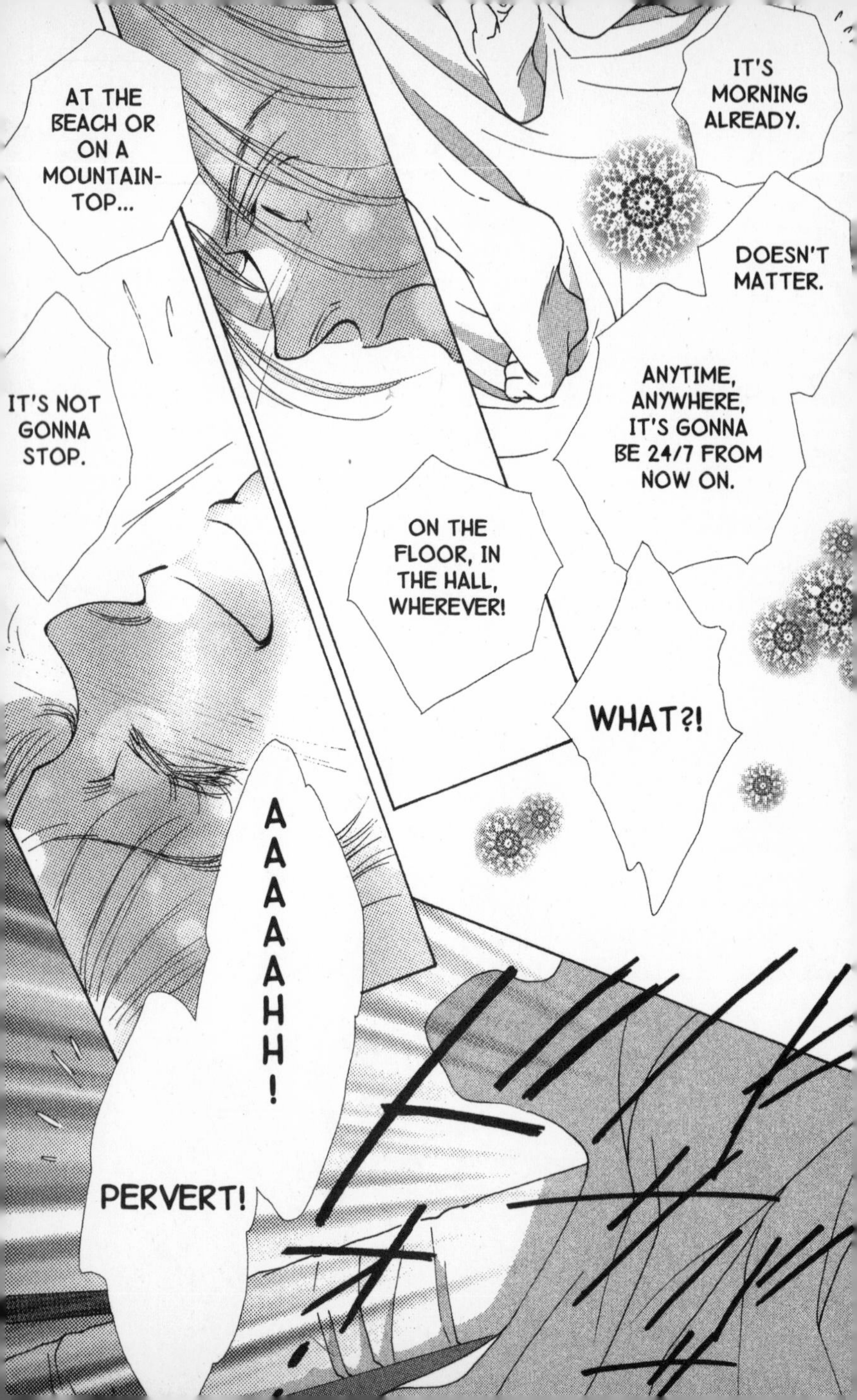
IT'S MORNING ALREADY.
DOESN'T MATTER.
ANYTIME, ANYWHERE, IT'S GONNA BE 24/7 FROM NOW ON.
ON THE FLOOR, IN THE HALL, WHEREVER!
AT THE BEACH OR ON A MOUNTAIN-TOP...
IT'S NOT GONNA STOP.
WHAT?!
AAAAAAHH!
PERVERT!

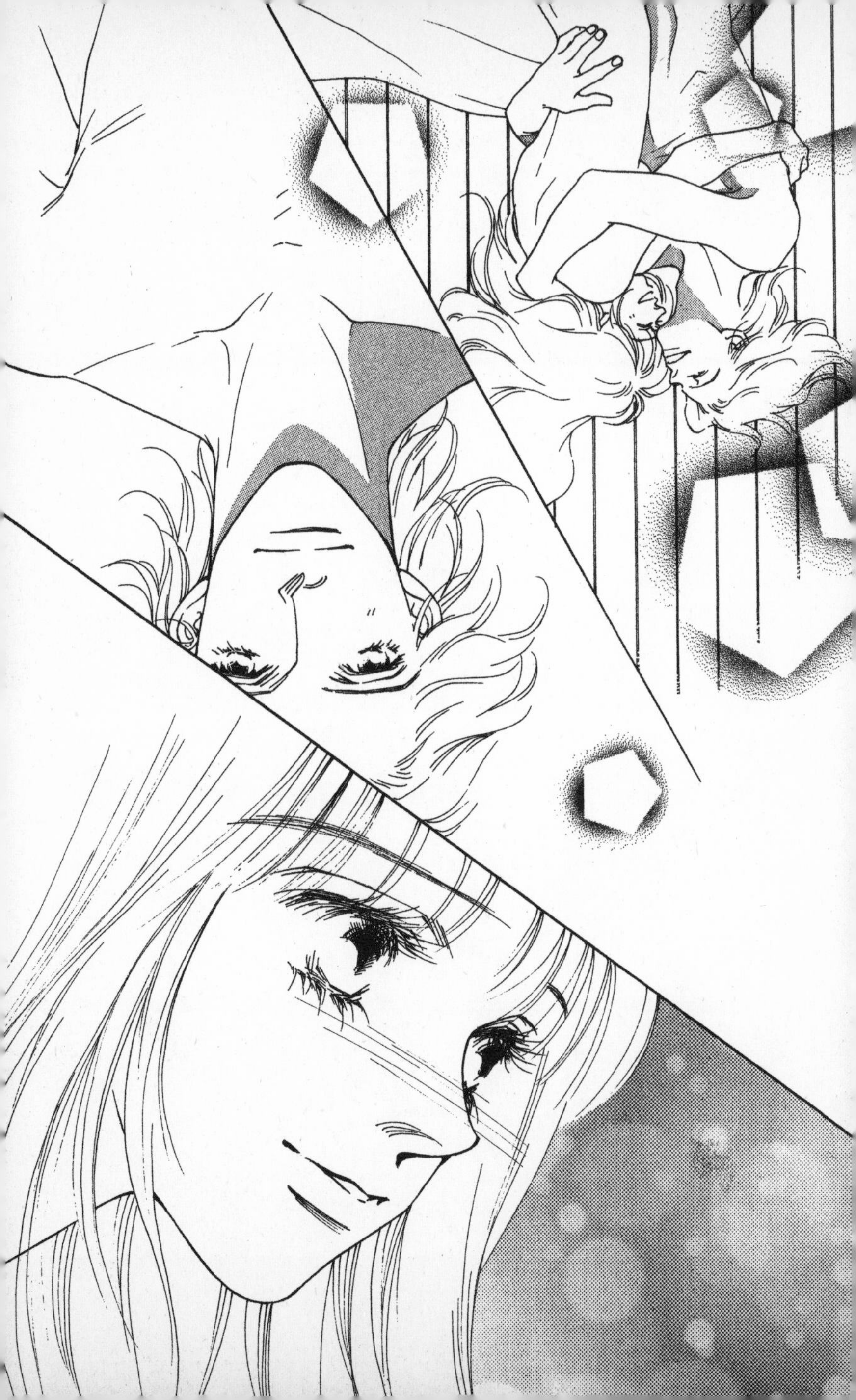

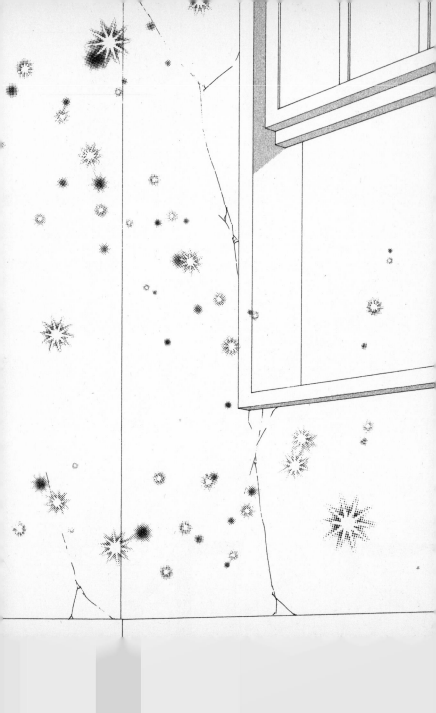

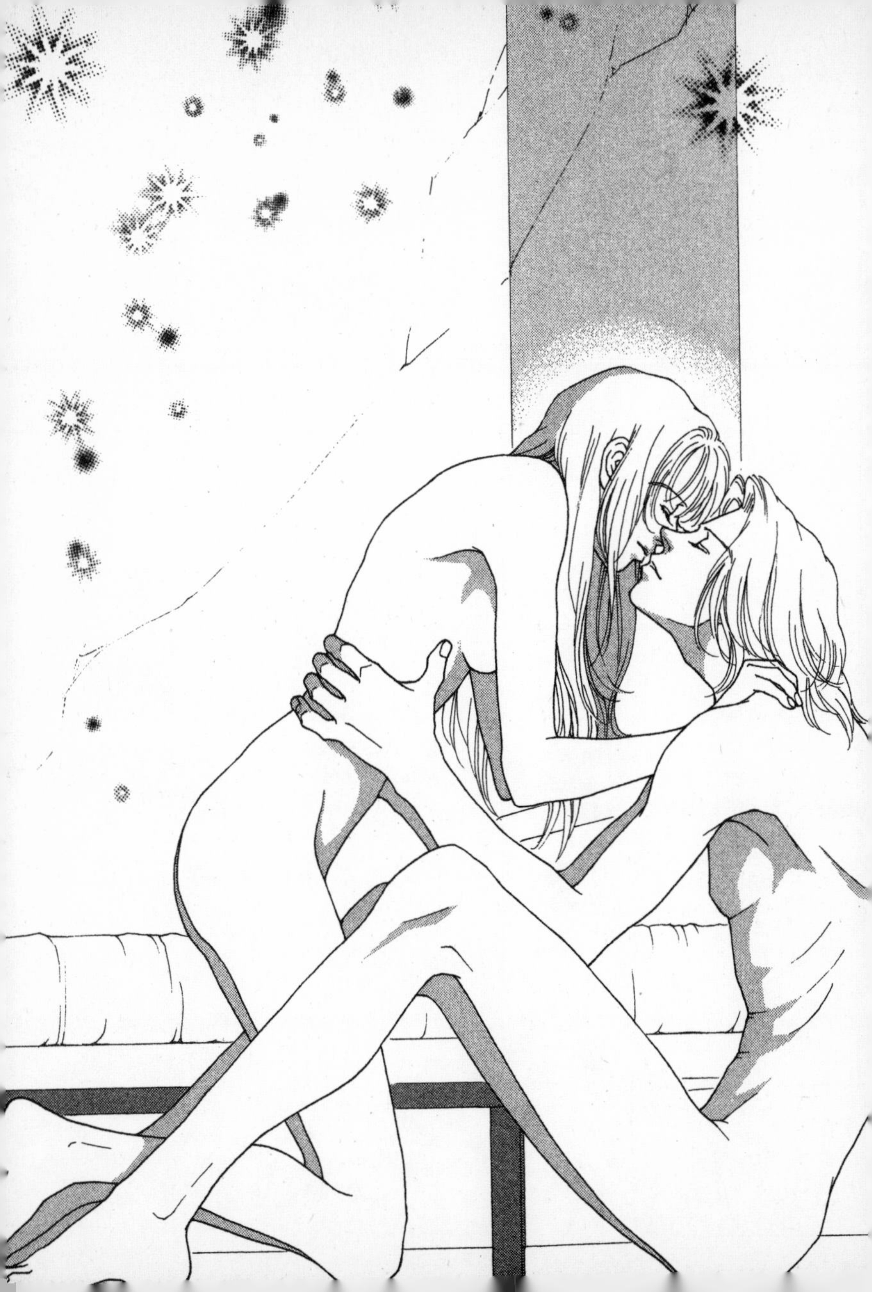

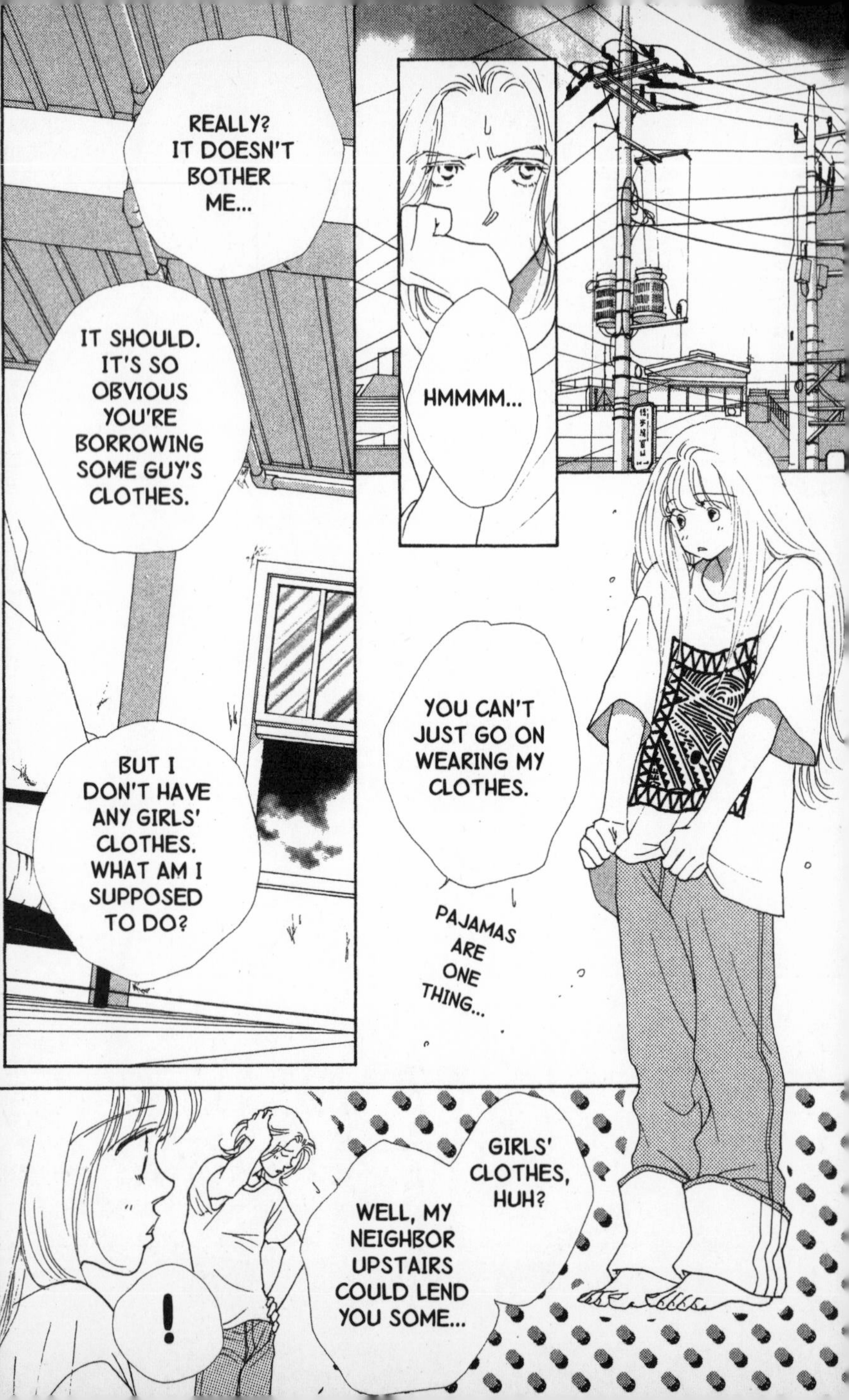
YOU CAN'T JUST GO ON WEARING MY CLOTHES.
PAJAMAS ARE ONE THING...
REALLY? IT DOESN'T BOTHER ME...
HMMMM...
IT SHOULD. IT'S SO OBVIOUS YOU'RE BORROWING SOME GUY'S CLOTHES.
BUT I DON'T HAVE ANY GIRLS' CLOTHES. WHAT AM I SUPPOSED TO DO?
GIRLS' CLOTHES, HUH?
WELL, MY NEIGHBOR UPSTAIRS COULD LEND YOU SOME...
!

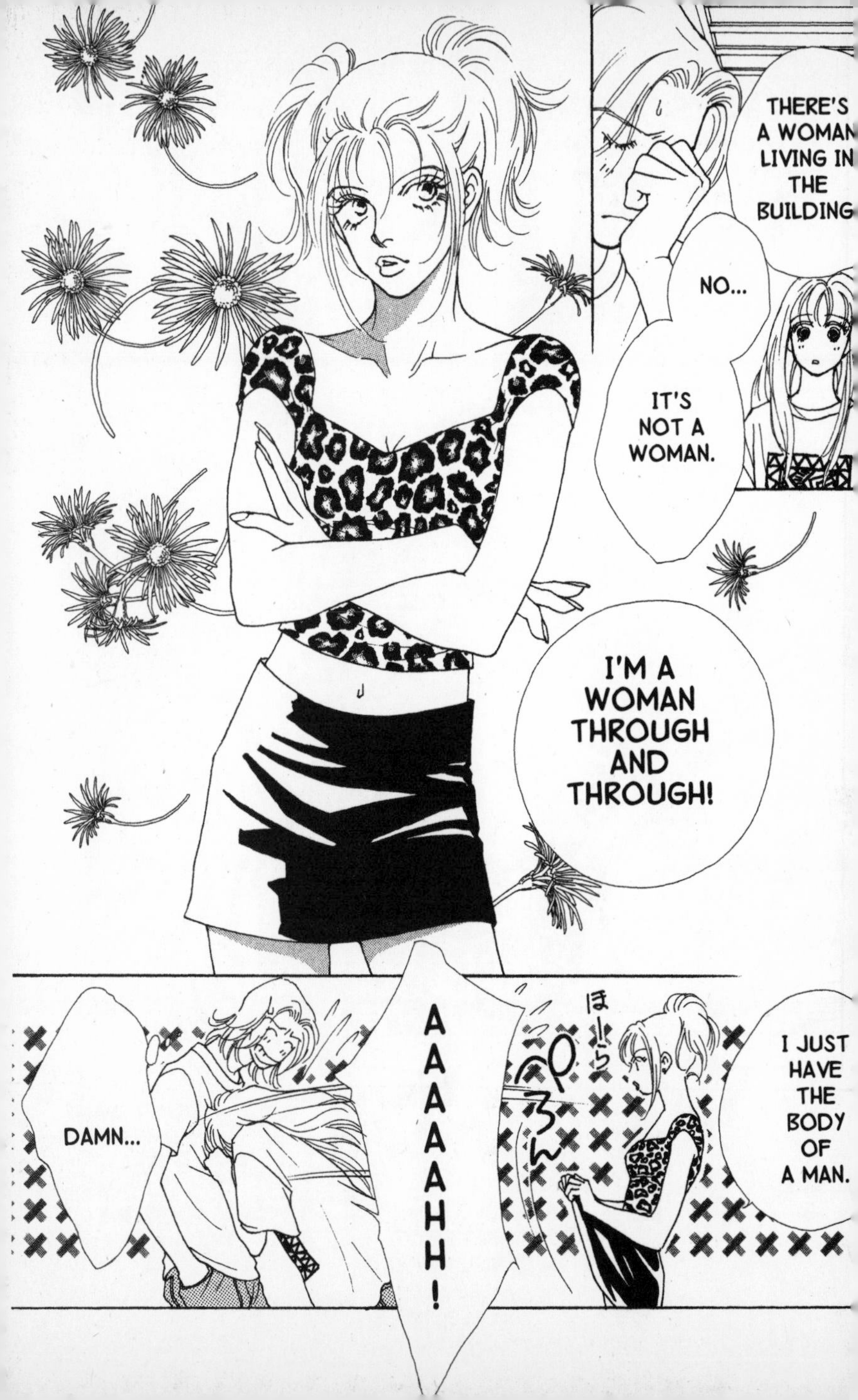

THERE'S A WOMAN LIVING IN THE BUILDING
NO...
IT'S NOT A WOMAN.
I'M A WOMAN THROUGH AND THROUGH!
I JUST HAVE THE BODY OF A MAN.
ほーら
ぺろん
AAAAAHH!
DAMN...

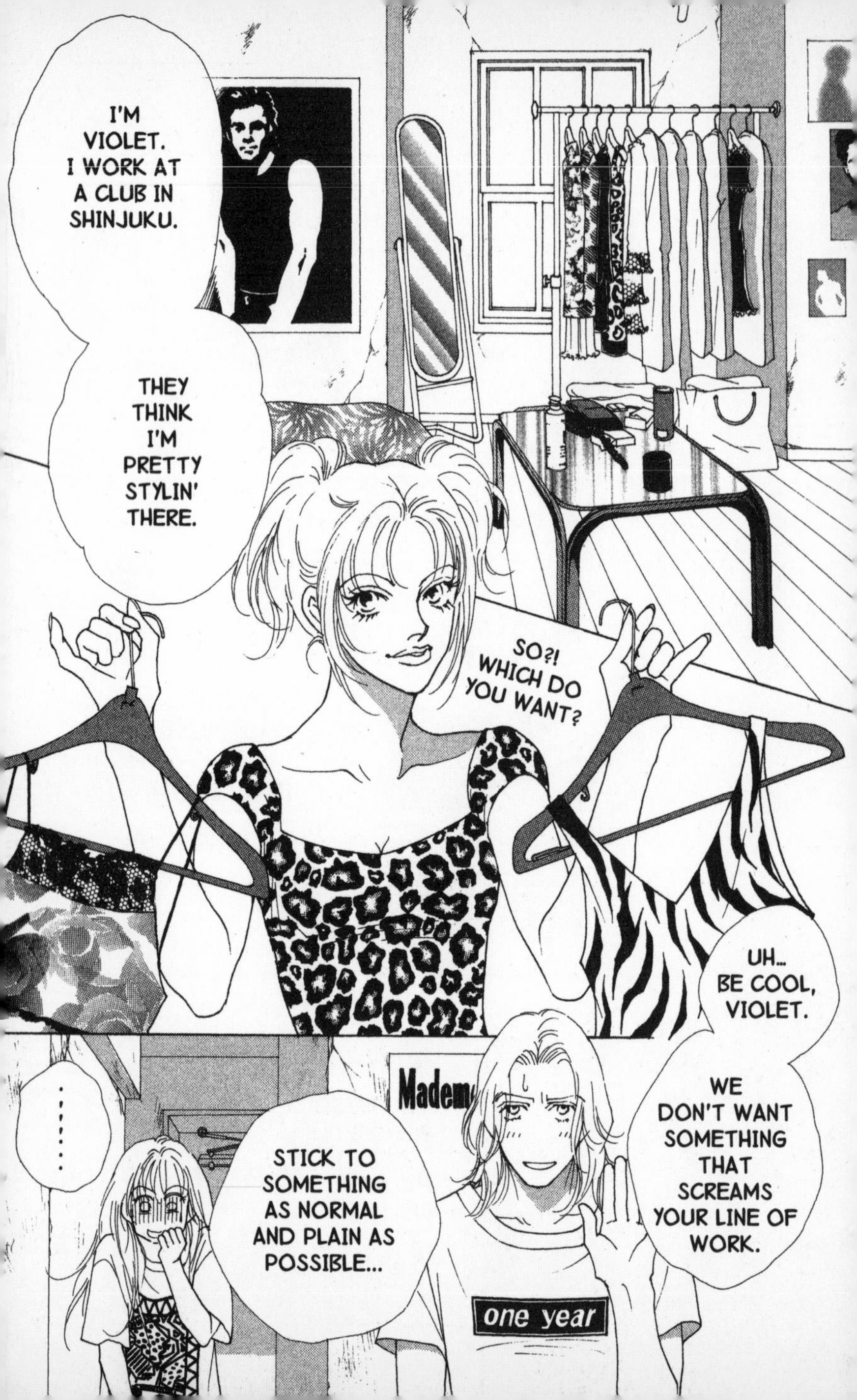
I'M VIOLET. I WORK AT A CLUB IN SHINJUKU.
THEY THINK I'M PRETTY STYLIN' THERE.
SO?! WHICH DO YOU WANT?
UH... BE COOL, VIOLET.
WE DON'T WANT SOMETHING THAT SCREAMS YOUR LINE OF WORK.
STICK TO SOMETHING AS NORMAL AND PLAIN AS POSSIBLE...
......
one year

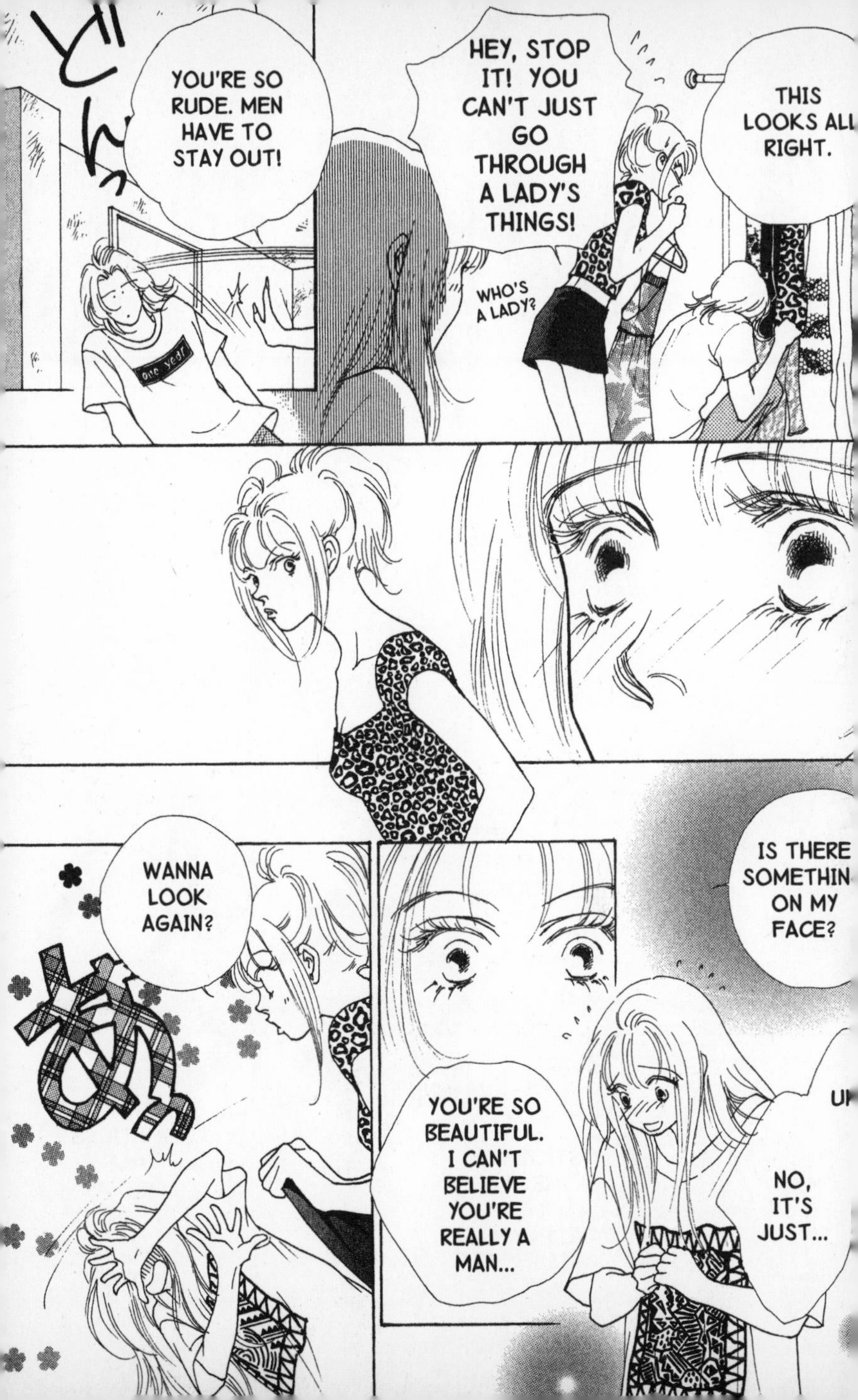
THIS LOOKS ALL RIGHT.
HEY, STOP IT! YOU CAN'T JUST GO THROUGH A LADY'S THINGS!
WHO'S A LADY?
YOU'RE SO RUDE. MEN HAVE TO STAY OUT!
IS THERE SOMETHIN ON MY FACE?
NO, IT'S JUST...
YOU'RE SO BEAUTIFUL. I CAN'T BELIEVE YOU'RE REALLY A MAN...
WANNA LOOK AGAIN?

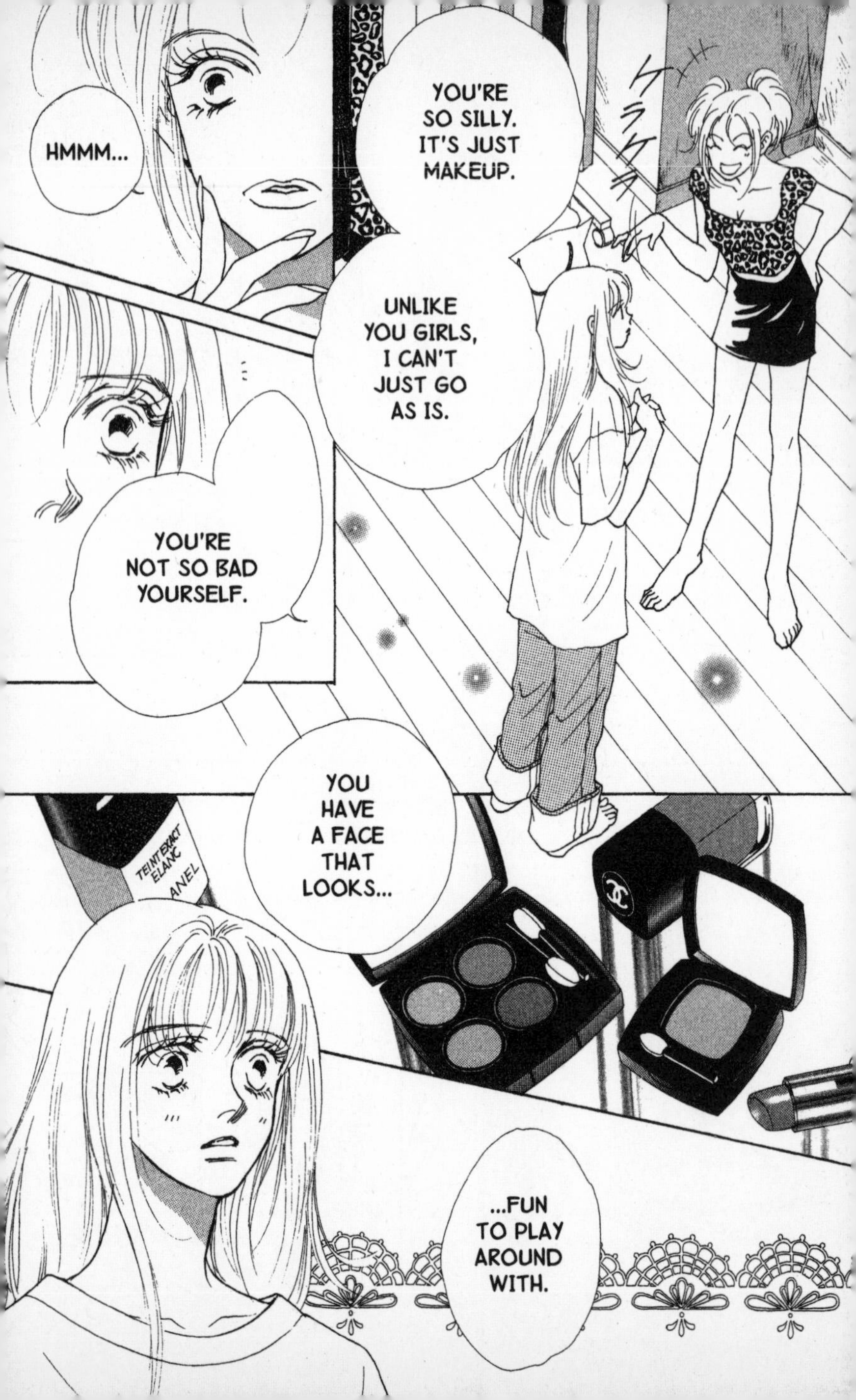

YOU'RE SO SILLY. IT'S JUST MAKEUP.
ケラケラ
UNLIKE YOU GIRLS, I CAN'T JUST GO AS IS.
HMMM...
YOU'RE NOT SO BAD YOURSELF.
YOU HAVE A FACE THAT LOOKS...
...FUN TO PLAY AROUND WITH.

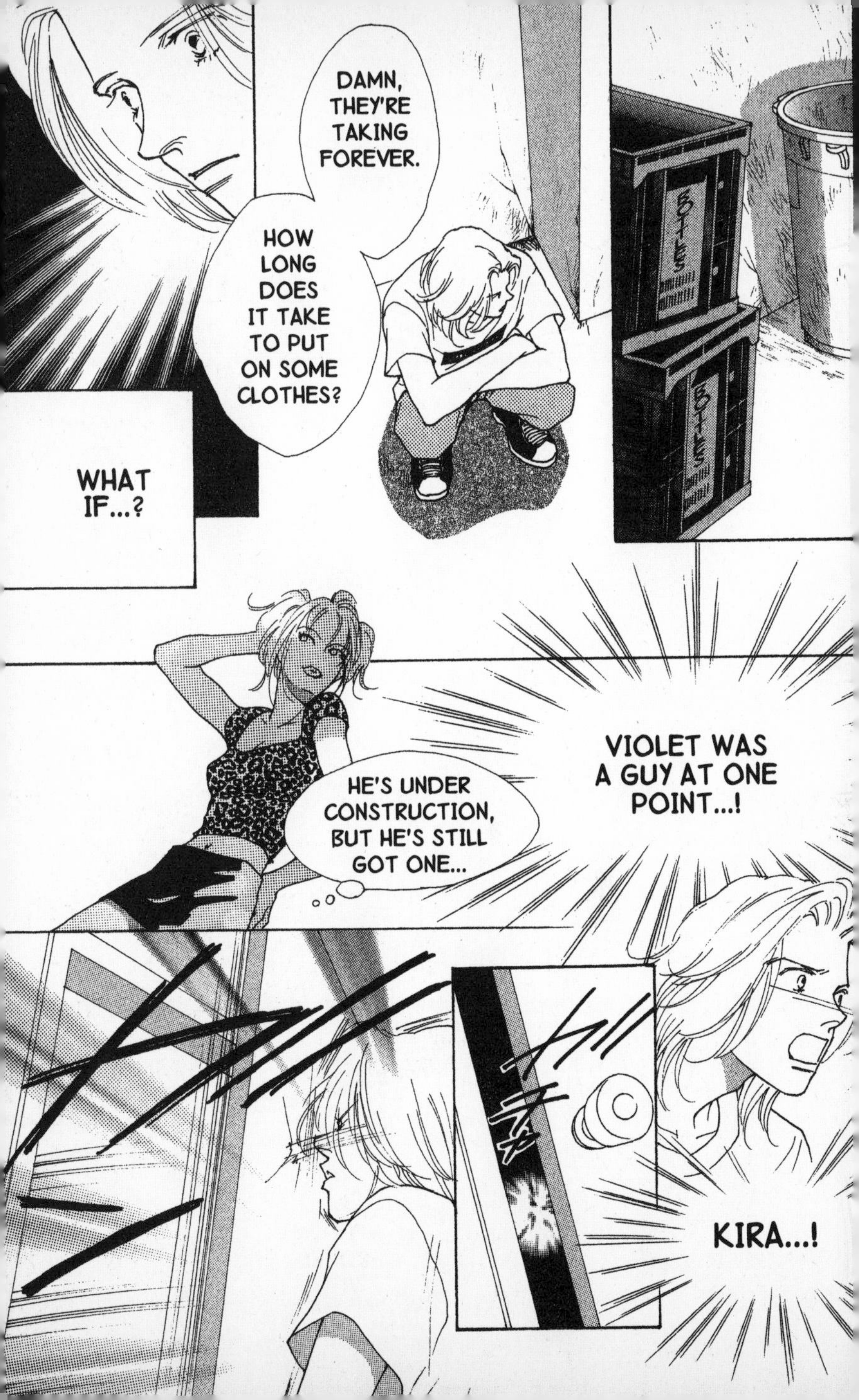
DAMN, THEY'RE TAKING FOREVER.
HOW LONG DOES IT TAKE TO PUT ON SOME CLOTHES?
BOTTLES
BOTTLES
WHAT IF...?
VIOLET WAS A GUY AT ONE POINT...!
HE'S UNDER CONSTRUCTION, BUT HE'S STILL GOT ONE...
KIRA...!

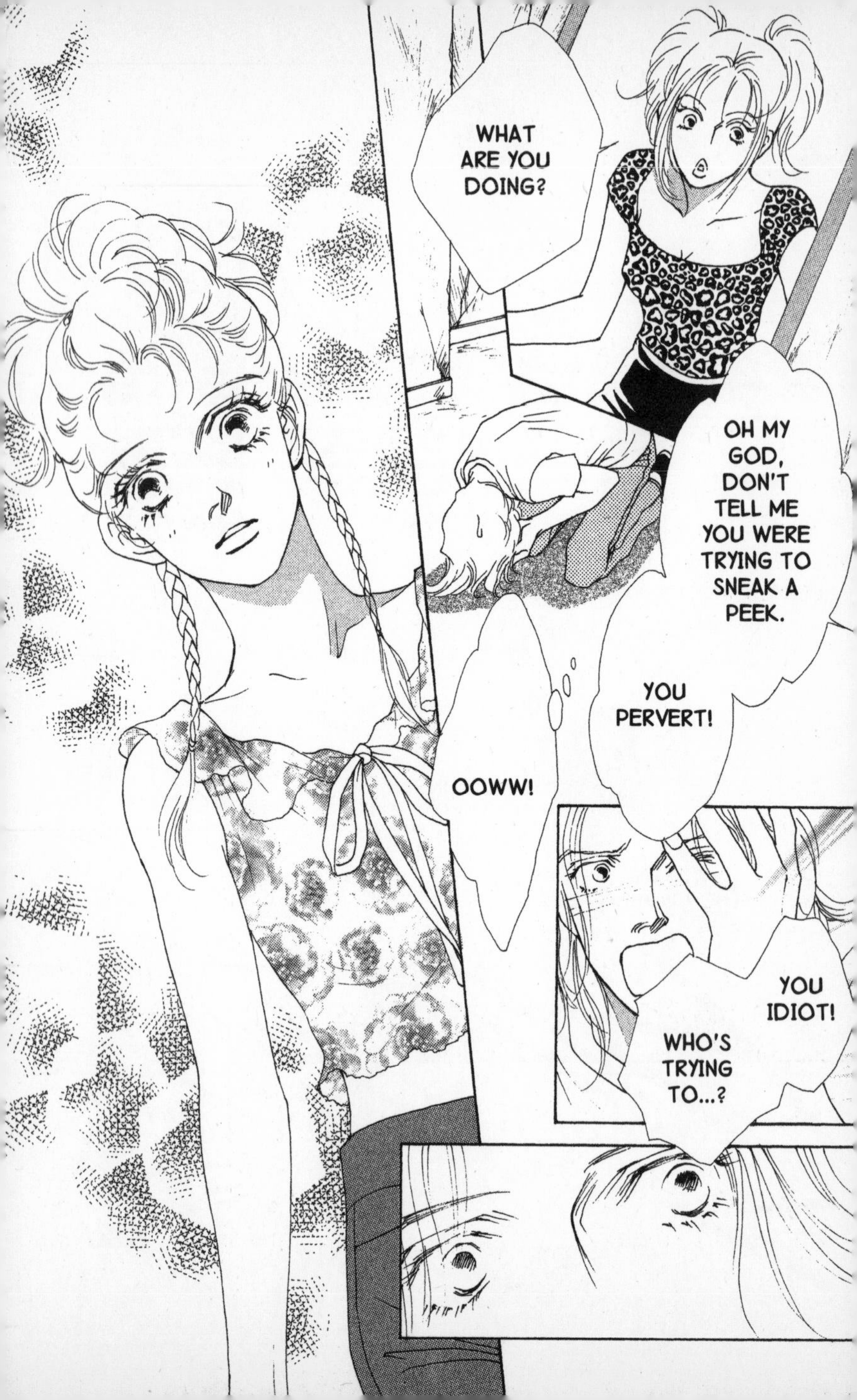
WHAT ARE YOU DOING?
OH MY GOD, DON'T TELL ME YOU WERE TRYING TO SNEAK A PEEK.
YOU PERVERT!
OOWW!
YOU IDIOT!
WHO'S TRYING TO...?

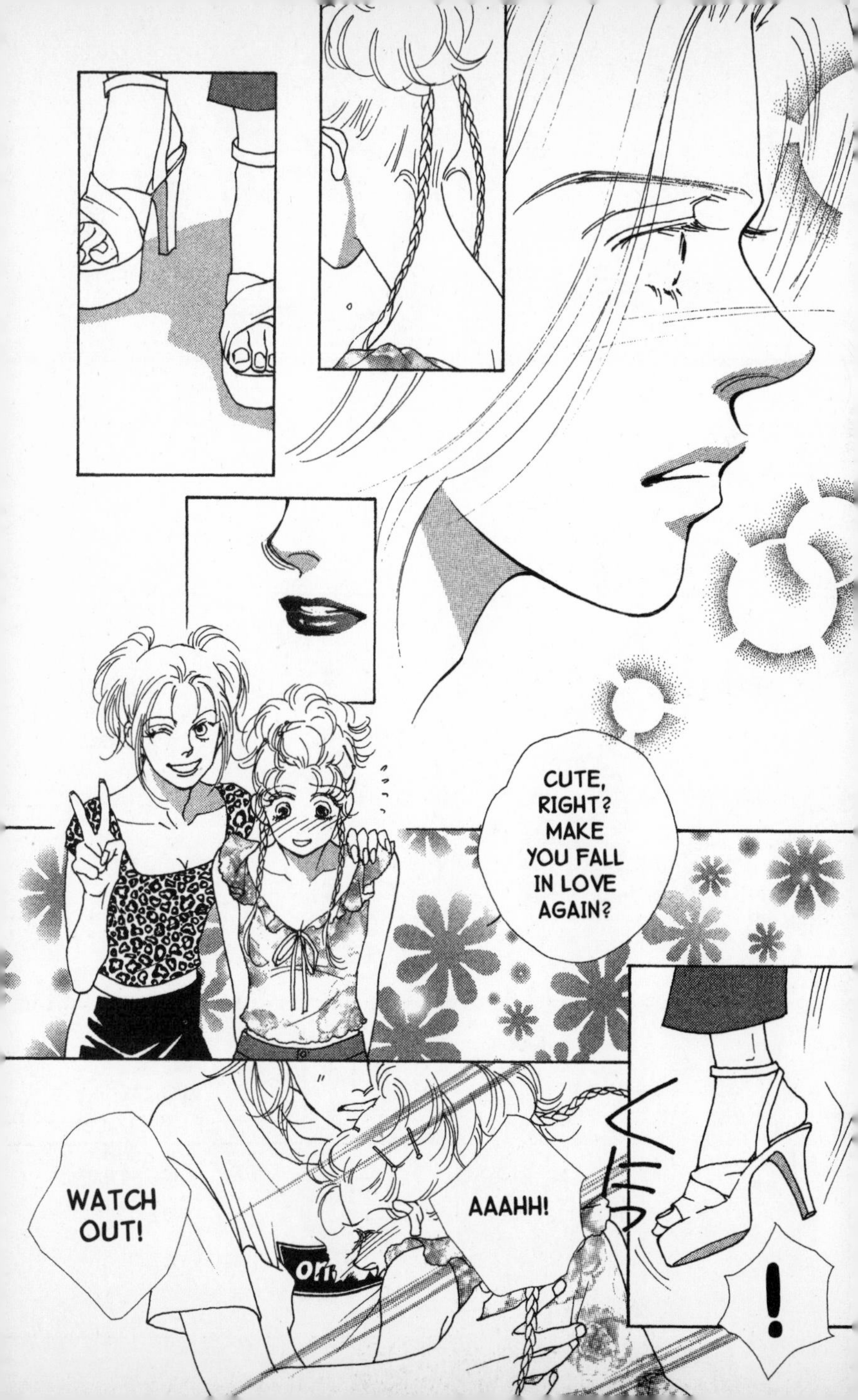
CUTE, RIGHT? MAKE YOU FALL IN LOVE AGAIN?
!
AAAHH!
WATCH OUT!

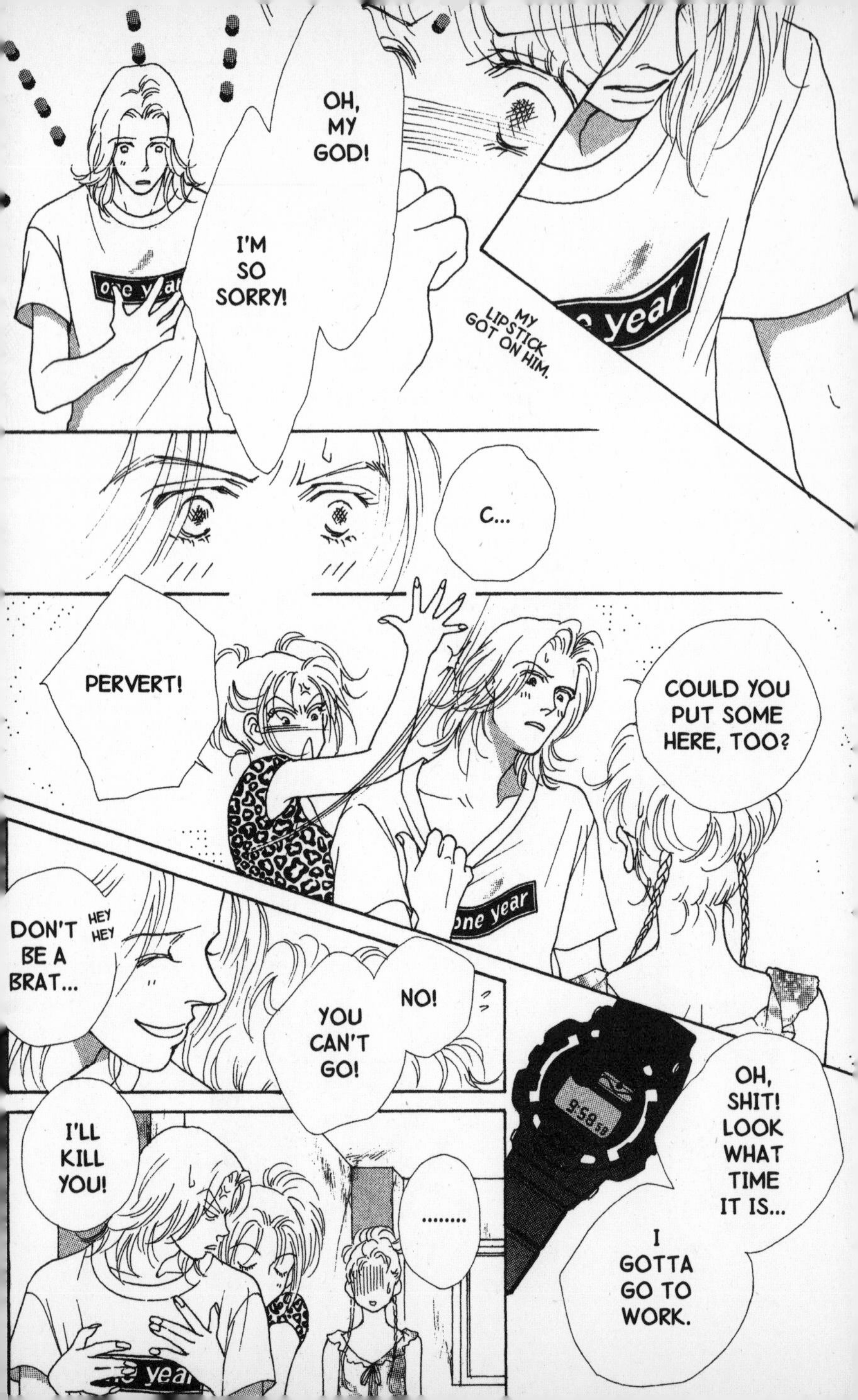

MY LIPSTICK GOT ON HIM.
OH, MY GOD!
I'M SO SORRY!
C...
COULD YOU PUT SOME HERE, TOO?
PERVERT!
one year
OH, SHIT! LOOK WHAT TIME IT IS...
I GOTTA GO TO WORK.
NO!
YOU CAN'T GO!
HEY HEY
DON'T BE A BRAT...
....
I'LL KILL YOU!

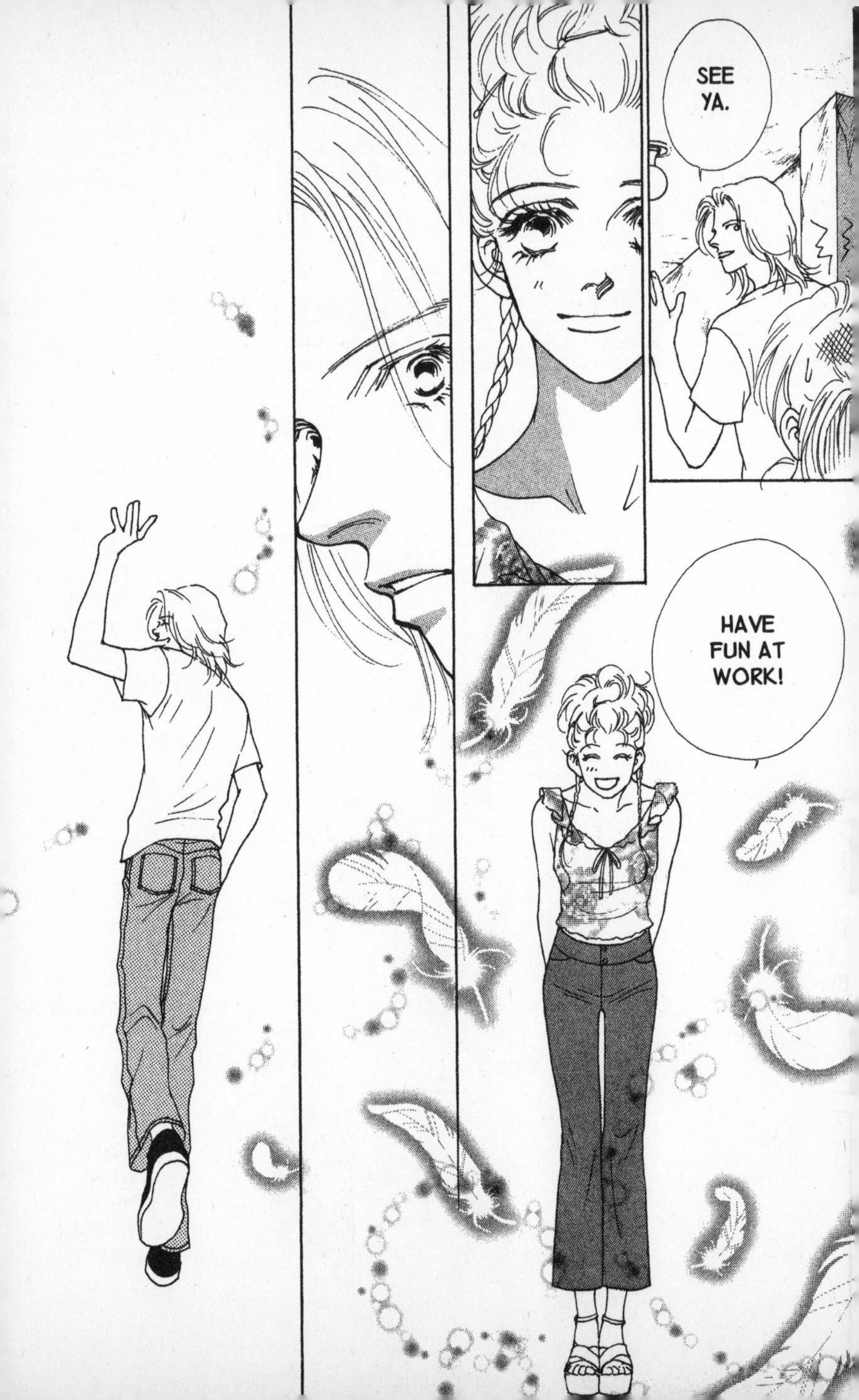
SEE YA.
HAVE FUN AT WORK!

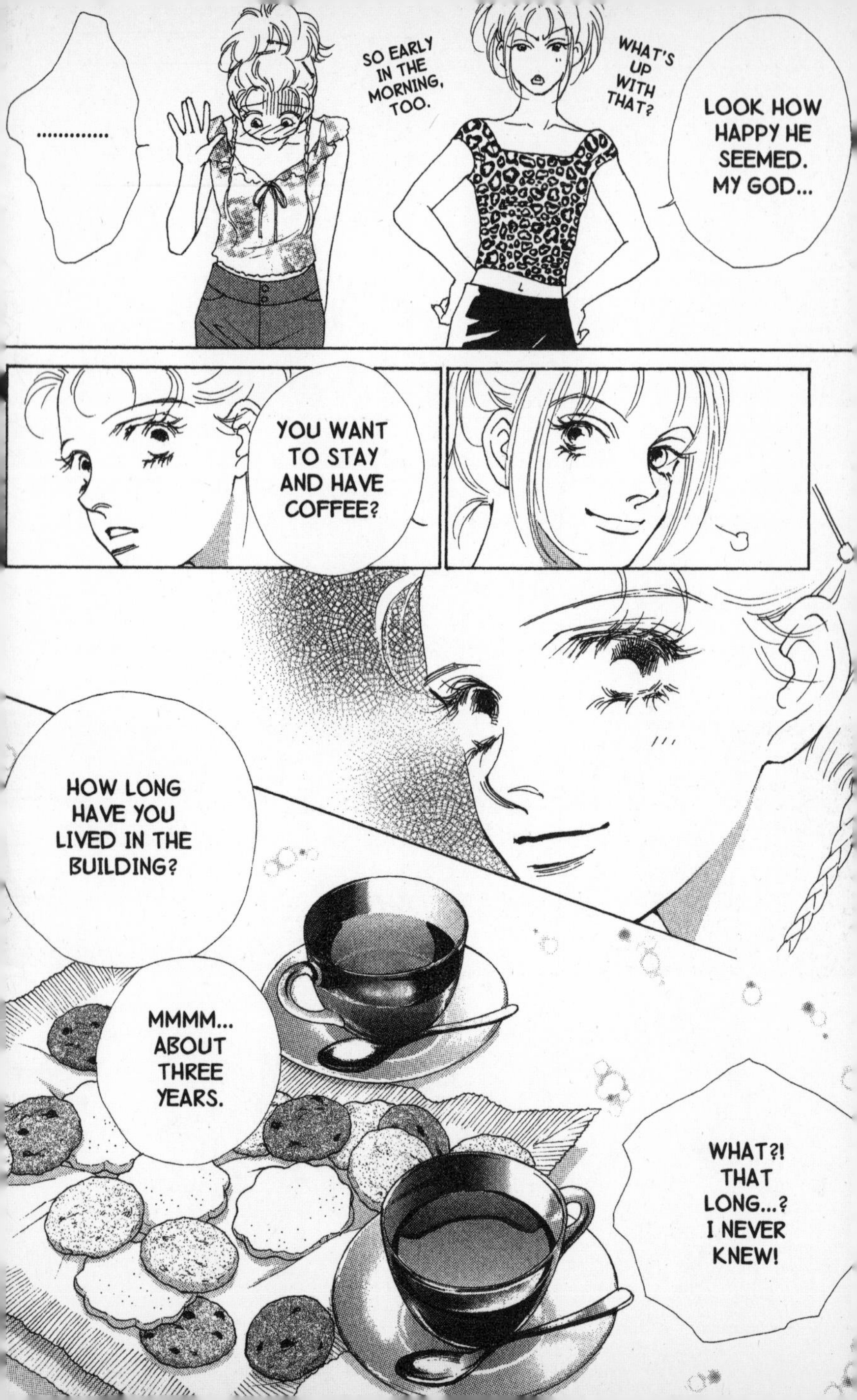
LOOK HOW HAPPY HE SEEMED. MY GOD...
WHAT'S UP WITH THAT?
SO EARLY IN THE MORNING, TOO.
....
YOU WANT TO STAY AND HAVE COFFEE?
HOW LONG HAVE YOU LIVED IN THE BUILDING?
MMMM... ABOUT THREE YEARS.
WHAT?! THAT LONG...? I NEVER KNEW!

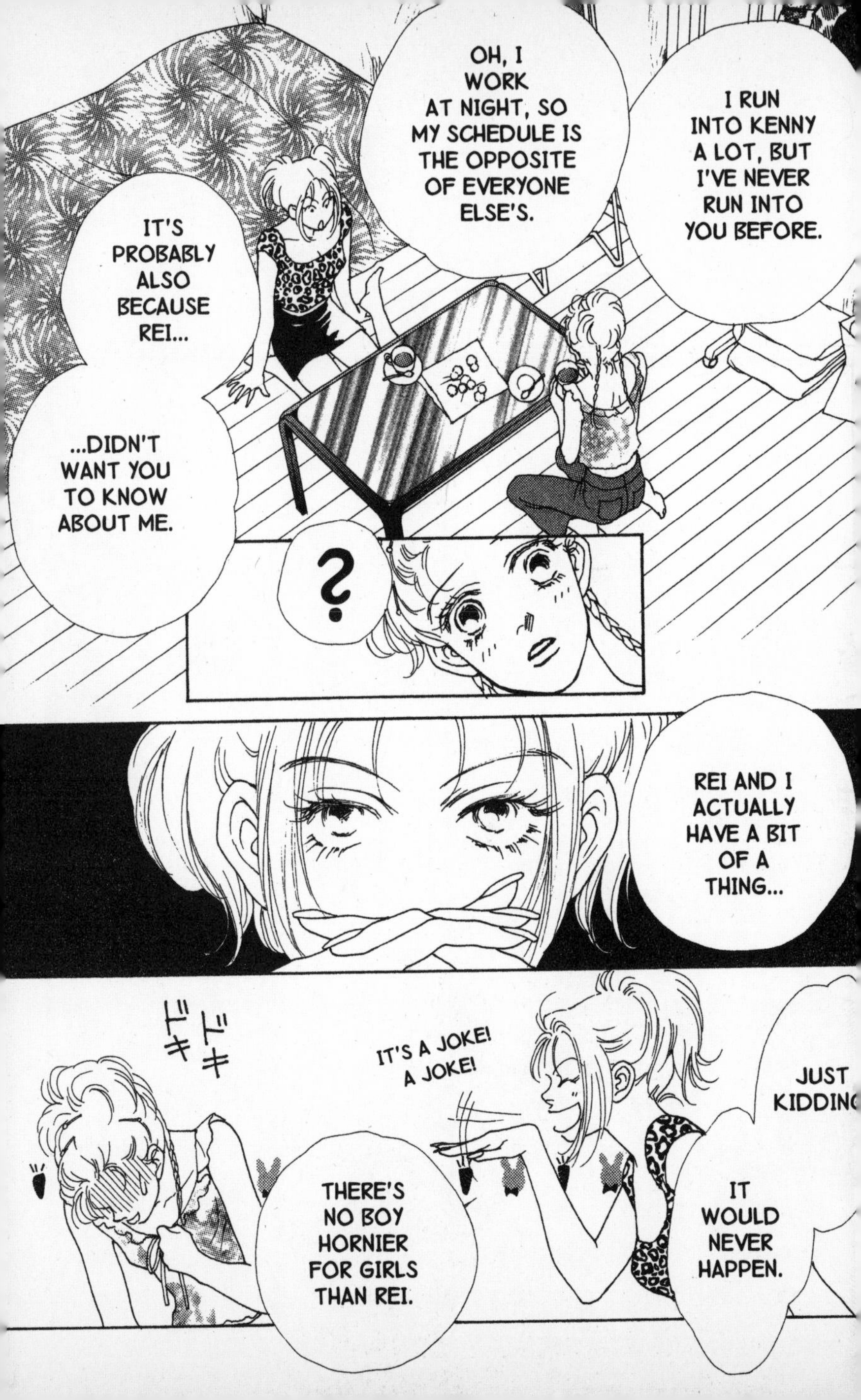
I RUN INTO KENNY A LOT, BUT I'VE NEVER RUN INTO YOU BEFORE.
OH, I WORK AT NIGHT, SO MY SCHEDULE IS THE OPPOSITE OF EVERYONE ELSE'S.
IT'S PROBABLY ALSO BECAUSE REI...
...DIDN'T WANT YOU TO KNOW ABOUT ME.
?
REI AND I ACTUALLY HAVE A BIT OF A THING...
JUST KIDDIN
IT WOULD NEVER HAPPEN.
IT'S A JOKE! A JOKE!
THERE'S NO BOY HORNIER FOR GIRLS THAN REI.
ドキドキ

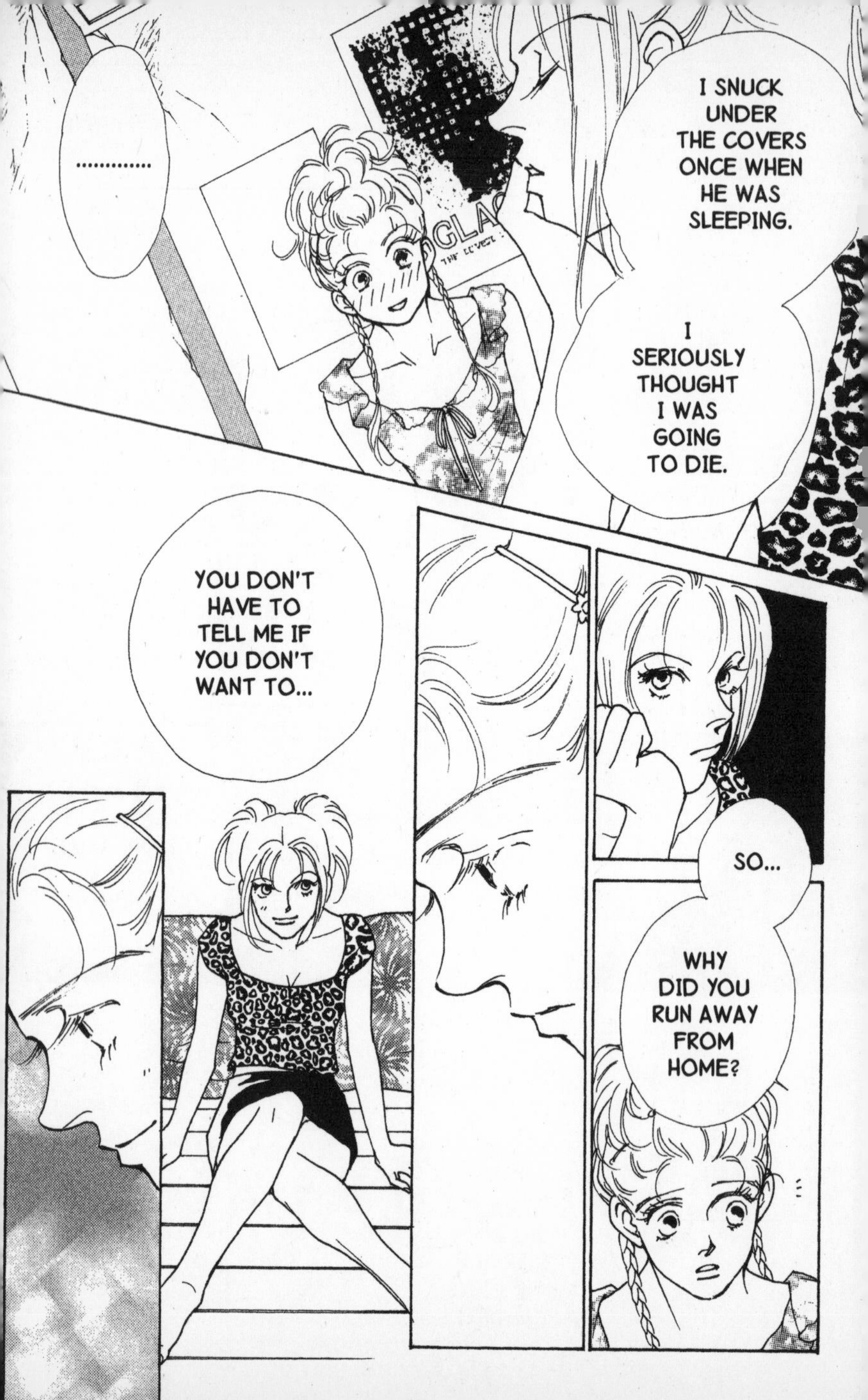
I SNUCK UNDER THE COVERS ONCE WHEN HE WAS SLEEPING.
I SERIOUSLY THOUGHT I WAS GOING TO DIE.
....
SO...
WHY DID YOU RUN AWAY FROM HOME?
YOU DON'T HAVE TO TELL ME IF YOU DON'T WANT TO...

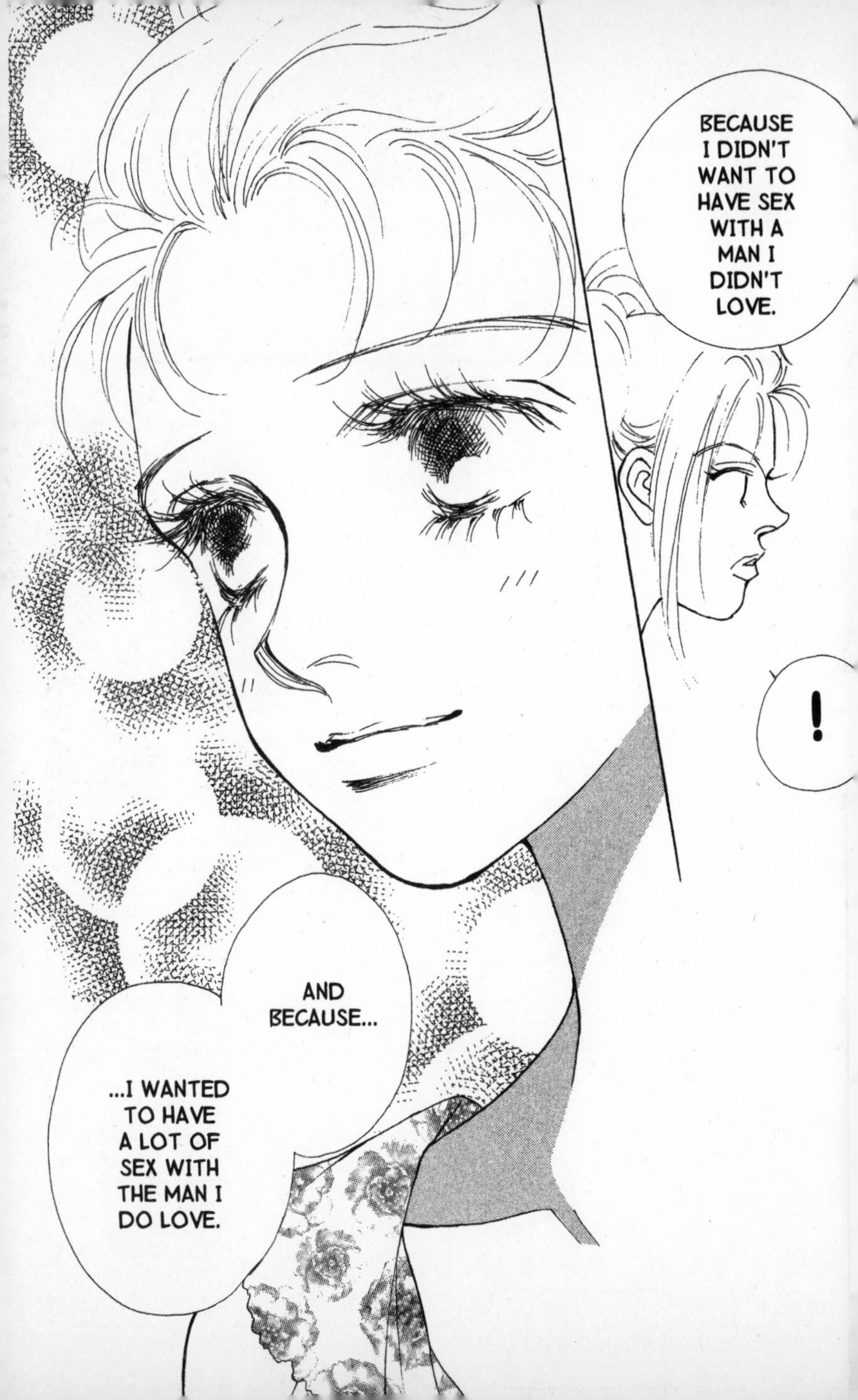
BECAUSE I DIDN'T WANT TO HAVE SEX WITH A MAN I DIDN'T LOVE.
!
AND BECAUSE...
...I WANTED TO HAVE A LOT OF SEX WITH THE MAN I DO LOVE.

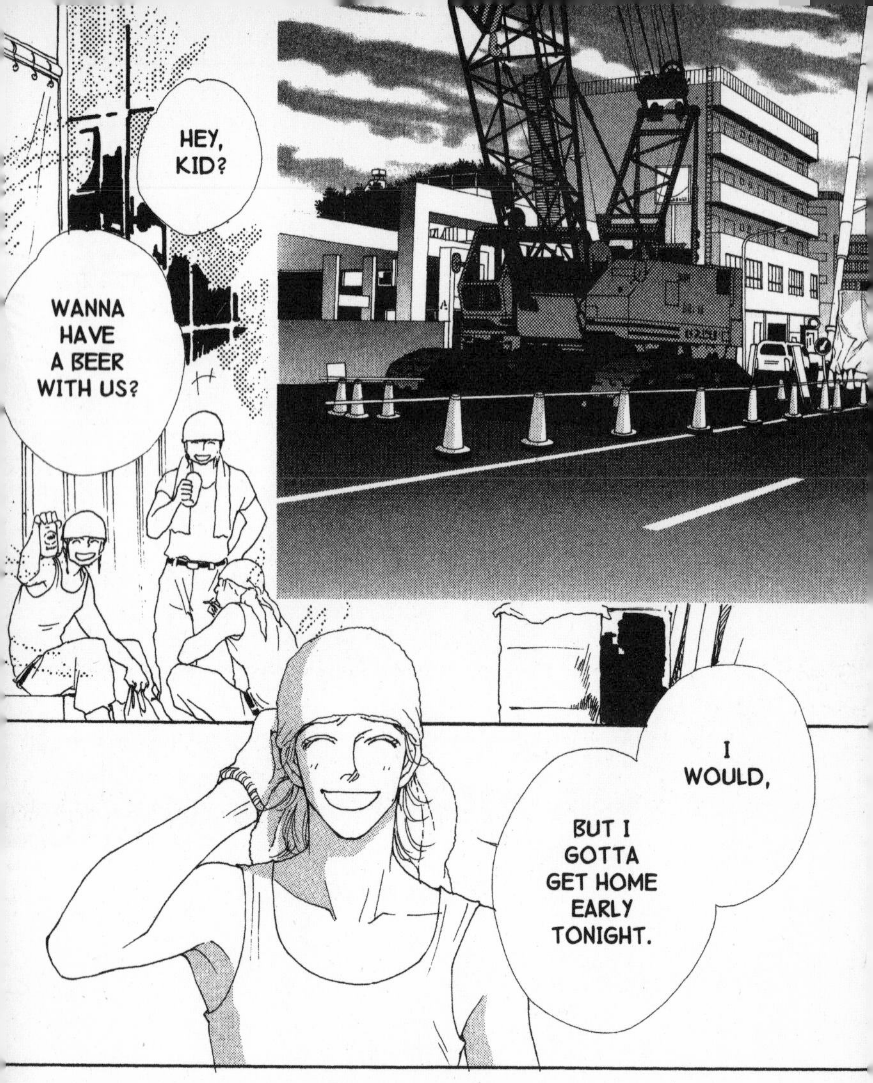
HEY, KID?
WANNA HAVE A BEER WITH US?
I WOULD,
BUT I GOTTA GET HOME EARLY TONIGHT.

I THINK I UNDERSTAND WHAT REINCARNATION IS LIKE...

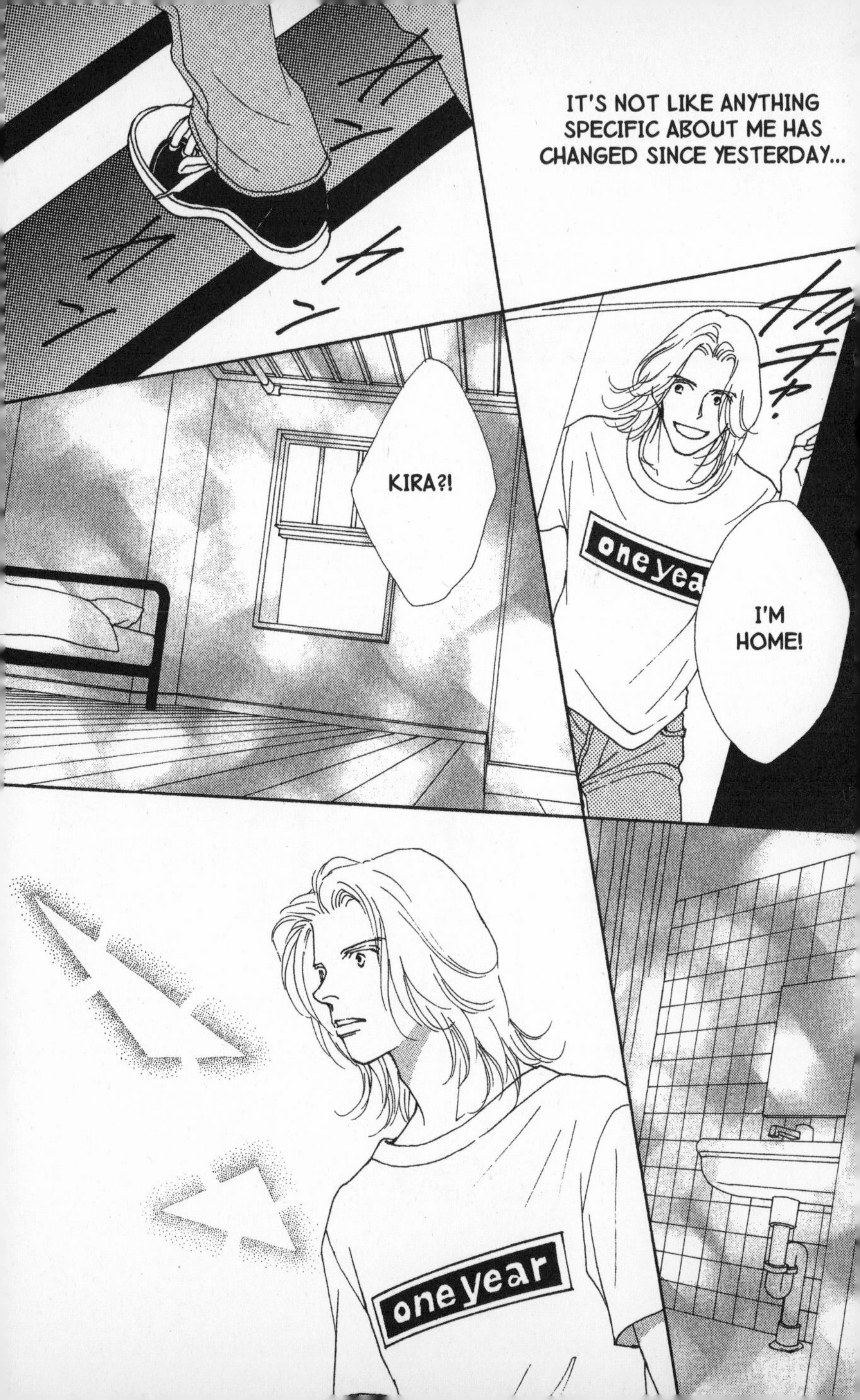
IT'S NOT LIKE ANYTHING SPECIFIC ABOUT ME HAS CHANGED SINCE YESTERDAY...
I'M HOME!
KIRA?!
one year
one year

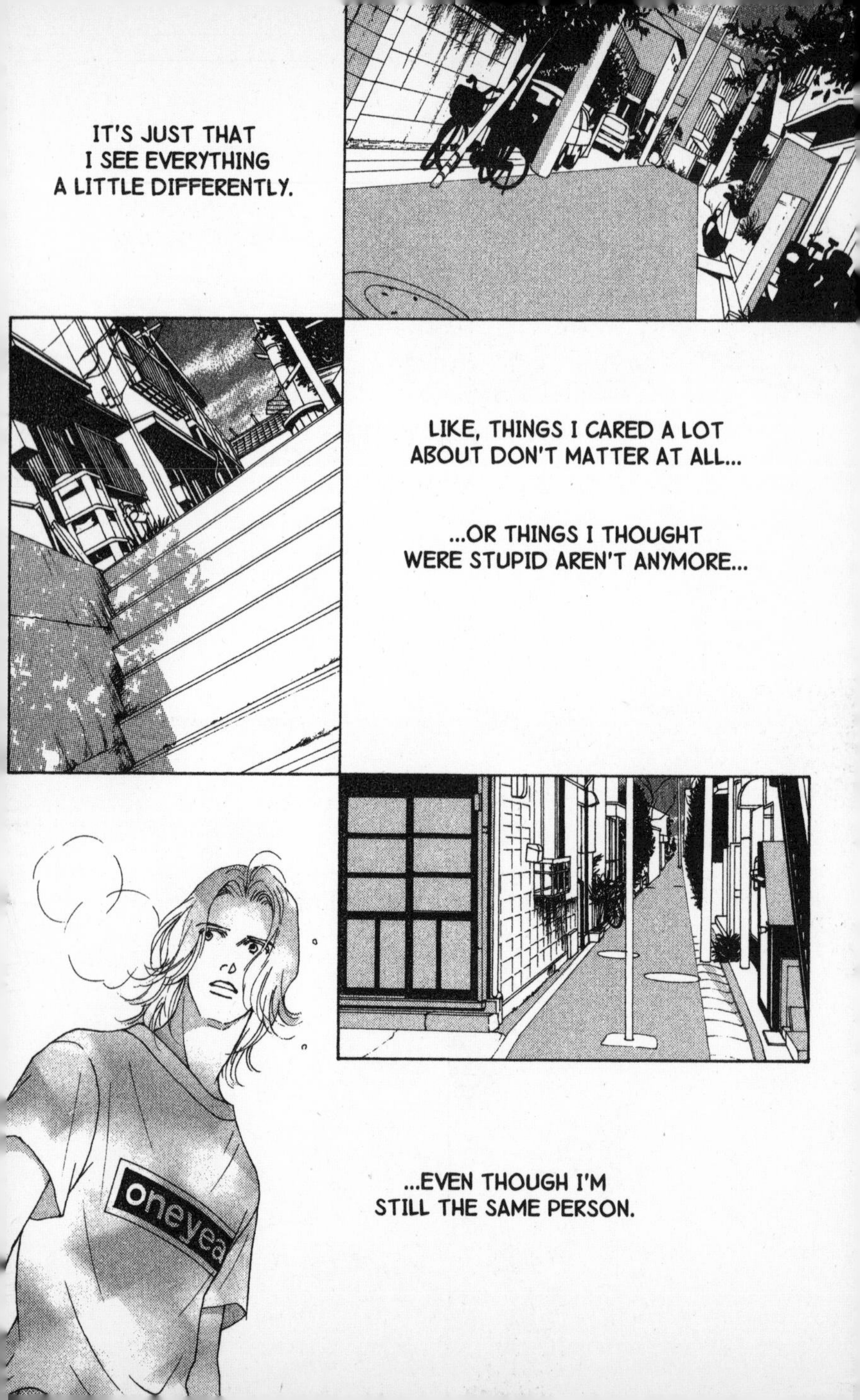
IT'S JUST THAT I SEE EVERYTHING A LITTLE DIFFERENTLY.
LIKE, THINGS I CARED A LOT ABOUT DON'T MATTER AT ALL...
...OR THINGS I THOUGHT WERE STUPID AREN'T ANYMORE...
...EVEN THOUGH I'M STILL THE SAME PERSON.

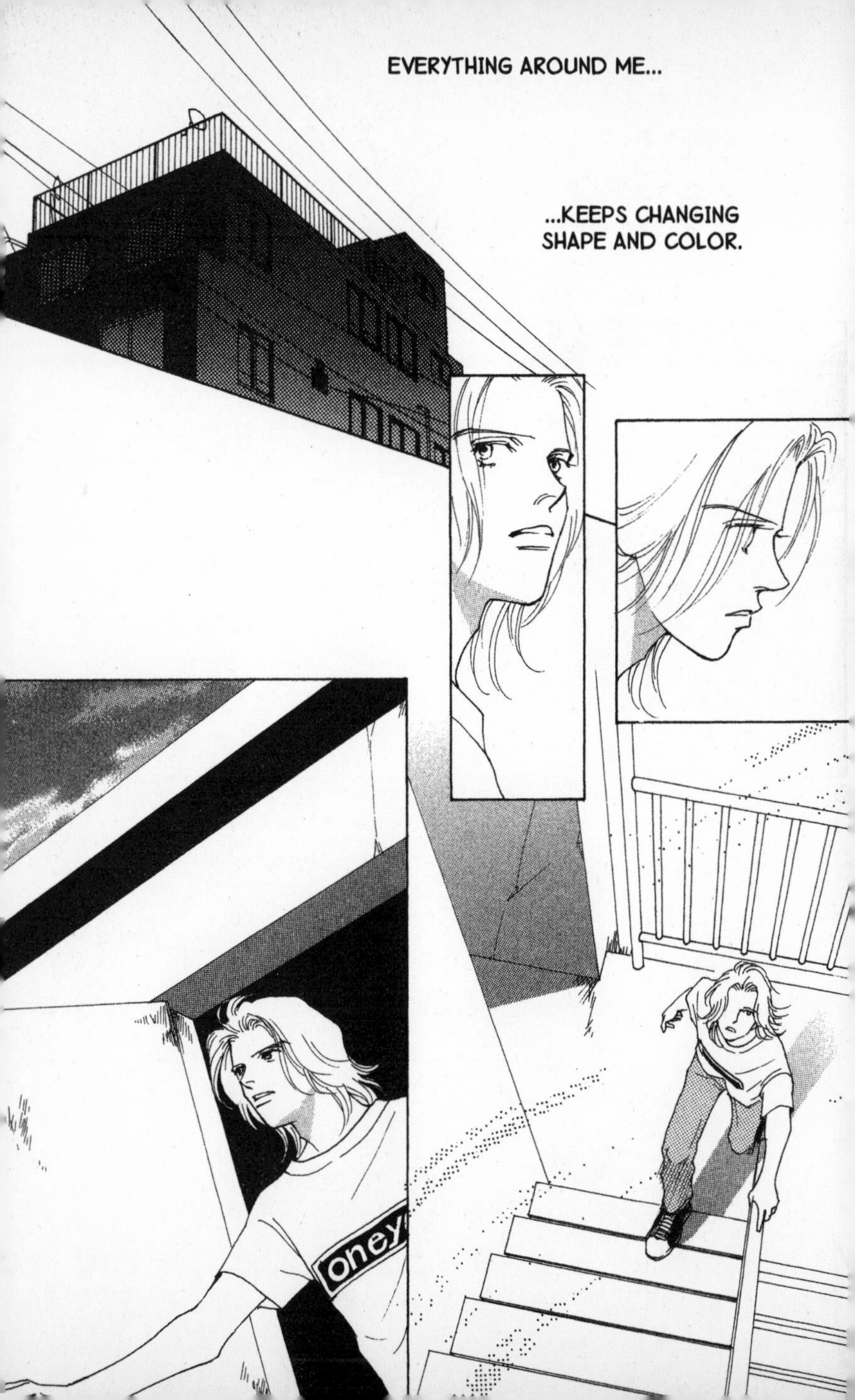
EVERYTHING AROUND ME...
...KEEPS CHANGING SHAPE AND COLOR.
oney

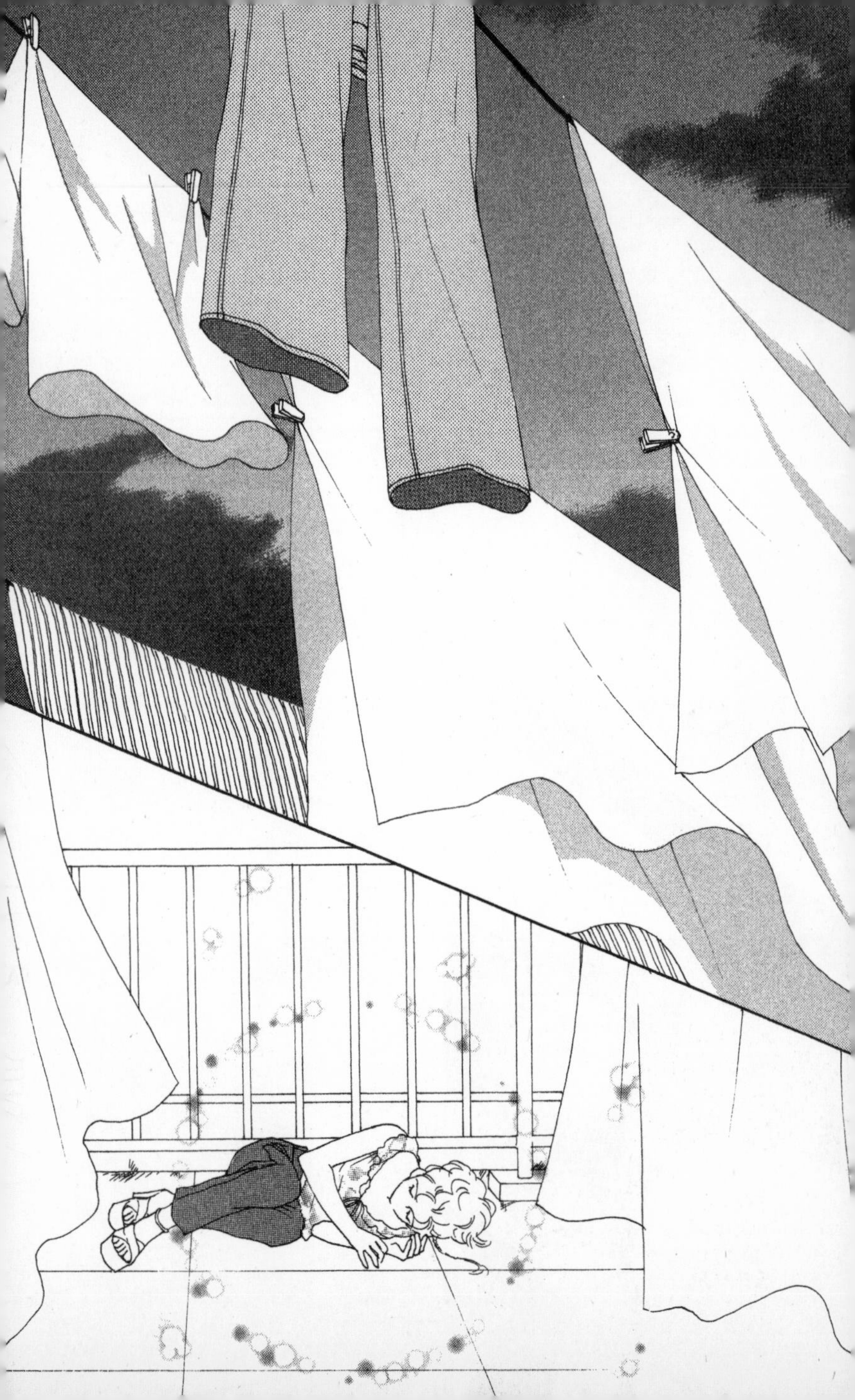

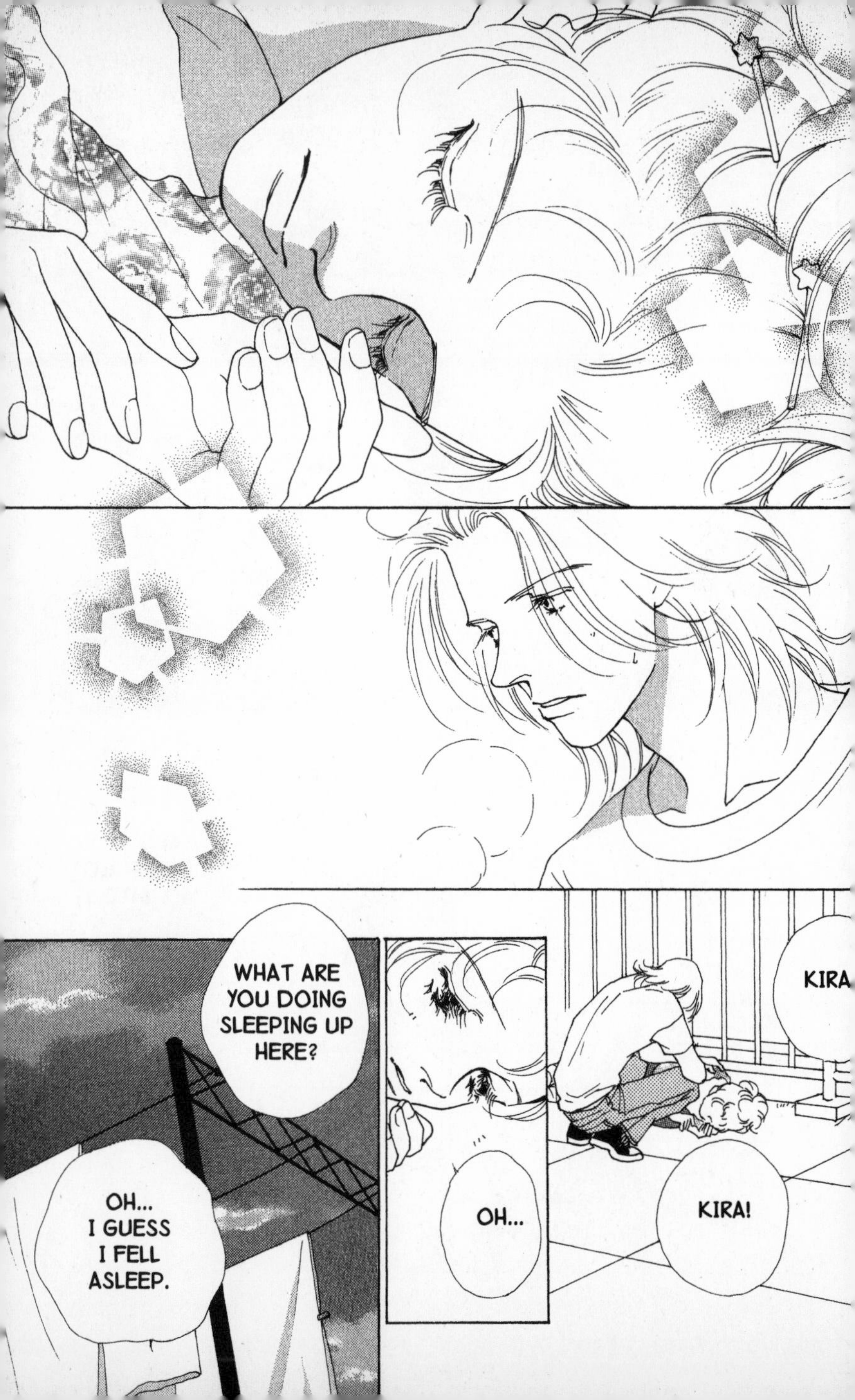
KIRA
KIRA!
OH...
WHAT ARE YOU DOING SLEEPING UP HERE?
OH... I GUESS I FELL ASLEEP.

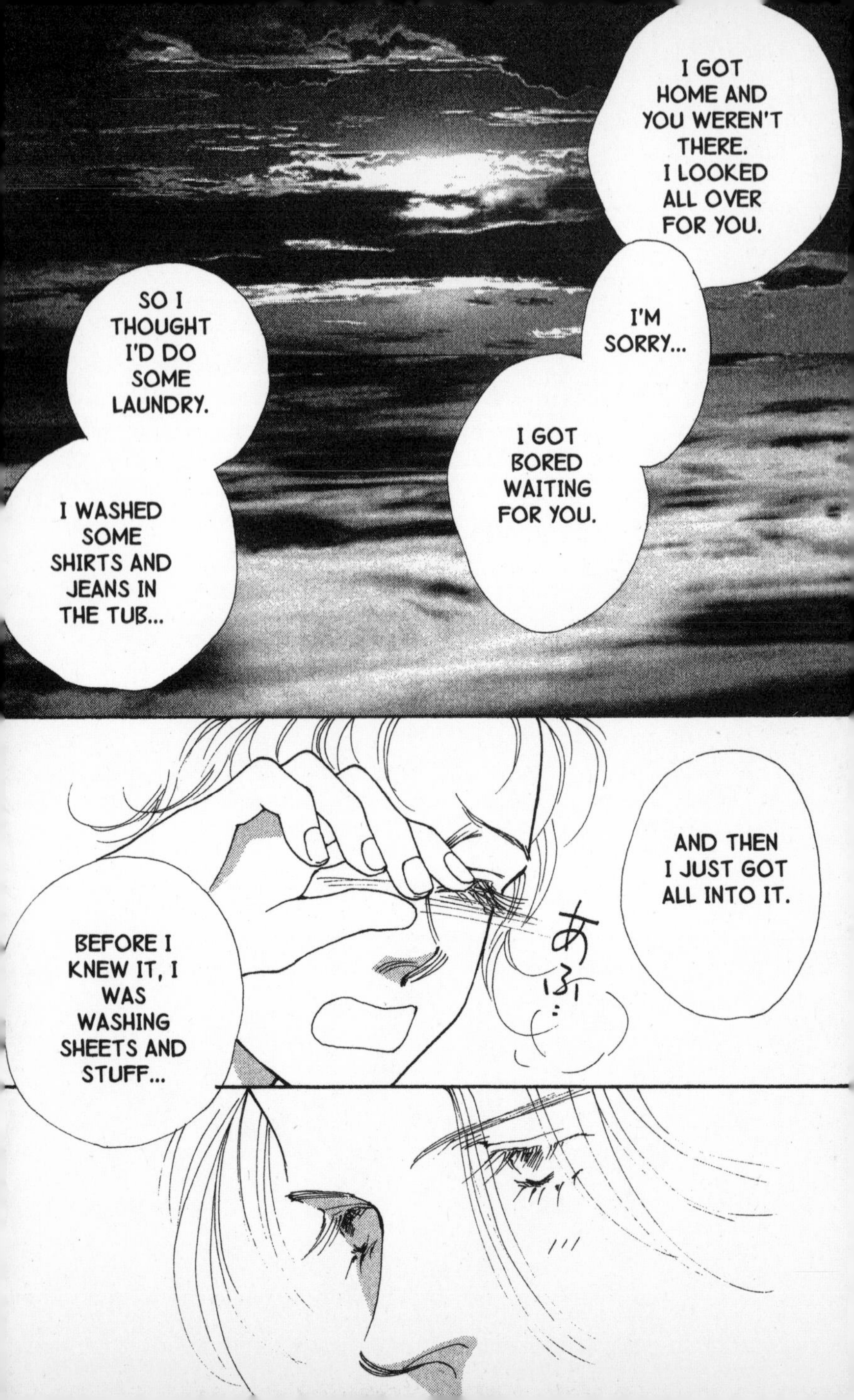
I GOT HOME AND YOU WEREN'T THERE. I LOOKED ALL OVER FOR YOU.
I'M SORRY...
I GOT BORED WAITING FOR YOU.
SO I THOUGHT I'D DO SOME LAUNDRY.
I WASHED SOME SHIRTS AND JEANS IN THE TUB...
AND THEN I JUST GOT ALL INTO IT.
あふ
BEFORE I KNEW IT, I WAS WASHING SHEETS AND STUFF...

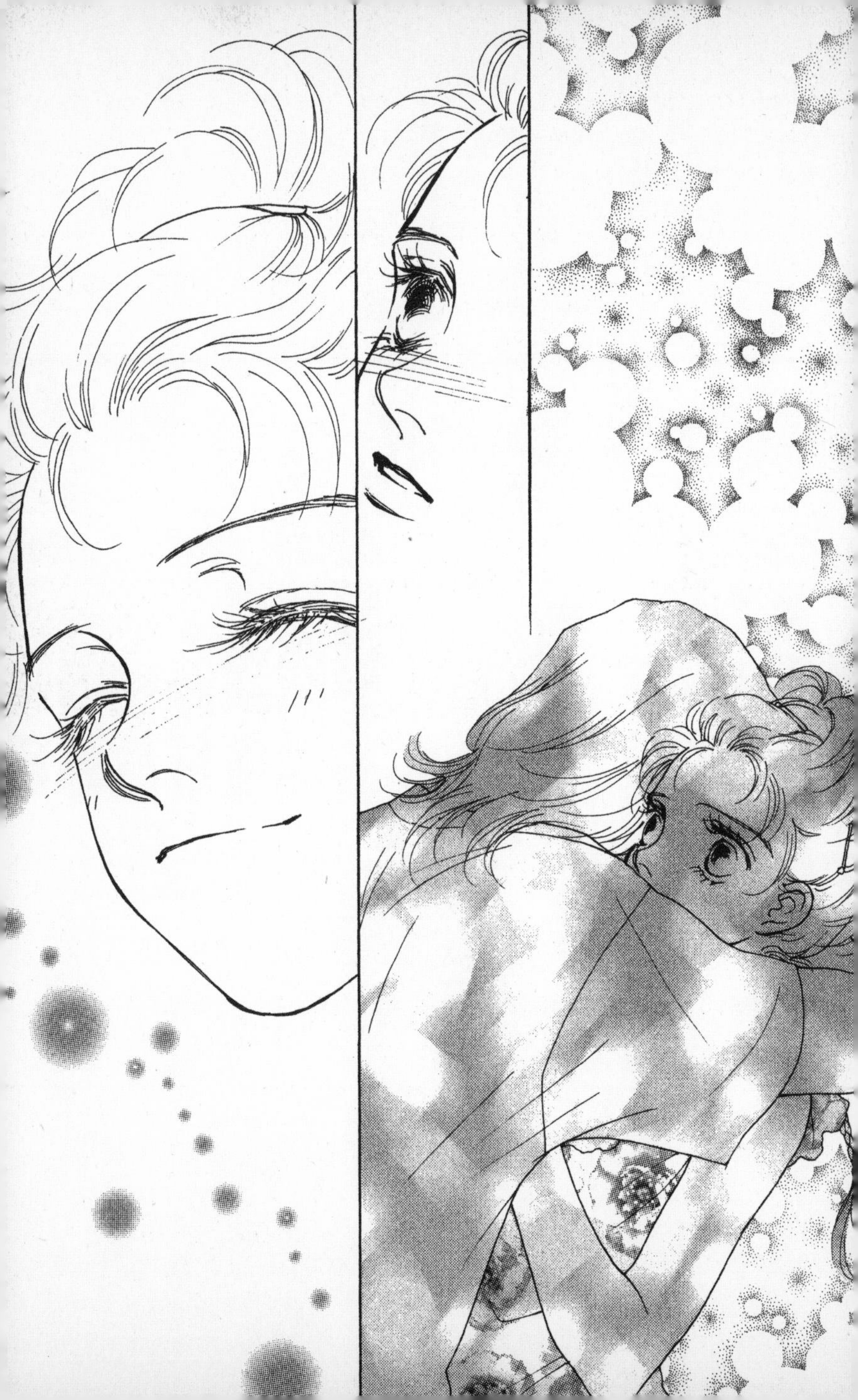

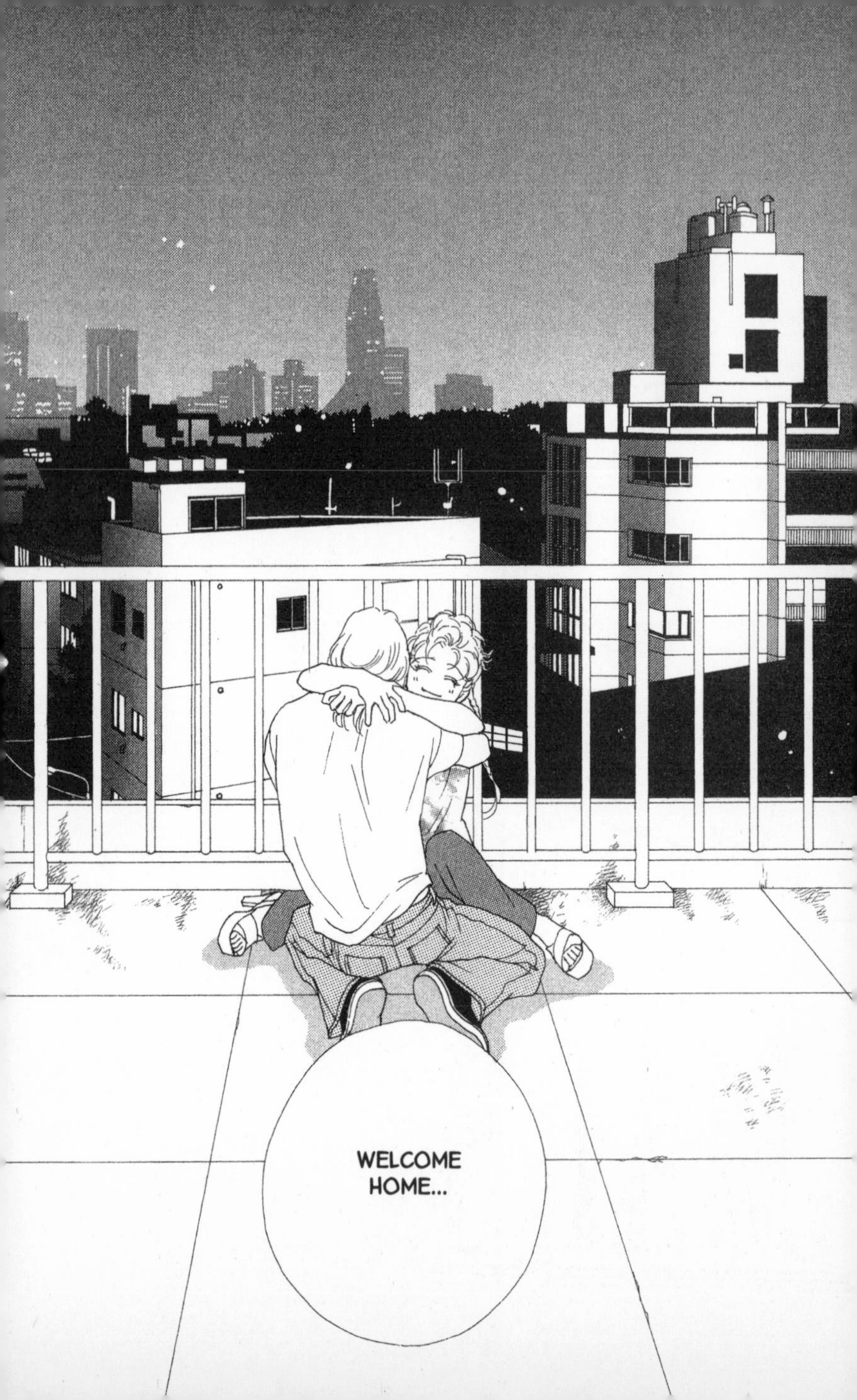
WELCOME HOME...

MARS

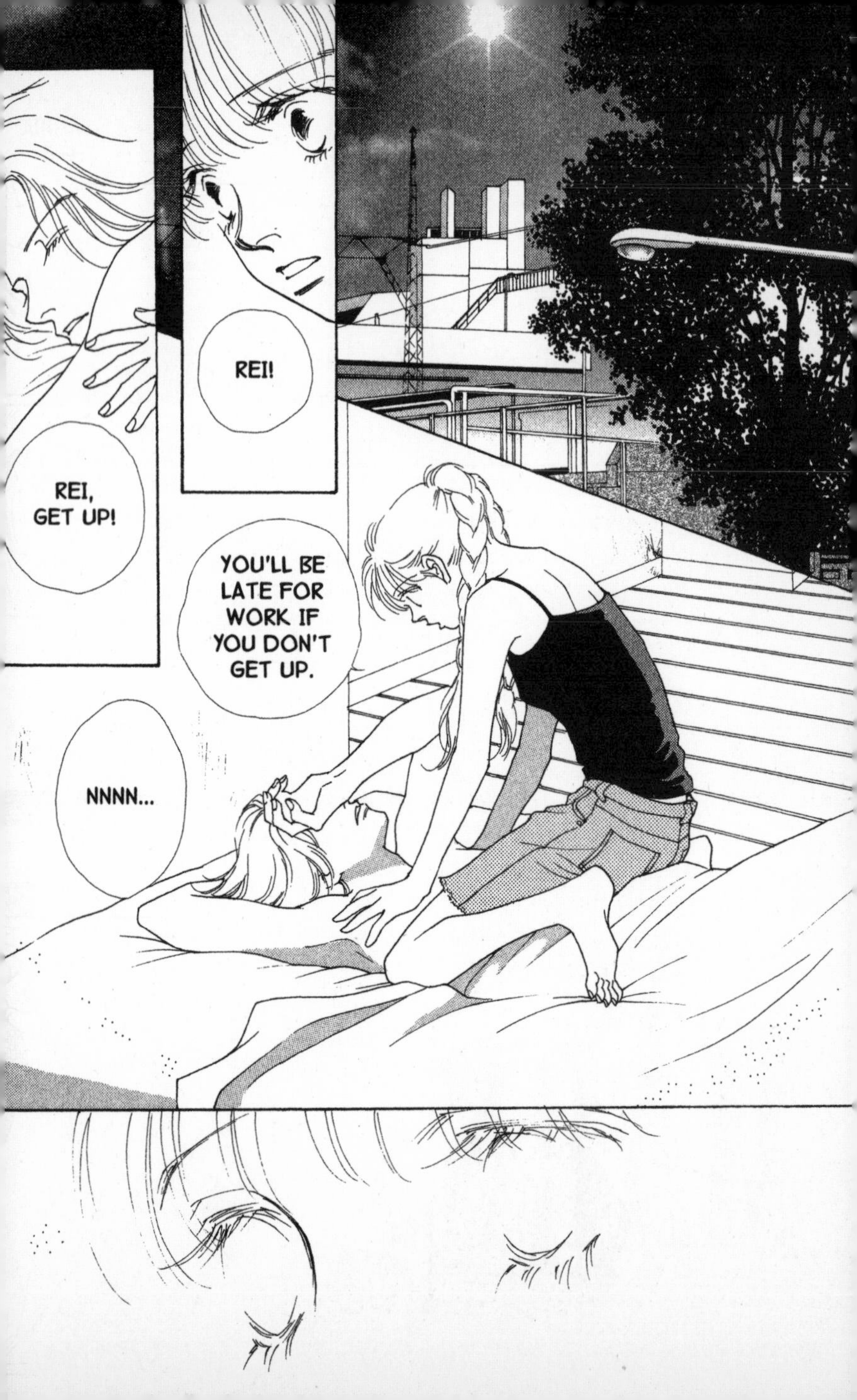
REI!
REI, GET UP!
YOU'LL BE LATE FOR WORK IF YOU DON'T GET UP.
NNNN...

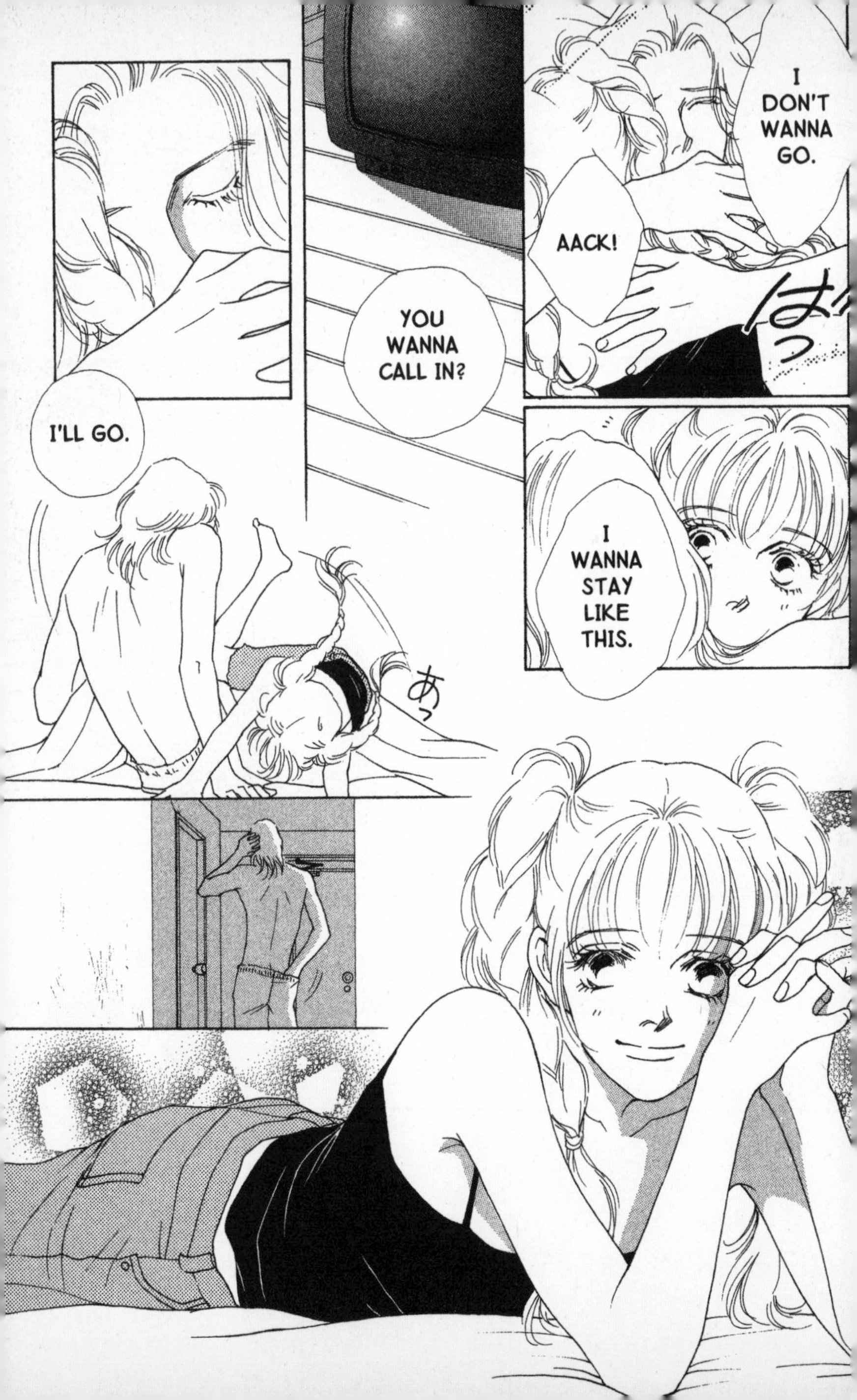
I DON'T WANNA GO.
AACK!
はっ
YOU WANNA CALL IN?
I WANNA STAY LIKE THIS.
I'LL GO.
あっ

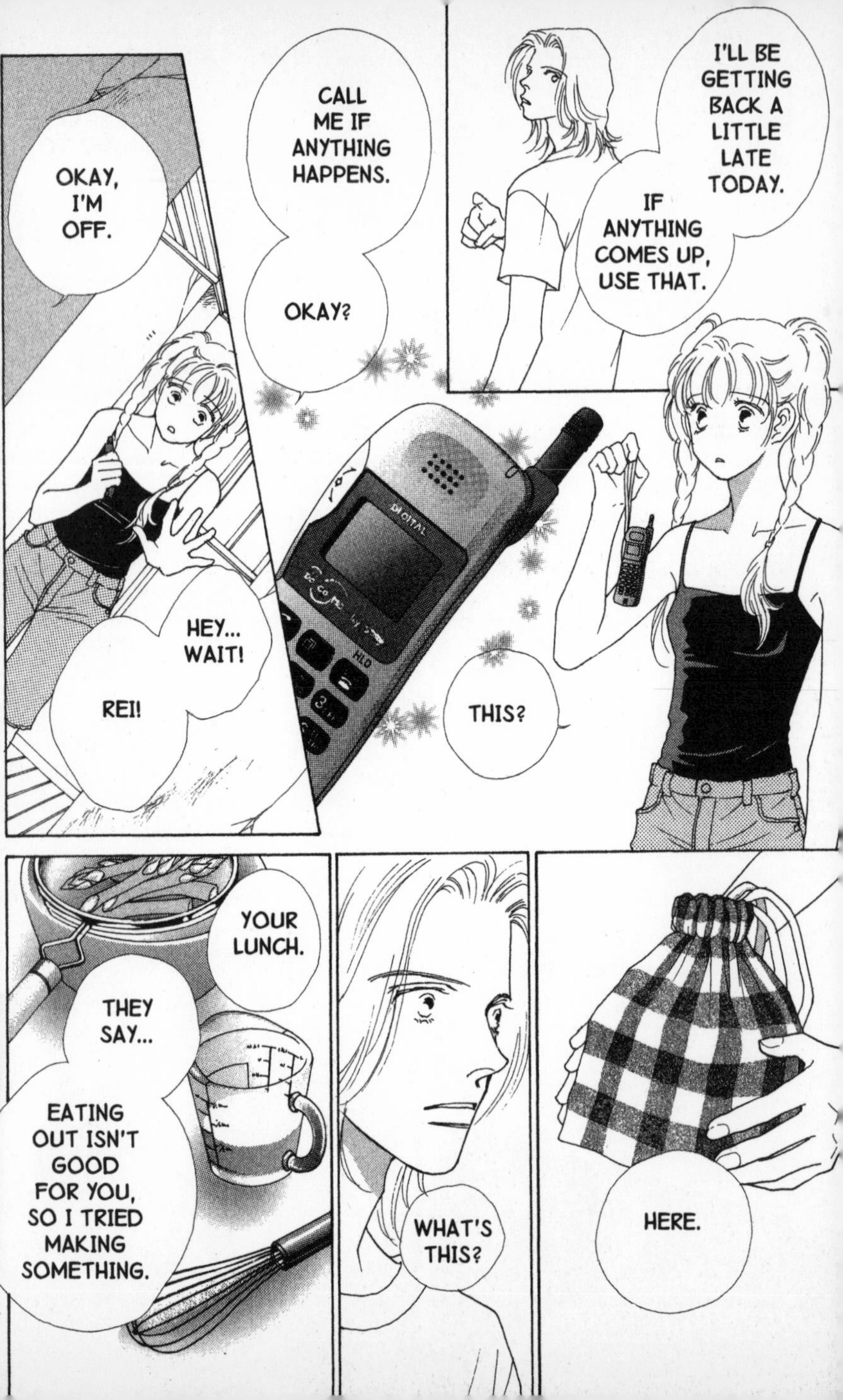
I'LL BE GETTING BACK A LITTLE LATE TODAY.
IF ANYTHING COMES UP, USE THAT.
THIS?
CALL ME IF ANYTHING HAPPENS.
OKAY?
OKAY, I'M OFF.
HEY... WAIT!
REI!
HERE.
WHAT'S THIS?
YOUR LUNCH.
THEY SAY...
EATING OUT ISN'T GOOD FOR YOU, SO I TRIED MAKING SOMETHING.

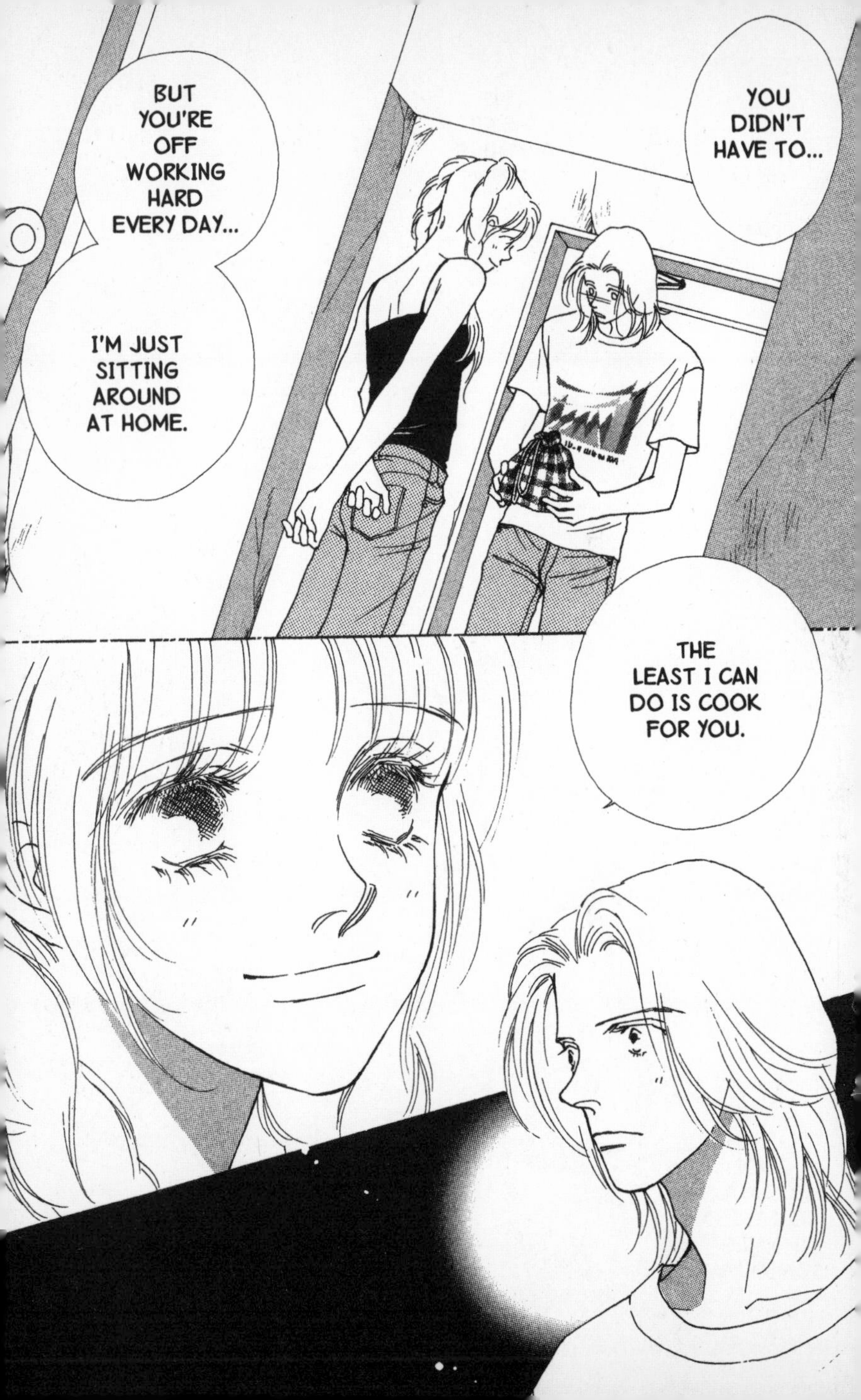
YOU DIDN'T HAVE TO...
BUT YOU'RE OFF WORKING HARD EVERY DAY...
I'M JUST SITTING AROUND AT HOME.
THE LEAST I CAN DO IS COOK FOR YOU.

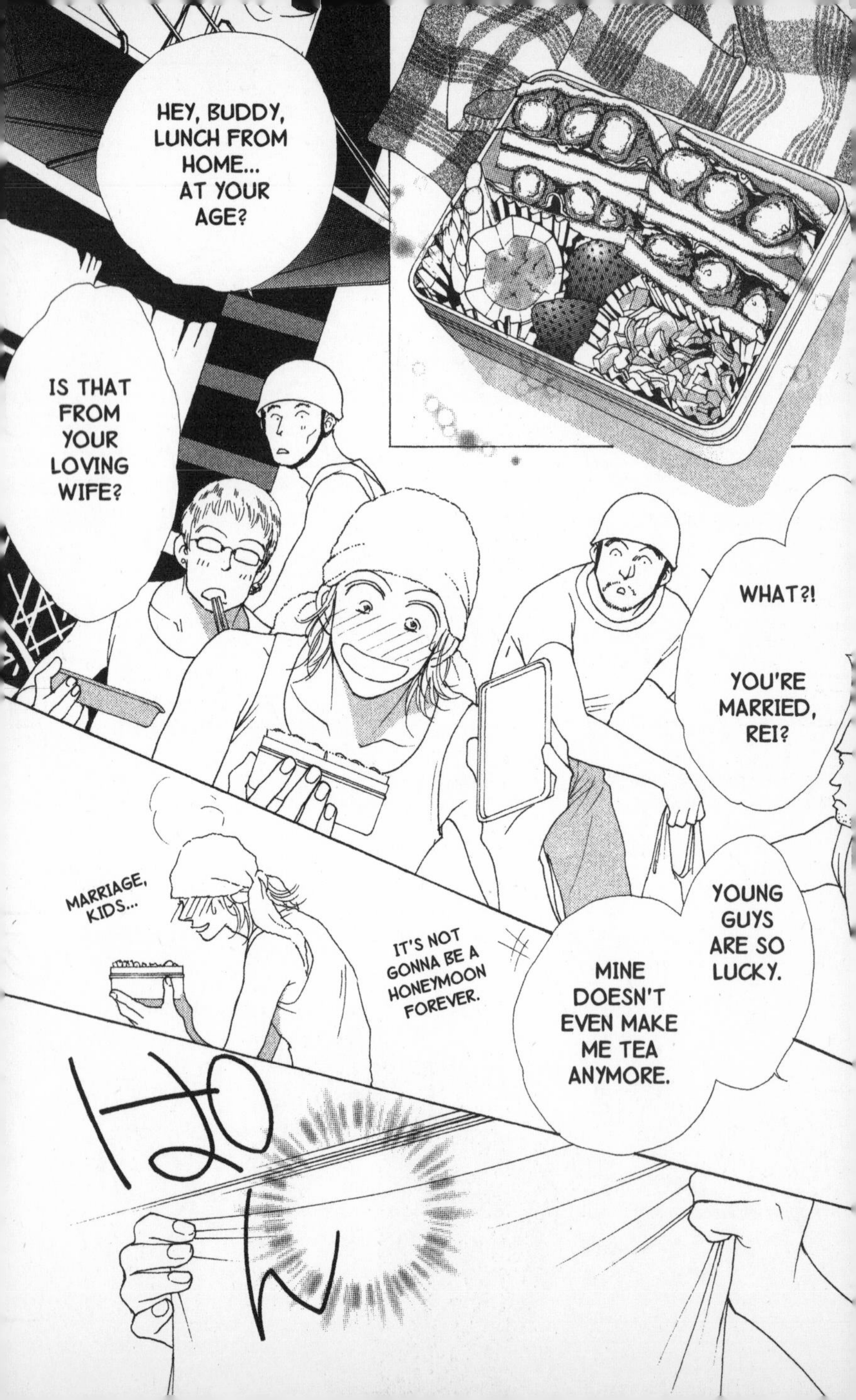
HEY, BUDDY, LUNCH FROM HOME... AT YOUR AGE?
IS THAT FROM YOUR LOVING WIFE?
WHAT?!
YOU'RE MARRIED, REI?
YOUNG GUYS ARE SO LUCKY.
MINE DOESN'T EVEN MAKE ME TEA ANYMORE.
IT'S NOT GONNA BE A HONEYMOON FOREVER.
MARRIAGE, KIDS...

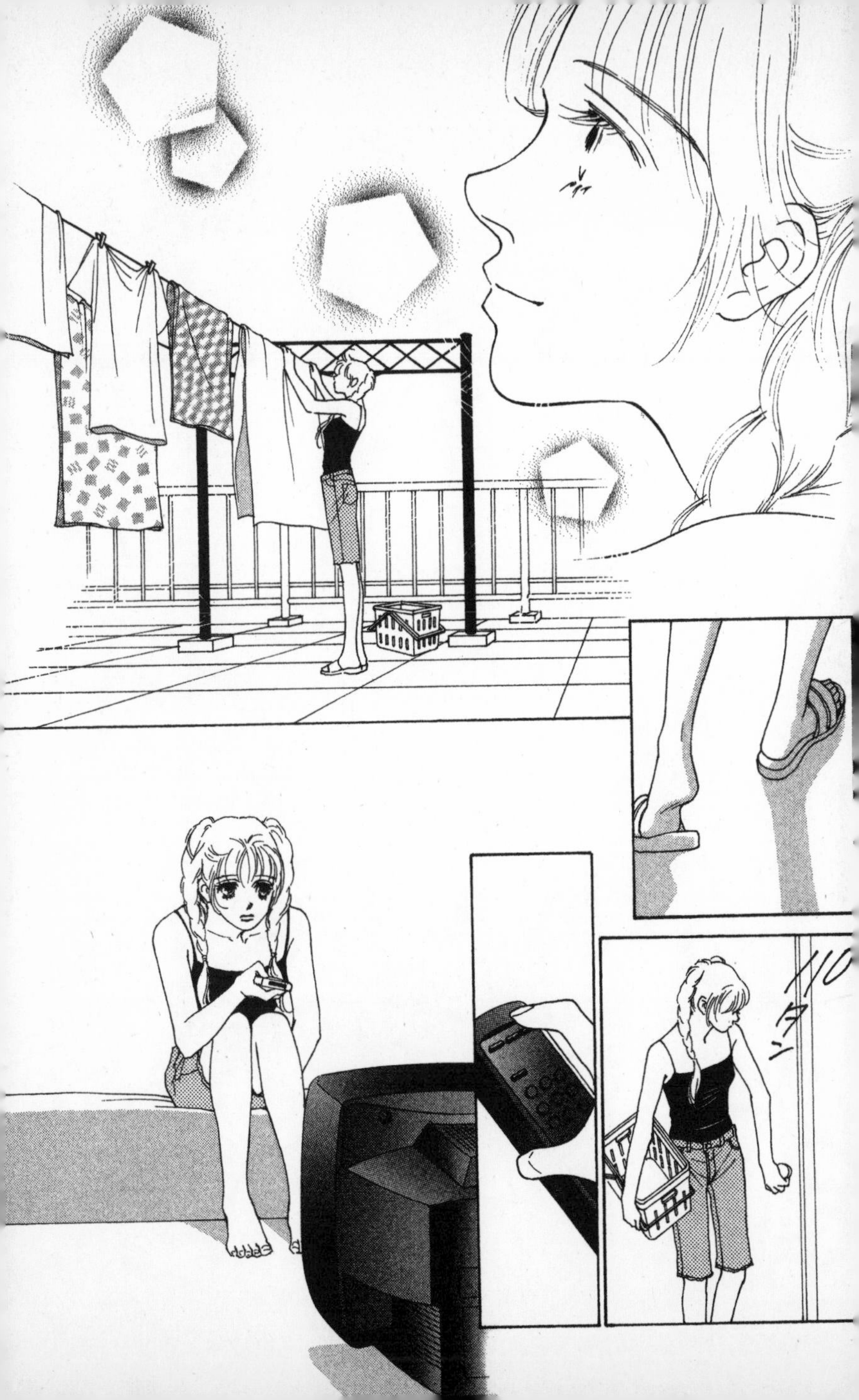
パタン

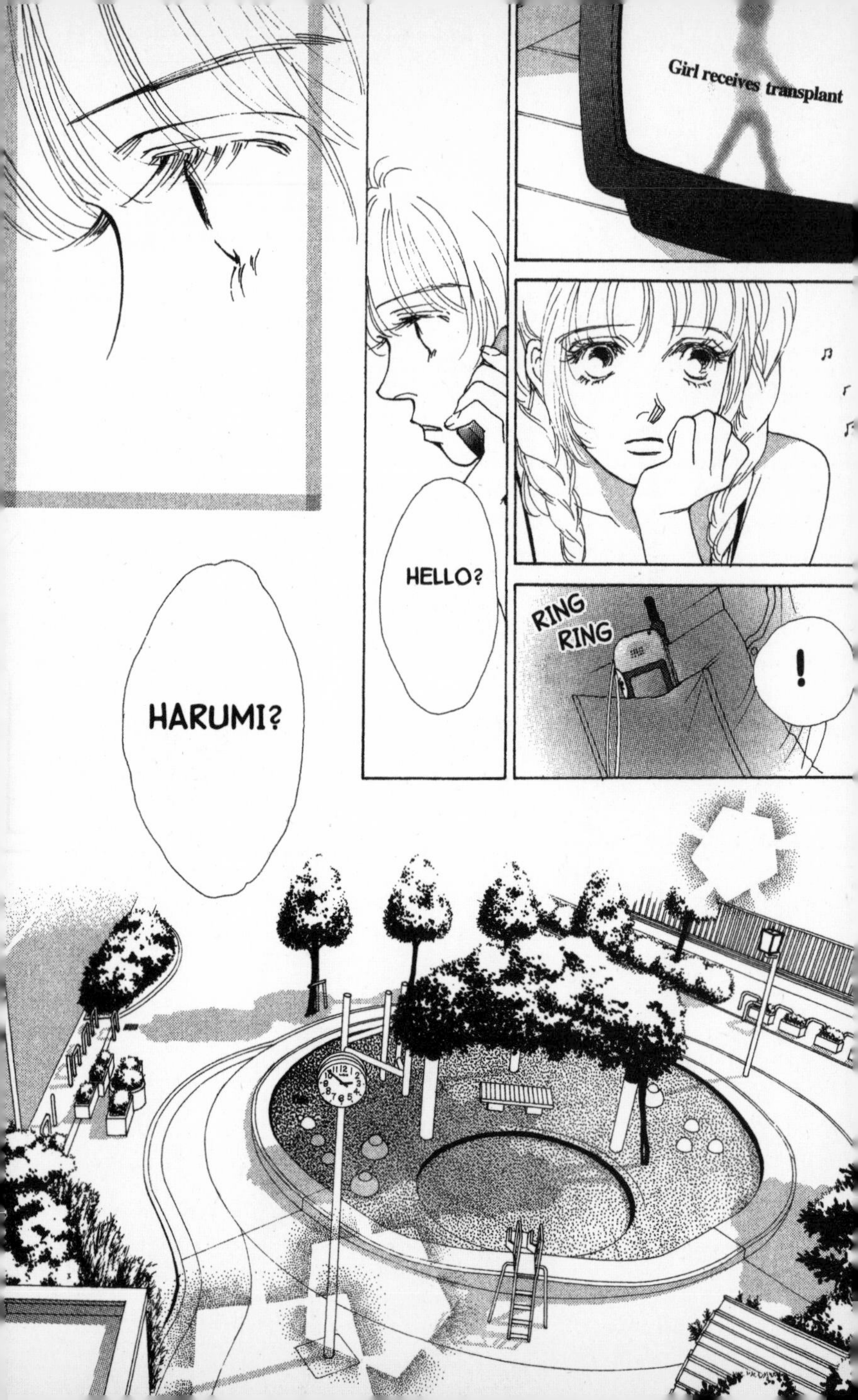
Girl receives transplant
RING RING
!
HELLO?
HARUMI?

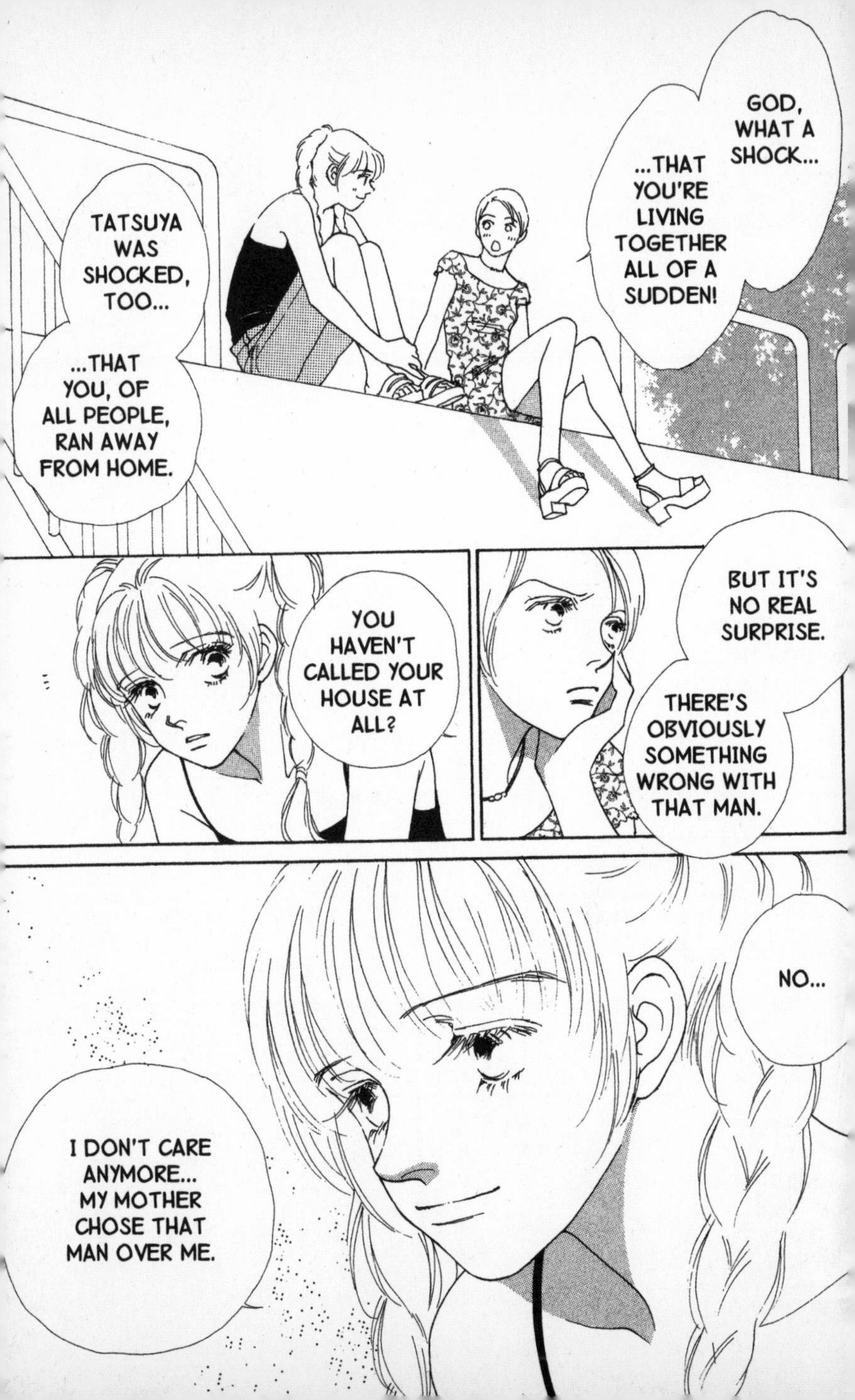
GOD, WHAT A SHOCK...
...THAT YOU'RE LIVING TOGETHER ALL OF A SUDDEN!
TATSUYA WAS SHOCKED, TOO...
...THAT YOU, OF ALL PEOPLE, RAN AWAY FROM HOME.
BUT IT'S NO REAL SURPRISE.
THERE'S OBVIOUSLY SOMETHING WRONG WITH THAT MAN.
YOU HAVEN'T CALLED YOUR HOUSE AT ALL?
NO...
I DON'T CARE ANYMORE... MY MOTHER CHOSE THAT MAN OVER ME.

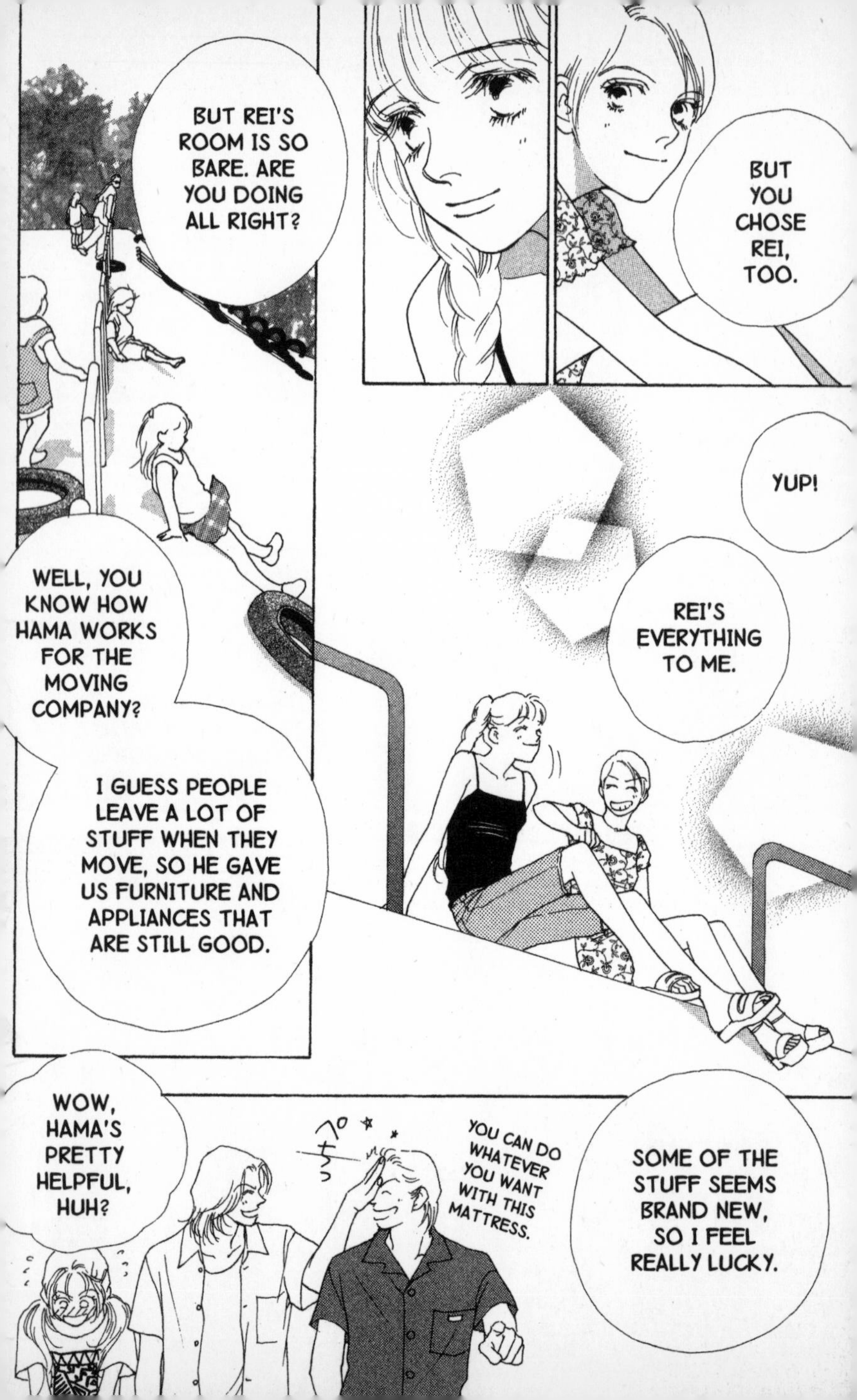

BUT YOU CHOSE REI, TOO.
YUP!
REI'S EVERYTHING TO ME.
BUT REI'S ROOM IS SO BARE. ARE YOU DOING ALL RIGHT?
WELL, YOU KNOW HOW HAMA WORKS FOR THE MOVING COMPANY?
I GUESS PEOPLE LEAVE A LOT OF STUFF WHEN THEY MOVE, SO HE GAVE US FURNITURE AND APPLIANCES THAT ARE STILL GOOD.
SOME OF THE STUFF SEEMS BRAND NEW, SO I FEEL REALLY LUCKY.
YOU CAN DO WHATEVER YOU WANT WITH THIS MATTRESS.
WOW, HAMA'S PRETTY HELPFUL, HUH?

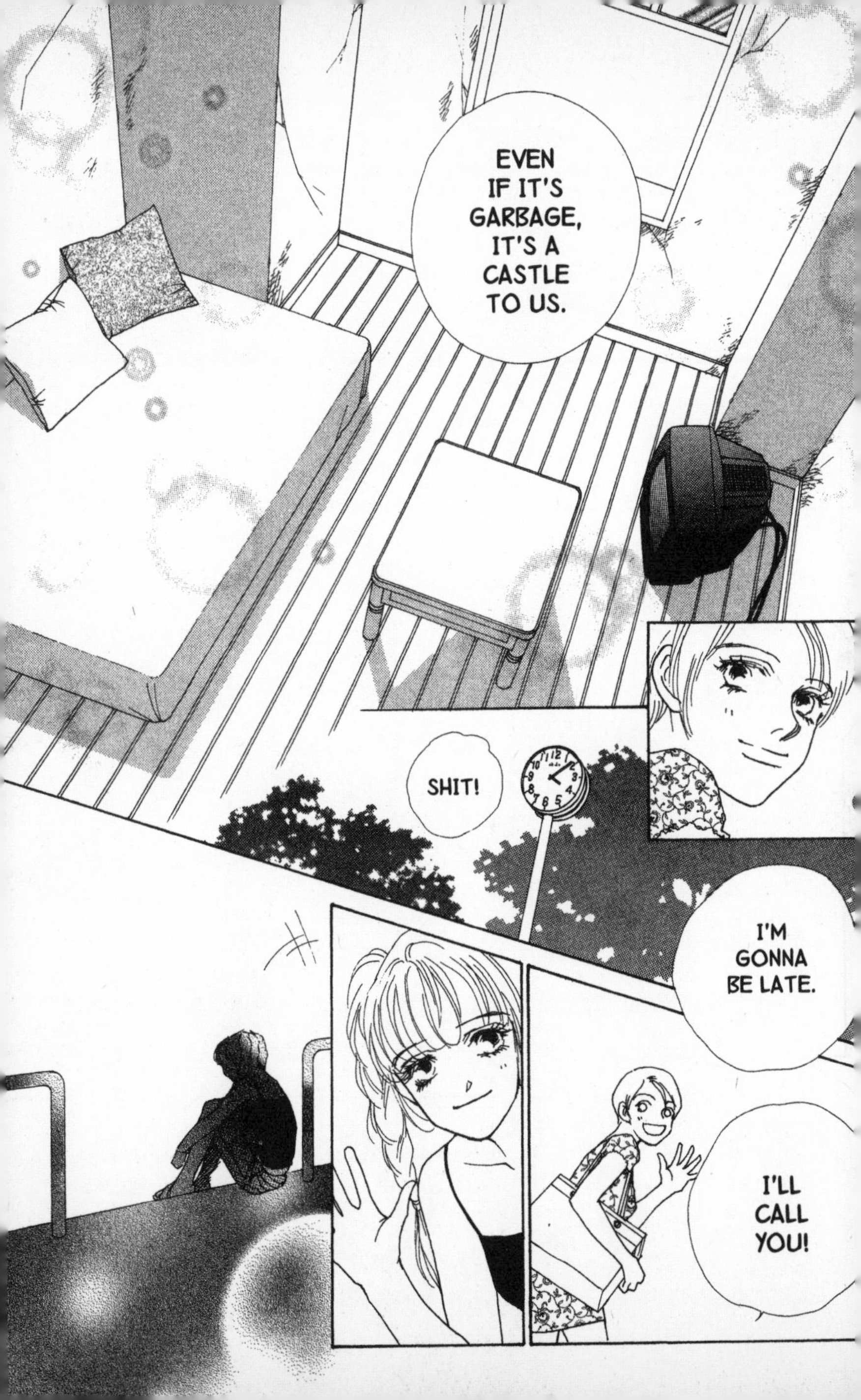
EVEN IF IT'S GARBAGE, IT'S A CASTLE TO US.
SHIT!
I'M GONNA BE LATE.
I'LL CALL YOU!

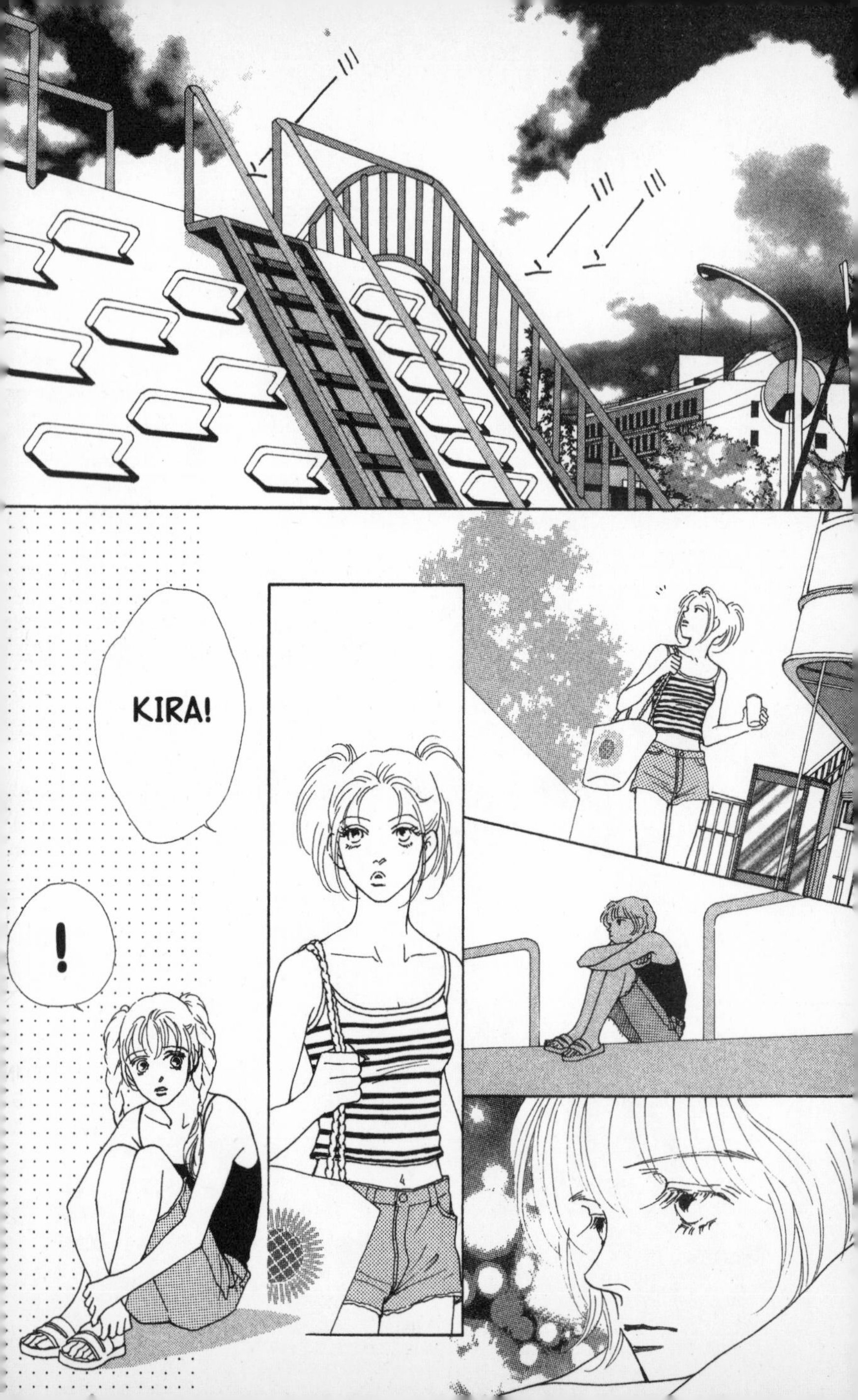

KIRA!
!

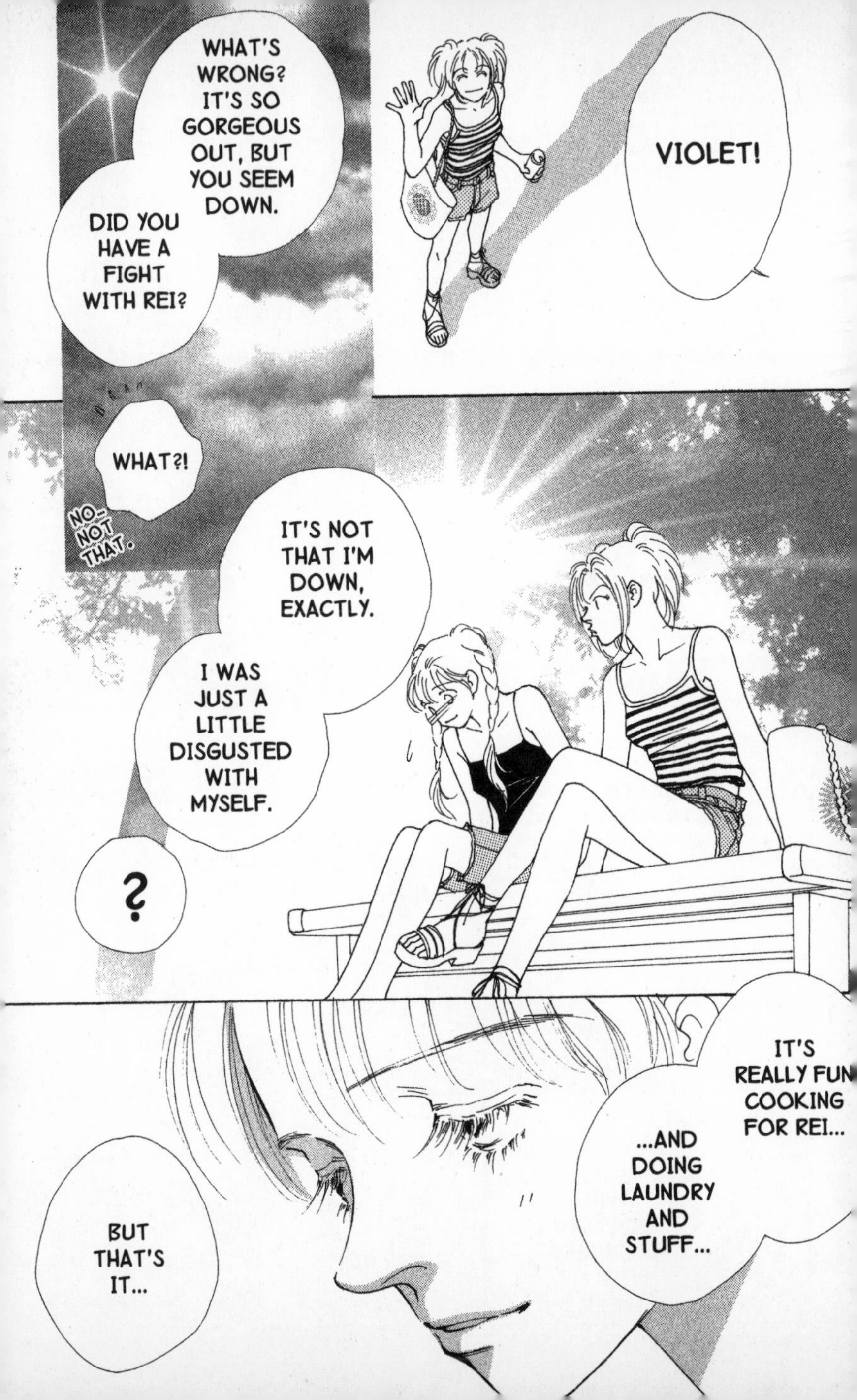

VIOLET!
WHAT'S WRONG? IT'S SO GORGEOUS OUT, BUT YOU SEEM DOWN.
DID YOU HAVE A FIGHT WITH REI?
WHAT?!
NO... NOT THAT.
IT'S NOT THAT I'M DOWN, EXACTLY.
I WAS JUST A LITTLE DISGUSTED WITH MYSELF.
?
IT'S REALLY FUN COOKING FOR REI...
...AND DOING LAUNDRY AND STUFF...
BUT THAT'S IT...

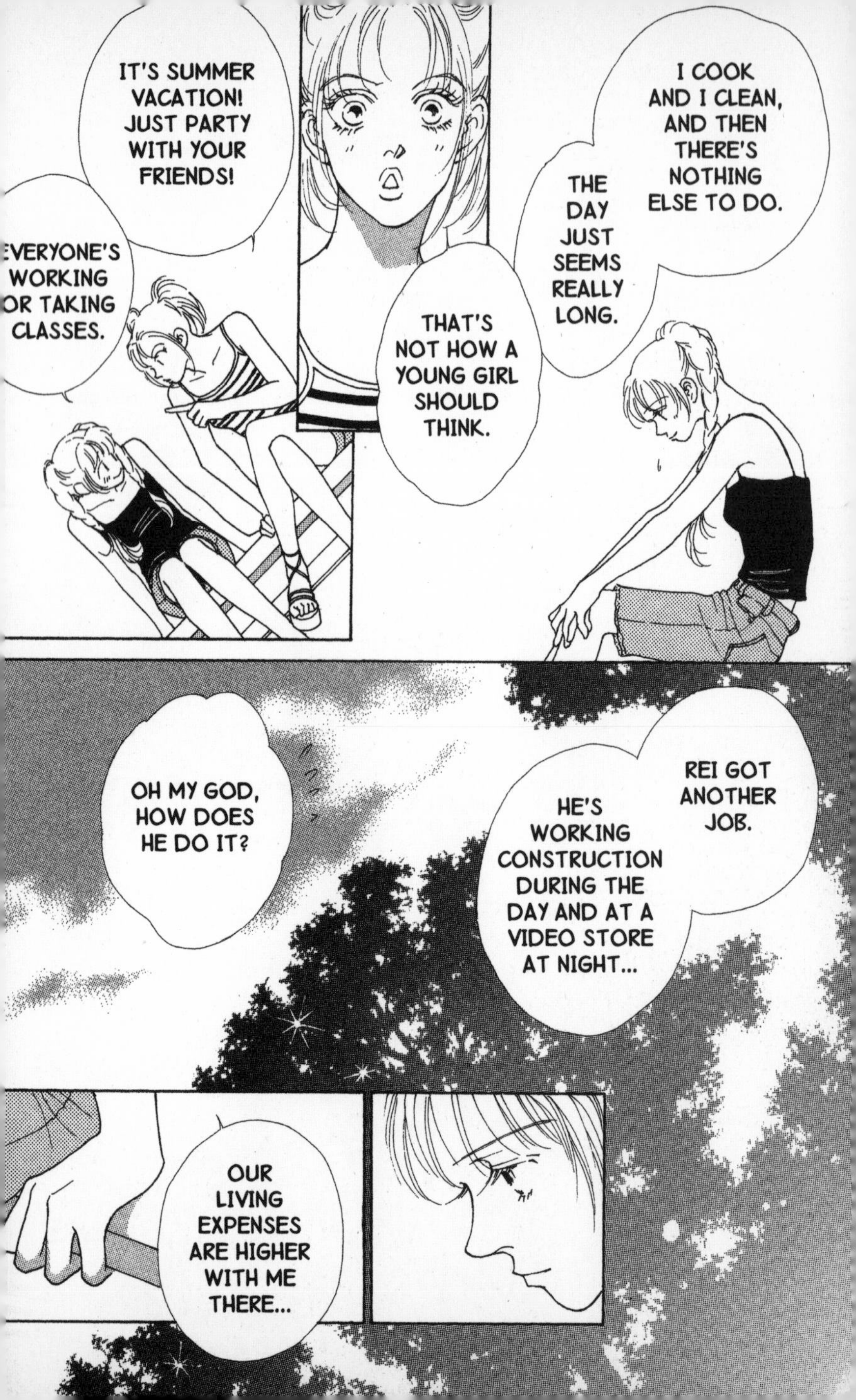
I COOK AND I CLEAN, AND THEN THERE'S NOTHING ELSE TO DO.
THE DAY JUST SEEMS REALLY LONG.
THAT'S NOT HOW A YOUNG GIRL SHOULD THINK.
IT'S SUMMER VACATION! JUST PARTY WITH YOUR FRIENDS!
EVERYONE'S WORKING OR TAKING CLASSES.
REI GOT ANOTHER JOB.
HE'S WORKING CONSTRUCTION DURING THE DAY AND AT A VIDEO STORE AT NIGHT...
OH MY GOD, HOW DOES HE DO IT?
OUR LIVING EXPENSES ARE HIGHER WITH ME THERE...

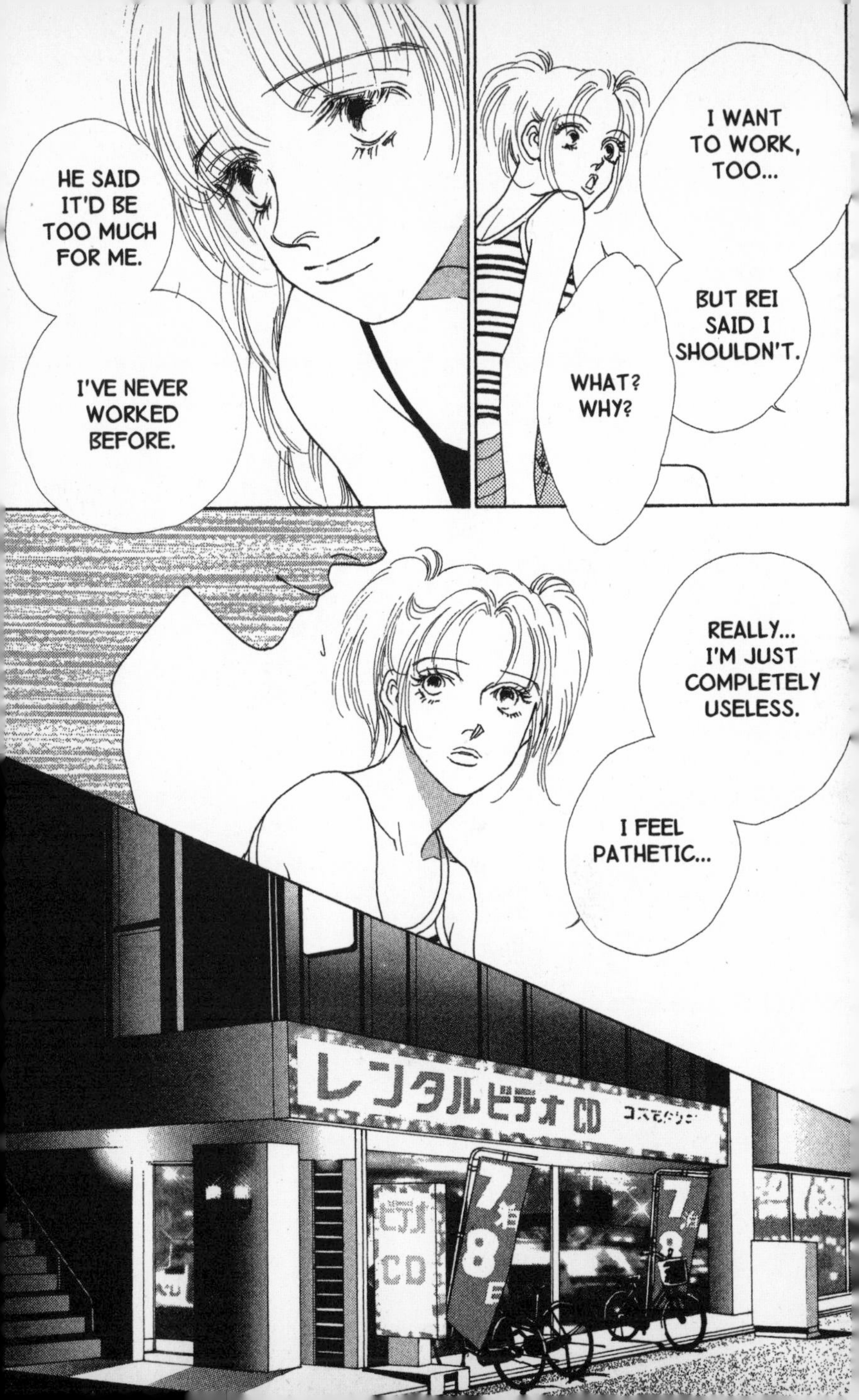
I WANT TO WORK, TOO...
BUT REI SAID I SHOULDN'T.
WHAT? WHY?
HE SAID IT'D BE TOO MUCH FOR ME.
I'VE NEVER WORKED BEFORE.
REALLY... I'M JUST COMPLETELY USELESS.
I FEEL PATHETIC...
レンタルビデオ CD

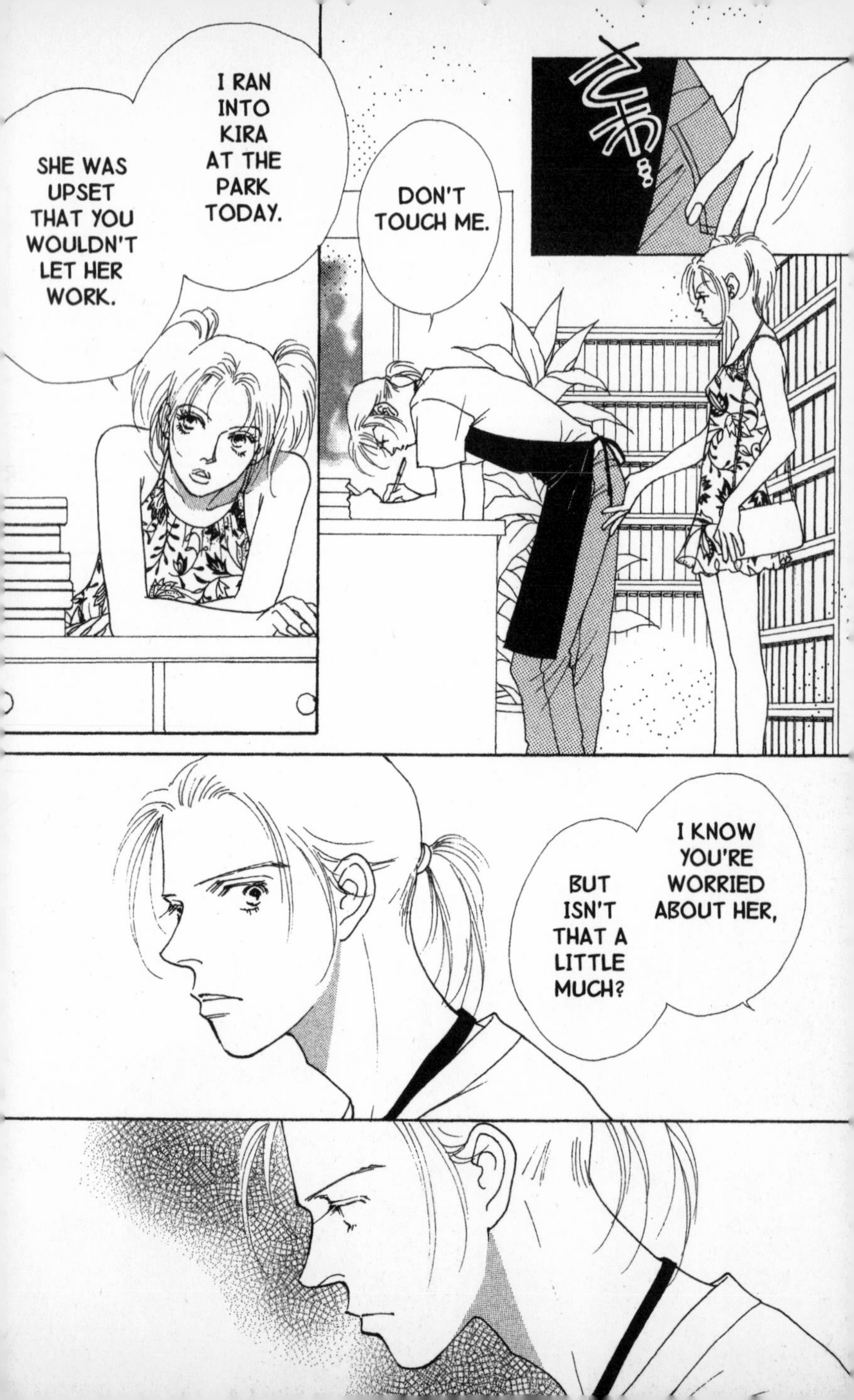
DON'T TOUCH ME.
I RAN INTO KIRA AT THE PARK TODAY.
SHE WAS UPSET THAT YOU WOULDN'T LET HER WORK.
I KNOW YOU'RE WORRIED ABOUT HER,
BUT ISN'T THAT A LITTLE MUCH?

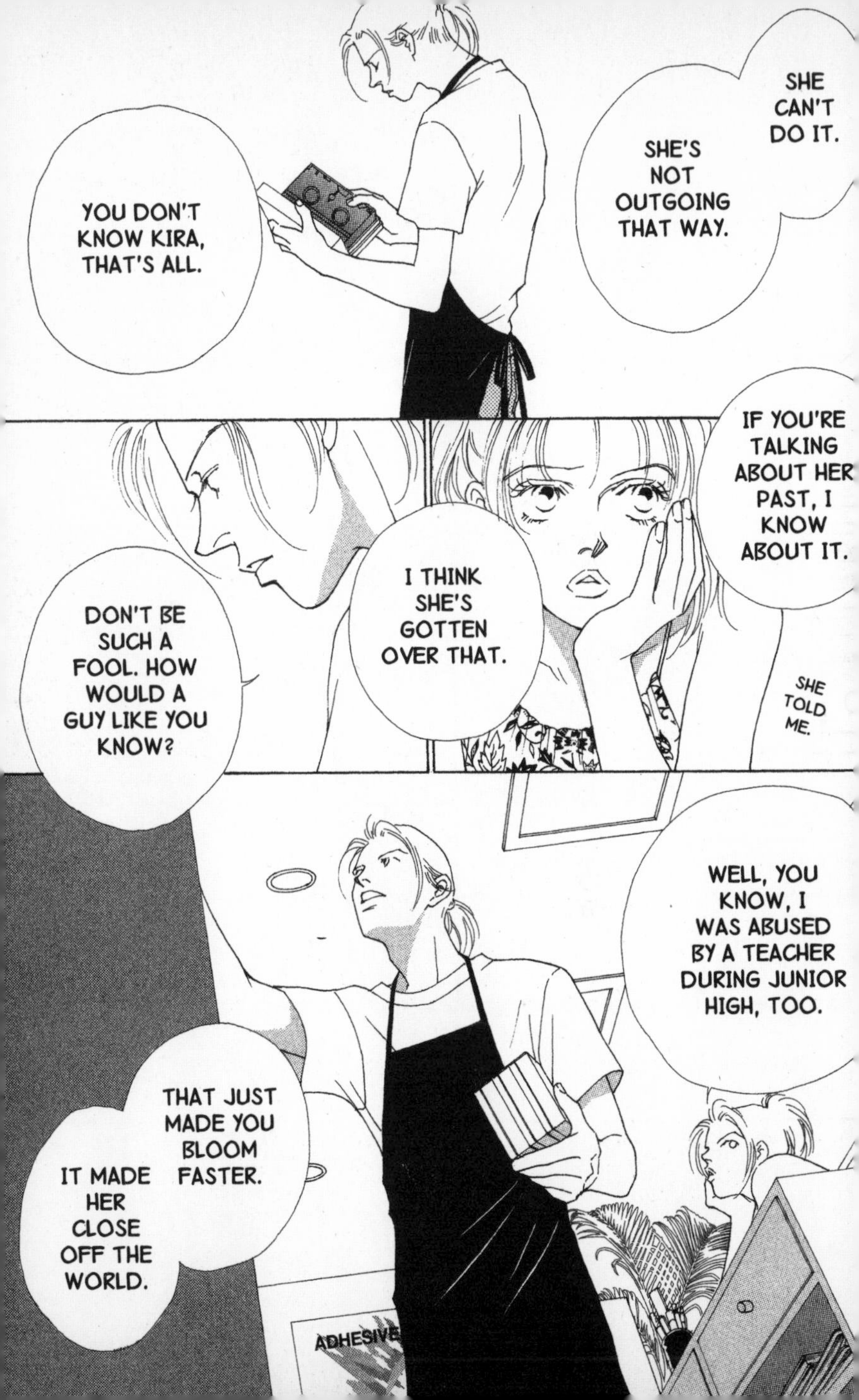
SHE CAN'T DO IT.
SHE'S NOT OUTGOING THAT WAY.
YOU DON'T KNOW KIRA, THAT'S ALL.
IF YOU'RE TALKING ABOUT HER PAST, I KNOW ABOUT IT.
SHE TOLD ME.
I THINK SHE'S GOTTEN OVER THAT.
DON'T BE SUCH A FOOL. HOW WOULD A GUY LIKE YOU KNOW?
WELL, YOU KNOW, I WAS ABUSED BY A TEACHER DURING JUNIOR HIGH, TOO.
THAT JUST MADE YOU BLOOM FASTER.
IT MADE HER CLOSE OFF THE WORLD.
ADHESIVE

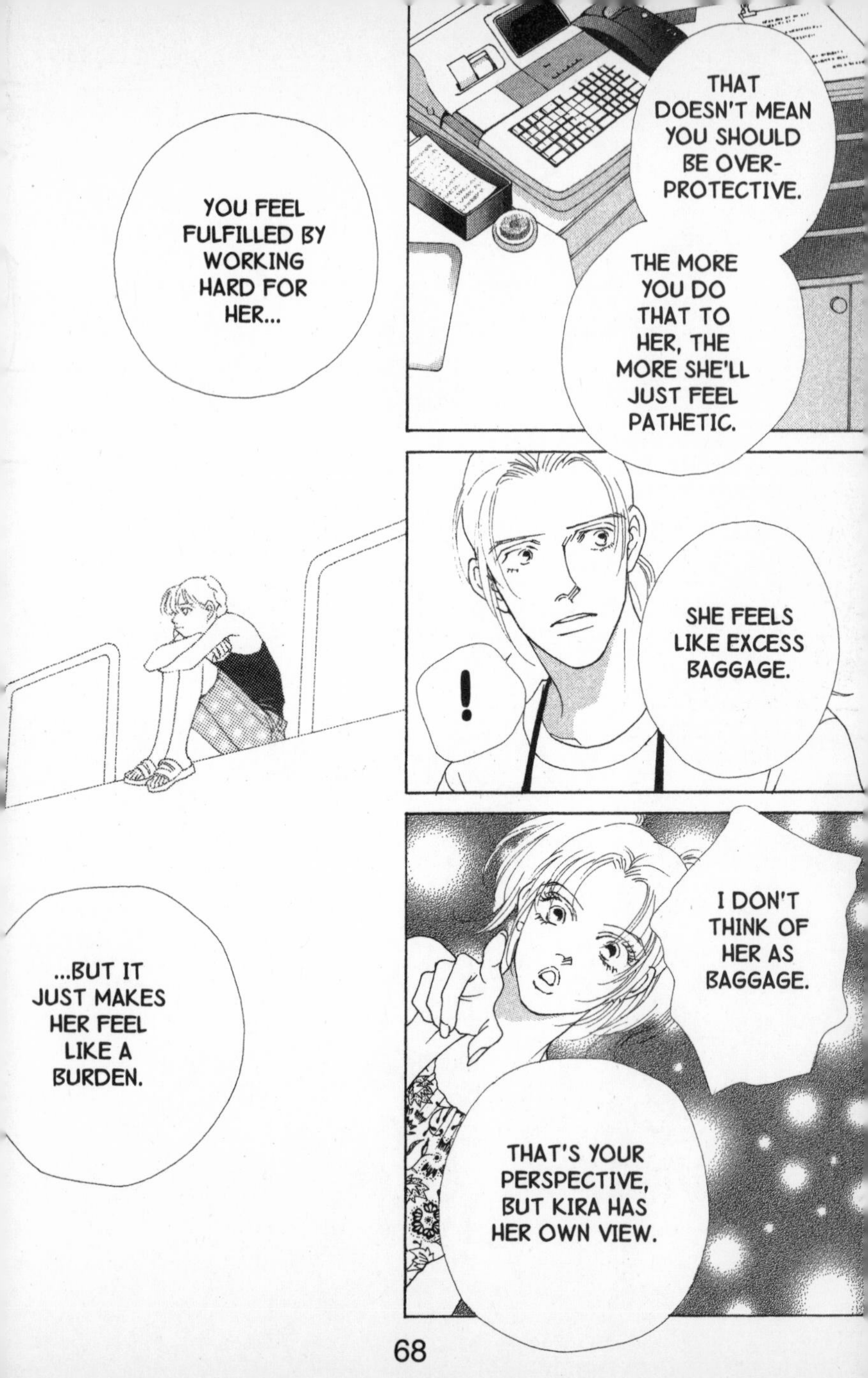
THAT DOESN'T MEAN YOU SHOULD BE OVER-PROTECTIVE.
THE MORE YOU DO THAT TO HER, THE MORE SHE'LL JUST FEEL PATHETIC.
SHE FEELS LIKE EXCESS BAGGAGE.
!
I DON'T THINK OF HER AS BAGGAGE.
THAT'S YOUR PERSPECTIVE, BUT KIRA HAS HER OWN VIEW.
YOU FEEL FULFILLED BY WORKING HARD FOR HER...
...BUT IT JUST MAKES HER FEEL LIKE A BURDEN.

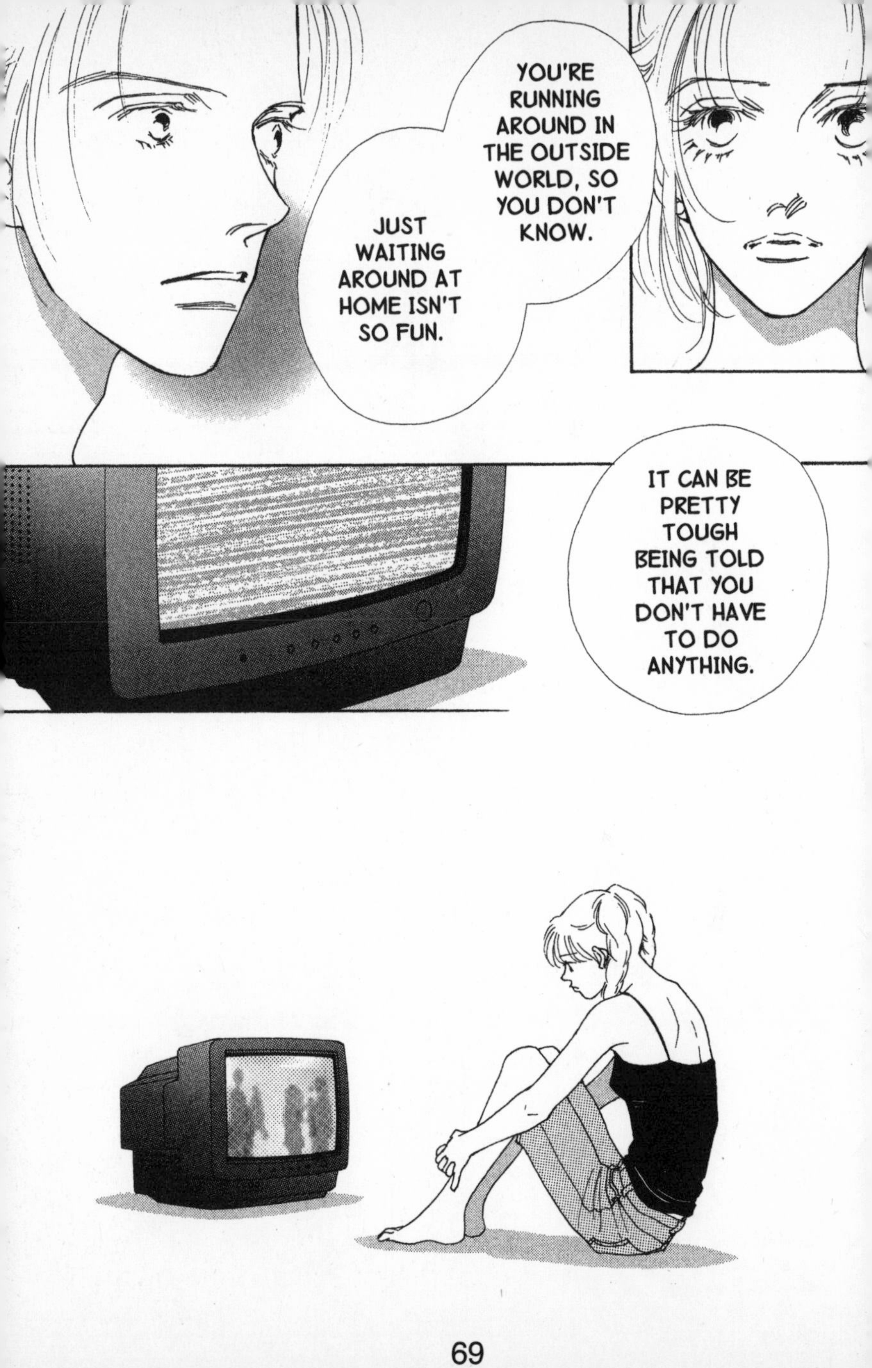
YOU'RE RUNNING AROUND IN THE OUTSIDE WORLD, SO YOU DON'T KNOW.
JUST WAITING AROUND AT HOME ISN'T SO FUN.
IT CAN BE PRETTY TOUGH BEING TOLD THAT YOU DON'T HAVE TO DO ANYTHING.

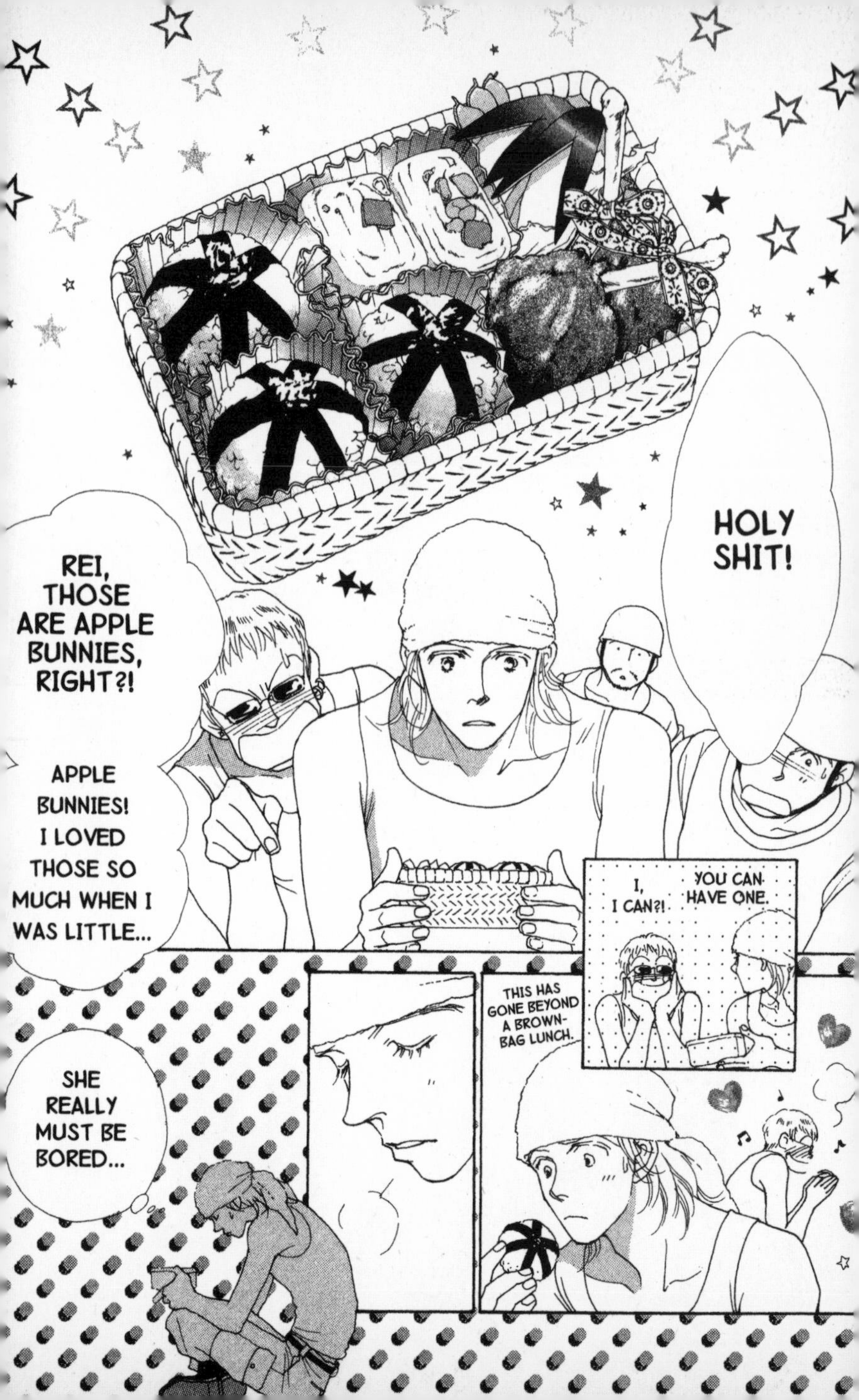
HOLY SHIT!
REI, THOSE ARE APPLE BUNNIES, RIGHT?!
APPLE BUNNIES! I LOVED THOSE SO MUCH WHEN I WAS LITTLE...
YOU CAN HAVE ONE.
I, I CAN?!
THIS HAS GONE BEYOND A BROWN-BAG LUNCH.
SHE REALLY MUST BE BORED...

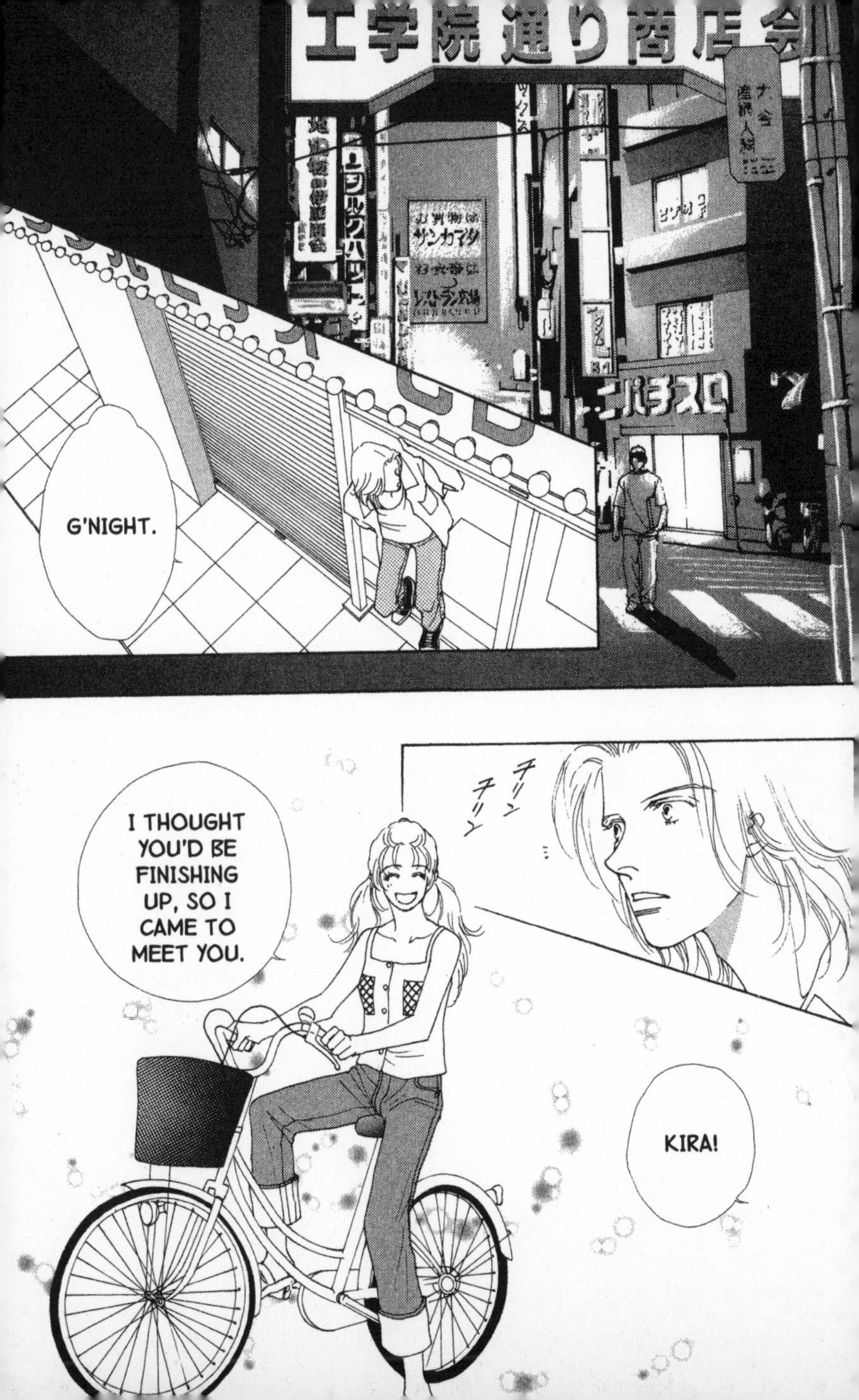

工学院通り商店
パチスロ
G'NIGHT.
チリン
チリン
KIRA!
I THOUGHT YOU'D BE FINISHING UP, SO I CAME TO MEET YOU.

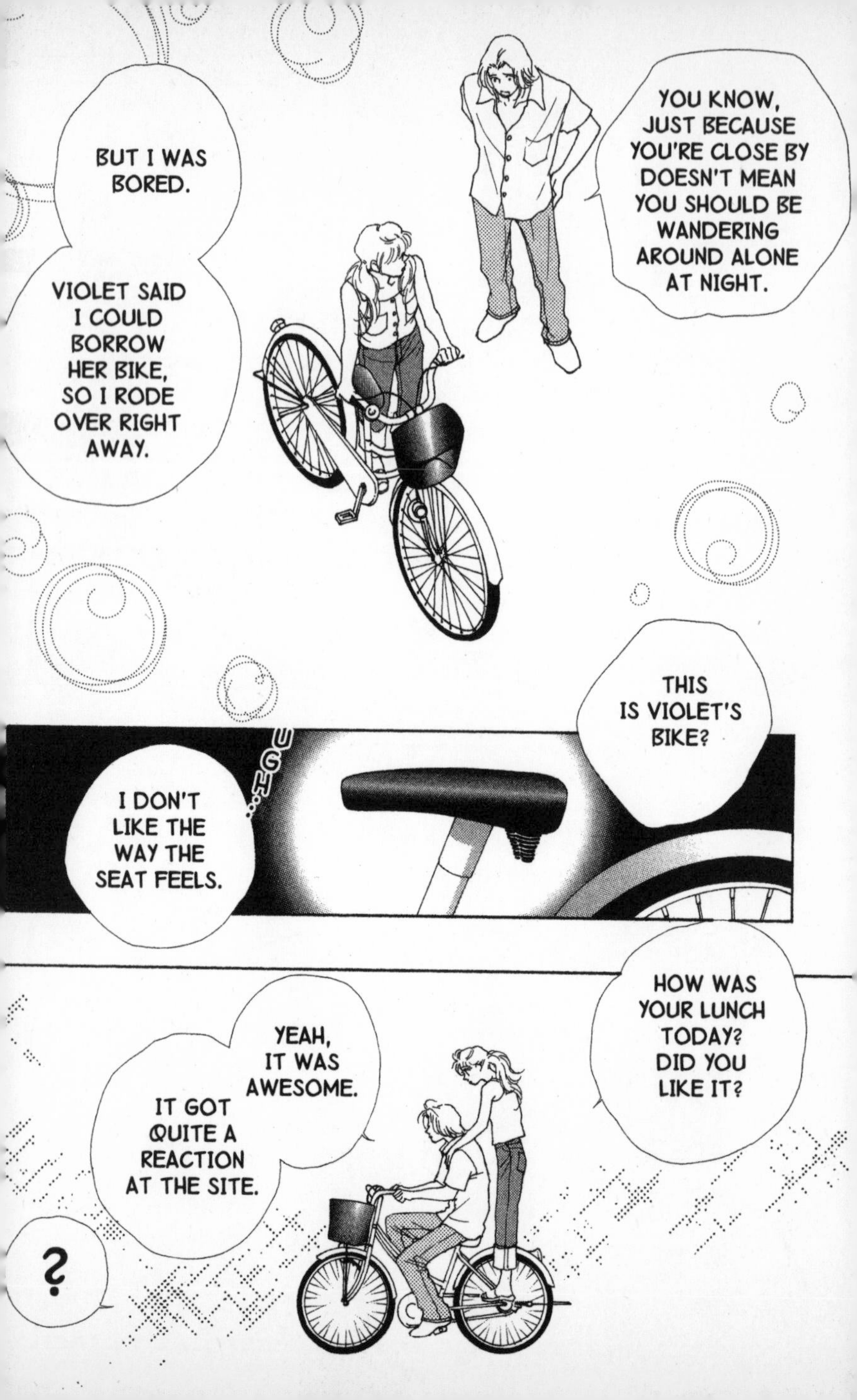
YOU KNOW, JUST BECAUSE YOU'RE CLOSE BY DOESN'T MEAN YOU SHOULD BE WANDERING AROUND ALONE AT NIGHT.
BUT I WAS BORED.
VIOLET SAID I COULD BORROW HER BIKE, SO I RODE OVER RIGHT AWAY.
THIS IS VIOLET'S BIKE?
UGH...
I DON'T LIKE THE WAY THE SEAT FEELS.
HOW WAS YOUR LUNCH TODAY? DID YOU LIKE IT?
YEAH, IT WAS AWESOME.
IT GOT QUITE A REACTION AT THE SITE.
?

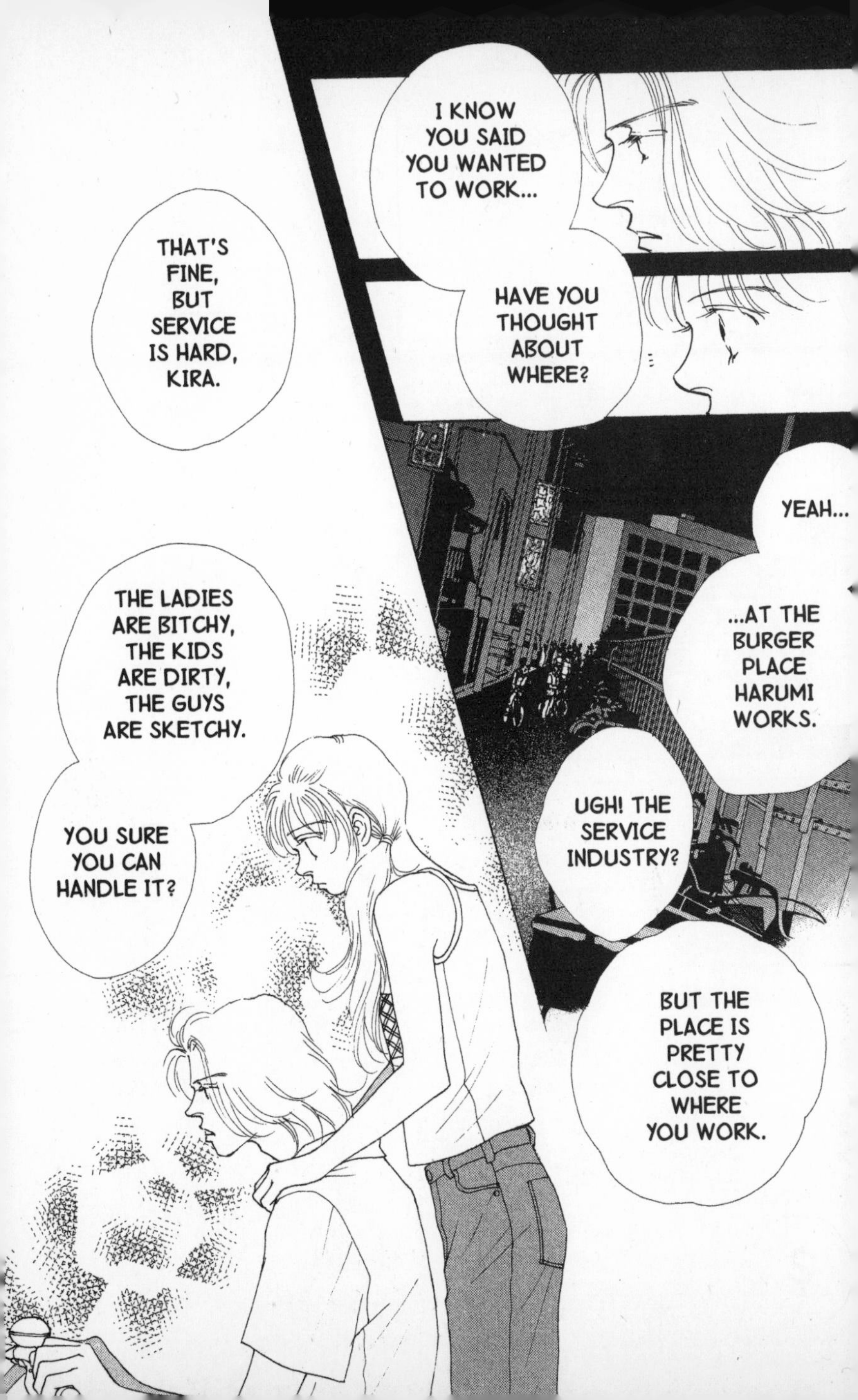
I KNOW YOU SAID YOU WANTED TO WORK...
HAVE YOU THOUGHT ABOUT WHERE?
YEAH...
...AT THE BURGER PLACE HARUMI WORKS.
UGH! THE SERVICE INDUSTRY?
BUT THE PLACE IS PRETTY CLOSE TO WHERE YOU WORK.
THAT'S FINE, BUT SERVICE IS HARD, KIRA.
THE LADIES ARE BITCHY, THE KIDS ARE DIRTY, THE GUYS ARE SKETCHY.
YOU SURE YOU CAN HANDLE IT?

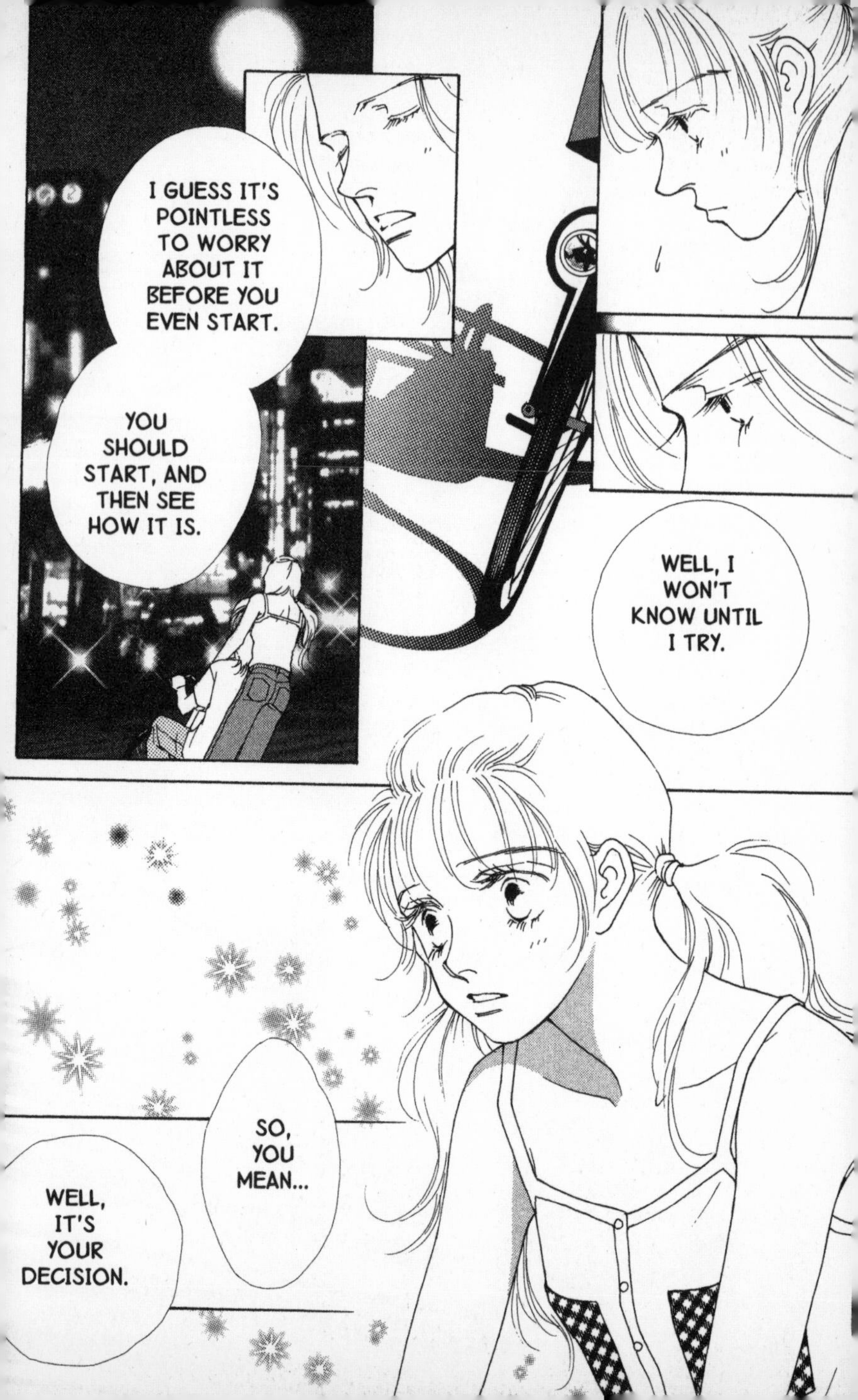
I GUESS IT'S POINTLESS TO WORRY ABOUT IT BEFORE YOU EVEN START.
YOU SHOULD START, AND THEN SEE HOW IT IS.
WELL, I WON'T KNOW UNTIL I TRY.
SO, YOU MEAN...
WELL, IT'S YOUR DECISION.

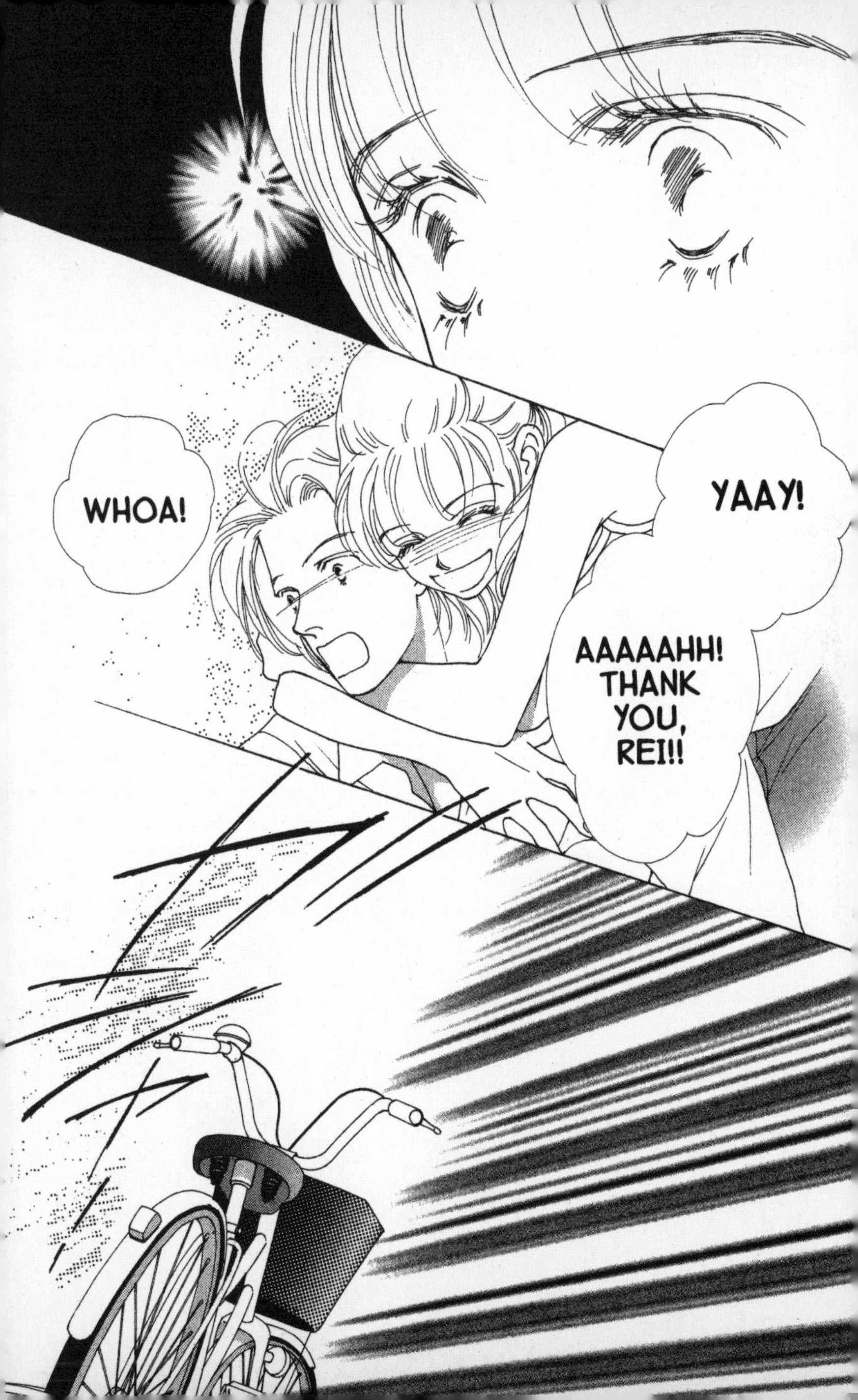
YAAY!
WHOA!
AAAAAHH! THANK YOU, REI!!

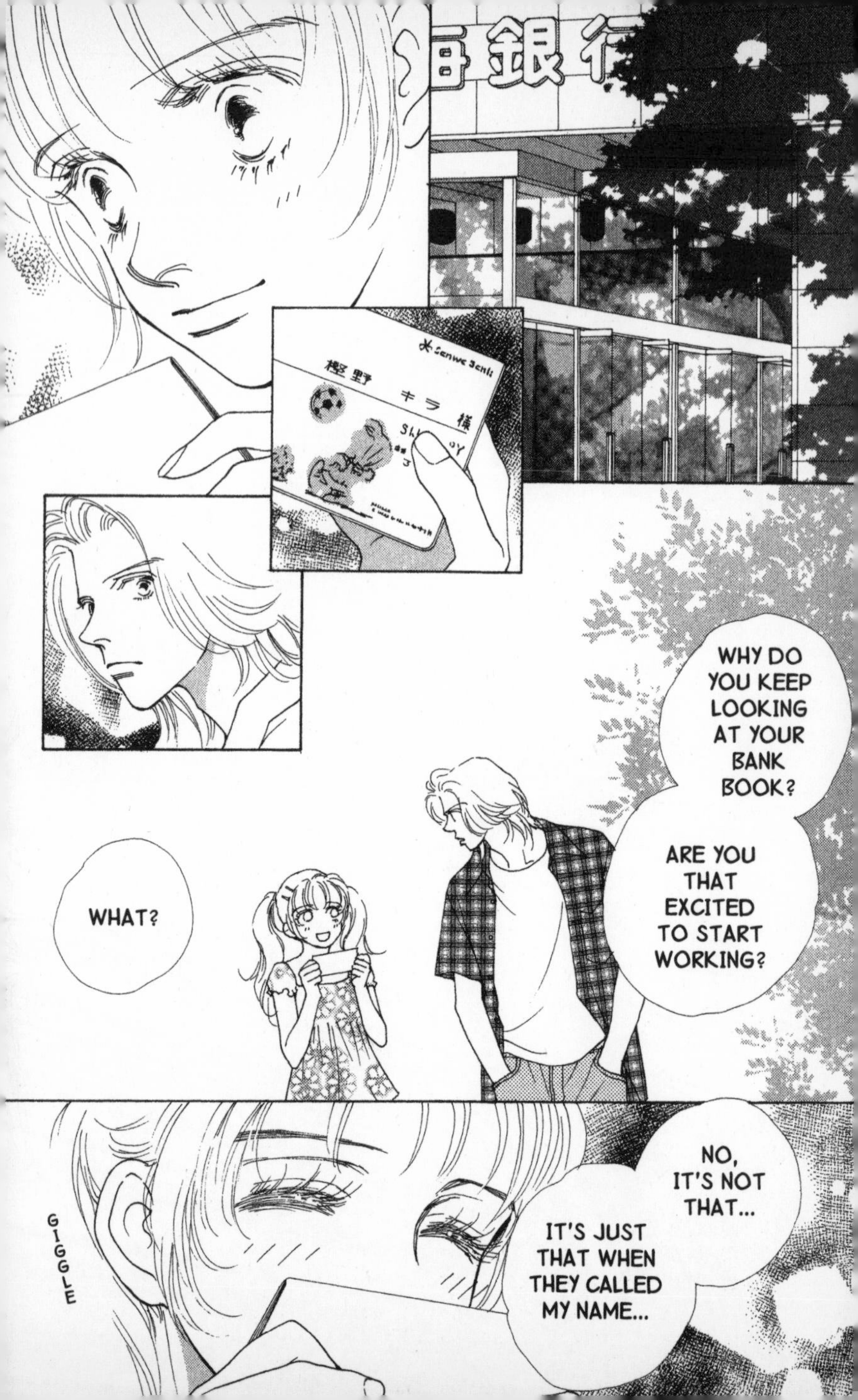
WHY DO YOU KEEP LOOKING AT YOUR BANK BOOK?
ARE YOU THAT EXCITED TO START WORKING?
WHAT?
NO, IT'S NOT THAT...
IT'S JUST THAT WHEN THEY CALLED MY NAME...
GIGGLE

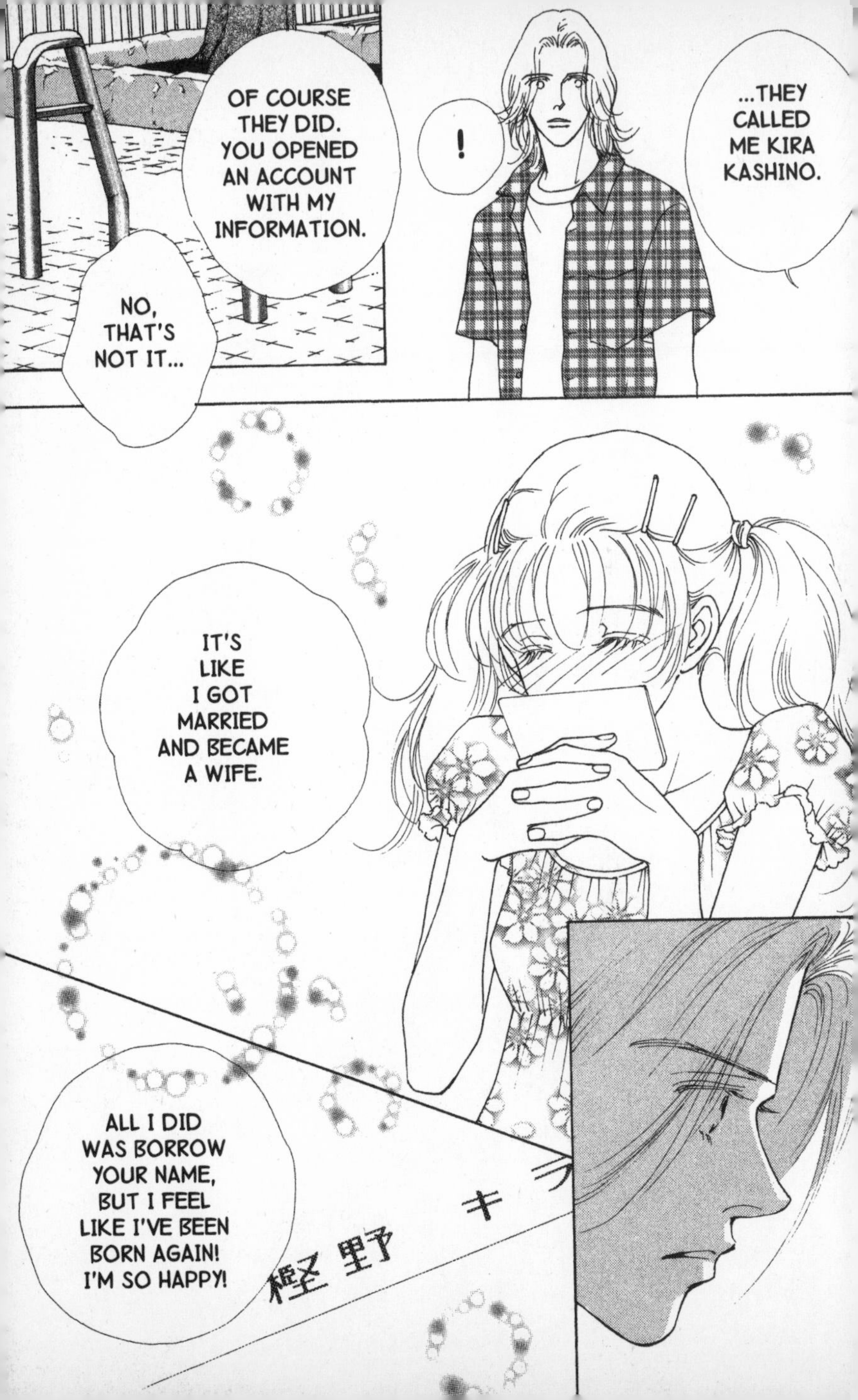
...THEY CALLED ME KIRA KASHINO.
!
OF COURSE THEY DID. YOU OPENED AN ACCOUNT WITH MY INFORMATION.
NO, THAT'S NOT IT...
IT'S LIKE I GOT MARRIED AND BECAME A WIFE.
ALL I DID WAS BORROW YOUR NAME, BUT I FEEL LIKE I'VE BEEN BORN AGAIN! I'M SO HAPPY!
樫野

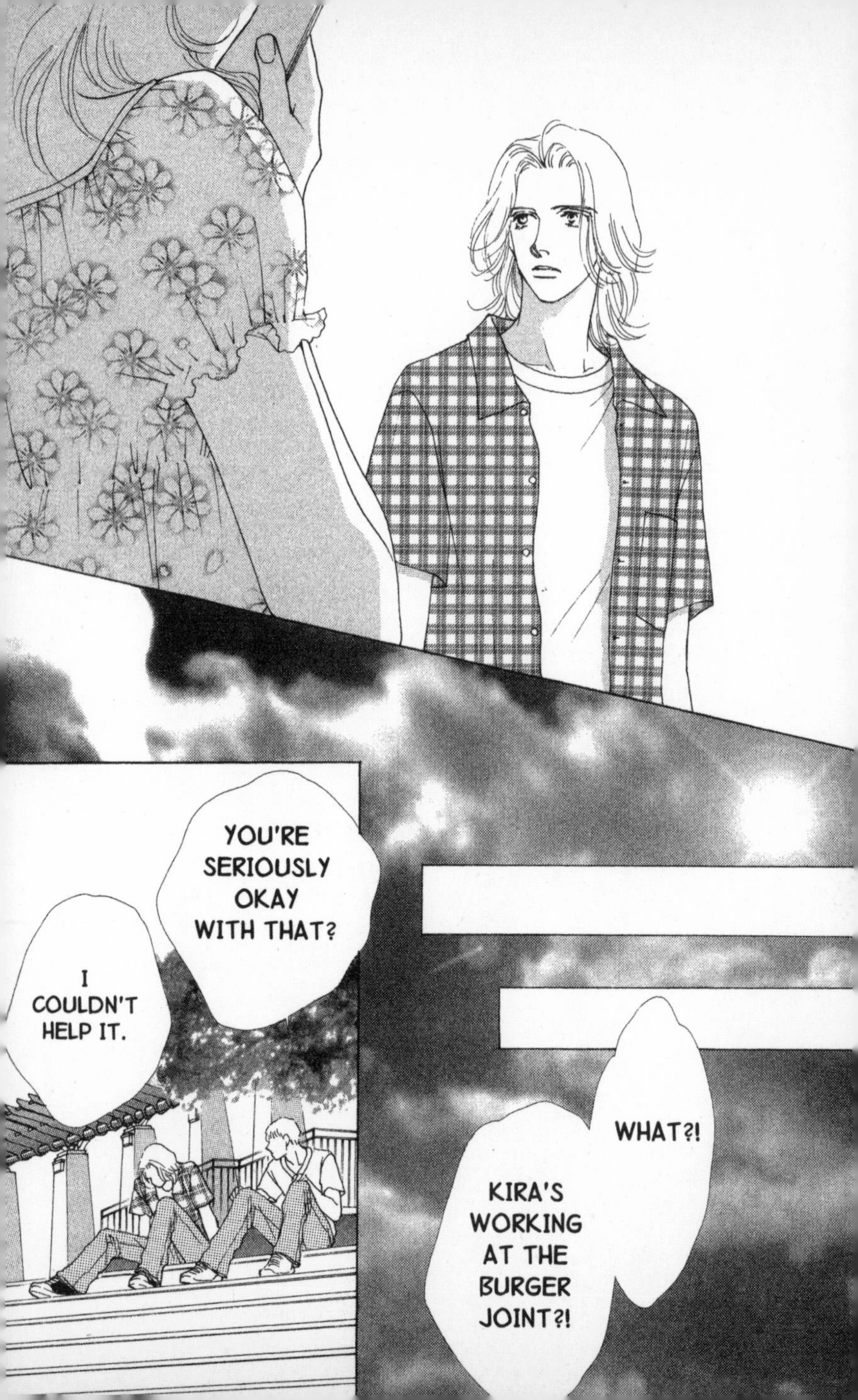
WHAT?!
KIRA'S WORKING AT THE BURGER JOINT?!
YOU'RE SERIOUSLY OKAY WITH THAT?
I COULDN'T HELP IT.

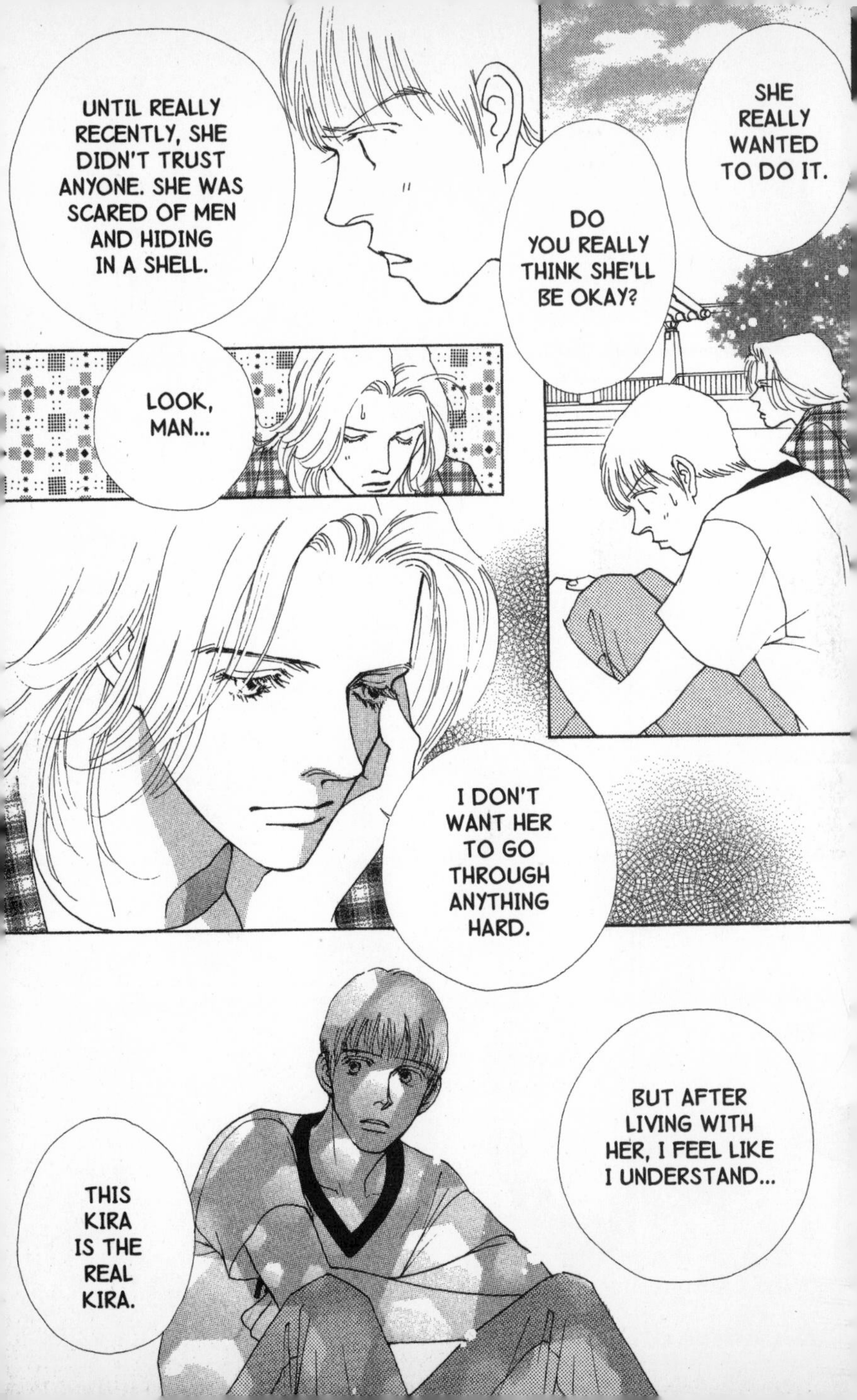
SHE REALLY WANTED TO DO IT.
DO YOU REALLY THINK SHE'LL BE OKAY?
UNTIL REALLY RECENTLY, SHE DIDN'T TRUST ANYONE. SHE WAS SCARED OF MEN AND HIDING IN A SHELL.
LOOK, MAN...
I DON'T WANT HER TO GO THROUGH ANYTHING HARD.
BUT AFTER LIVING WITH HER, I FEEL LIKE I UNDERSTAND...
THIS KIRA IS THE REAL KIRA.

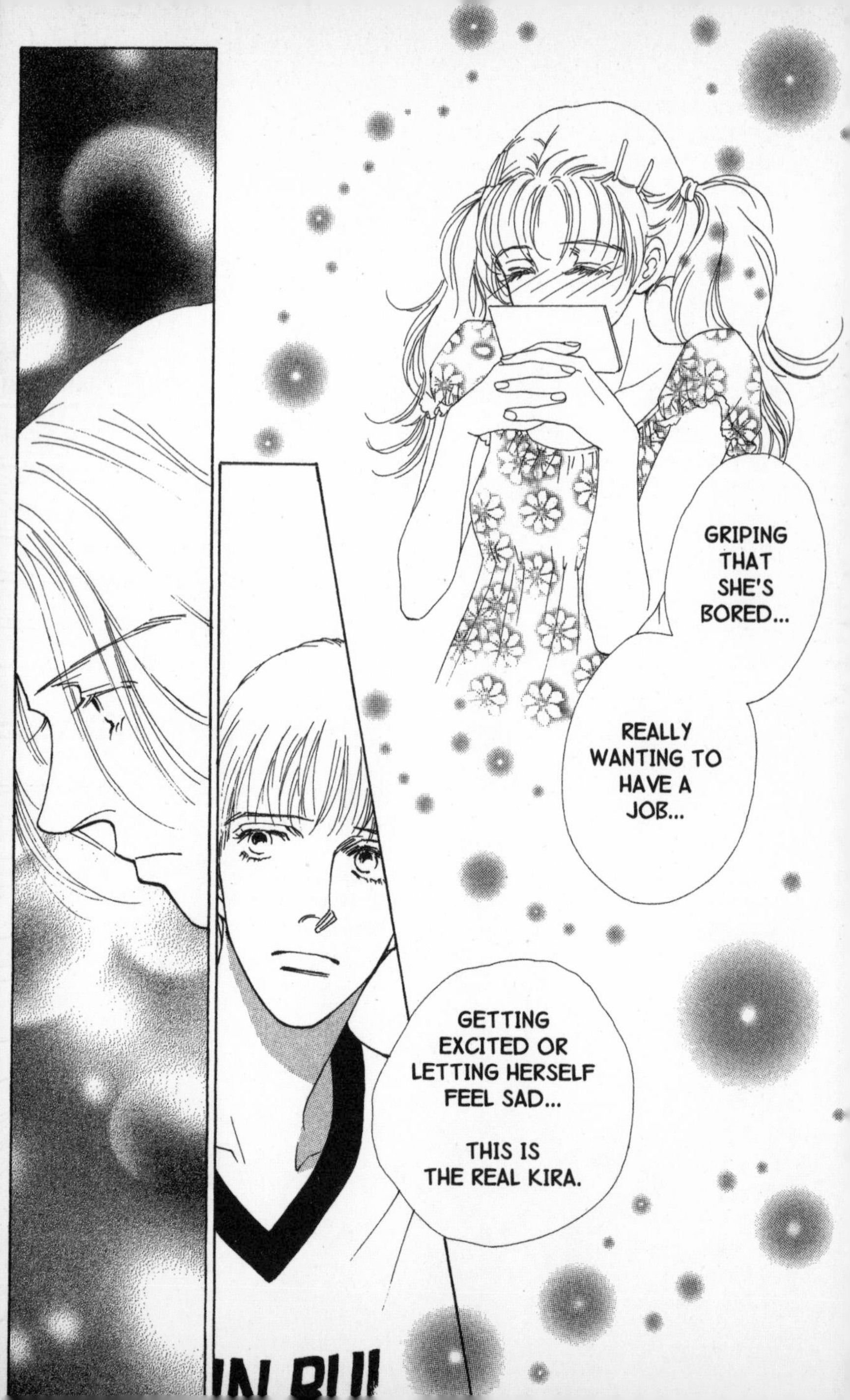
GRIPING THAT SHE'S BORED...
REALLY WANTING TO HAVE A JOB...
GETTING EXCITED OR LETTING HERSELF FEEL SAD...
THIS IS THE REAL KIRA.

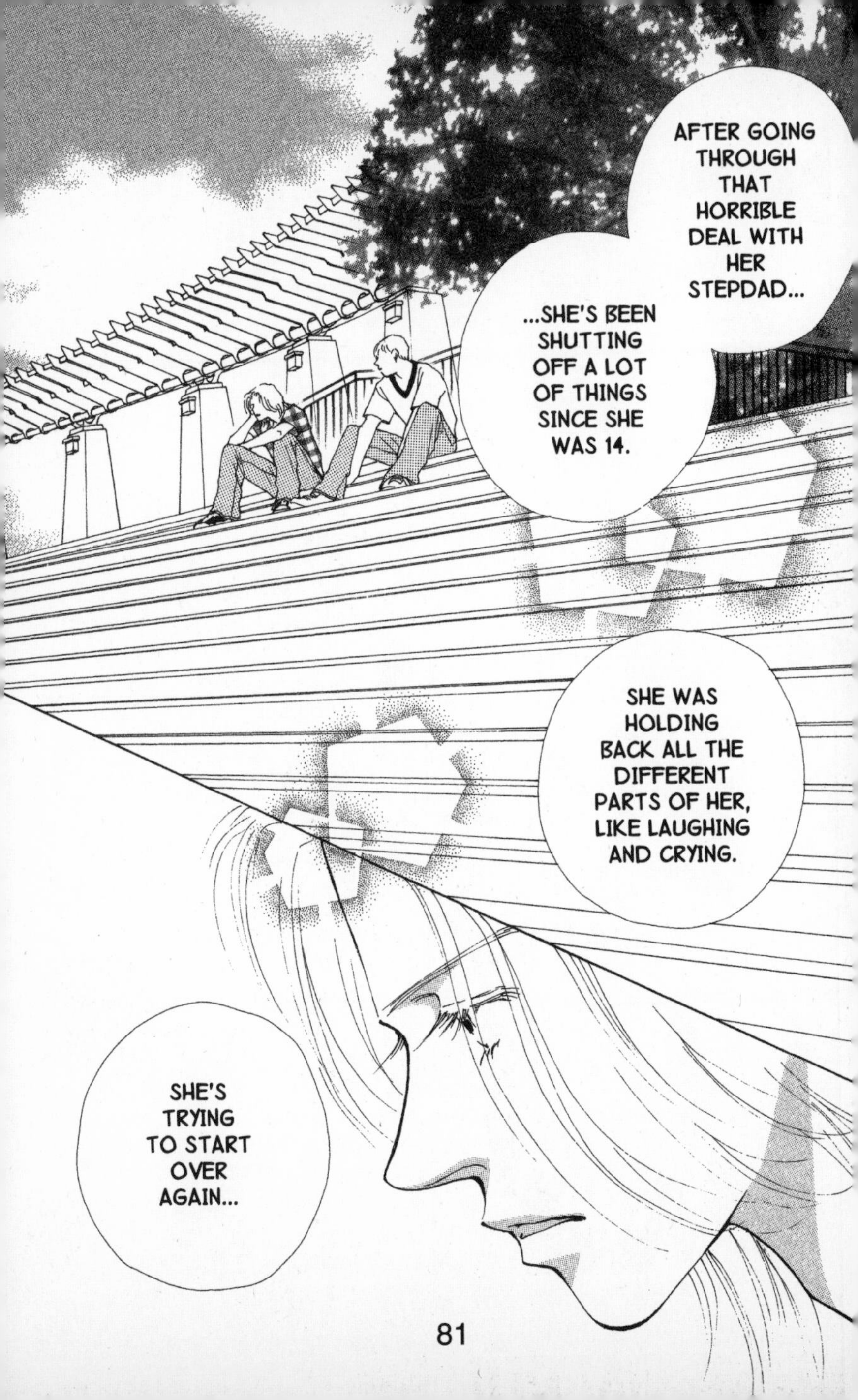
AFTER GOING THROUGH THAT HORRIBLE DEAL WITH HER STEPDAD...
...SHE'S BEEN SHUTTING OFF A LOT OF THINGS SINCE SHE WAS 14.
SHE WAS HOLDING BACK ALL THE DIFFERENT PARTS OF HER, LIKE LAUGHING AND CRYING.
SHE'S TRYING TO START OVER AGAIN...

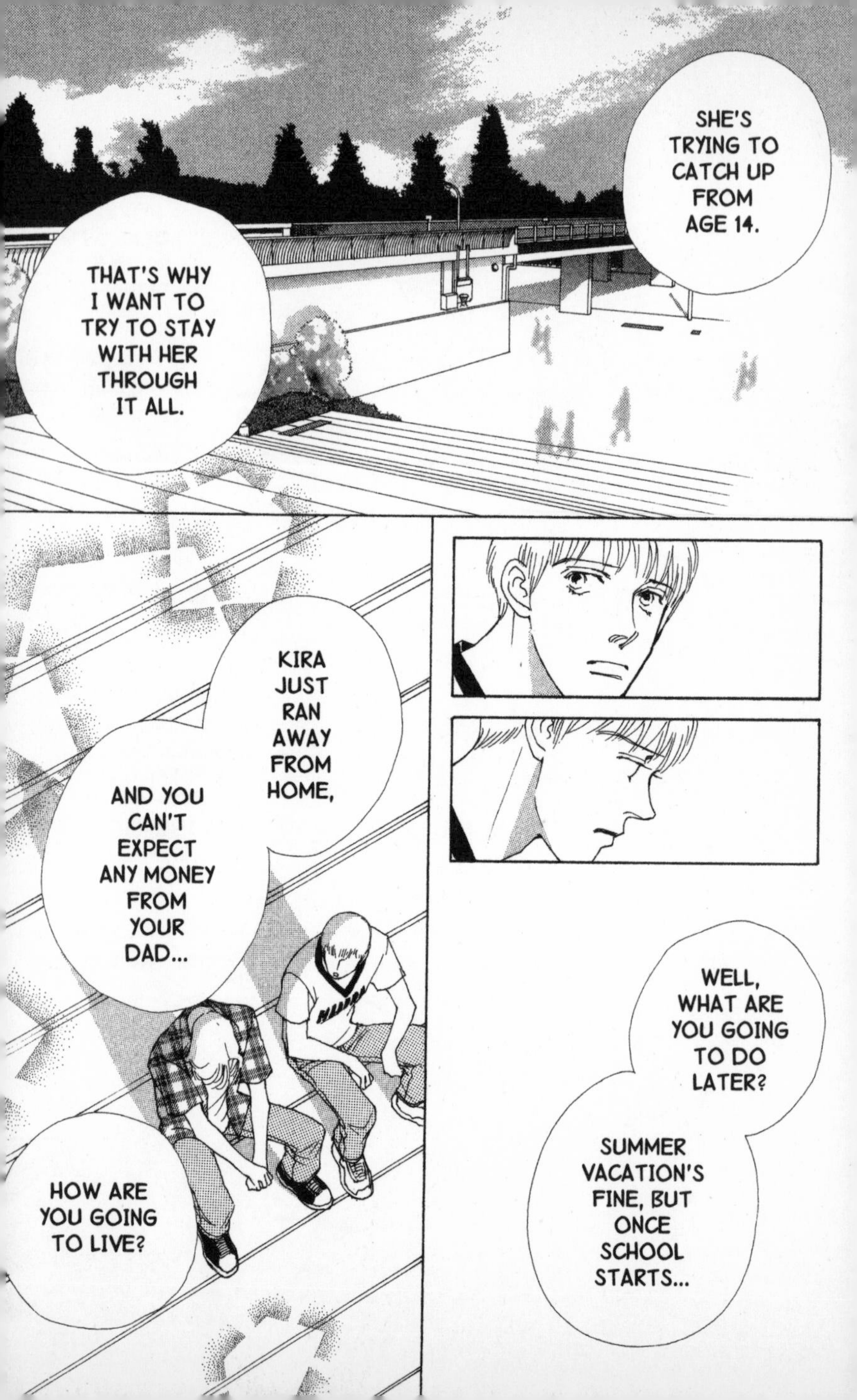
SHE'S TRYING TO CATCH UP FROM AGE 14.
THAT'S WHY I WANT TO TRY TO STAY WITH HER THROUGH IT ALL.
WELL, WHAT ARE YOU GOING TO DO LATER?
SUMMER VACATION'S FINE, BUT ONCE SCHOOL STARTS...
KIRA JUST RAN AWAY FROM HOME,
AND YOU CAN'T EXPECT ANY MONEY FROM YOUR DAD...
HOW ARE YOU GOING TO LIVE?

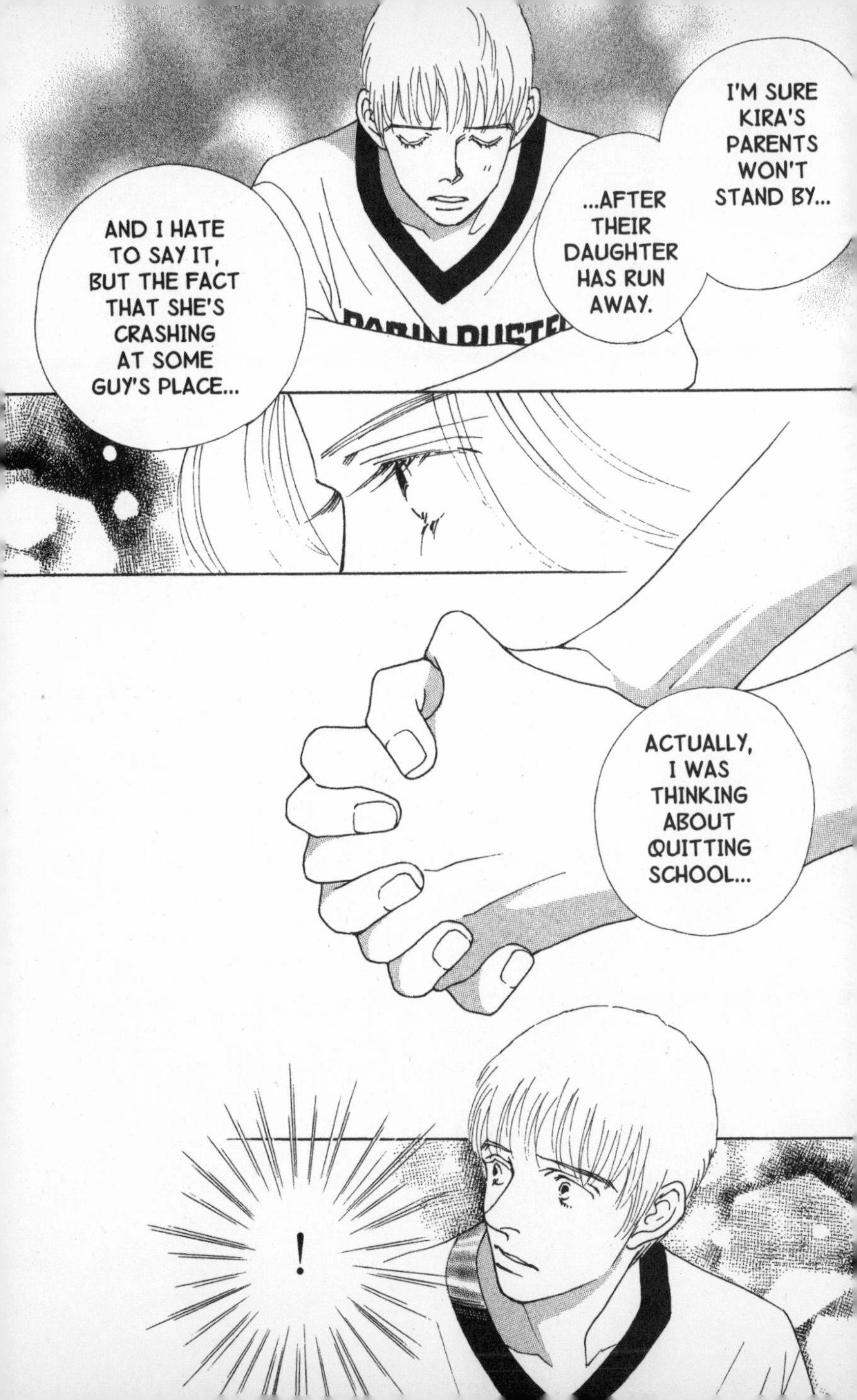
I'M SURE KIRA'S PARENTS WON'T STAND BY...
...AFTER THEIR DAUGHTER HAS RUN AWAY.
AND I HATE TO SAY IT, BUT THE FACT THAT SHE'S CRASHING AT SOME GUY'S PLACE...
ACTUALLY, I WAS THINKING ABOUT QUITTING SCHOOL...
!

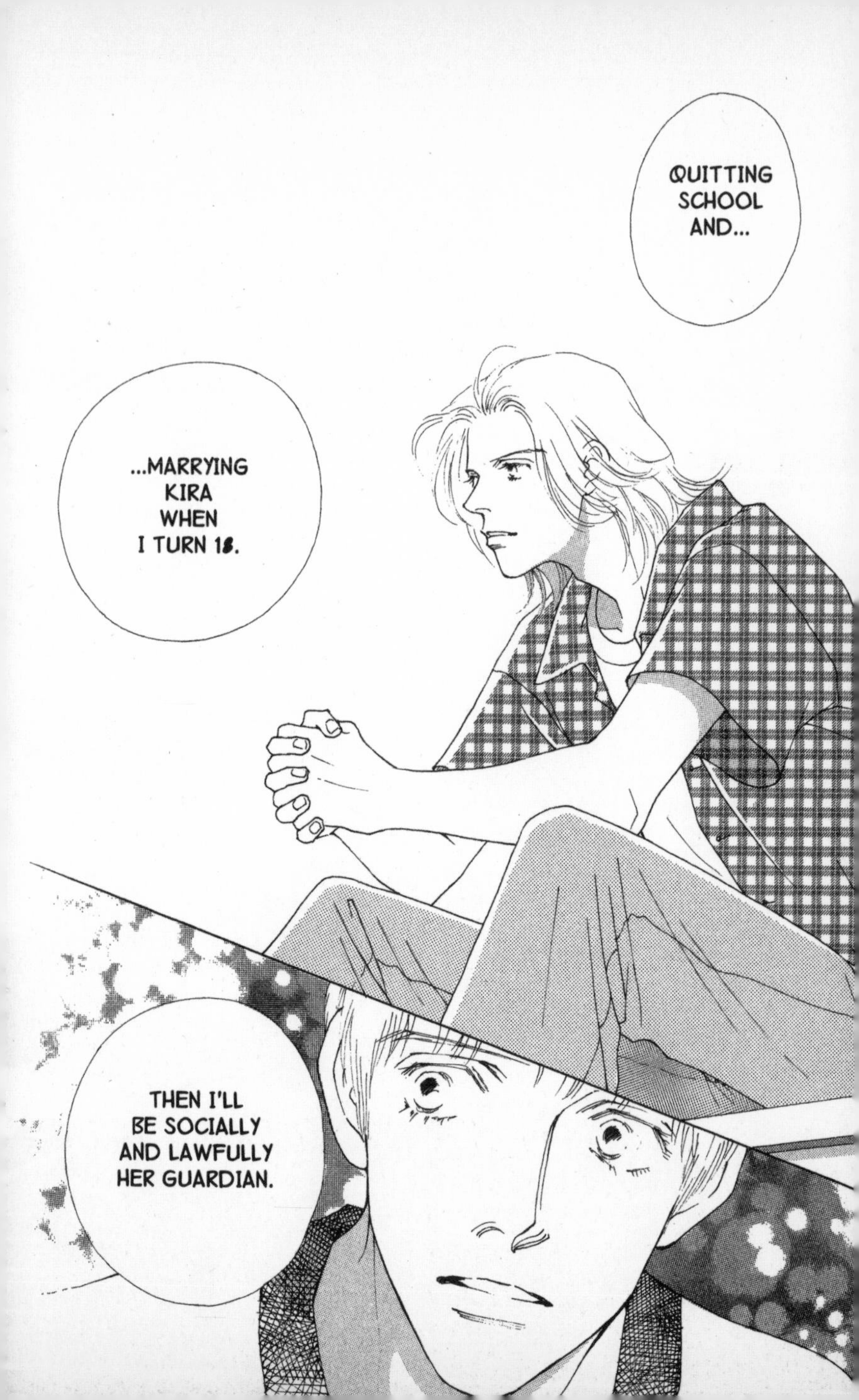
QUITTING SCHOOL AND...
...MARRYING KIRA WHEN I TURN 18.
THEN I'LL BE SOCIALLY AND LAWFULLY HER GUARDIAN.

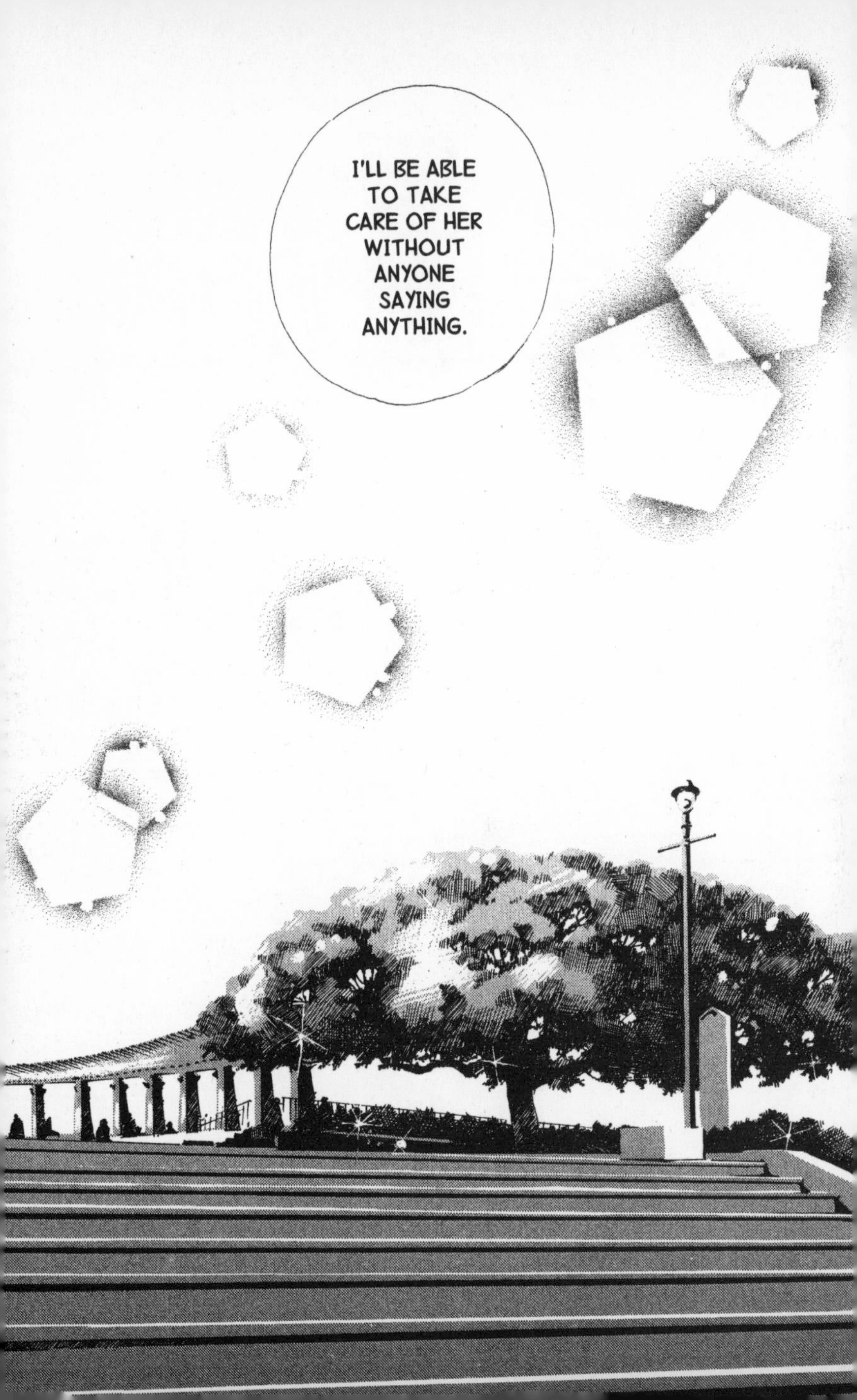
I'LL BE ABLE TO TAKE CARE OF HER WITHOUT ANYONE SAYING ANYTHING.

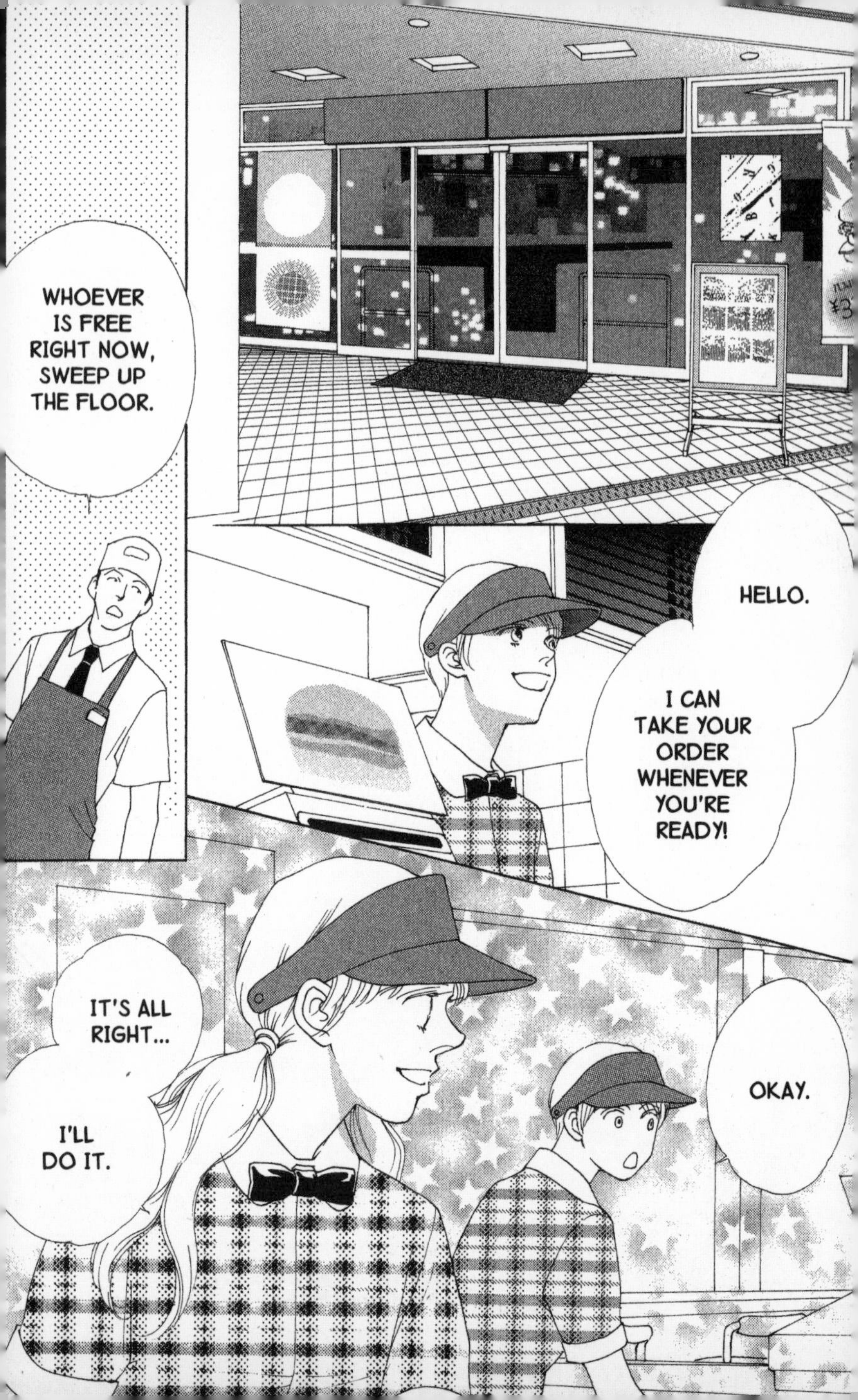

HELLO.
I CAN TAKE YOUR ORDER WHENEVER YOU'RE READY!
WHOEVER IS FREE RIGHT NOW, SWEEP UP THE FLOOR.
OKAY.
IT'S ALL RIGHT...
I'LL DO IT.

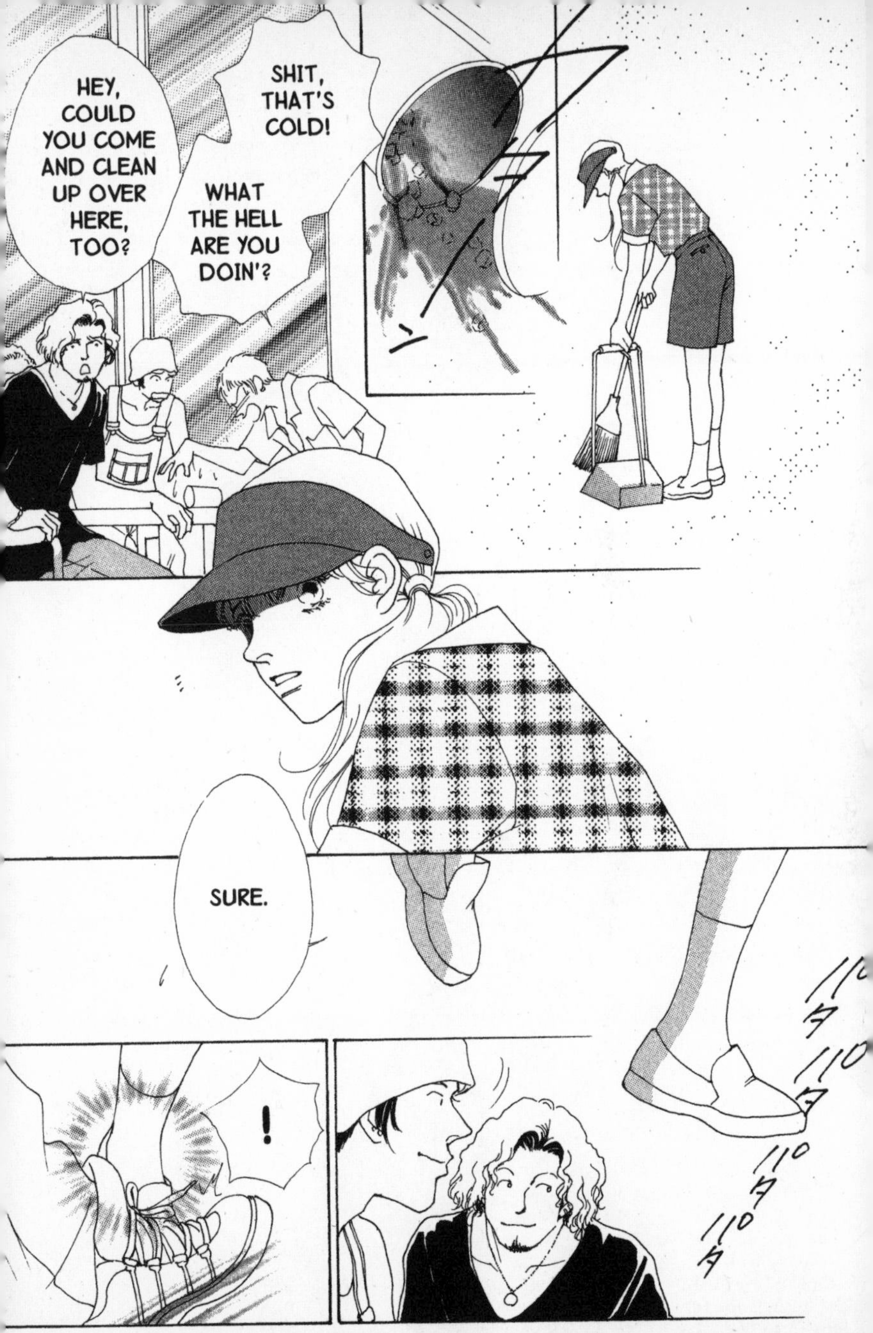
SHIT, THAT'S COLD!
WHAT THE HELL ARE YOU DOIN'?
HEY, COULD YOU COME AND CLEAN UP OVER HERE, TOO?
SURE.
!

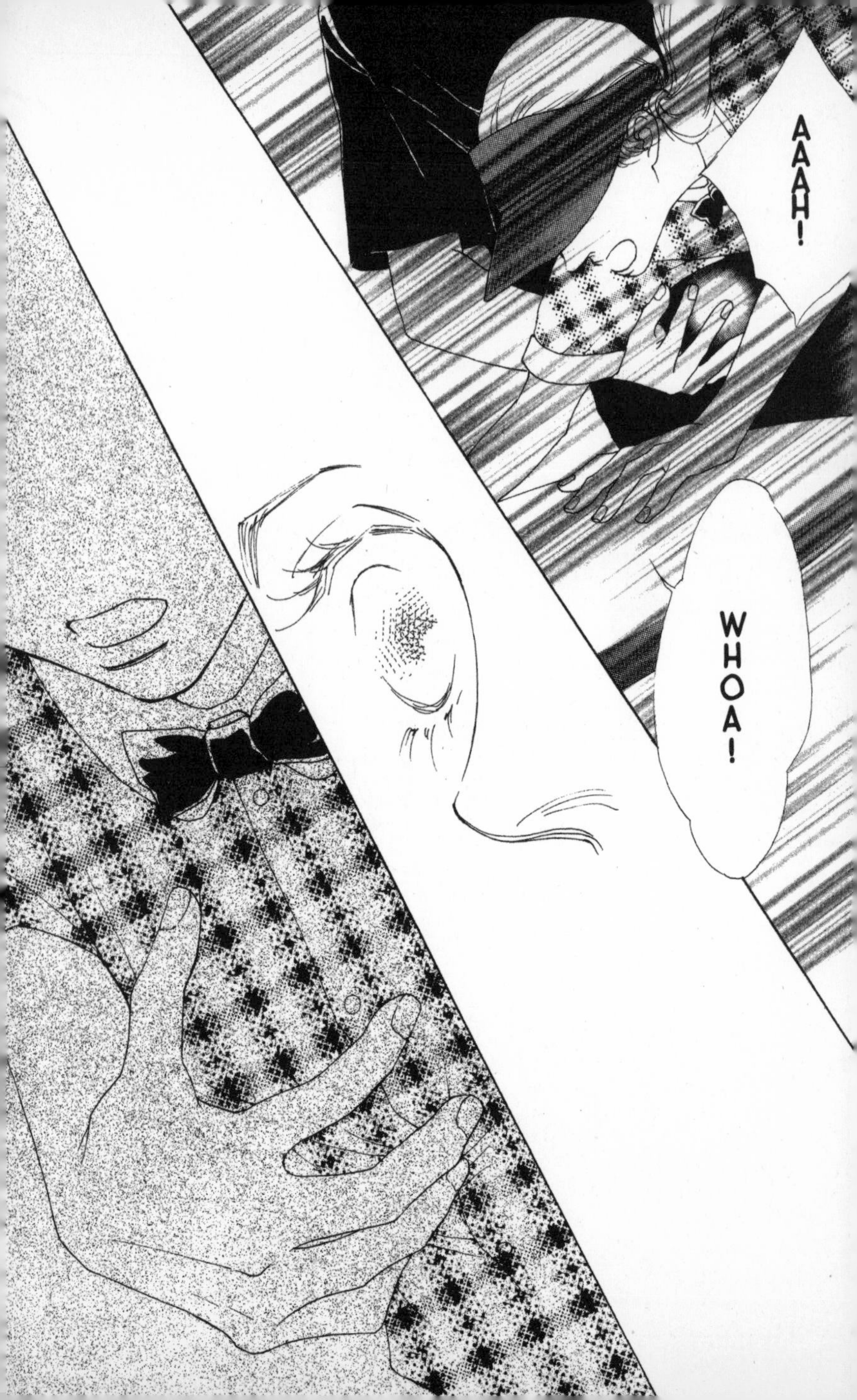
AAAH!
WHOA!

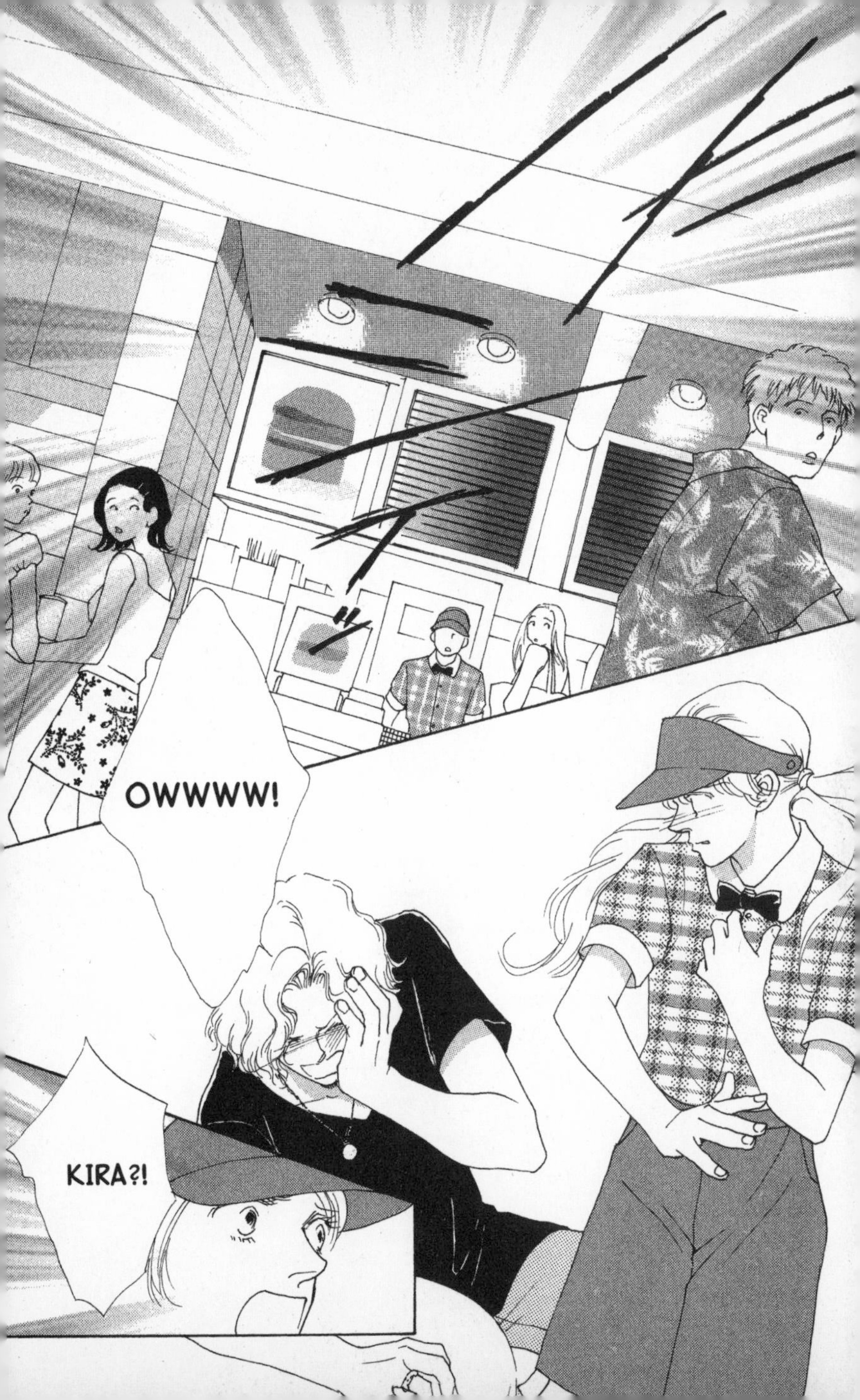
OWWWW!
KIRA?!

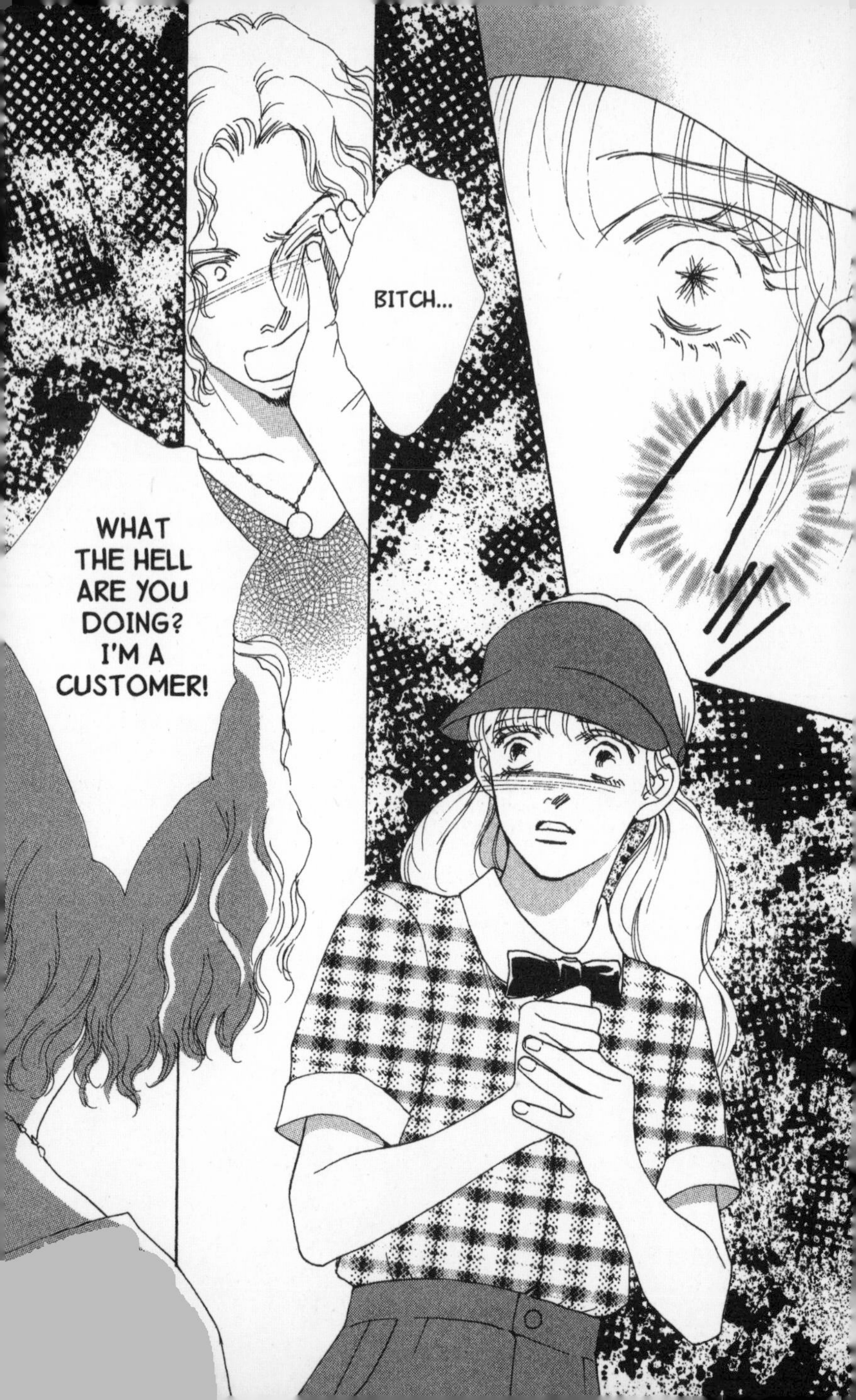
BITCH...
WHAT THE HELL ARE YOU DOING? I'M A CUSTOMER!

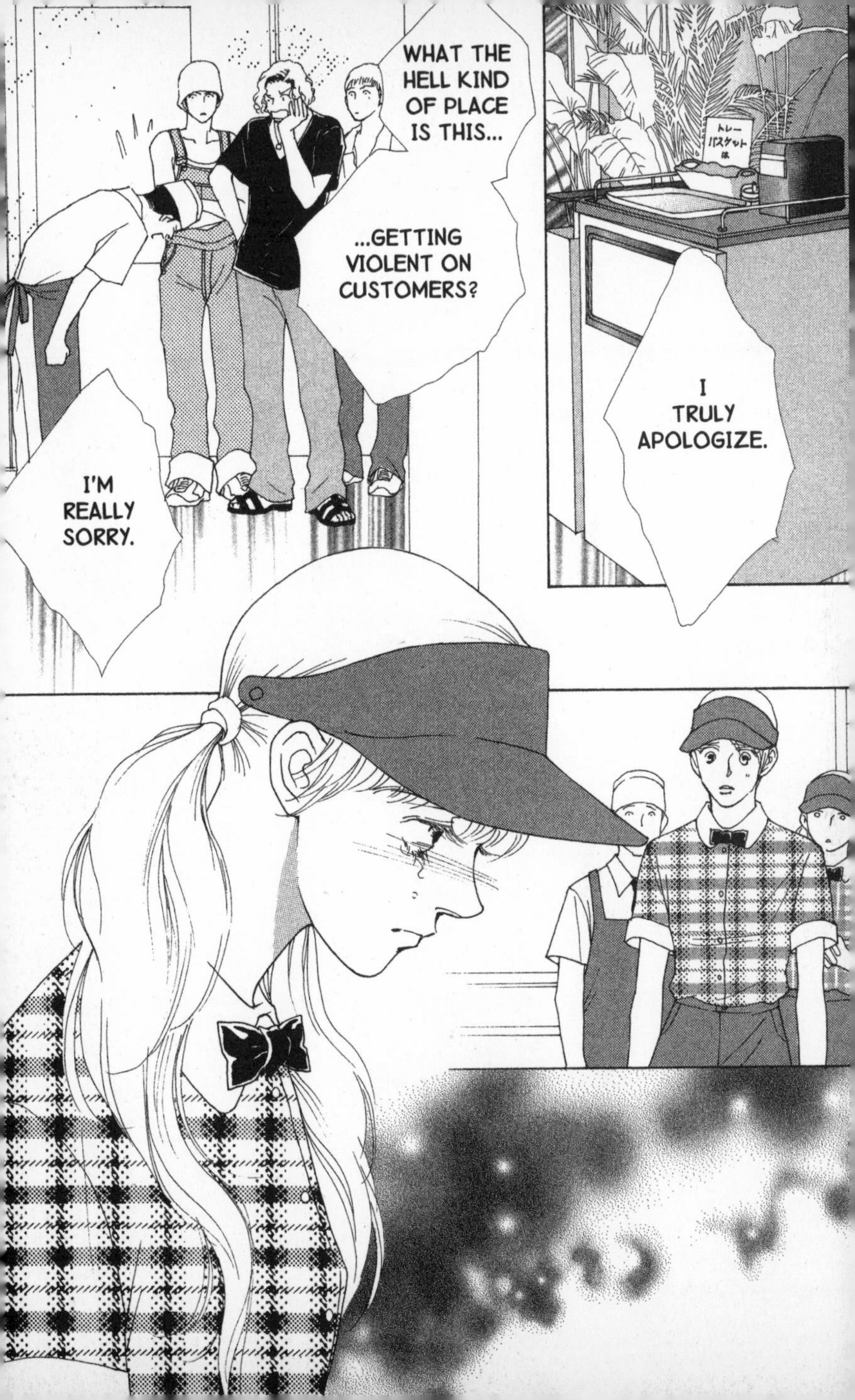
トレー バスケット は
I TRULY APOLOGIZE.
WHAT THE HELL KIND OF PLACE IS THIS...
...GETTING VIOLENT ON CUSTOMERS?
I'M REALLY SORRY.

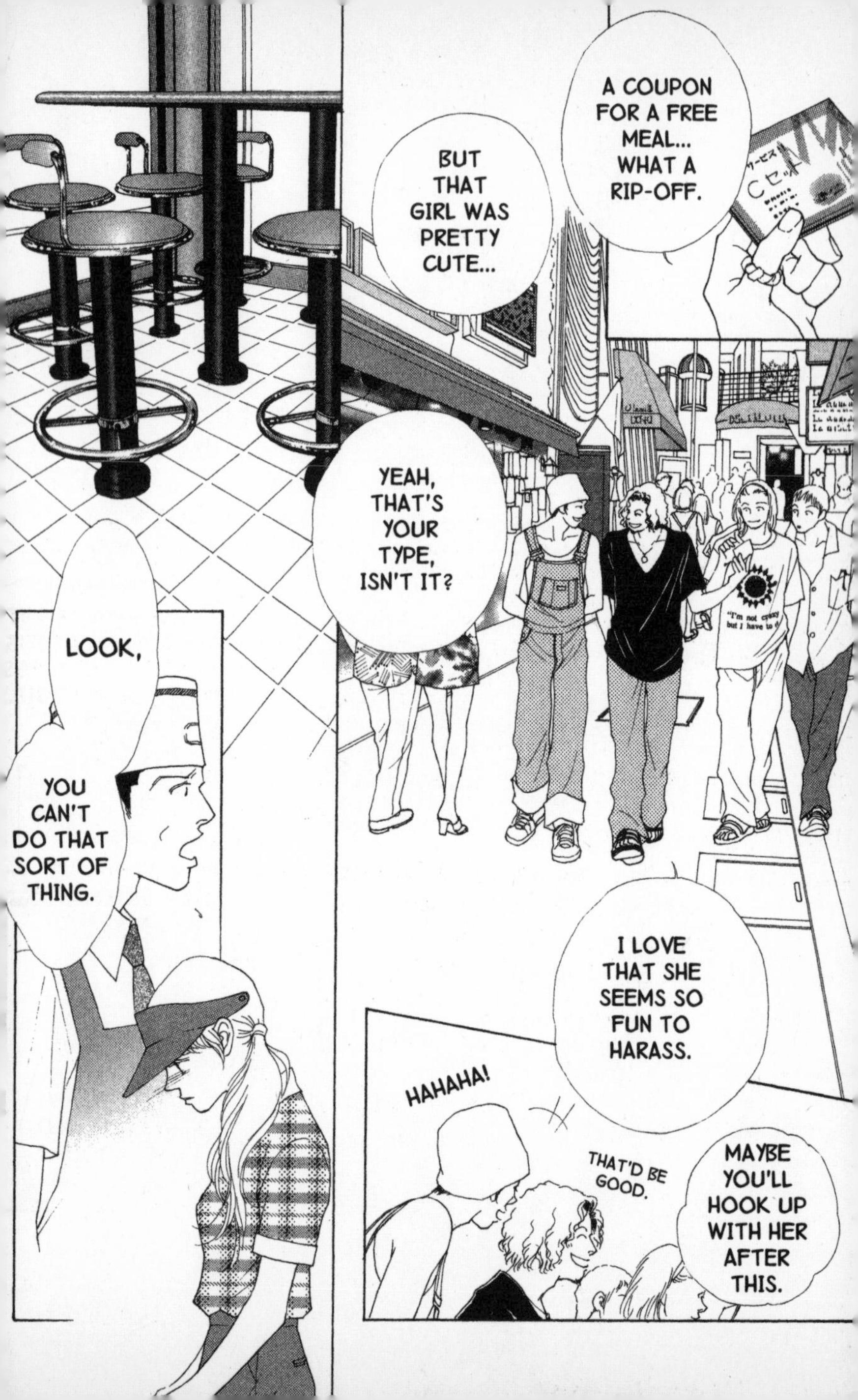
A COUPON FOR A FREE MEAL... WHAT A RIP-OFF.
BUT THAT GIRL WAS PRETTY CUTE...
YEAH, THAT'S YOUR TYPE, ISN'T IT?
I LOVE THAT SHE SEEMS SO FUN TO HARASS.
MAYBE YOU'LL HOOK UP WITH HER AFTER THIS.
THAT'D BE GOOD.
HAHAHA!
LOOK,
YOU CAN'T DO THAT SORT OF THING.

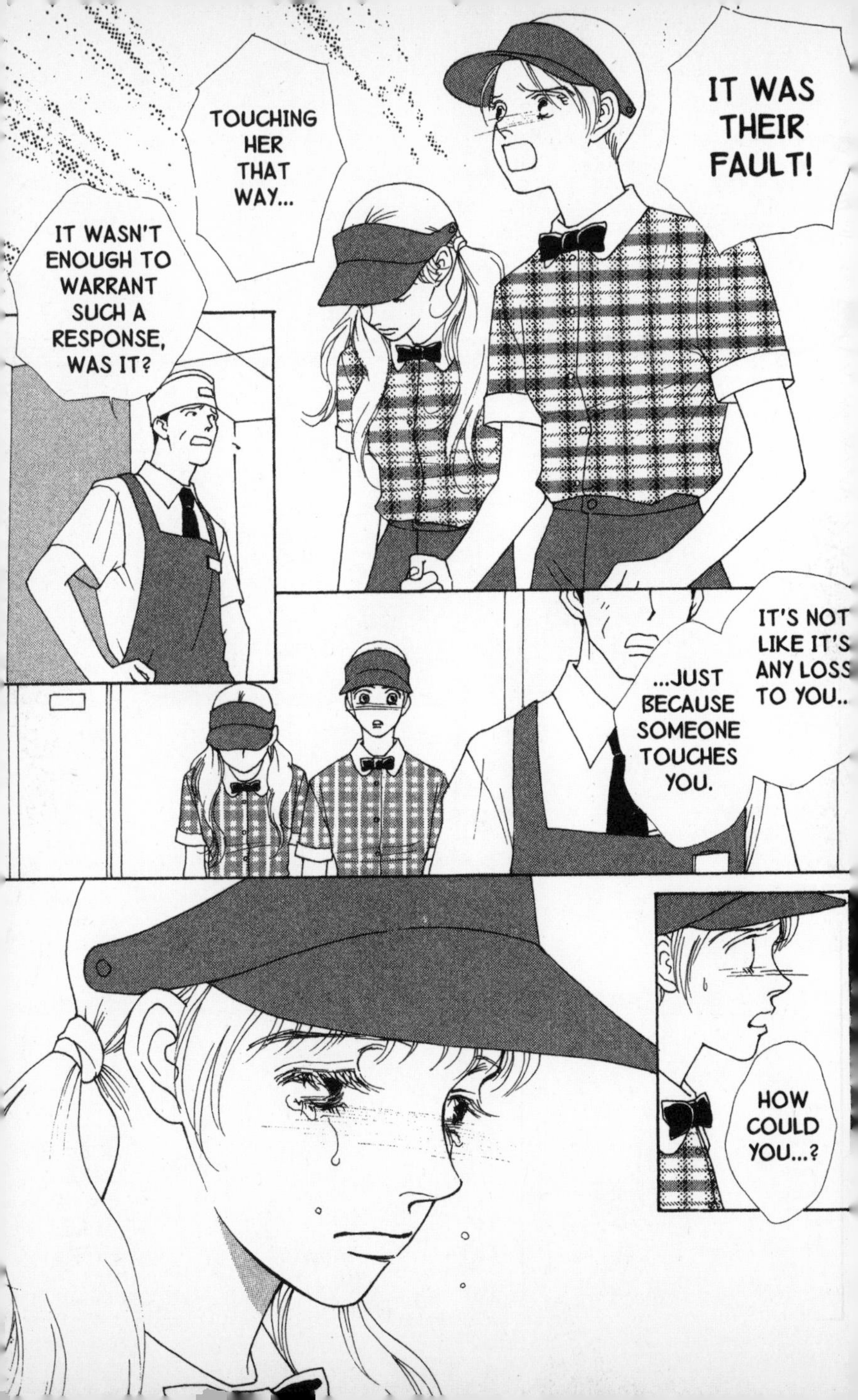
IT WAS THEIR FAULT!
TOUCHING HER THAT WAY...
IT WASN'T ENOUGH TO WARRANT SUCH A RESPONSE, WAS IT?
IT'S NOT LIKE IT'S ANY LOSS TO YOU..
...JUST BECAUSE SOMEONE TOUCHES YOU.
HOW COULD YOU...?

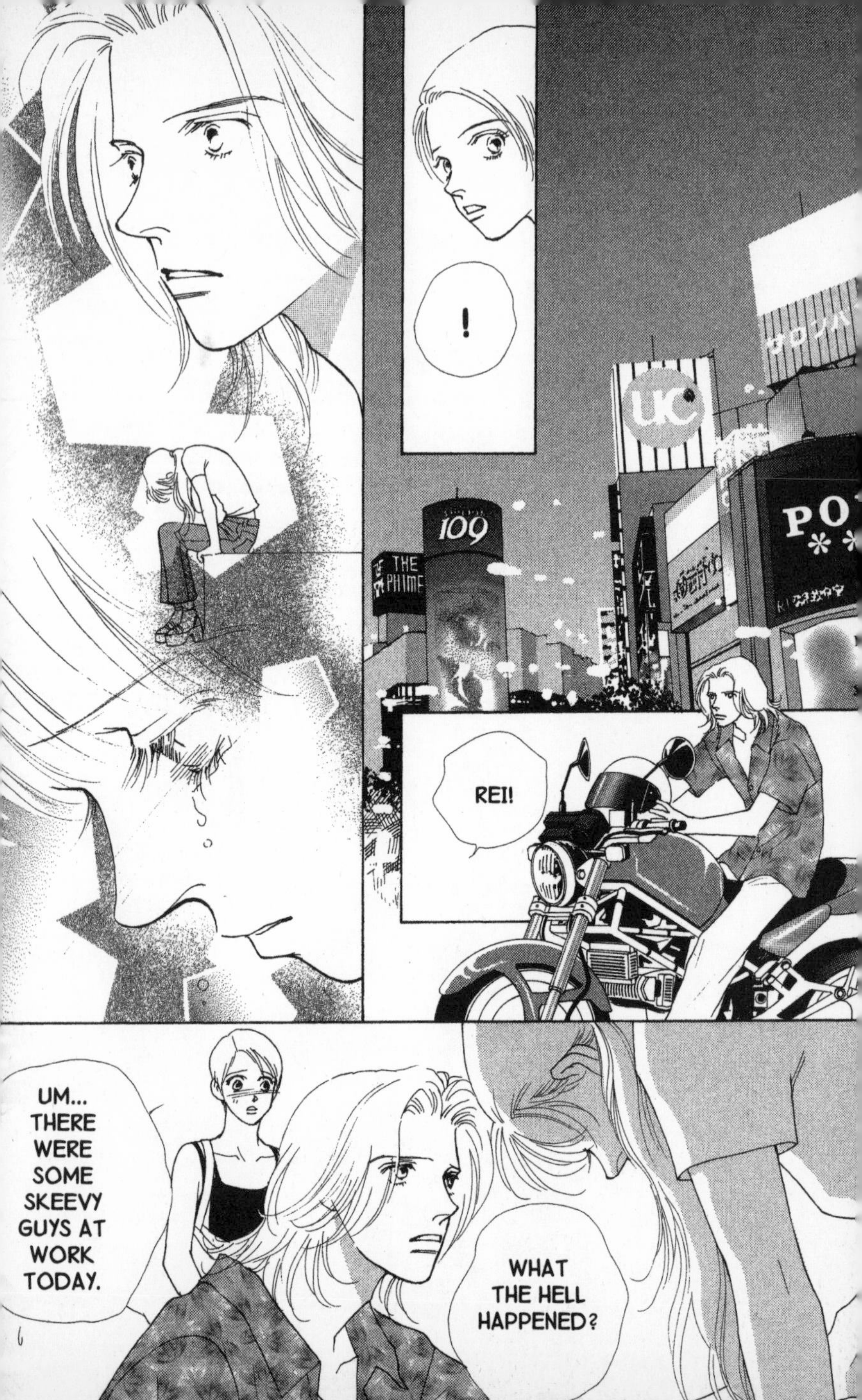
サロンパ
UC
109
POL
REI!
!
WHAT THE HELL HAPPENED?
UM... THERE WERE SOME SKEEVY GUYS AT WORK TODAY.

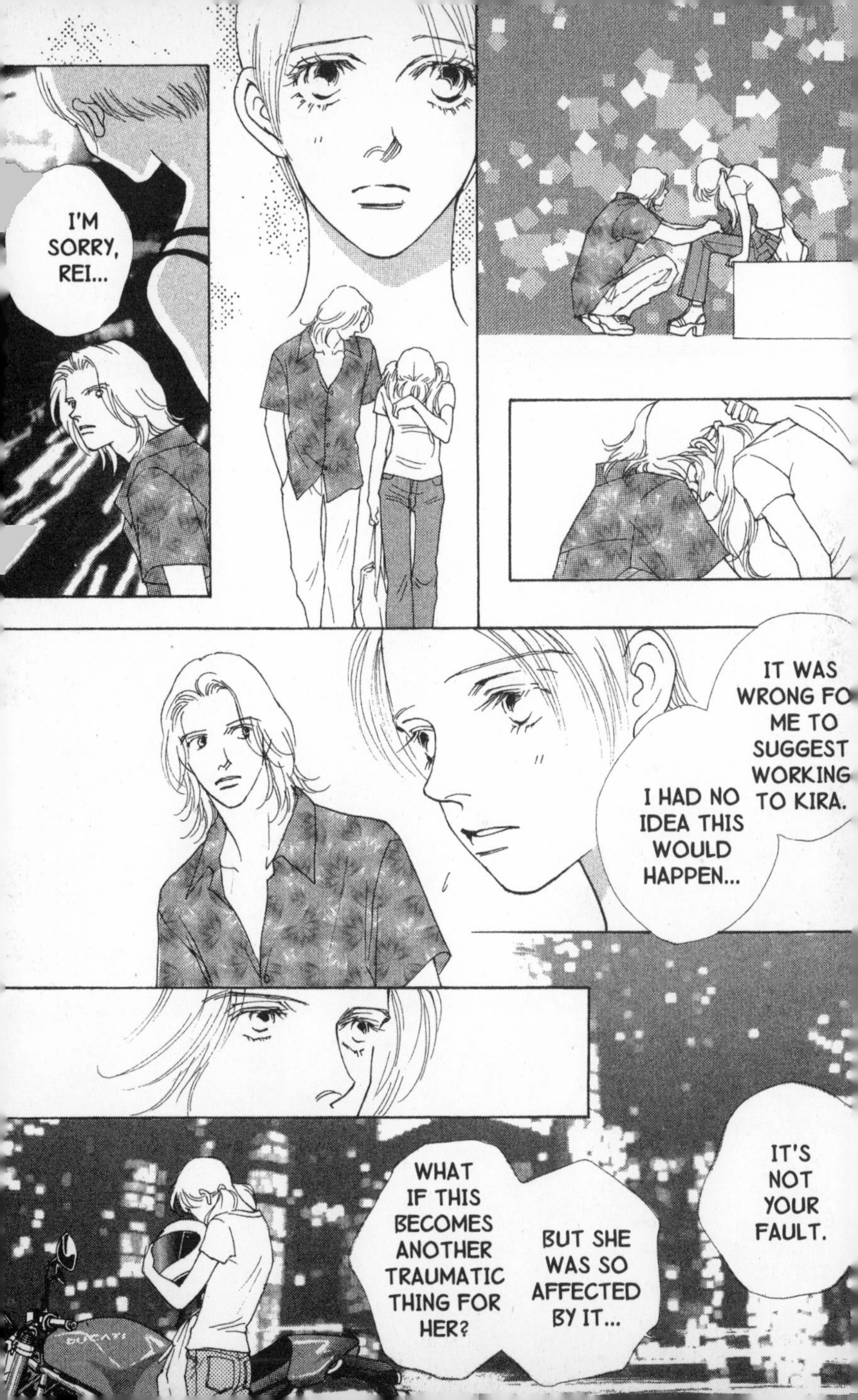
I'M SORRY, REI...
IT WAS WRONG FO ME TO SUGGEST WORKING TO KIRA.
I HAD NO IDEA THIS WOULD HAPPEN...
IT'S NOT YOUR FAULT.
BUT SHE WAS SO AFFECTED BY IT...
WHAT IF THIS BECOMES ANOTHER TRAUMATIC THING FOR HER?

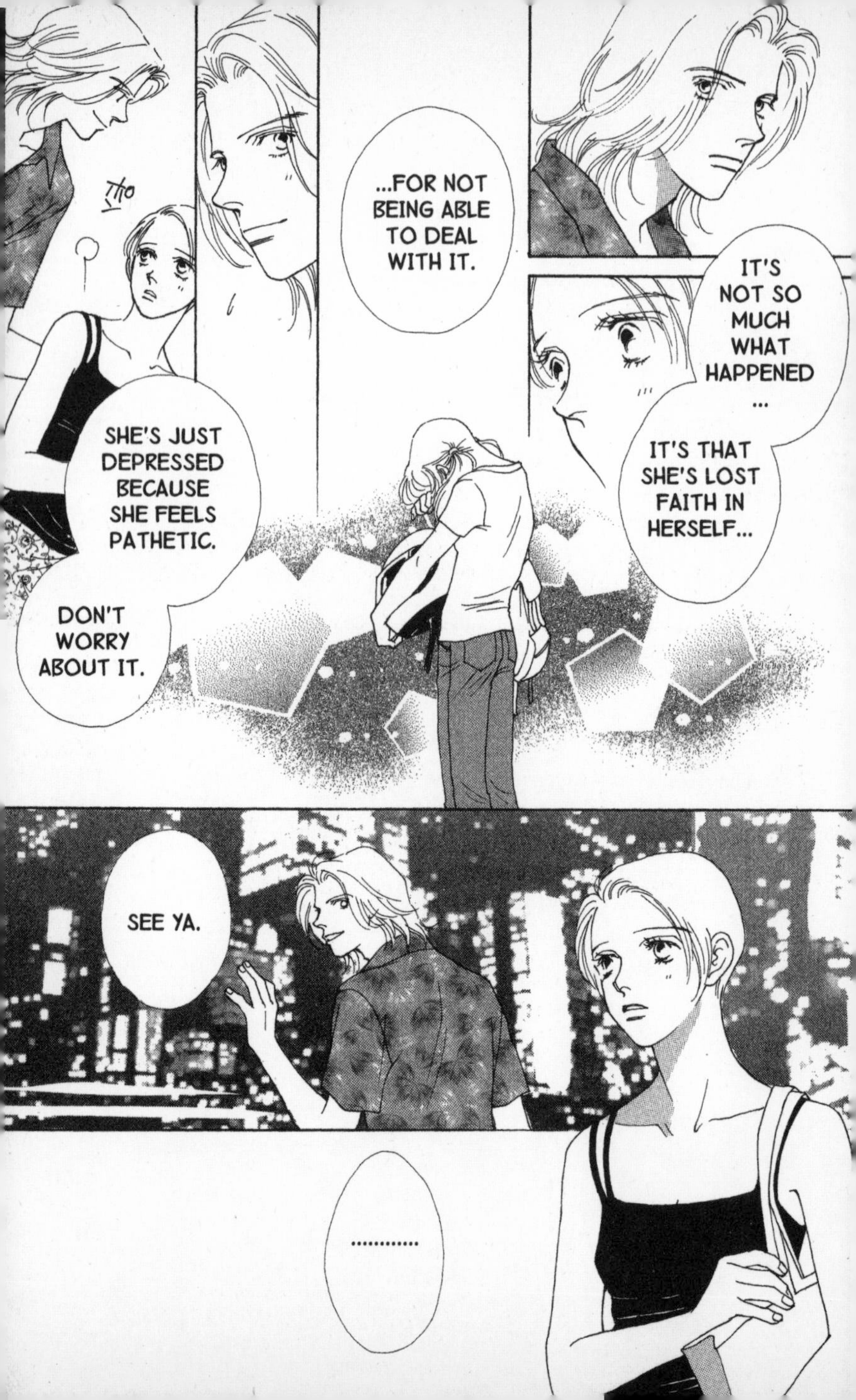
IT'S NOT SO MUCH WHAT HAPPENED...
IT'S THAT SHE'S LOST FAITH IN HERSELF...
...FOR NOT BEING ABLE TO DEAL WITH IT.
SHE'S JUST DEPRESSED BECAUSE SHE FEELS PATHETIC.
DON'T WORRY ABOUT IT.
SEE YA.
....

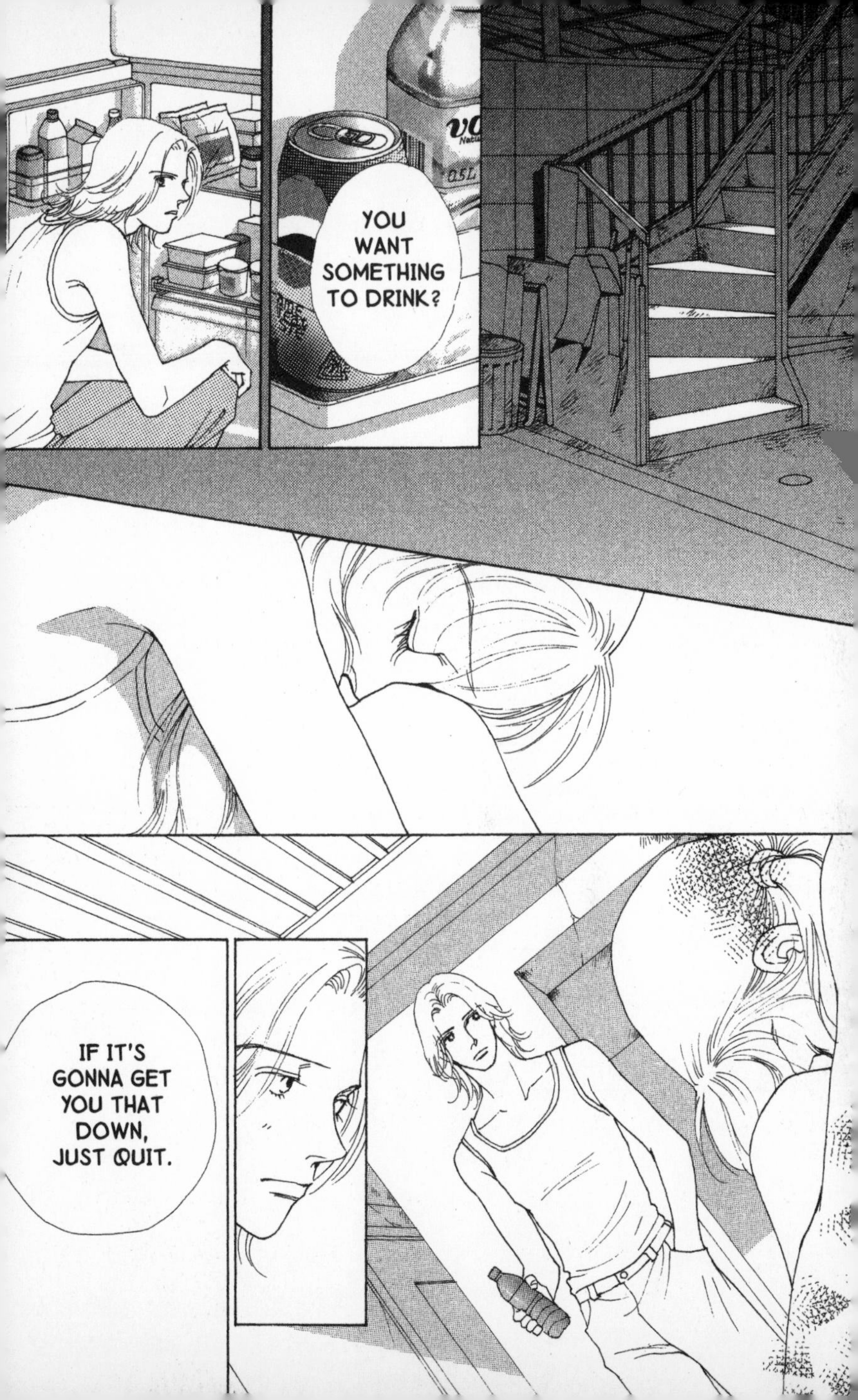
YOU WANT SOMETHING TO DRINK?
IF IT'S GONNA GET YOU THAT DOWN, JUST QUIT.

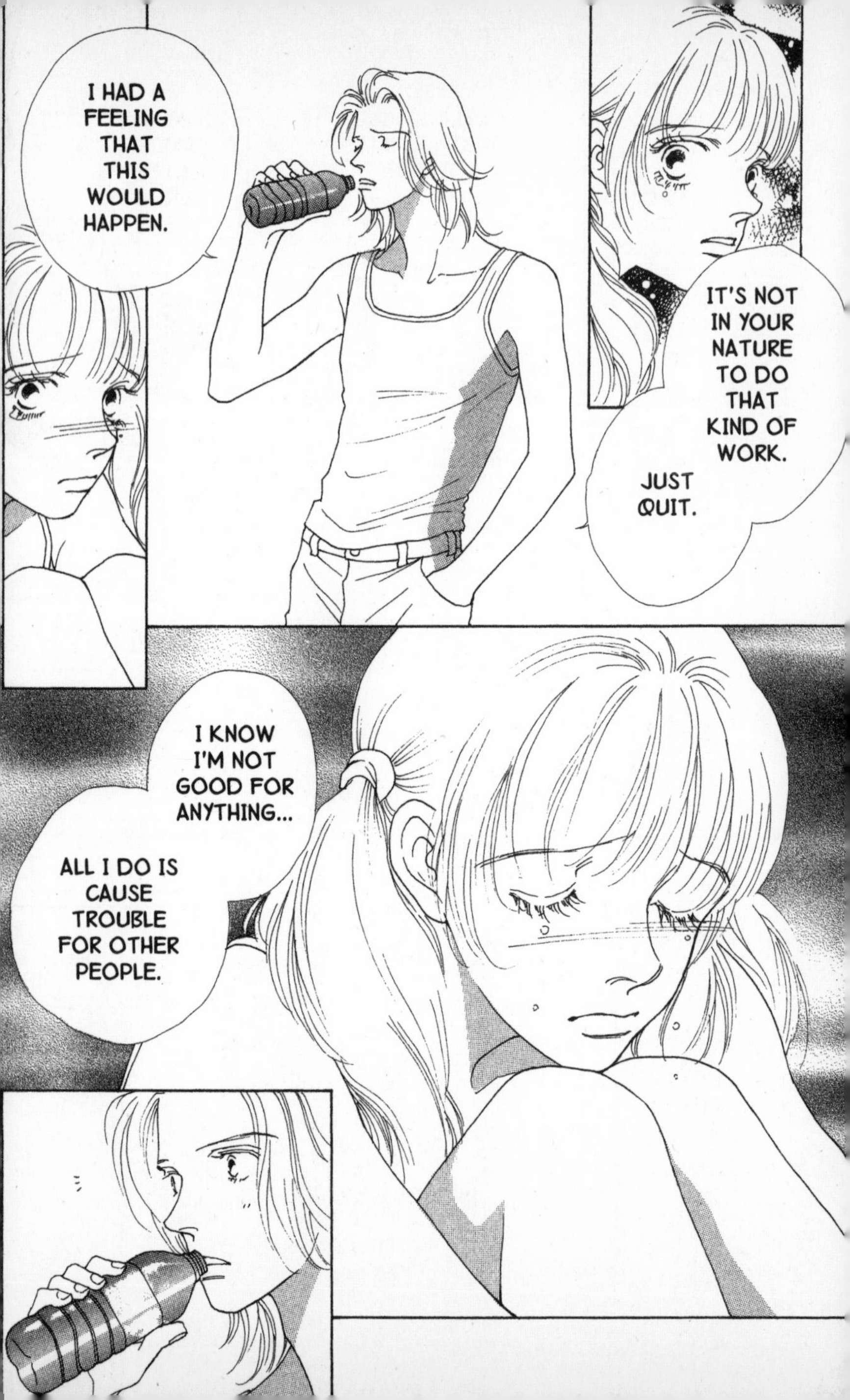
I HAD A FEELING THAT THIS WOULD HAPPEN.
IT'S NOT IN YOUR NATURE TO DO THAT KIND OF WORK.
JUST QUIT.
I KNOW I'M NOT GOOD FOR ANYTHING...
ALL I DO IS CAUSE TROUBLE FOR OTHER PEOPLE.

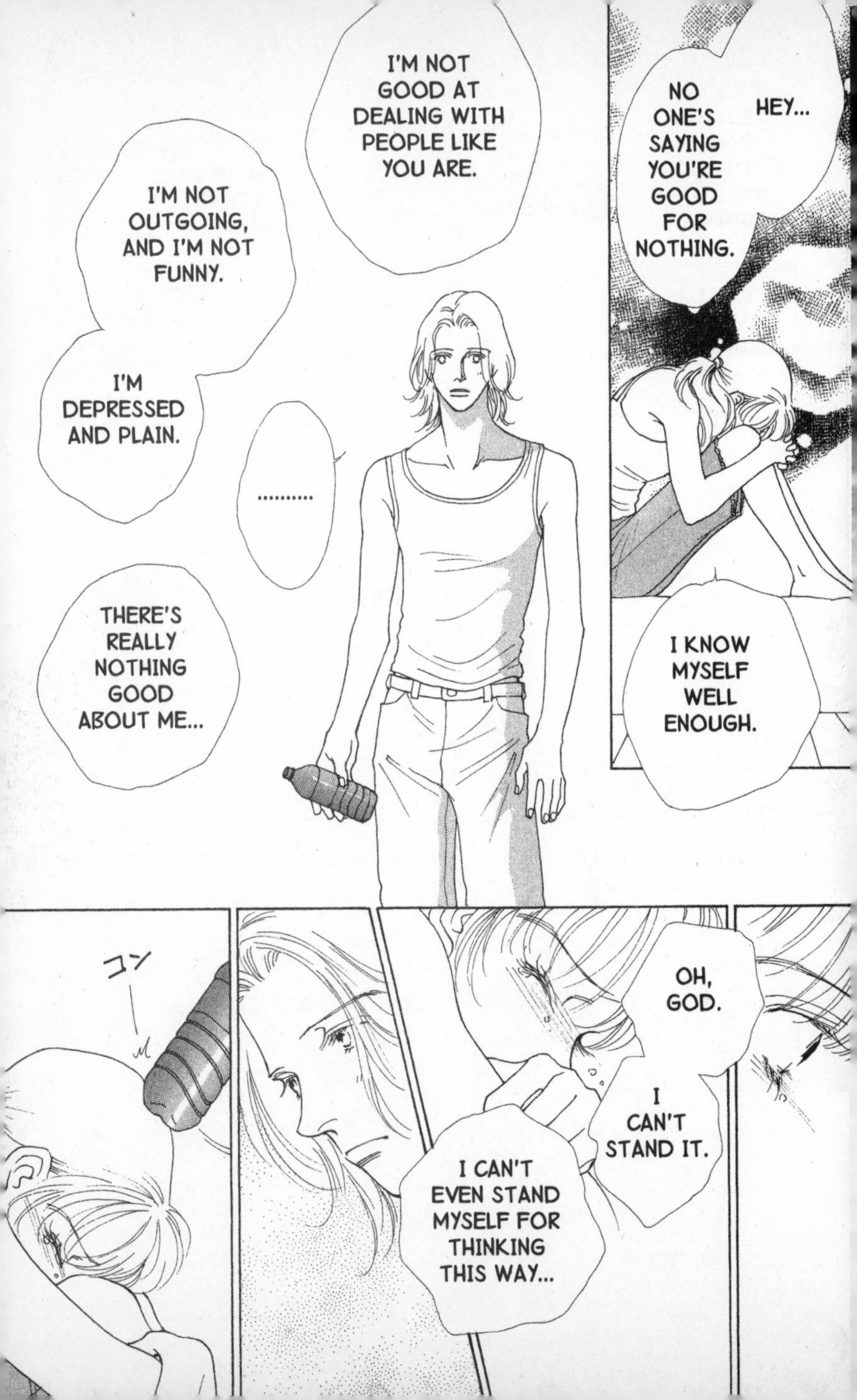
HEY...
NO ONE'S SAYING YOU'RE GOOD FOR NOTHING.
I KNOW MYSELF WELL ENOUGH.
I'M NOT GOOD AT DEALING WITH PEOPLE LIKE YOU ARE.
I'M NOT OUTGOING, AND I'M NOT FUNNY.
I'M DEPRESSED AND PLAIN.
....
THERE'S REALLY NOTHING GOOD ABOUT ME...
OH, GOD.
I CAN'T STAND IT.
I CAN'T EVEN STAND MYSELF FOR THINKING THIS WAY...
コン

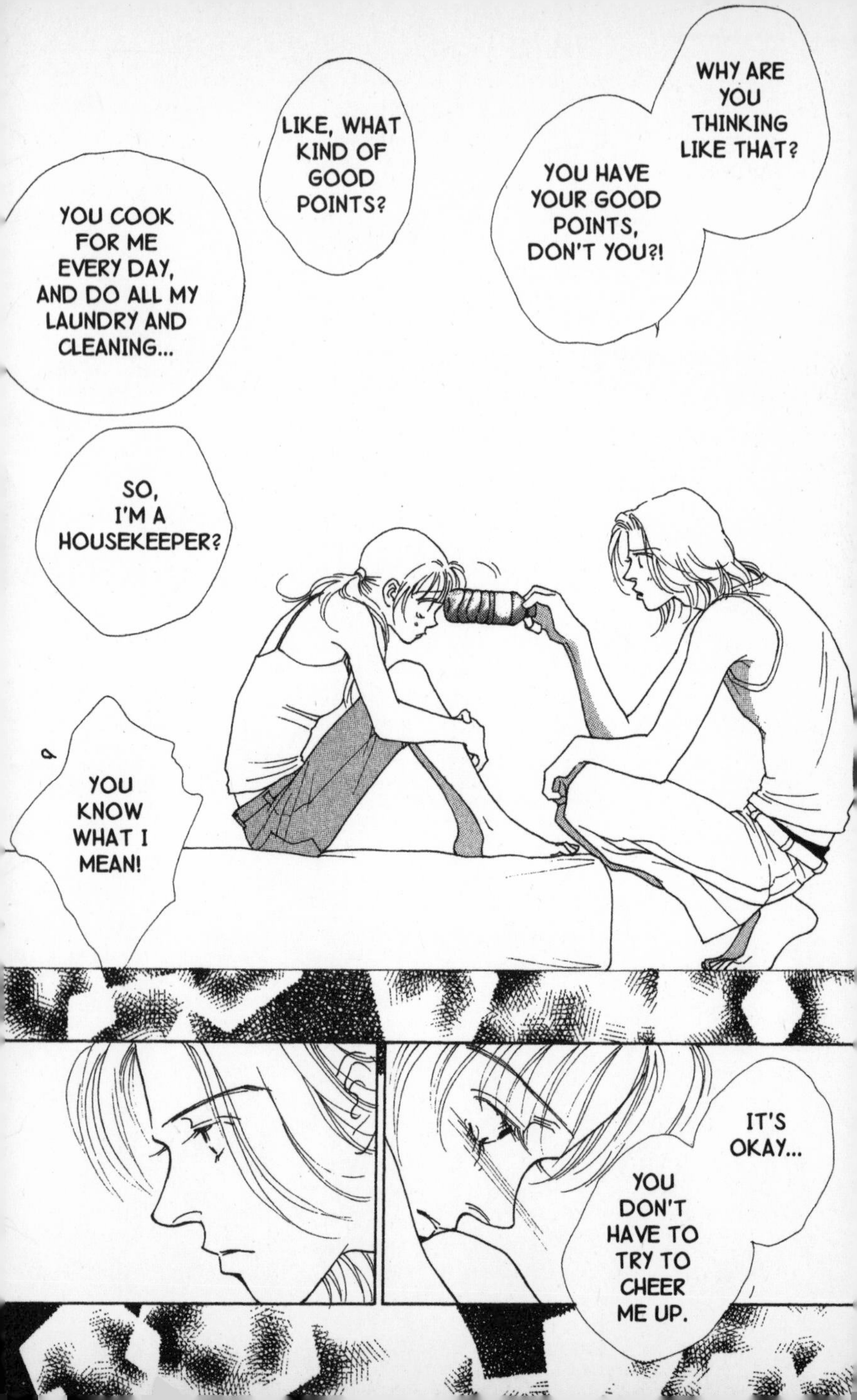
WHY ARE YOU THINKING LIKE THAT?
YOU HAVE YOUR GOOD POINTS, DON'T YOU?!
LIKE, WHAT KIND OF GOOD POINTS?
YOU COOK FOR ME EVERY DAY, AND DO ALL MY LAUNDRY AND CLEANING...
SO, I'M A HOUSEKEEPER?
YOU KNOW WHAT I MEAN!
IT'S OKAY...
YOU DON'T HAVE TO TRY TO CHEER ME UP.

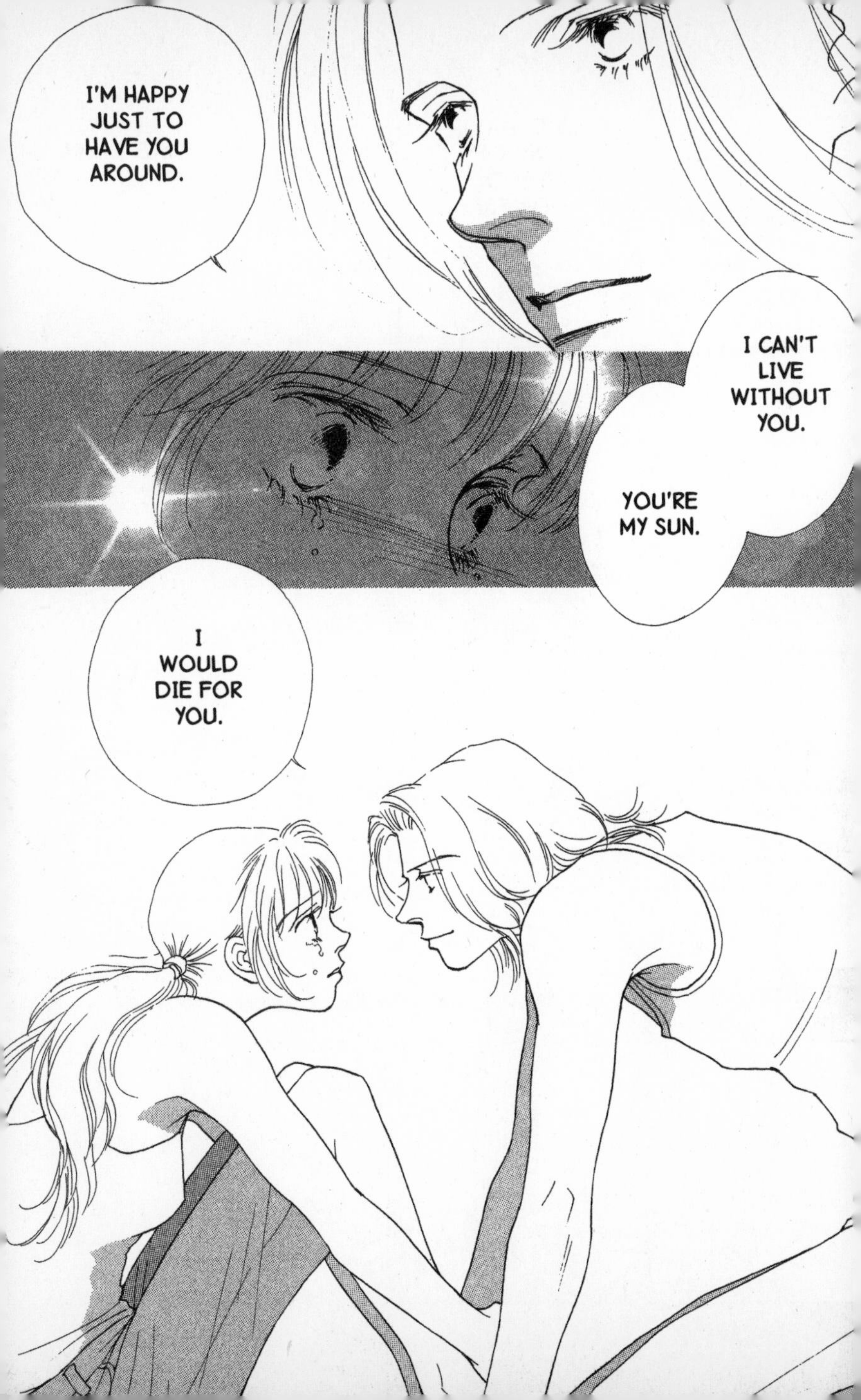
I'M HAPPY JUST TO HAVE YOU AROUND.
I CAN'T LIVE WITHOUT YOU.
YOU'RE MY SUN.
I WOULD DIE FOR YOU.

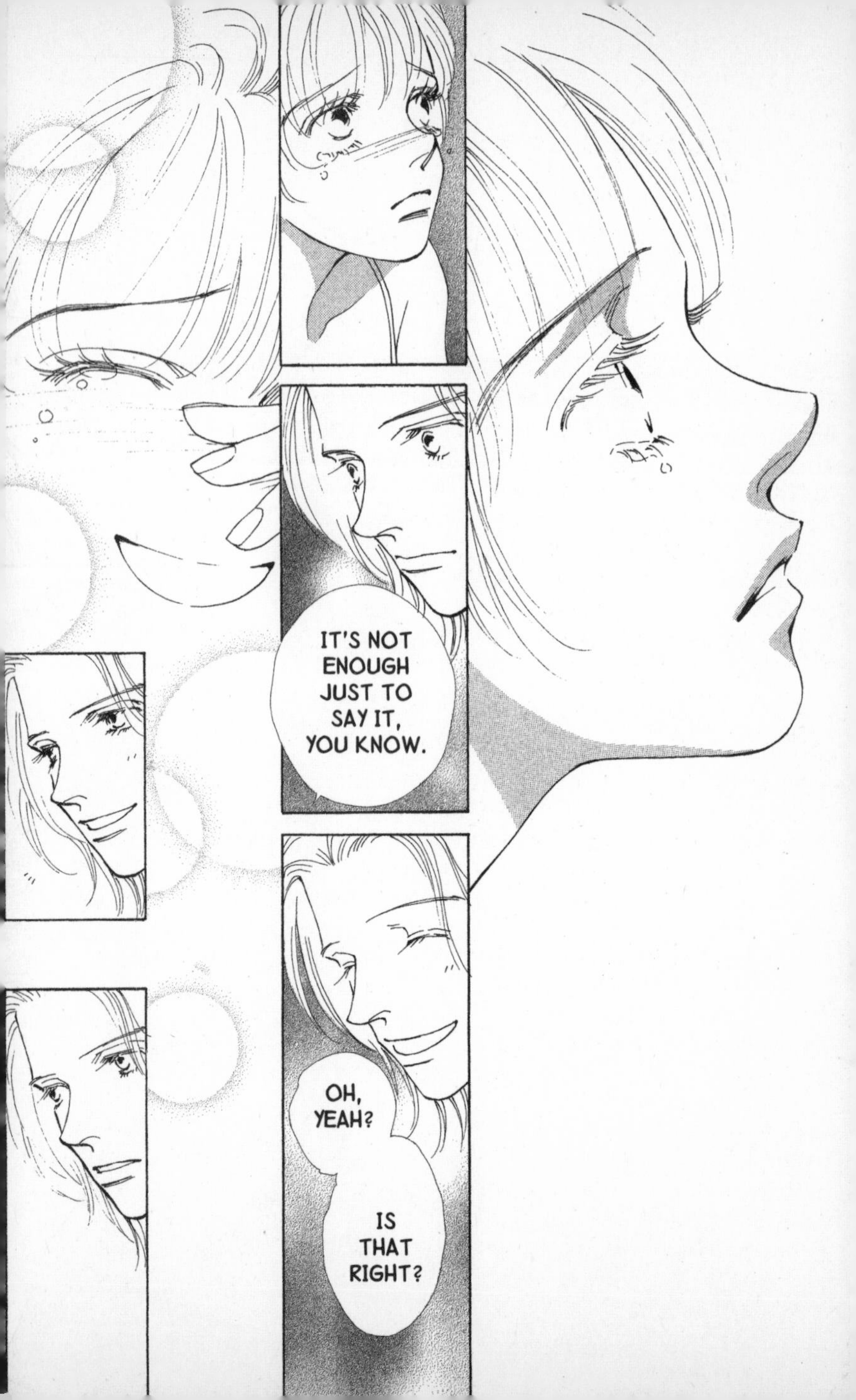
IT'S NOT ENOUGH JUST TO SAY IT, YOU KNOW.
OH, YEAH?
IS THAT RIGHT?

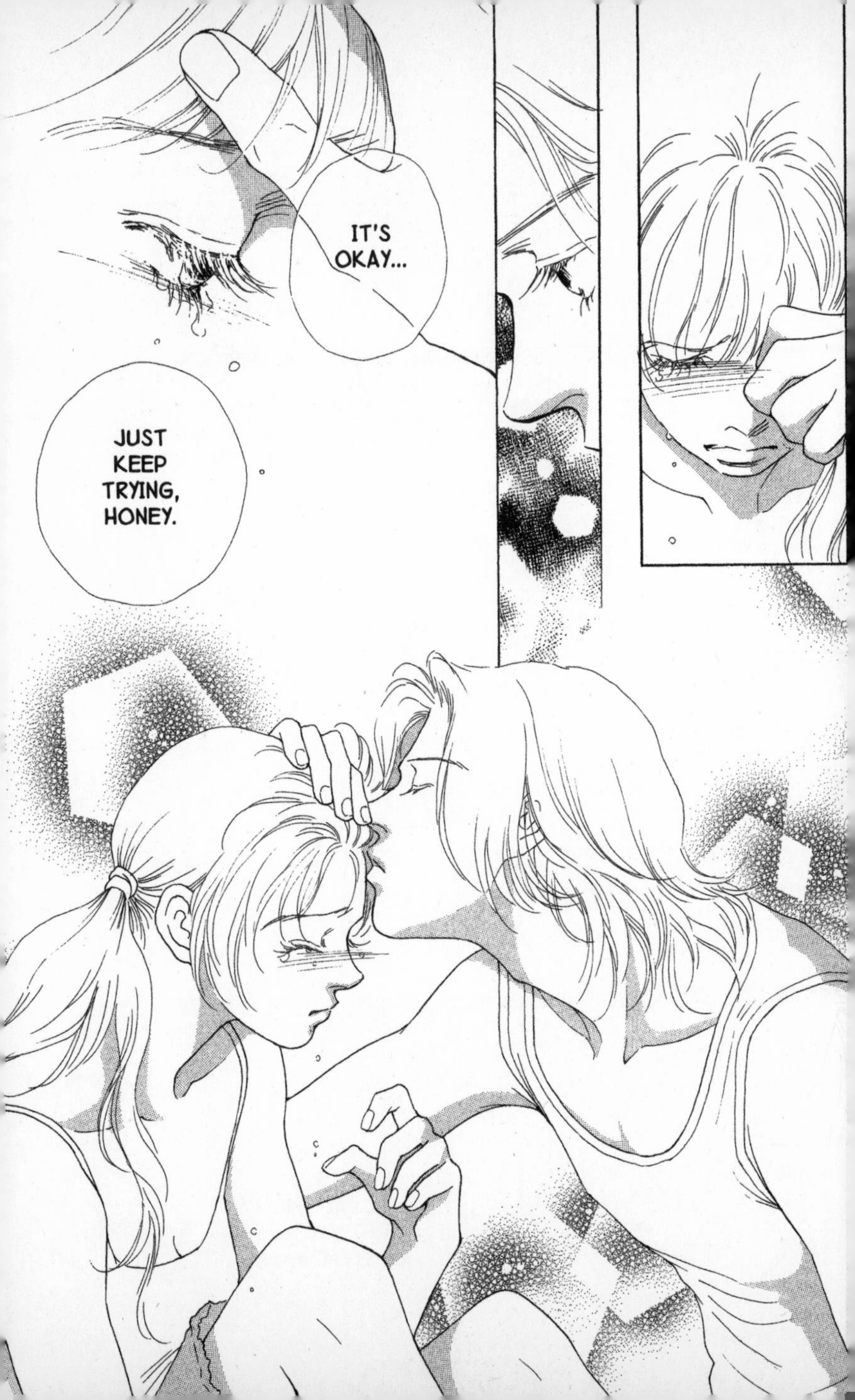
IT'S OKAY...
JUST KEEP TRYING, HONEY.

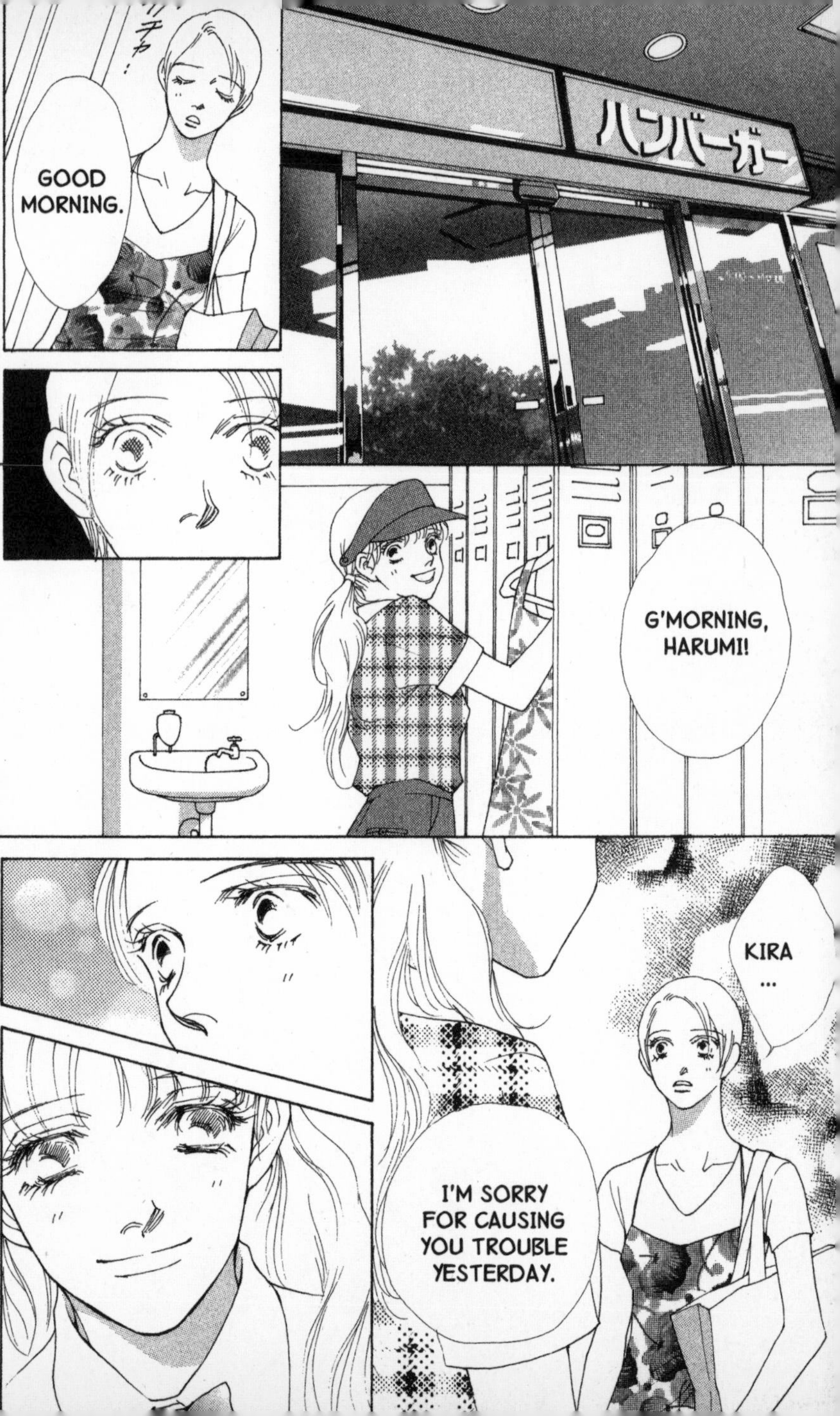
ハンバーガー
GOOD MORNING.
G'MORNING, HARUMI!
KIRA ...
I'M SORRY FOR CAUSING YOU TROUBLE YESTERDAY.

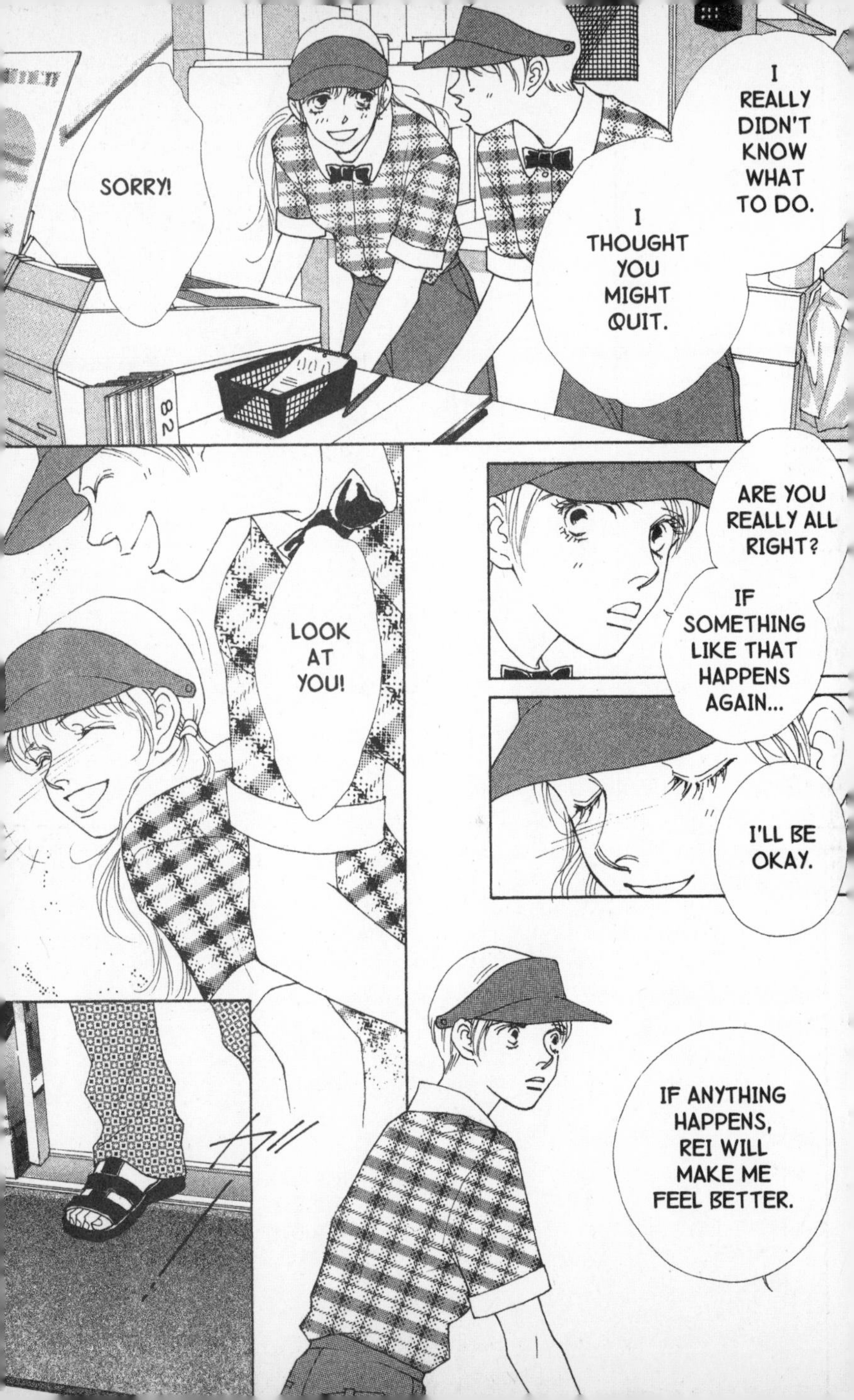
I REALLY DIDN'T KNOW WHAT TO DO.
I THOUGHT YOU MIGHT QUIT.
SORRY!
ARE YOU REALLY ALL RIGHT?
IF SOMETHING LIKE THAT HAPPENS AGAIN...
I'LL BE OKAY.
LOOK AT YOU!
IF ANYTHING HAPPENS, REI WILL MAKE ME FEEL BETTER.

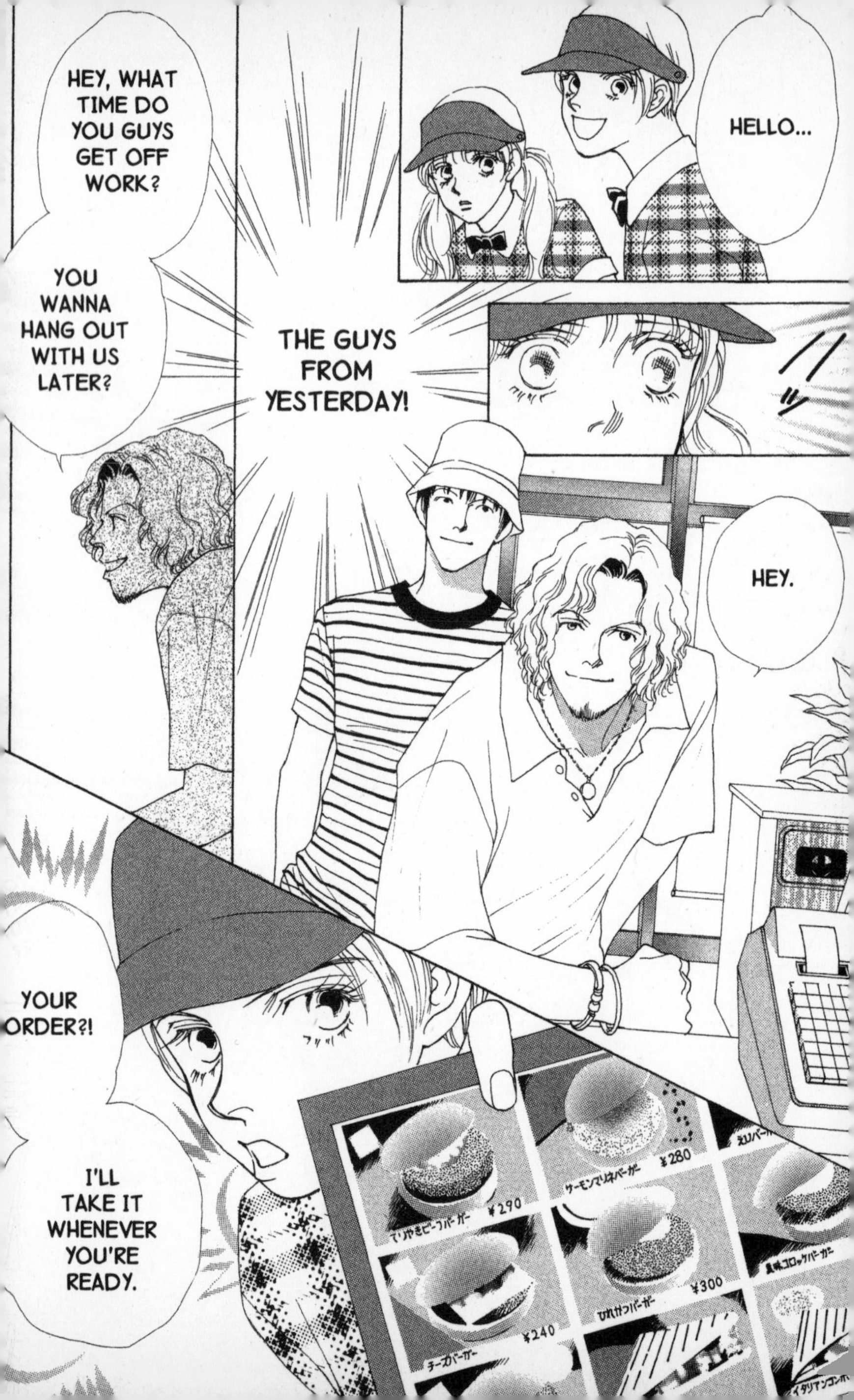
HELLO...
HEY.
THE GUYS FROM YESTERDAY!
HEY, WHAT TIME DO YOU GUYS GET OFF WORK?
YOU WANNA HANG OUT WITH US LATER?
YOUR ORDER?!
I'LL TAKE IT WHENEVER YOU'RE READY.
サーモンマリネバーガー ¥280
てりやきビーフバーガー ¥290
美味コロッケバーガー
ひれかつバーガー ¥300
チーズバーガー ¥240

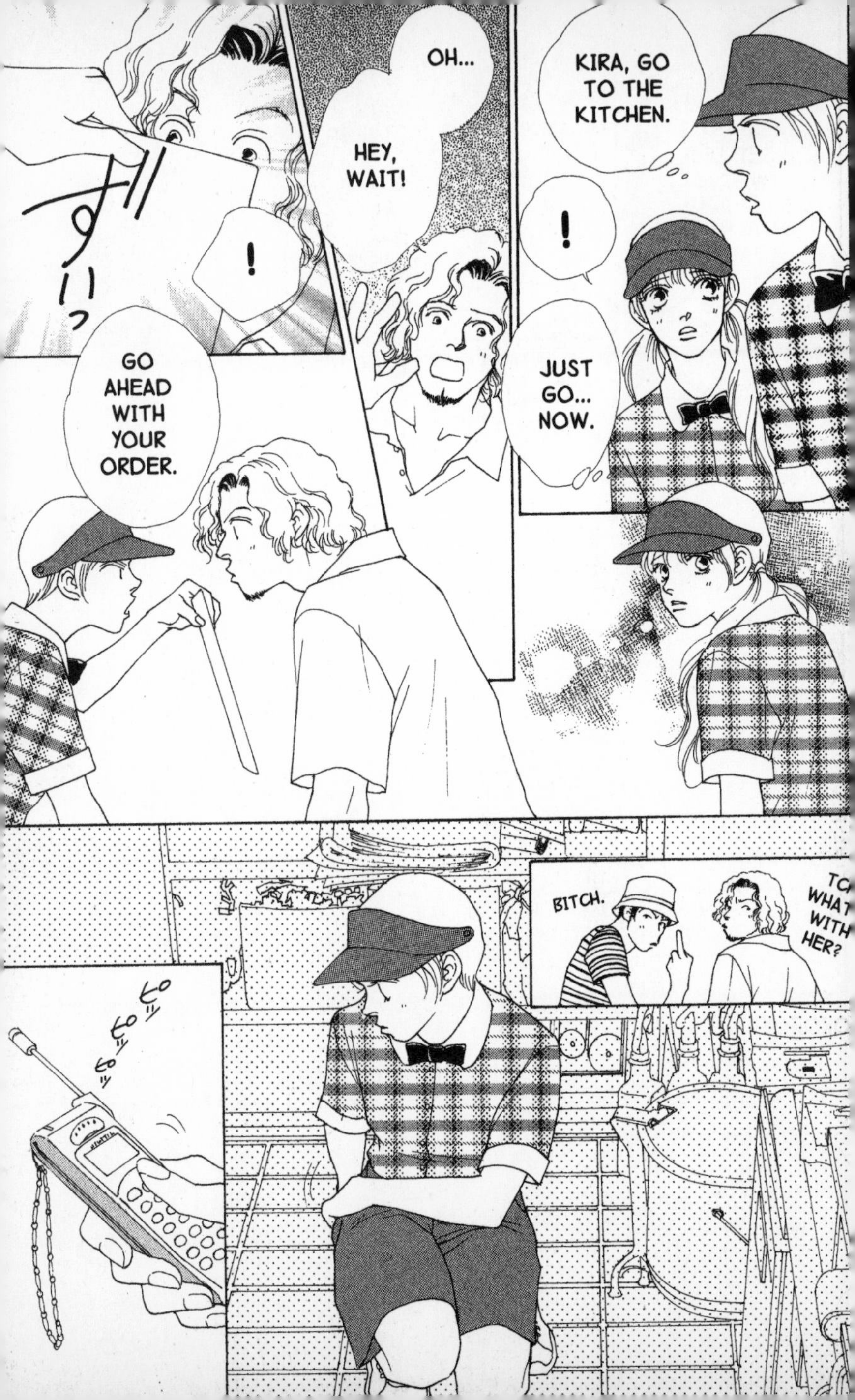
KIRA, GO TO THE KITCHEN.
!
JUST GO... NOW.
OH...
HEY, WAIT!
!
ずいっ
GO AHEAD WITH YOUR ORDER.
BITCH.
TC WHAT WITH HER?
ピッ ピッ ピッ

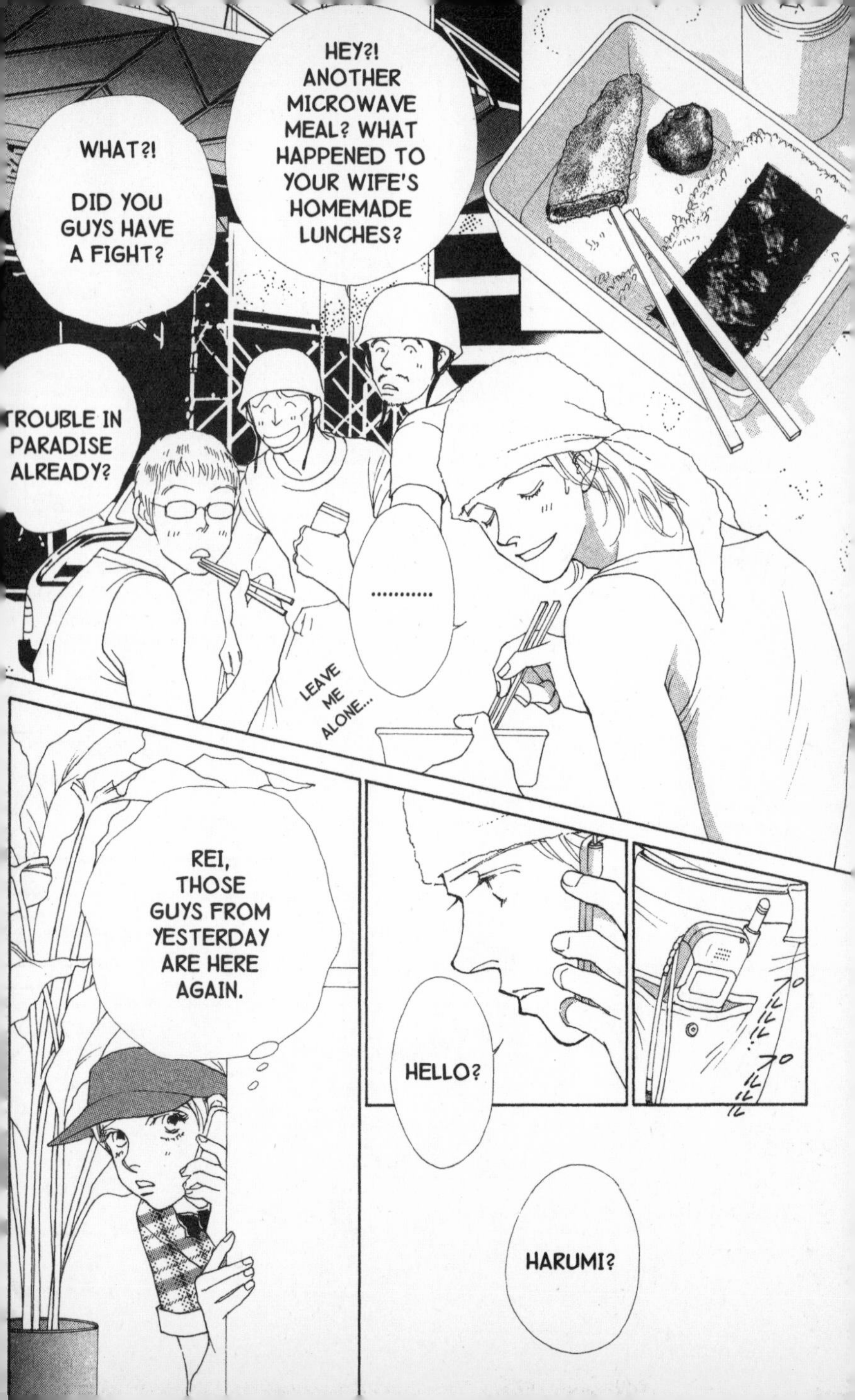
HEY?! ANOTHER MICROWAVE MEAL? WHAT HAPPENED TO YOUR WIFE'S HOMEMADE LUNCHES?
WHAT?! DID YOU GUYS HAVE A FIGHT?
TROUBLE IN PARADISE ALREADY?
....
LEAVE ME ALONE...
フルルル!
フルルル
HELLO?
HARUMI?
REI, THOSE GUYS FROM YESTERDAY ARE HERE AGAIN.

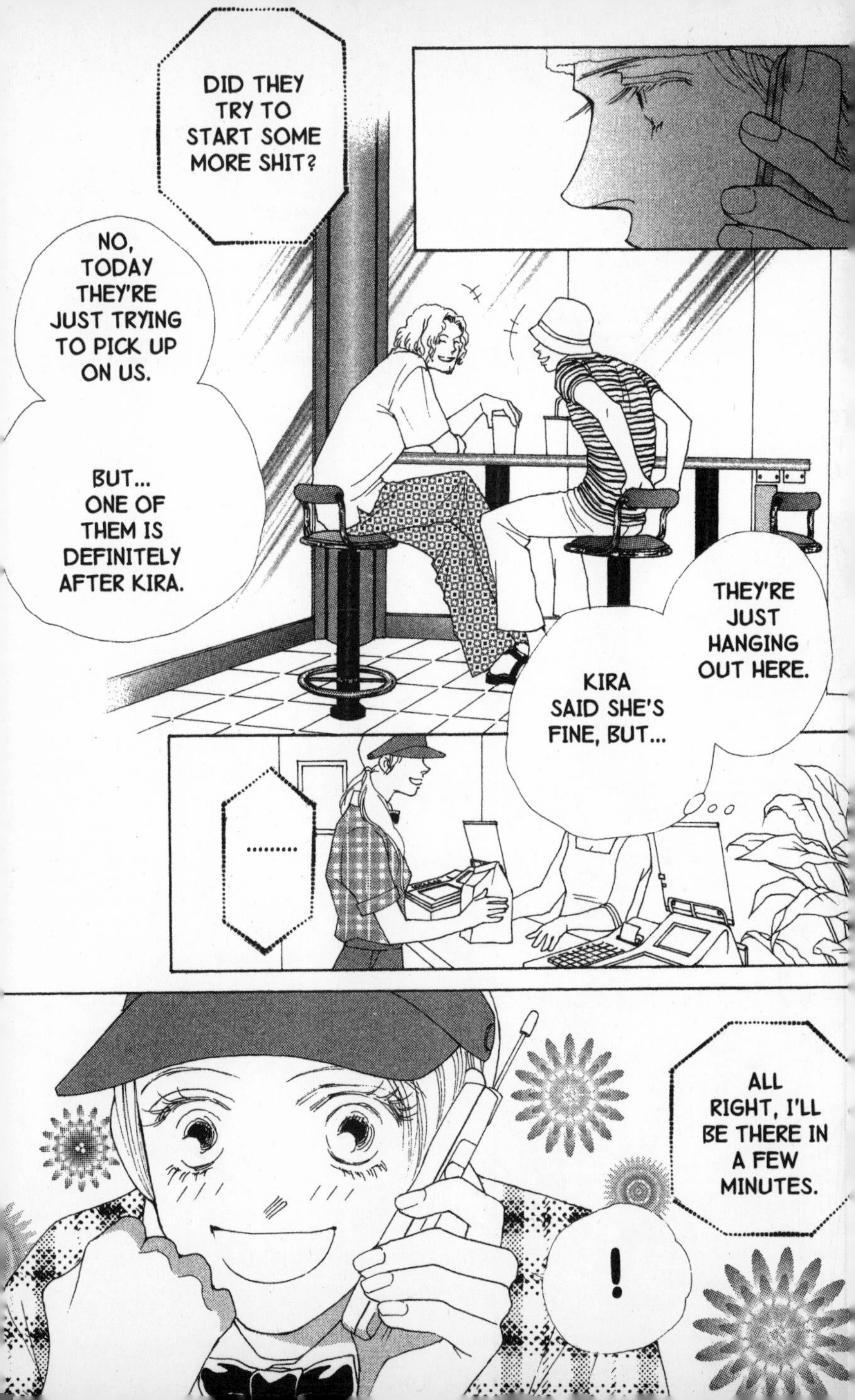
DID THEY TRY TO START SOME MORE SHIT?
NO, TODAY THEY'RE JUST TRYING TO PICK UP ON US.
BUT... ONE OF THEM IS DEFINITELY AFTER KIRA.
THEY'RE JUST HANGING OUT HERE.
KIRA SAID SHE'S FINE, BUT...
....
ALL RIGHT, I'LL BE THERE IN A FEW MINUTES.
!

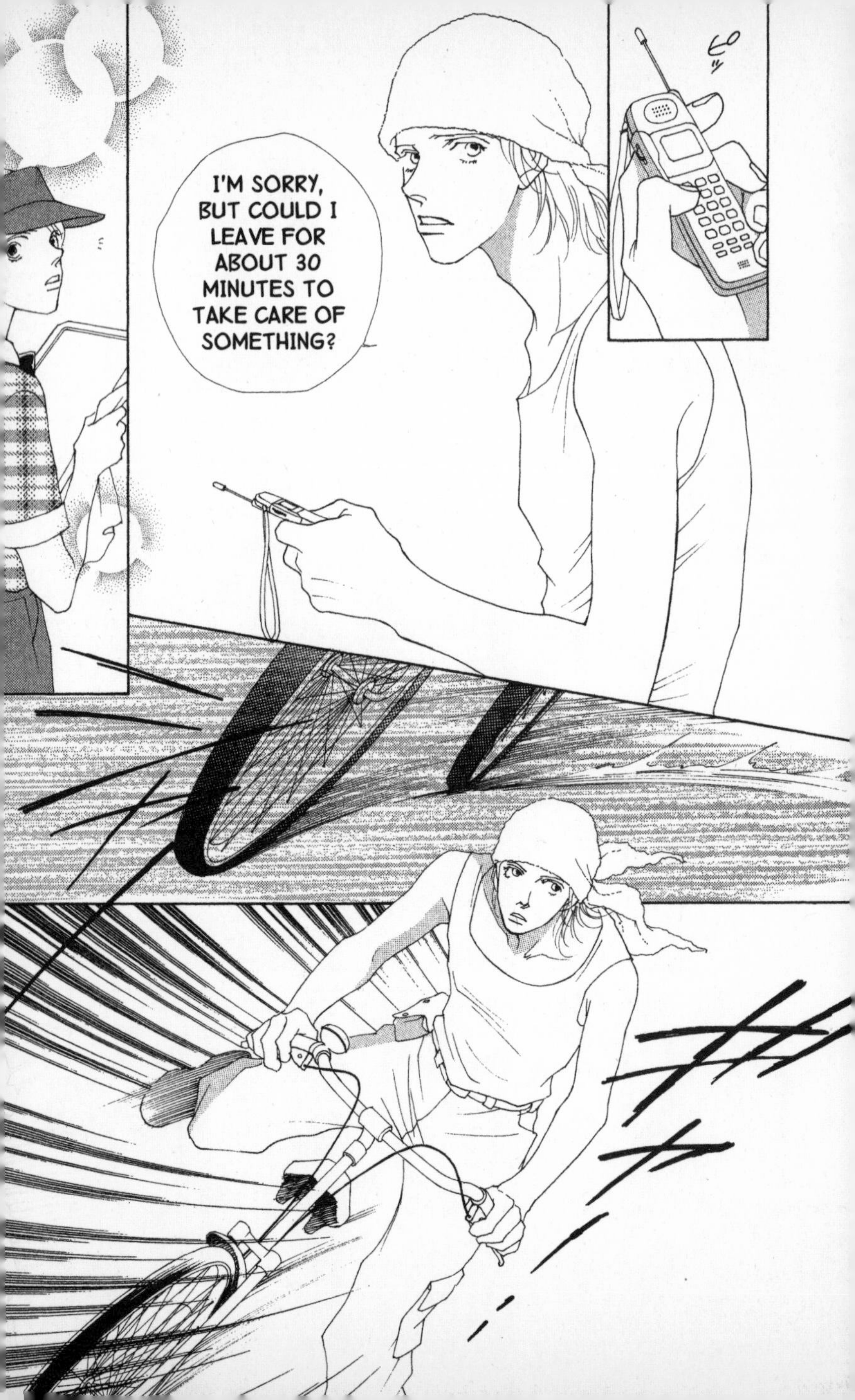
I'M SORRY, BUT COULD I LEAVE FOR ABOUT 30 MINUTES TO TAKE CARE OF SOMETHING?

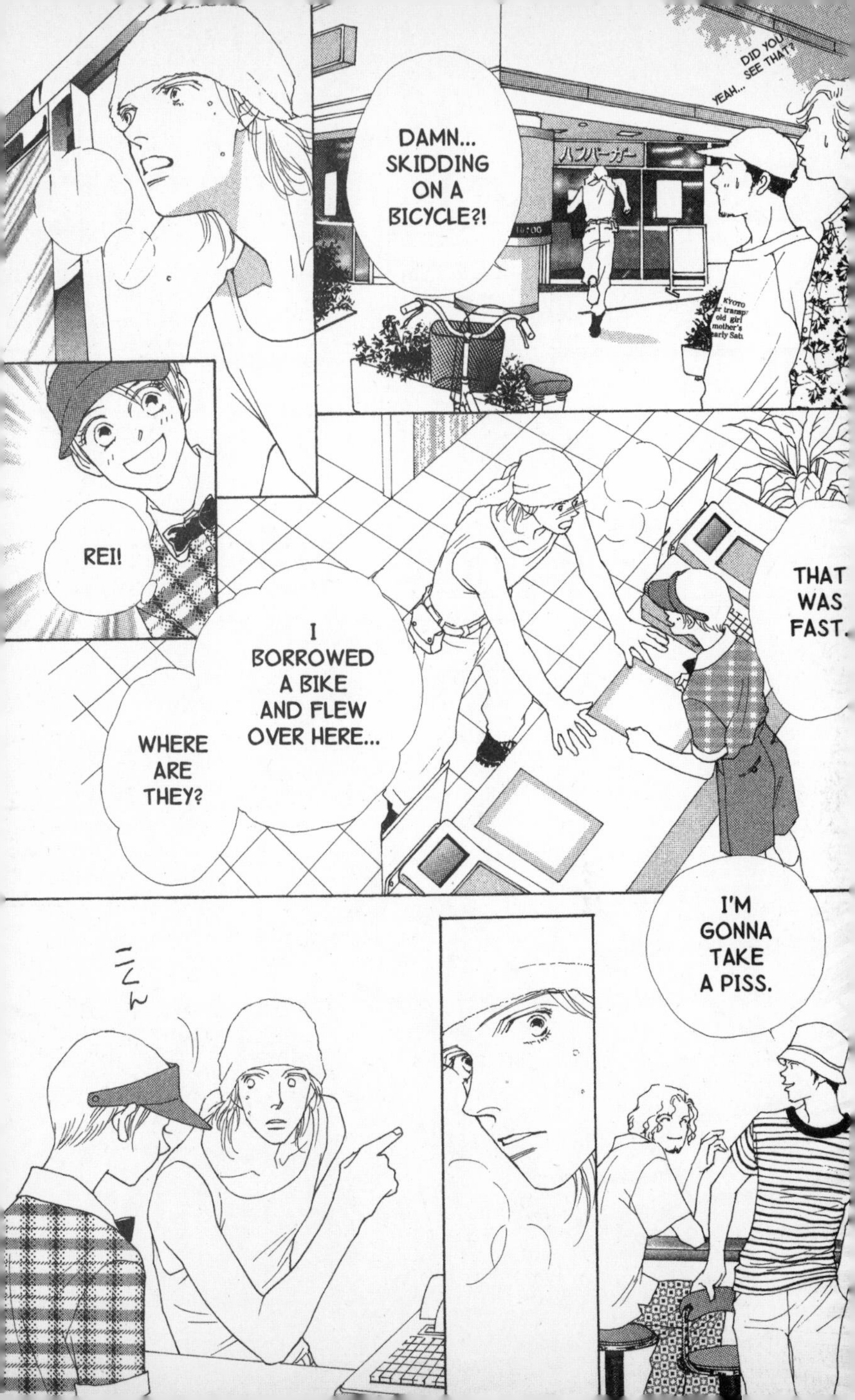
DID YOU SEE THAT?
YEAH...
DAMN... SKIDDING ON A BICYCLE?!
REI!
THAT WAS FAST.
I BORROWED A BIKE AND FLEW OVER HERE...
WHERE ARE THEY?
I'M GONNA TAKE A PISS.

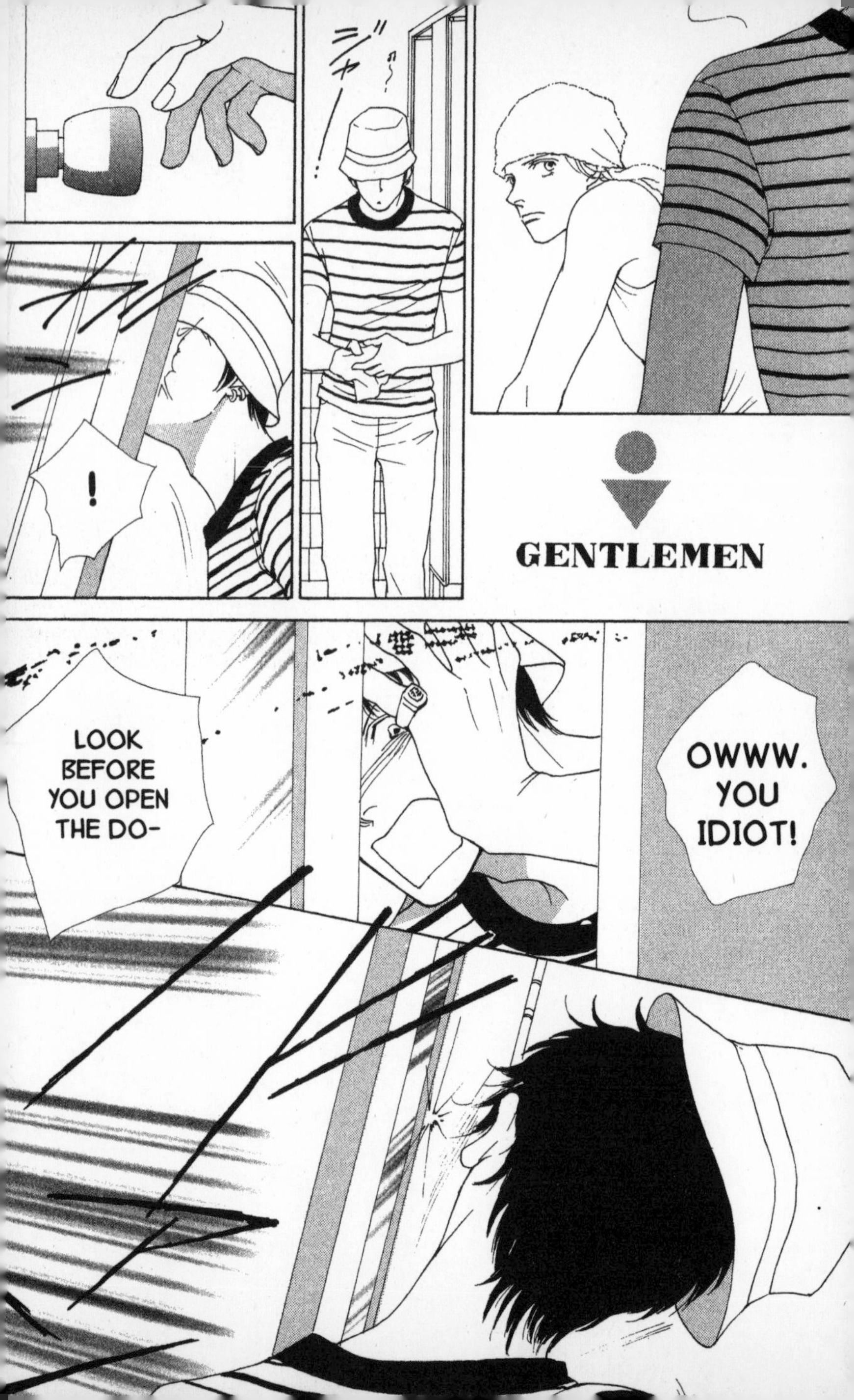
GENTLEMEN
ジャ
!
OWWW. YOU IDIOT!
LOOK BEFORE YOU OPEN THE DO-

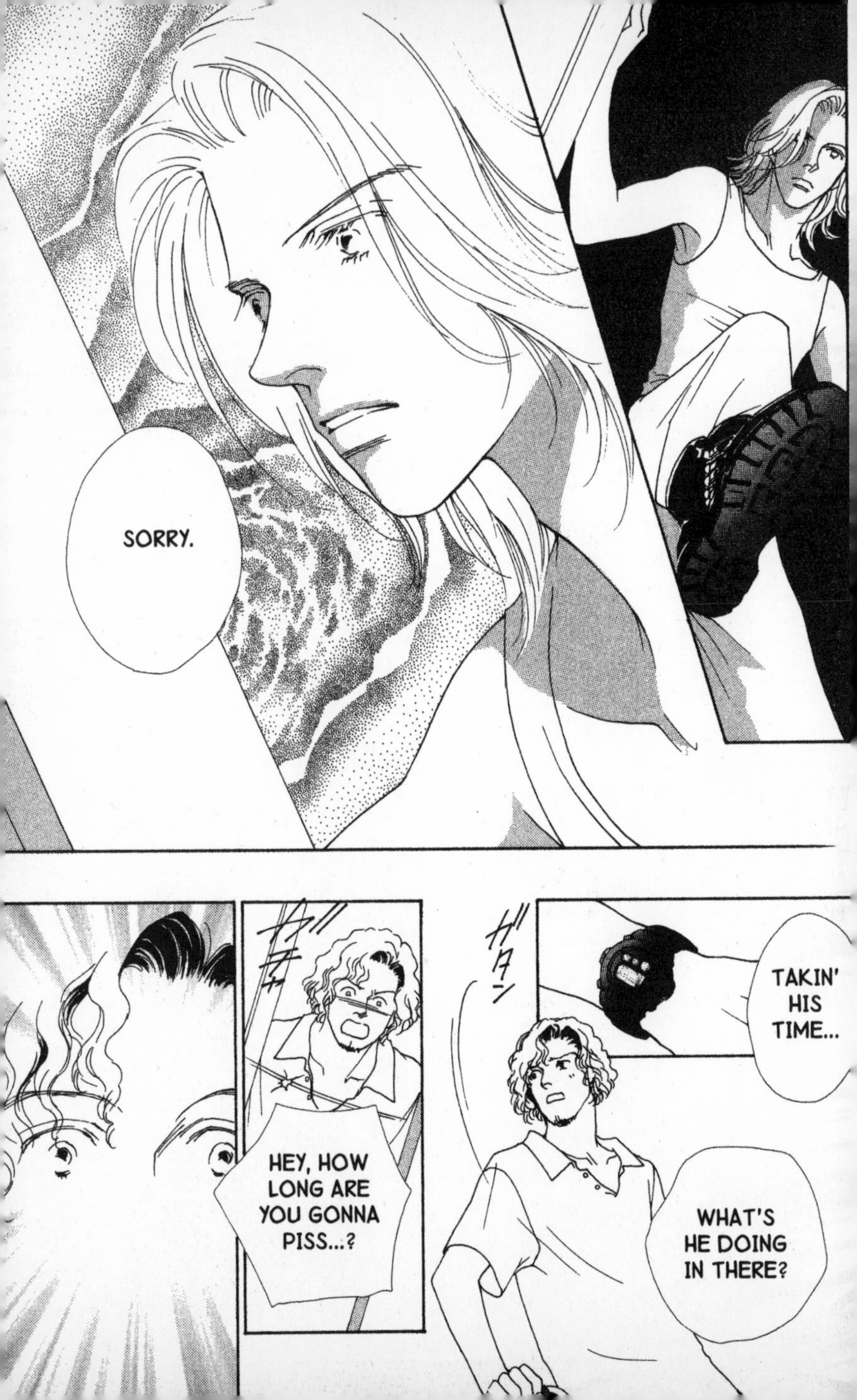
SORRY.
TAKIN' HIS TIME...
ガタン
WHAT'S HE DOING IN THERE?
HEY, HOW LONG ARE YOU GONNA PISS...?

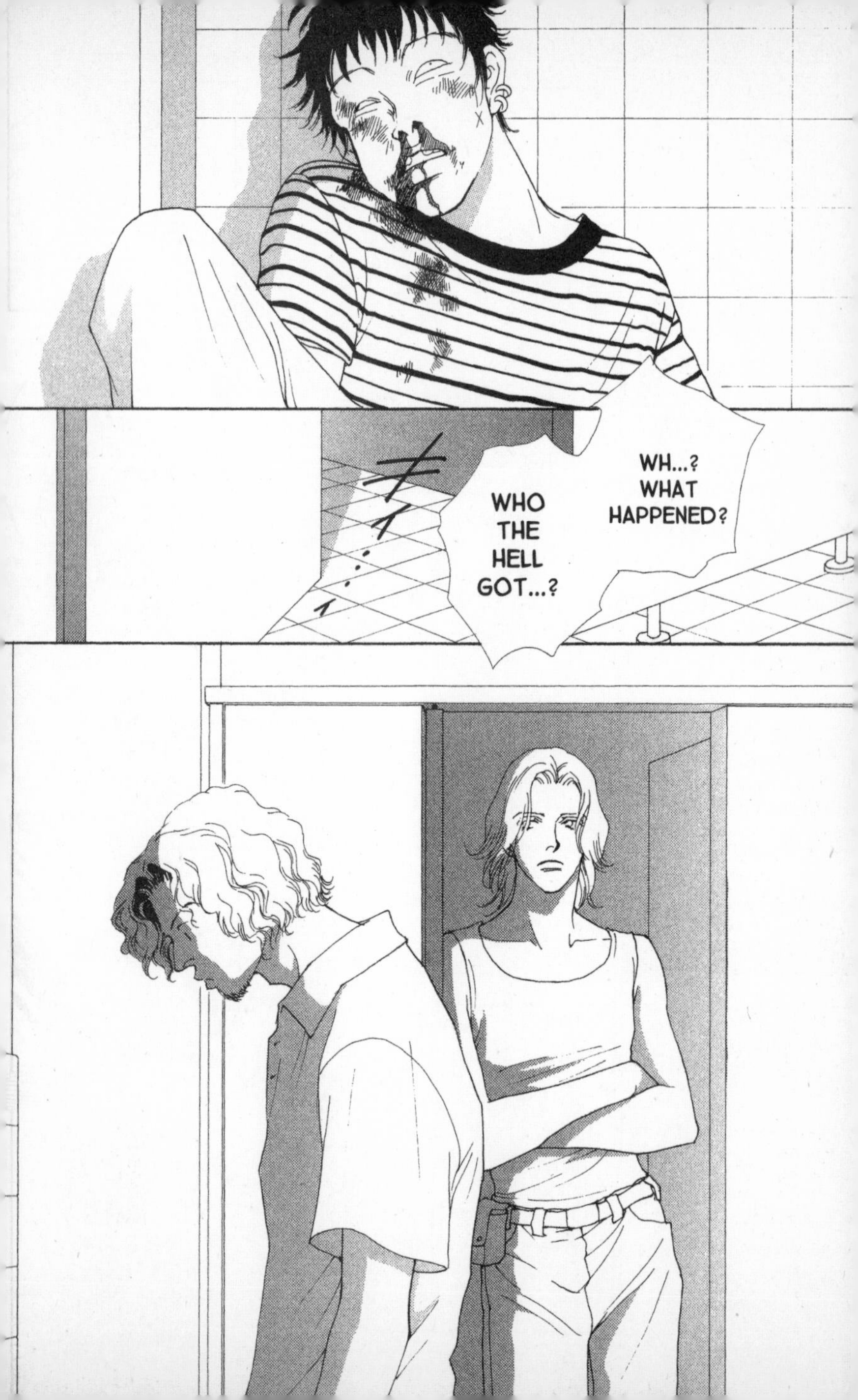
WH...? WHAT HAPPENED?
WHO THE HELL GOT...?

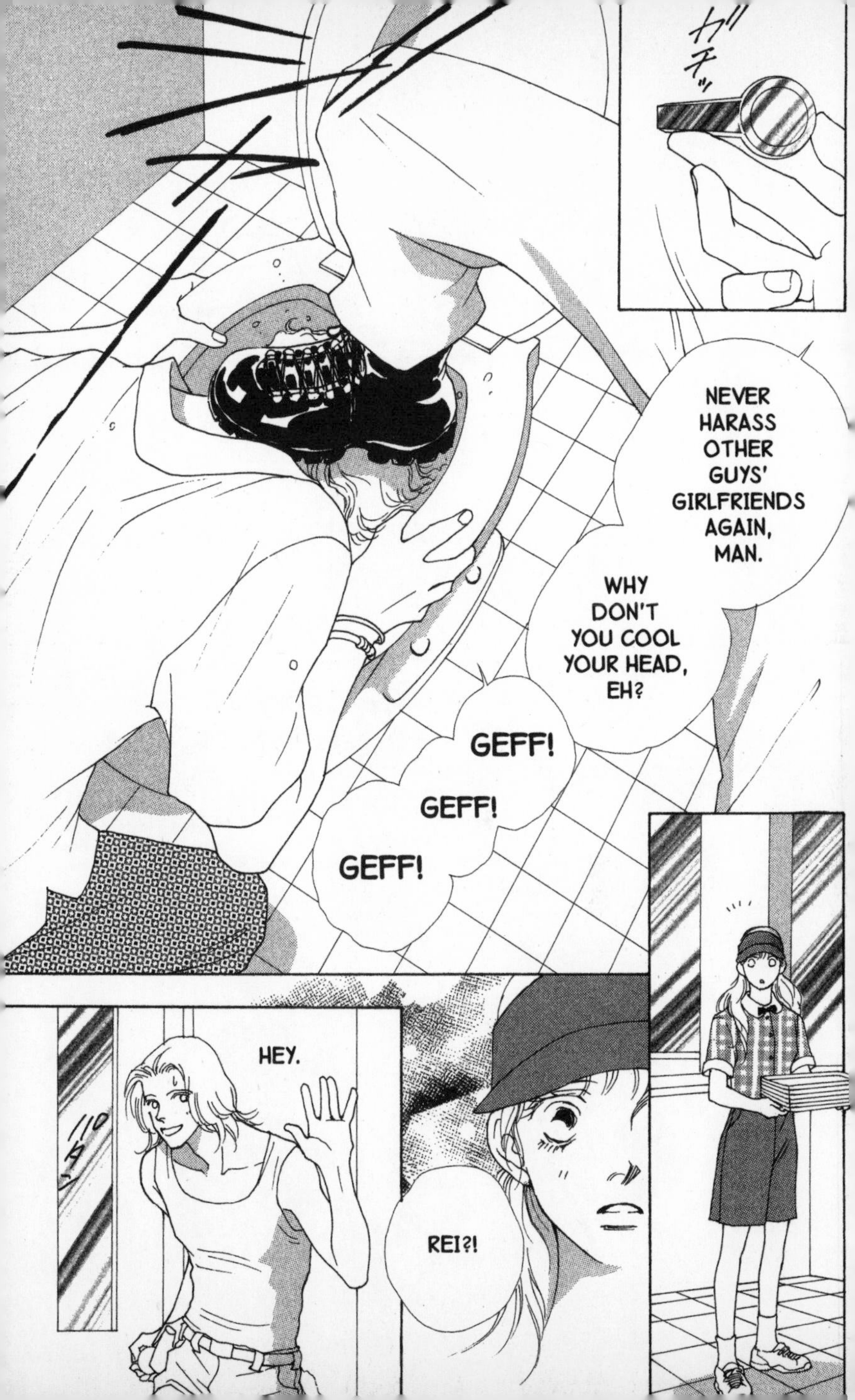
ガチッ
NEVER HARASS OTHER GUYS' GIRLFRIENDS AGAIN, MAN.
WHY DON'T YOU COOL YOUR HEAD, EH?
GEFF!
GEFF!
GEFF!
REI?!
パタン
HEY.

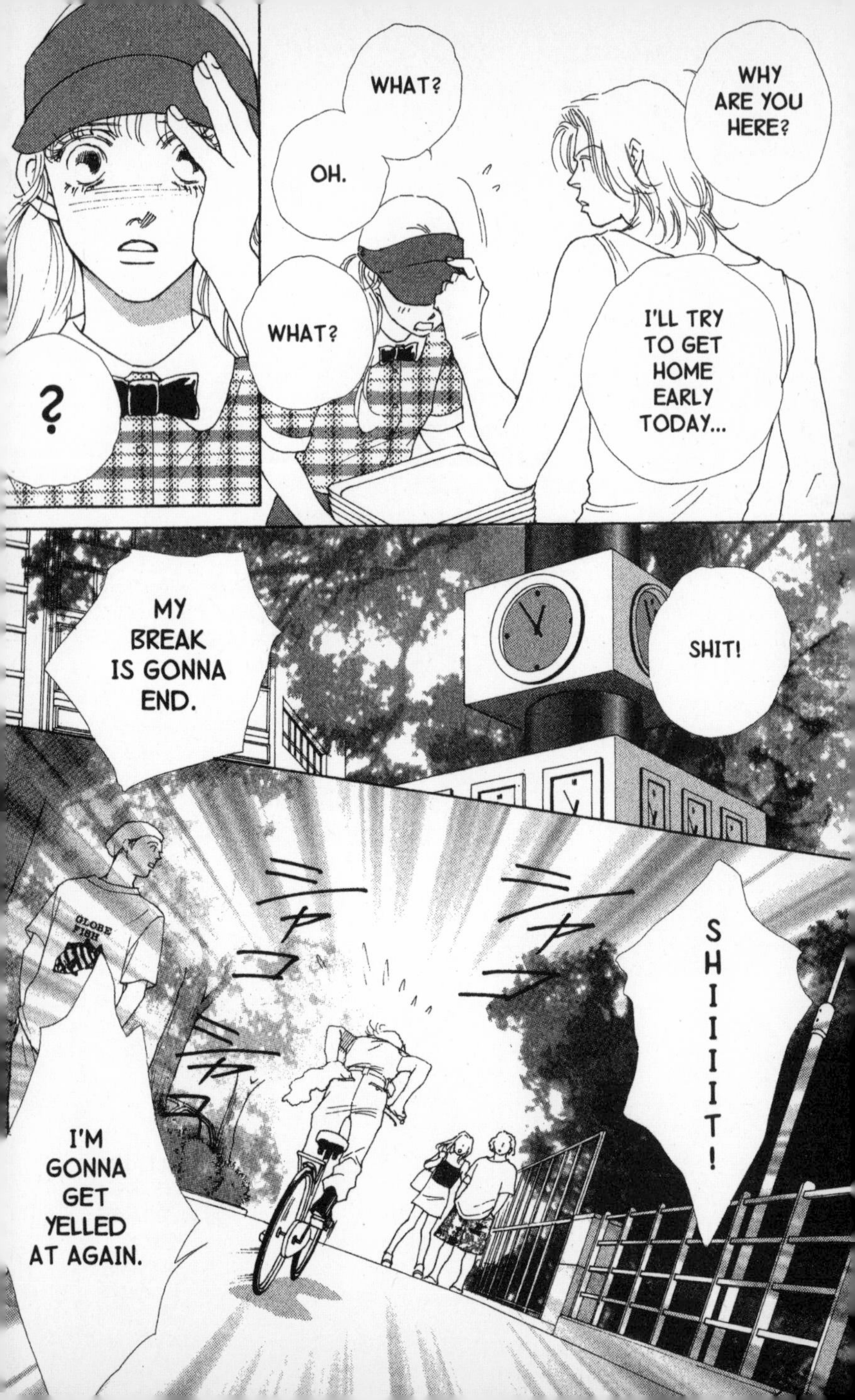
WHY ARE YOU HERE?
WHAT?
OH.
I'LL TRY TO GET HOME EARLY TODAY...
WHAT?
?
SHIT!
MY BREAK IS GONNA END.
SHIIIIIT!
GLOBE FISH
I'M GONNA GET YELLED AT AGAIN.

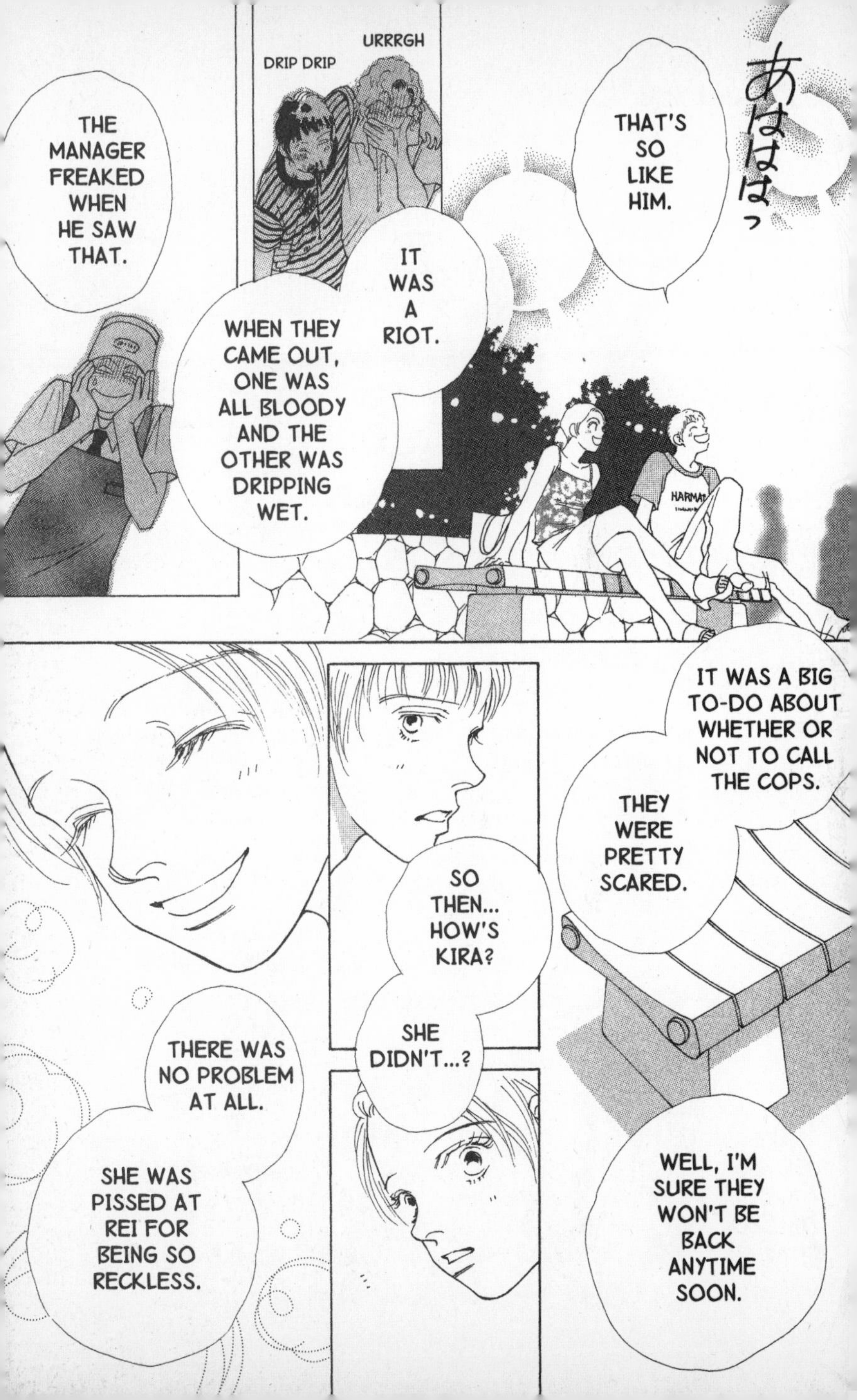
あははっ
THAT'S SO LIKE HIM.
IT WAS A RIOT.
WHEN THEY CAME OUT, ONE WAS ALL BLOODY AND THE OTHER WAS DRIPPING WET.
URRRGH
DRIP DRIP
THE MANAGER FREAKED WHEN HE SAW THAT.
IT WAS A BIG TO-DO ABOUT WHETHER OR NOT TO CALL THE COPS.
THEY WERE PRETTY SCARED.
WELL, I'M SURE THEY WON'T BE BACK ANYTIME SOON.
SO THEN... HOW'S KIRA?
SHE DIDN'T...?
THERE WAS NO PROBLEM AT ALL.
SHE WAS PISSED AT REI FOR BEING SO RECKLESS.

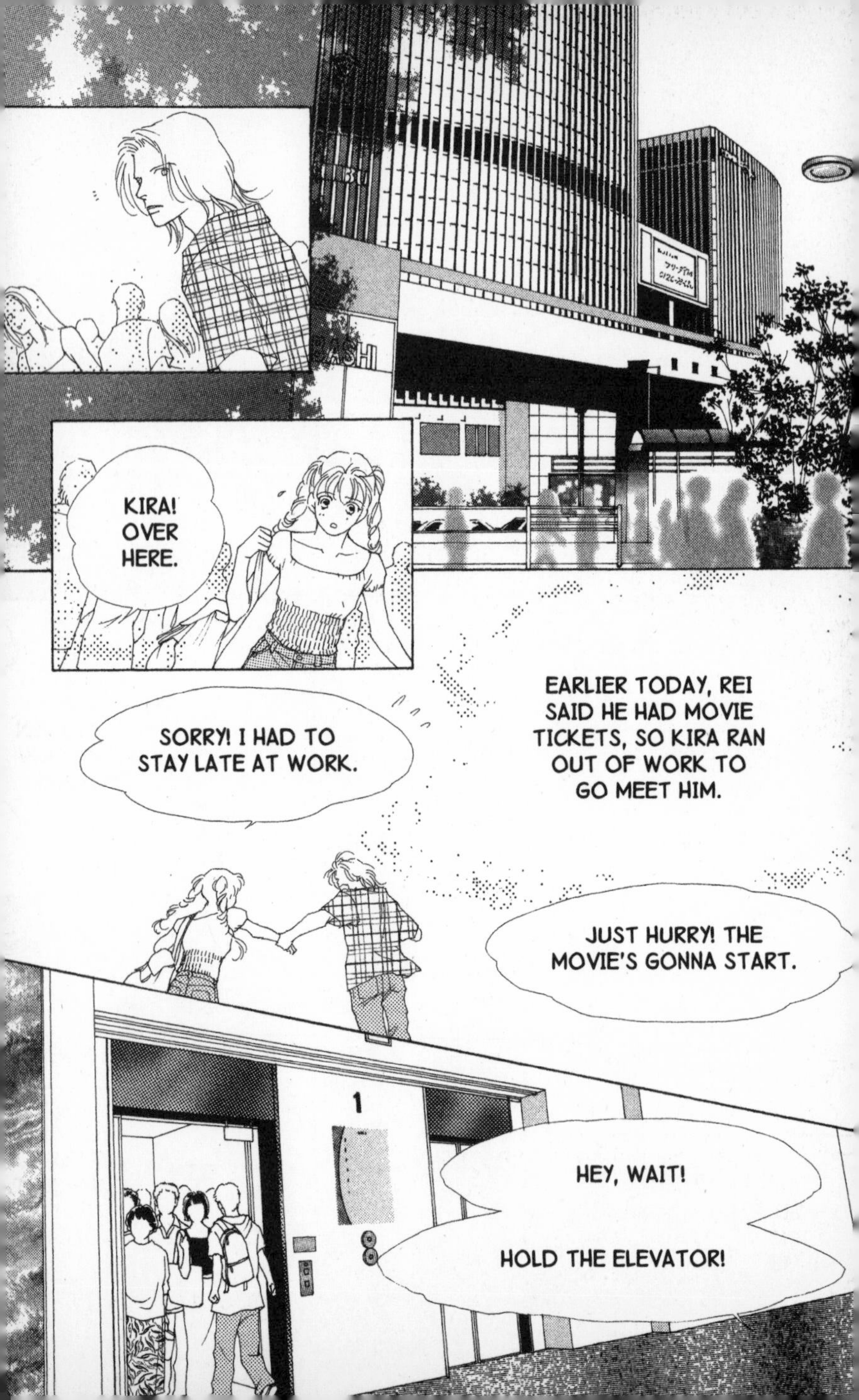
KIRA! OVER HERE.
EARLIER TODAY, REI SAID HE HAD MOVIE TICKETS, SO KIRA RAN OUT OF WORK TO GO MEET HIM.
SORRY! I HAD TO STAY LATE AT WORK.
JUST HURRY! THE MOVIE'S GONNA START.
HEY, WAIT!
HOLD THE ELEVATOR!

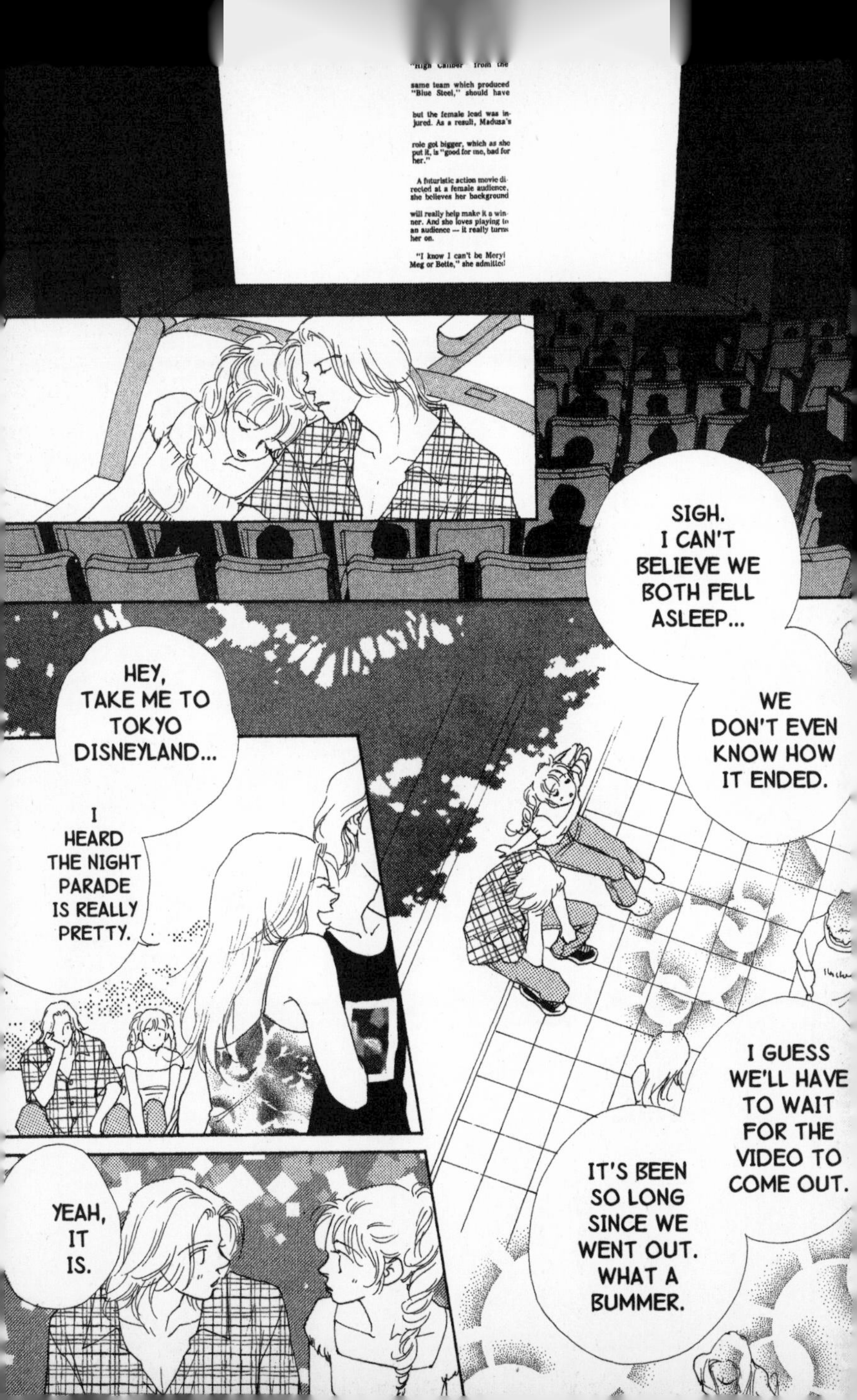
"High Caliber" from the
same team which produced "Blue Steel," should have
but the female lead was injured. As a result, Madusa's
role got bigger, which as she put it, is "good for me, bad for her."
A futuristic action movie directed at a female audience, she believes her background
will really help make it a winner. And she loves playing to an audience — it really turns her on.
"I know I can't be Meryl, Meg or Bette," she admitted
SIGH. I CAN'T BELIEVE WE BOTH FELL ASLEEP...
WE DON'T EVEN KNOW HOW IT ENDED.
I GUESS WE'LL HAVE TO WAIT FOR THE VIDEO TO COME OUT.
IT'S BEEN SO LONG SINCE WE WENT OUT. WHAT A BUMMER.
HEY, TAKE ME TO TOKYO DISNEYLAND...
I HEARD THE NIGHT PARADE IS REALLY PRETTY.
YEAH, IT IS.

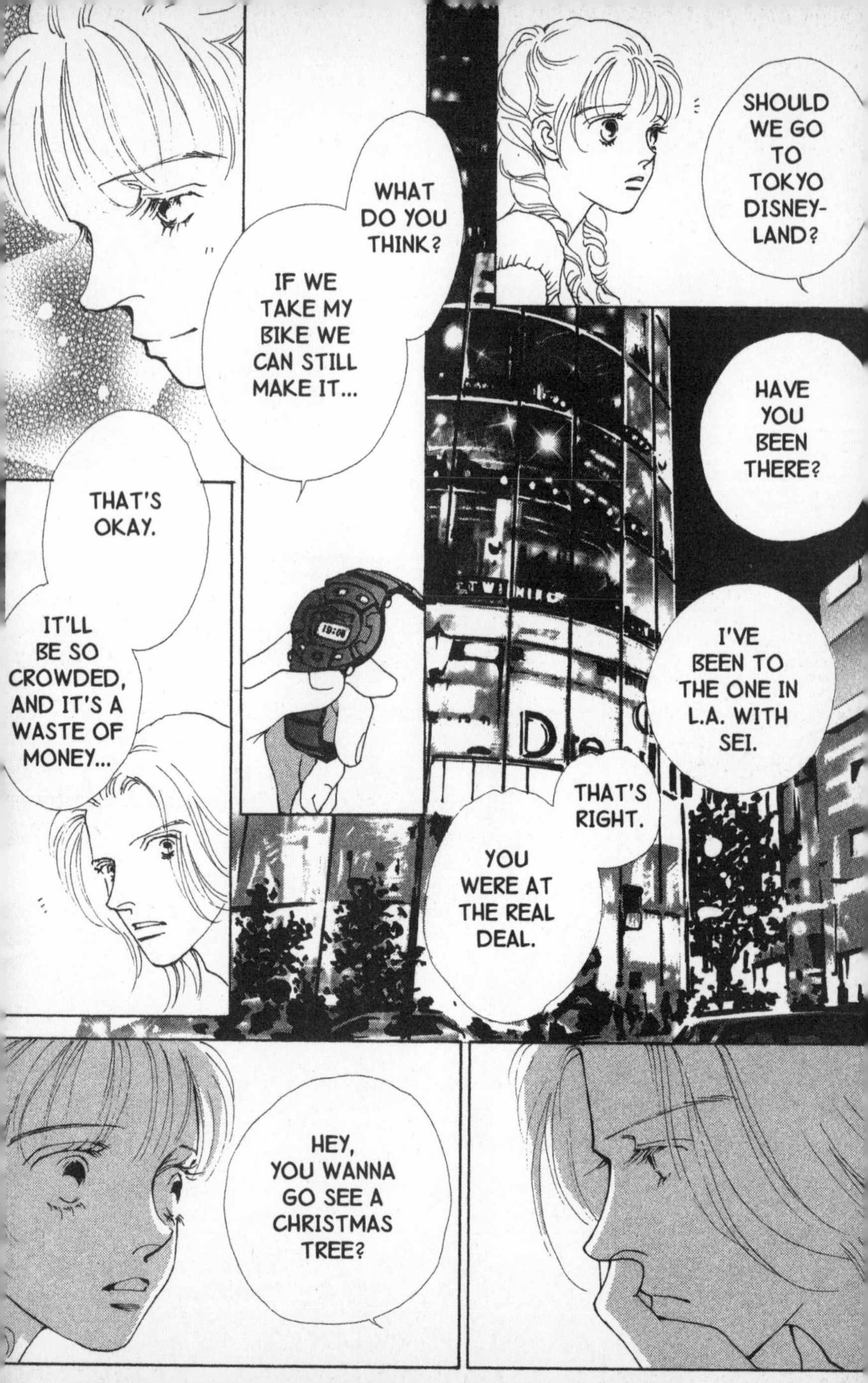

SHOULD WE GO TO TOKYO DISNEY-LAND?
WHAT DO YOU THINK?
IF WE TAKE MY BIKE WE CAN STILL MAKE IT...
THAT'S OKAY.
IT'LL BE SO CROWDED, AND IT'S A WASTE OF MONEY...
HAVE YOU BEEN THERE?
I'VE BEEN TO THE ONE IN L.A. WITH SEI.
THAT'S RIGHT.
YOU WERE AT THE REAL DEAL.
HEY, YOU WANNA GO SEE A CHRISTMAS TREE?

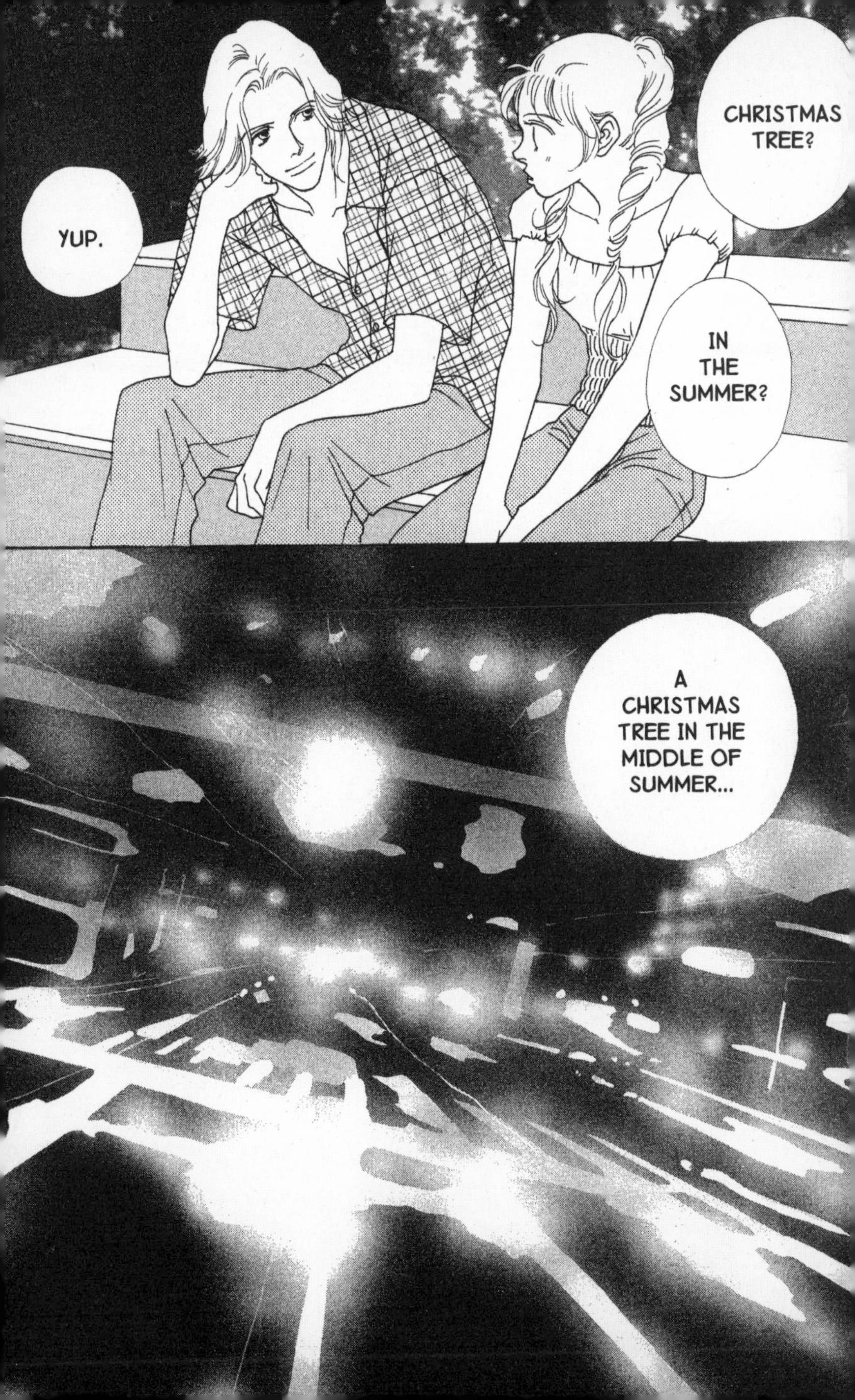
CHRISTMAS TREE?
IN THE SUMMER?
YUP.
A CHRISTMAS TREE IN THE MIDDLE OF SUMMER...

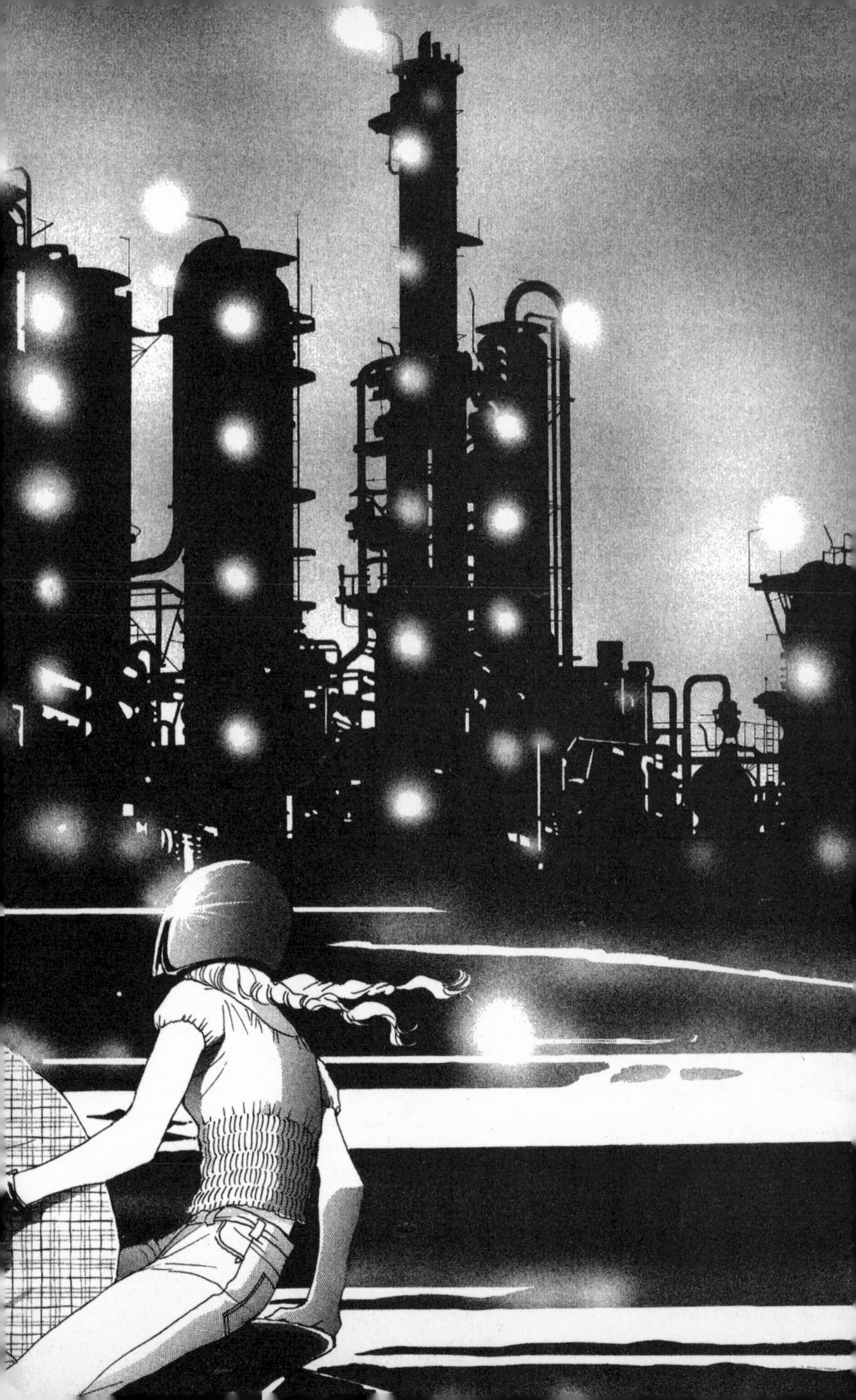

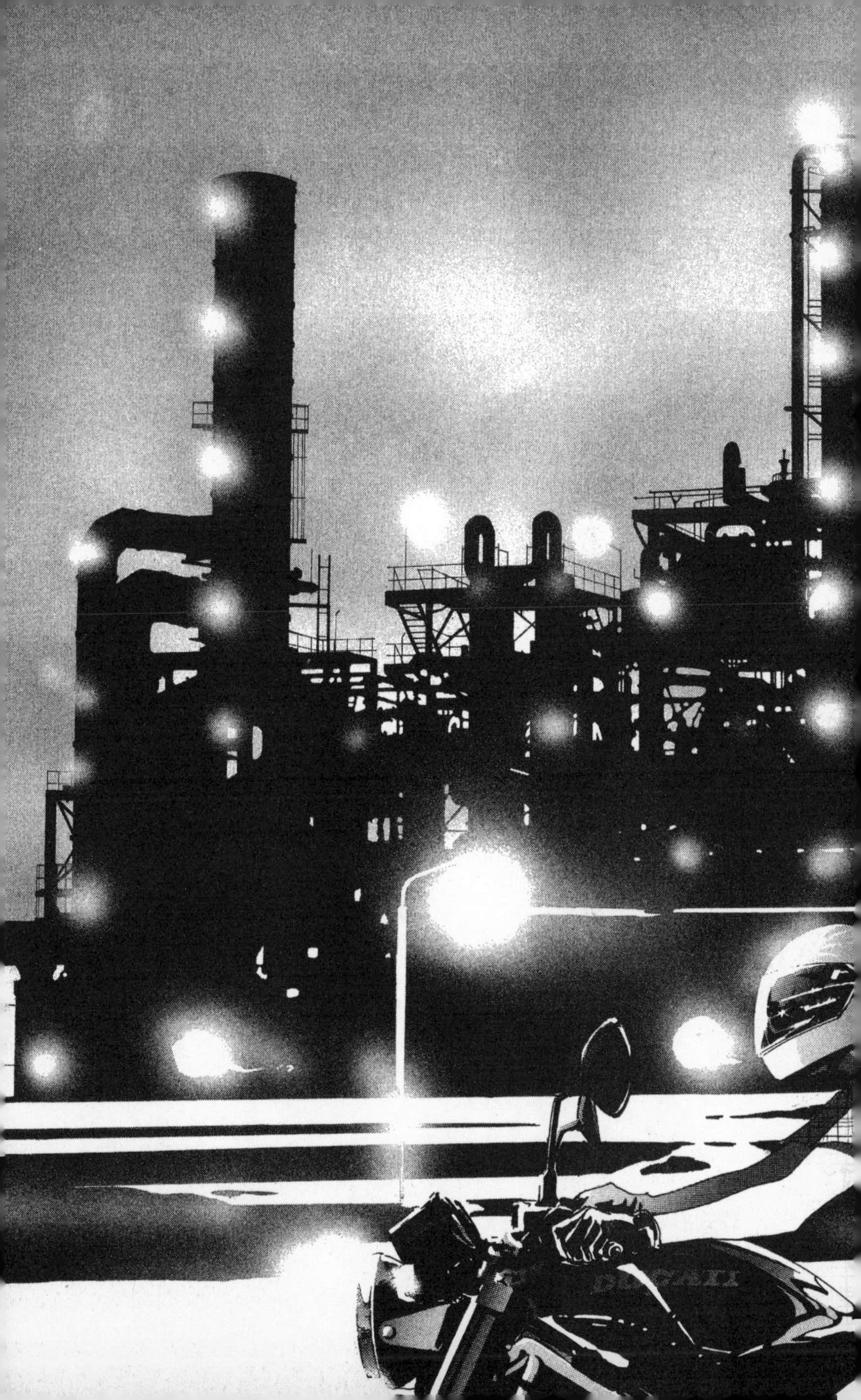

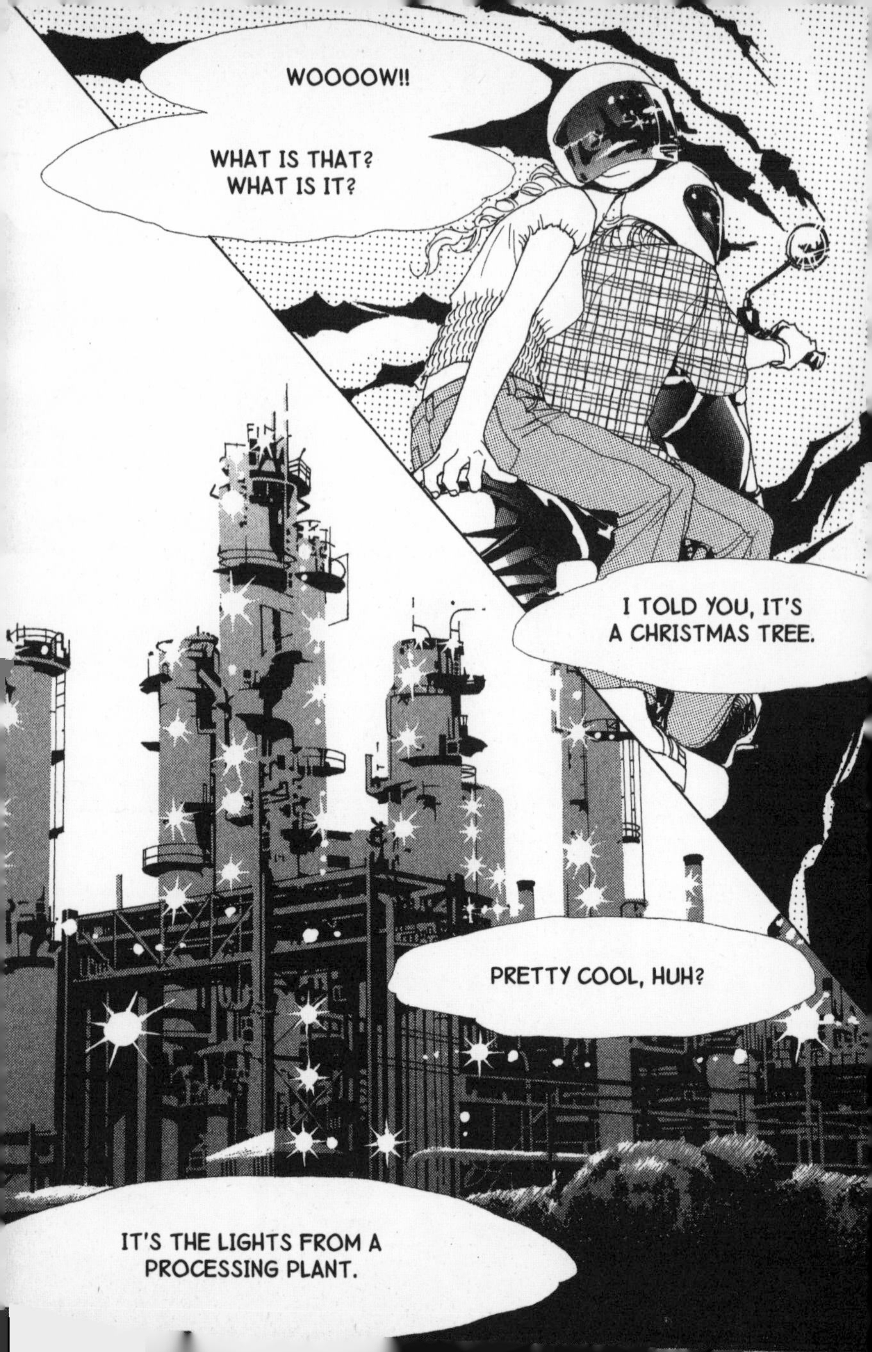
WOOOOW!!
WHAT IS THAT? WHAT IS IT?
I TOLD YOU, IT'S A CHRISTMAS TREE.
PRETTY COOL, HUH?
IT'S THE LIGHTS FROM A PROCESSING PLANT.

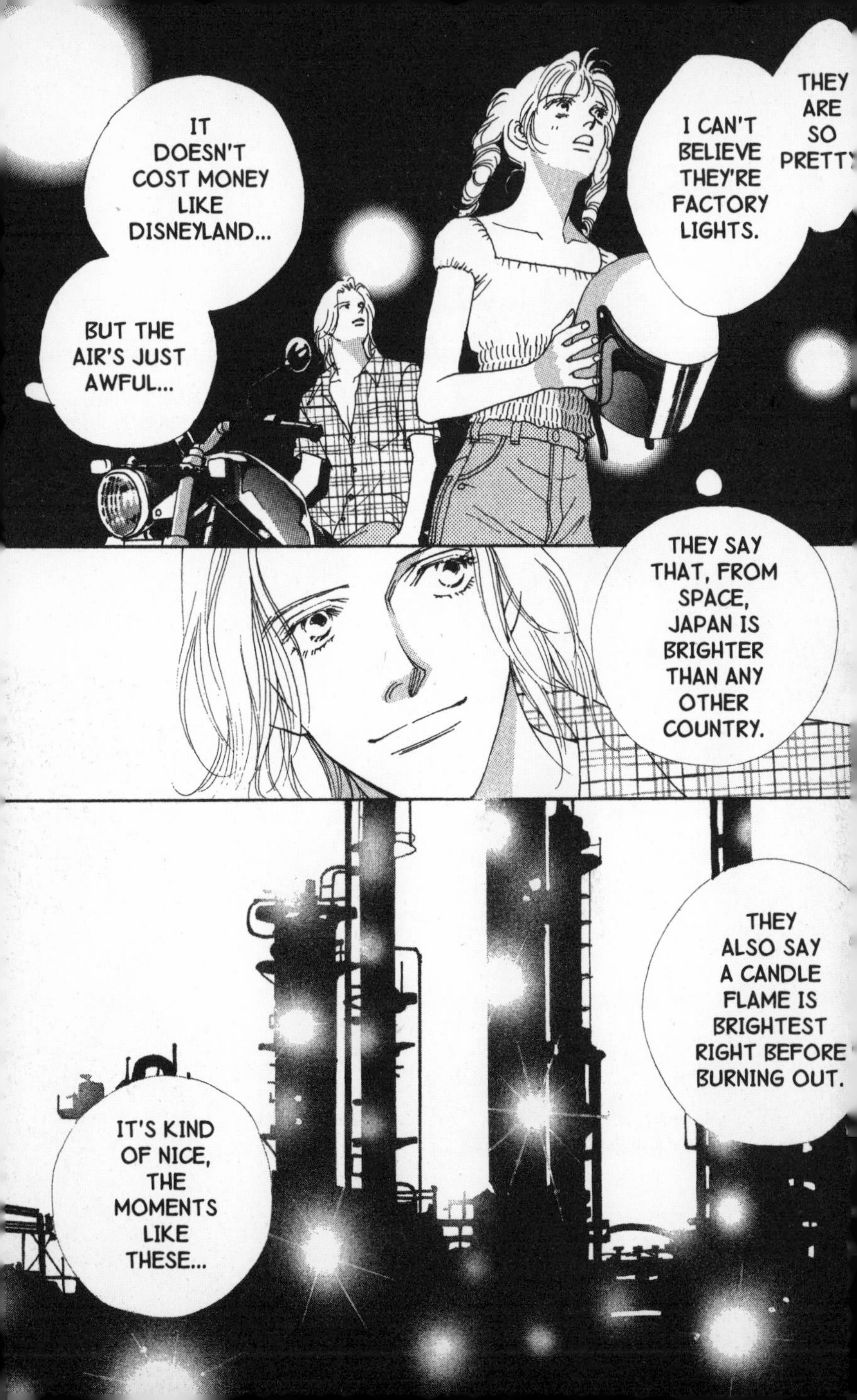
THEY ARE SO PRETT
I CAN'T BELIEVE THEY'RE FACTORY LIGHTS.
IT DOESN'T COST MONEY LIKE DISNEYLAND...
BUT THE AIR'S JUST AWFUL...
THEY SAY THAT, FROM SPACE, JAPAN IS BRIGHTER THAN ANY OTHER COUNTRY.
THEY ALSO SAY A CANDLE FLAME IS BRIGHTEST RIGHT BEFORE BURNING OUT.
IT'S KIND OF NICE, THE MOMENTS LIKE THESE...

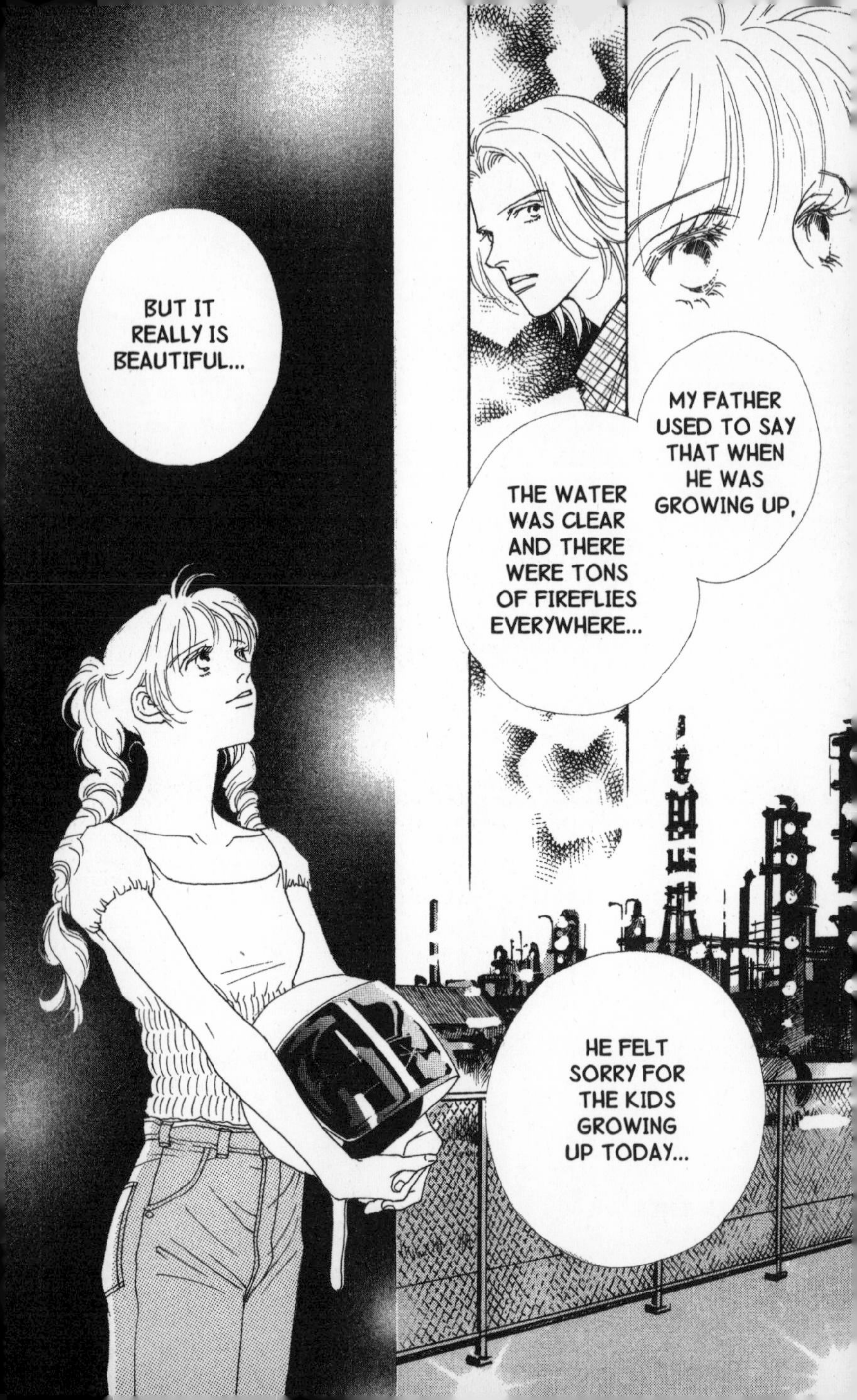
MY FATHER USED TO SAY THAT WHEN HE WAS GROWING UP,
THE WATER WAS CLEAR AND THERE WERE TONS OF FIREFLIES EVERYWHERE...
HE FELT SORRY FOR THE KIDS GROWING UP TODAY...
BUT IT REALLY IS BEAUTIFUL...

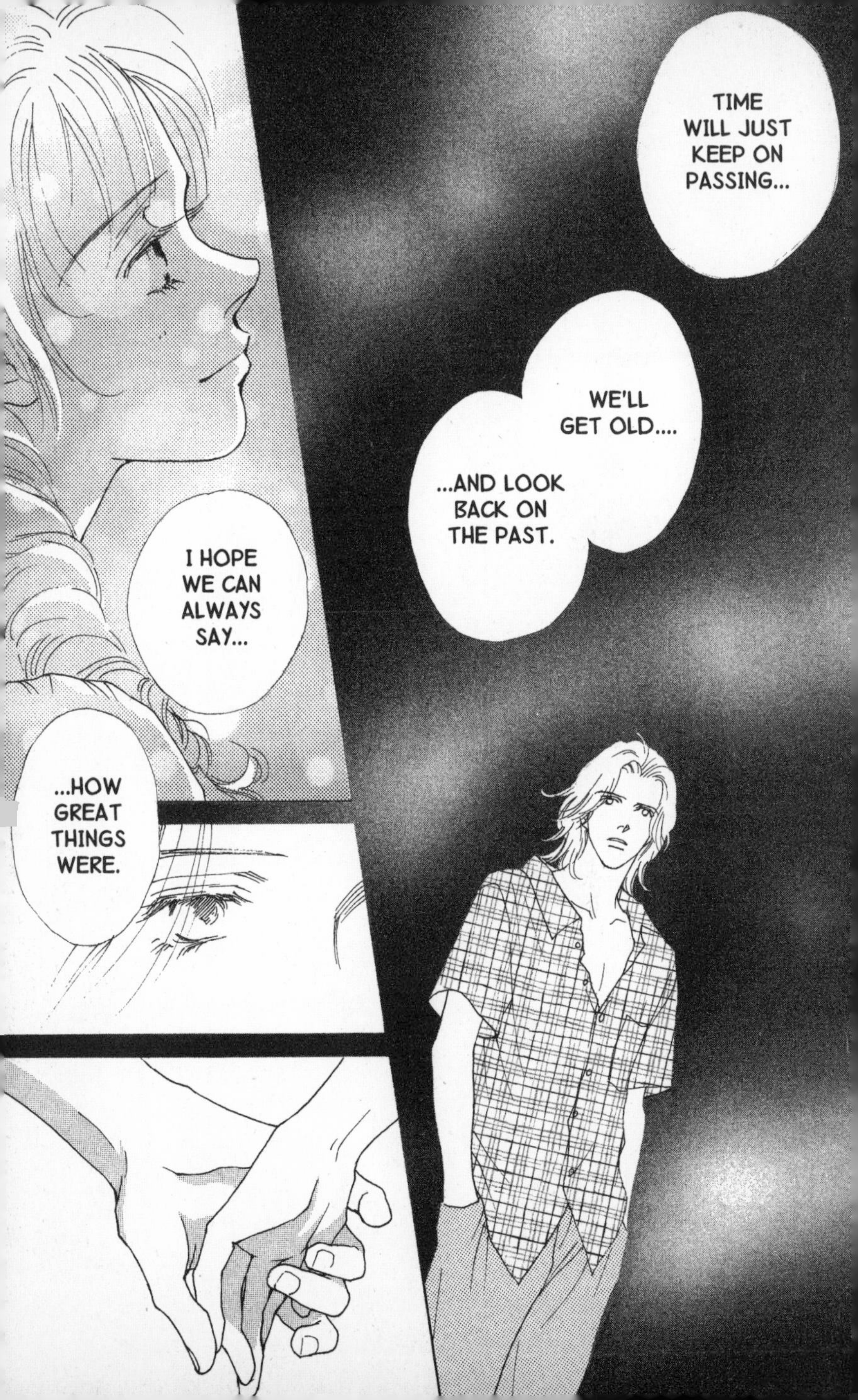
TIME WILL JUST KEEP ON PASSING...
WE'LL GET OLD....
...AND LOOK BACK ON THE PAST.
I HOPE WE CAN ALWAYS SAY...
...HOW GREAT THINGS WERE.

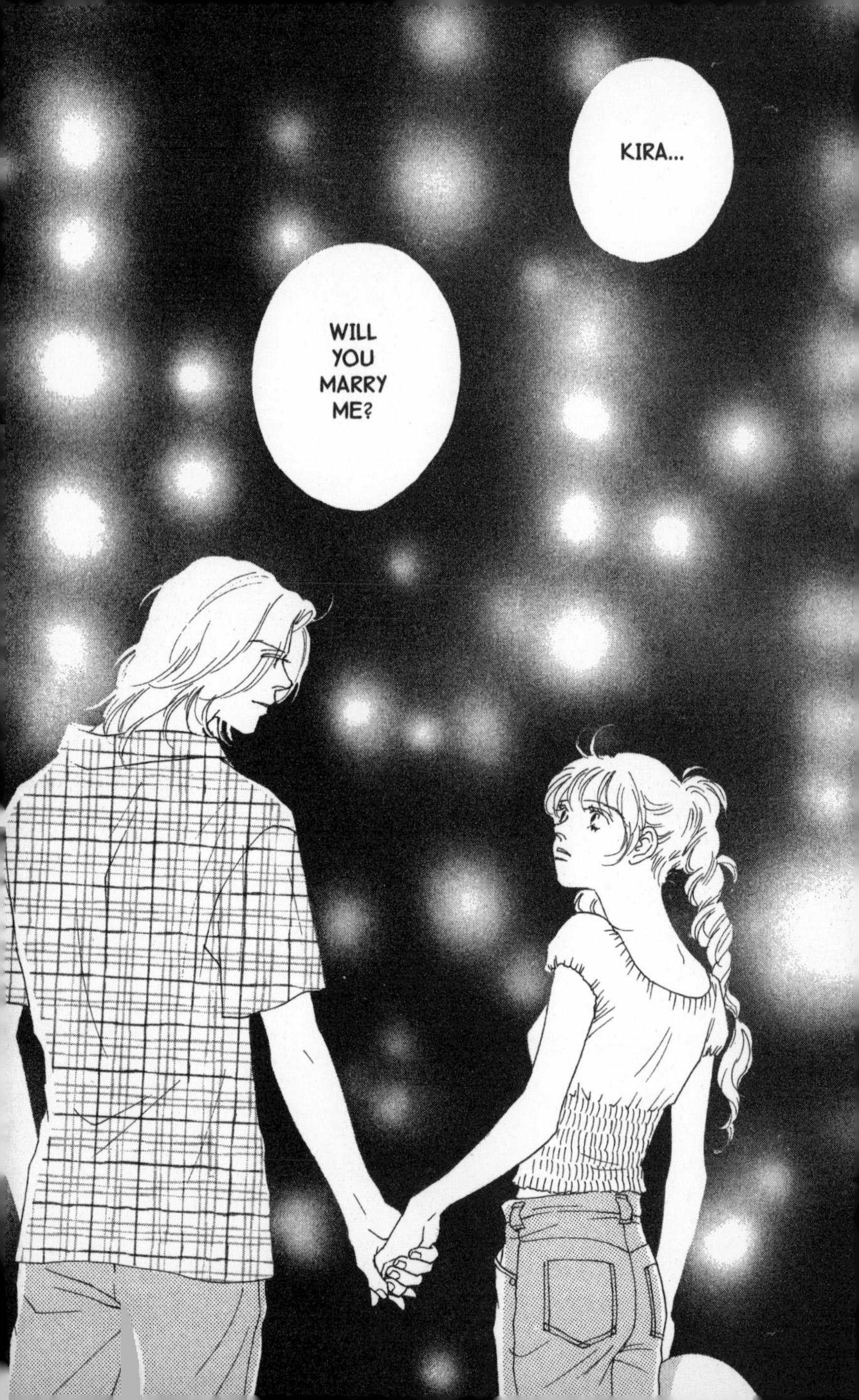
KIRA...
WILL YOU MARRY ME?

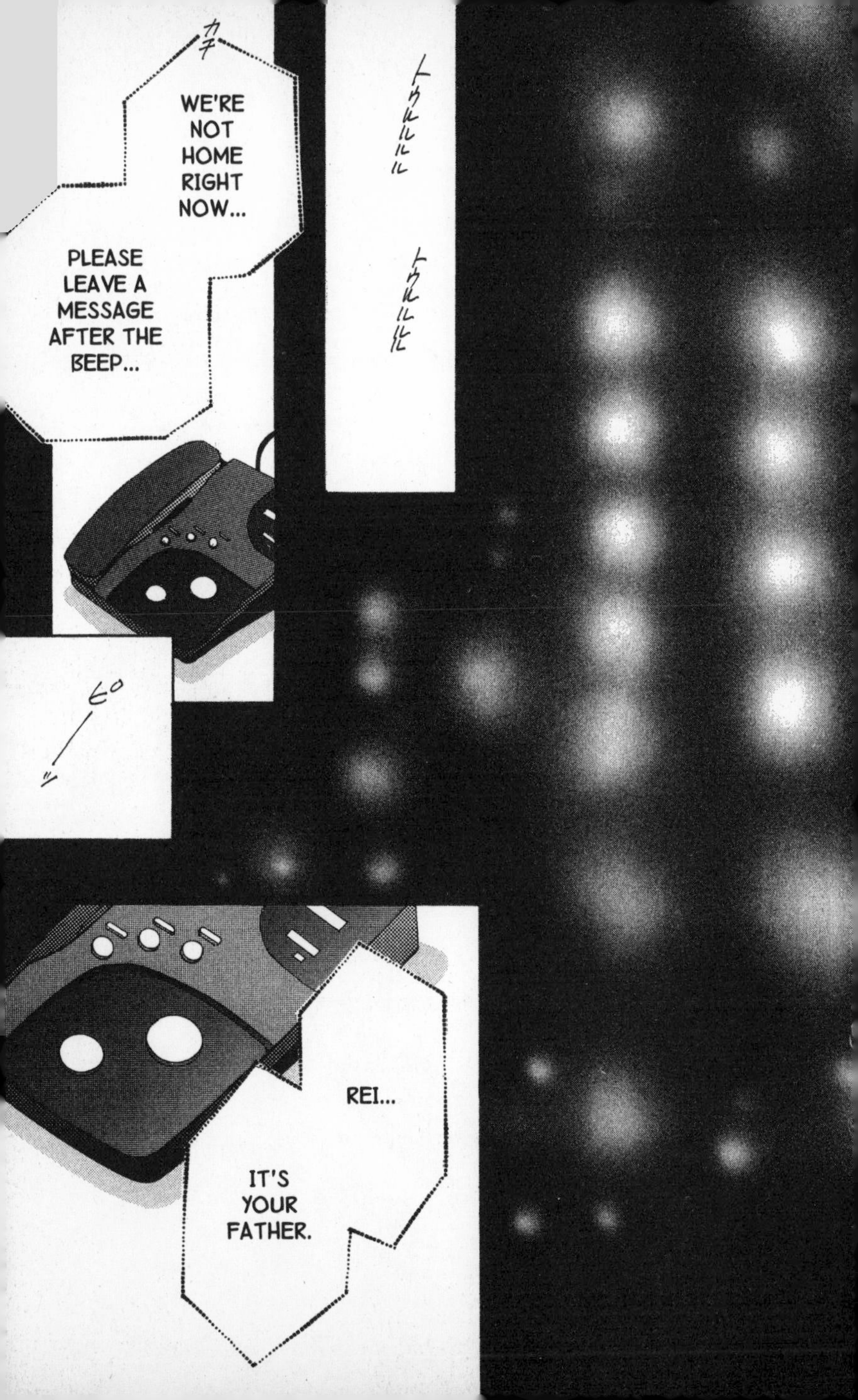
トゥルルル
トゥルルル
カチ
WE'RE NOT HOME RIGHT NOW...
PLEASE LEAVE A MESSAGE AFTER THE BEEP...
ピーッ
REI...
IT'S YOUR FATHER.

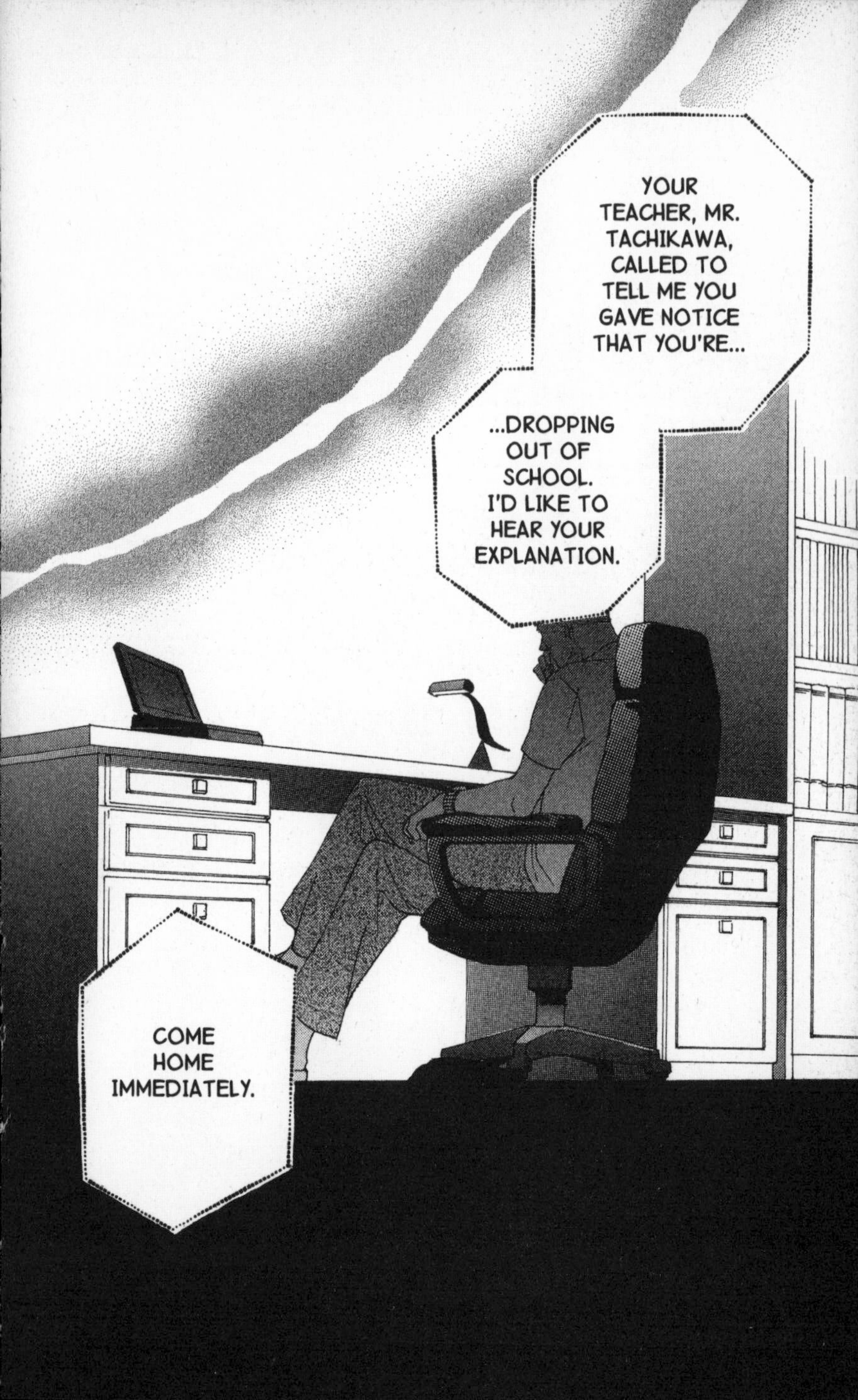
YOUR TEACHER, MR. TACHIKAWA, CALLED TO TELL ME YOU GAVE NOTICE THAT YOU'RE...
...DROPPING OUT OF SCHOOL. I'D LIKE TO HEAR YOUR EXPLANATION.
COME HOME IMMEDIATELY.

MARS

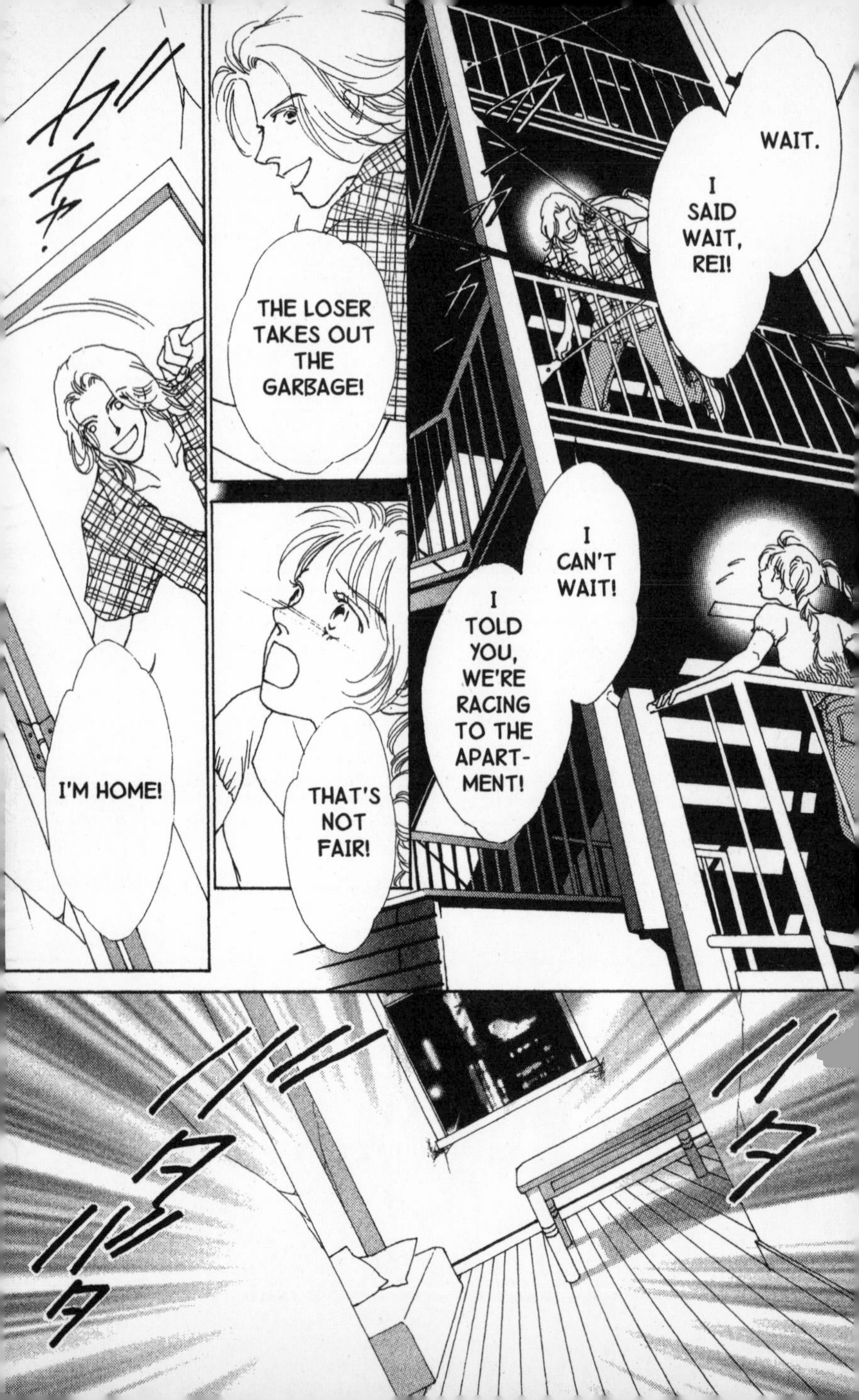
WAIT.
I SAID WAIT, REI!
I CAN'T WAIT!
I TOLD YOU, WE'RE RACING TO THE APART-MENT!
THE LOSER TAKES OUT THE GARBAGE!
THAT'S NOT FAIR!
I'M HOME!

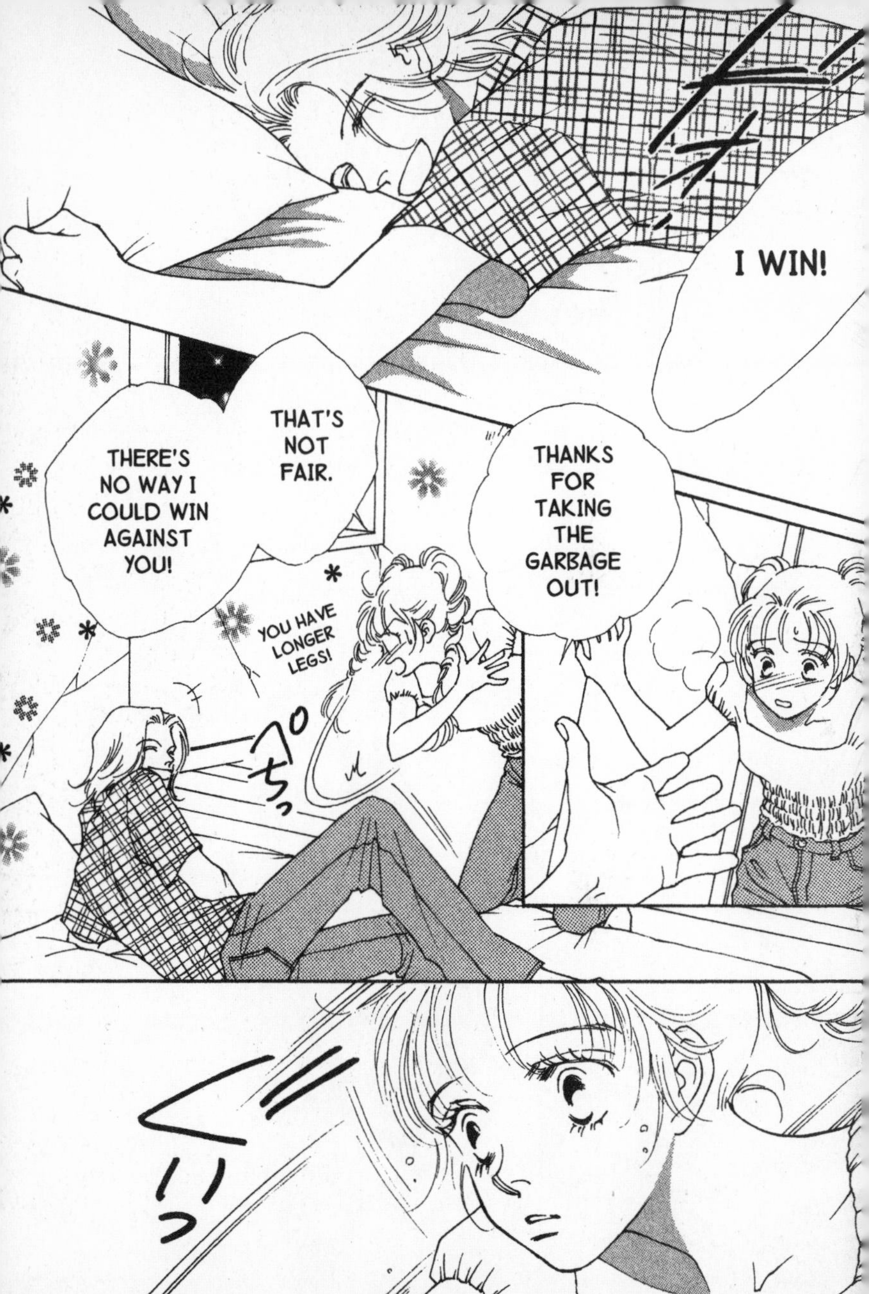
I WIN!
THANKS FOR TAKING THE GARBAGE OUT!
THAT'S NOT FAIR.
THERE'S NO WAY I COULD WIN AGAINST YOU!
YOU HAVE LONGER LEGS!

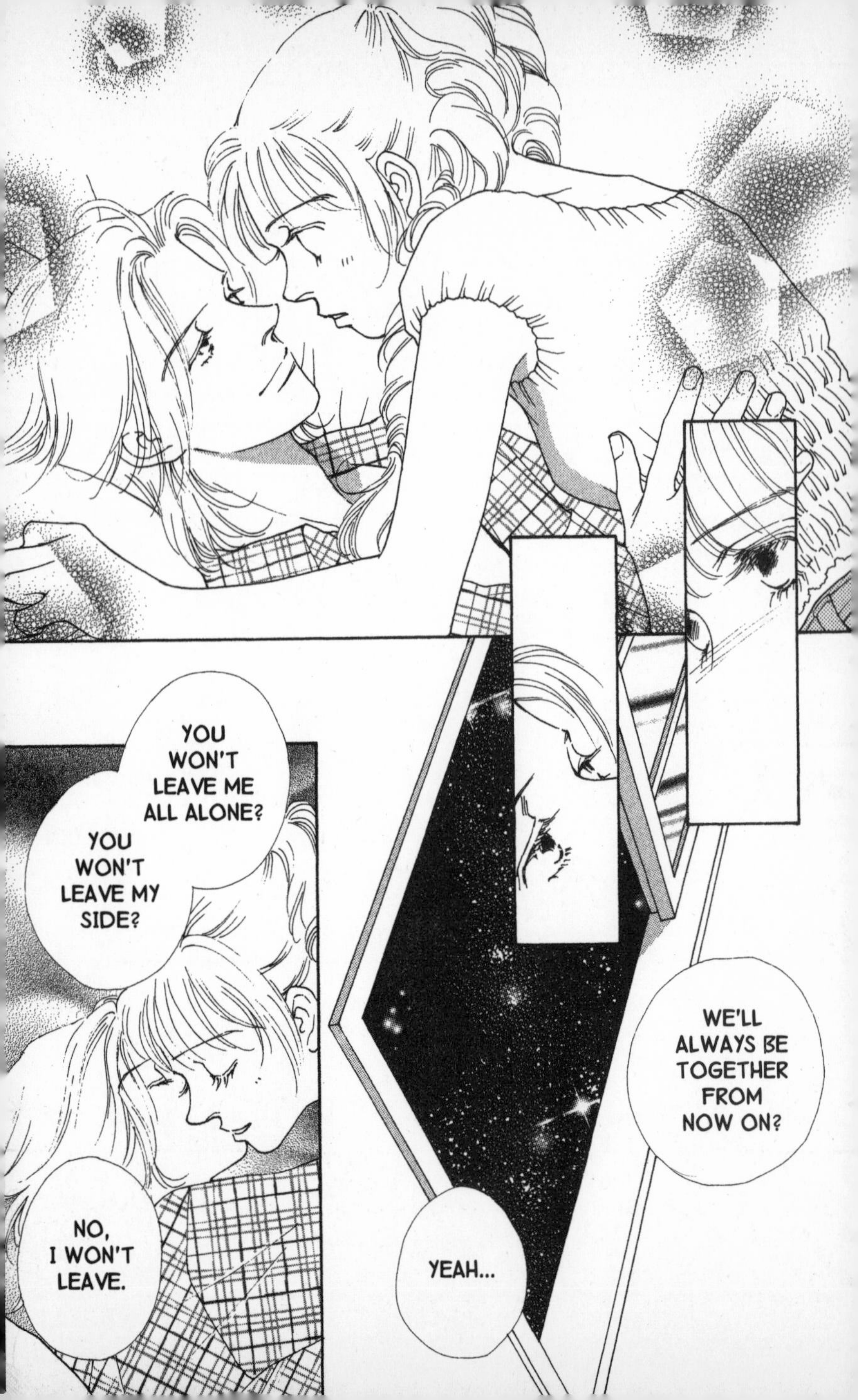
WE'LL ALWAYS BE TOGETHER FROM NOW ON?
YEAH...
YOU WON'T LEAVE ME ALL ALONE?
YOU WON'T LEAVE MY SIDE?
NO, I WON'T LEAVE.

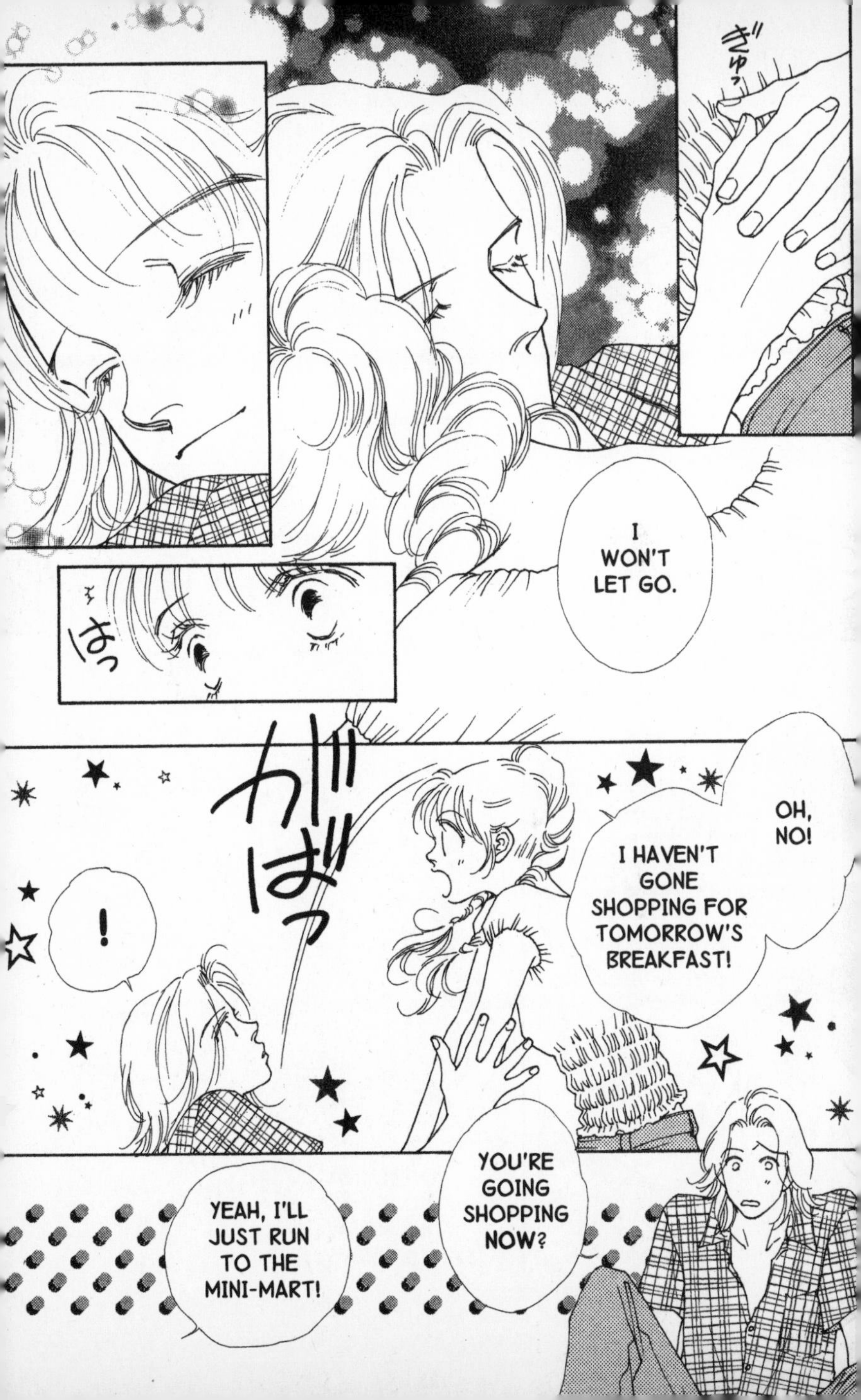
ぎゅっ
I WON'T LET GO.
はっ
OH, NO!
I HAVEN'T GONE SHOPPING FOR TOMORROW'S BREAKFAST!
がばっ
!
YOU'RE GOING SHOPPING NOW?
YEAH, I'LL JUST RUN TO THE MINI-MART!

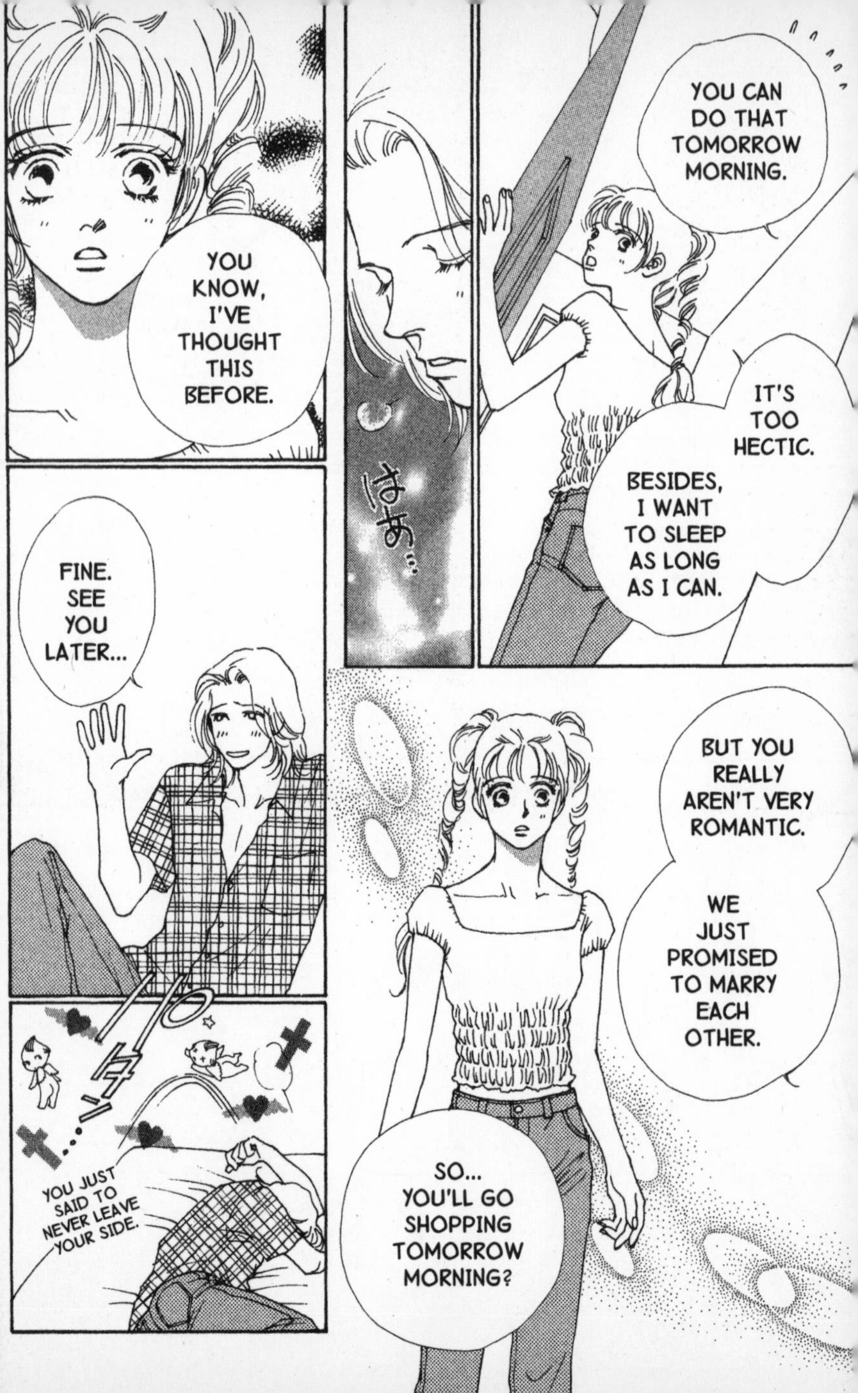
YOU CAN DO THAT TOMORROW MORNING.
IT'S TOO HECTIC.
BESIDES, I WANT TO SLEEP AS LONG AS I CAN.
はあ…
BUT YOU REALLY AREN'T VERY ROMANTIC.
WE JUST PROMISED TO MARRY EACH OTHER.
SO... YOU'LL GO SHOPPING TOMORROW MORNING?
YOU KNOW, I'VE THOUGHT THIS BEFORE.
FINE. SEE YOU LATER...
YOU JUST SAID TO NEVER LEAVE YOUR SIDE.

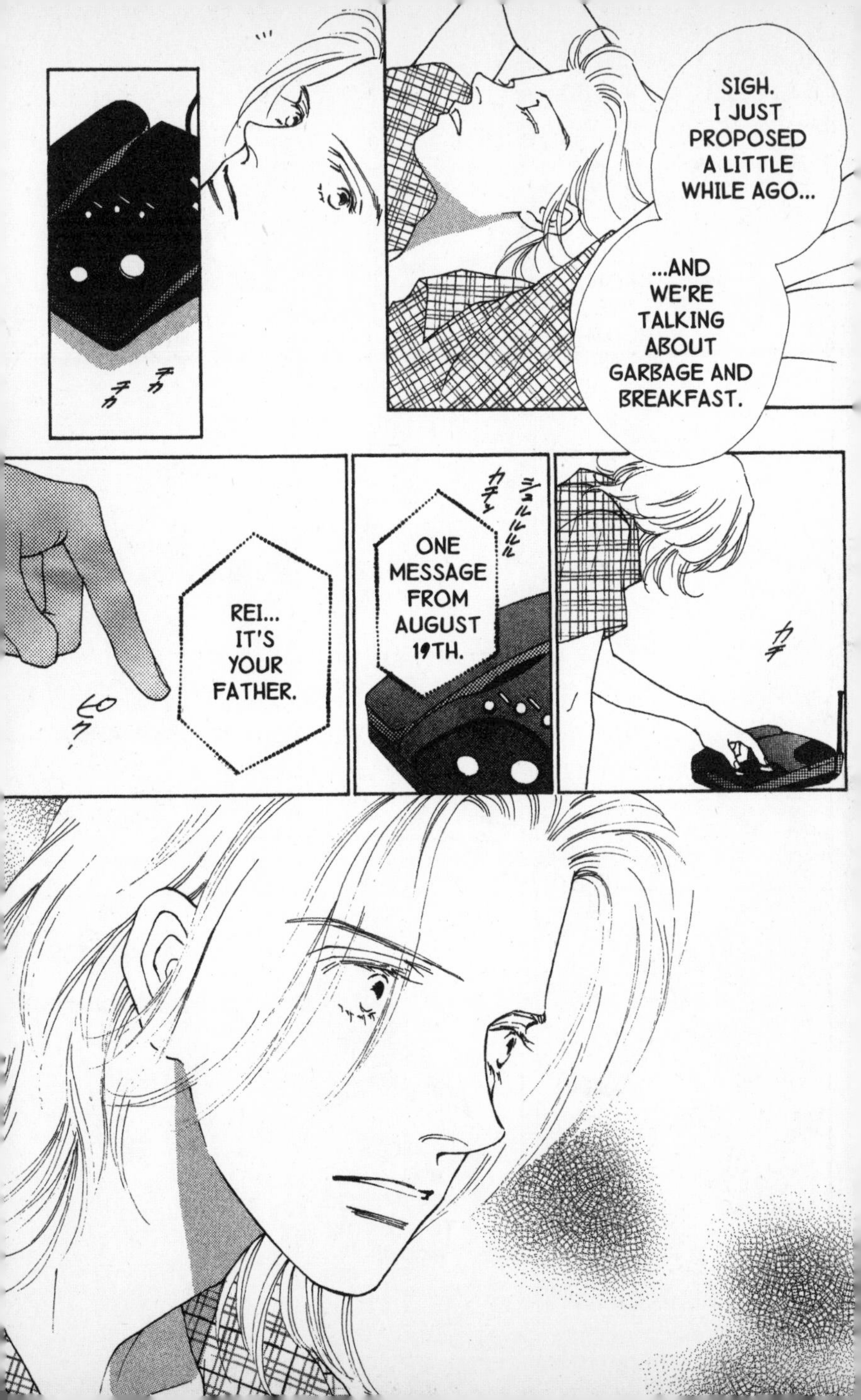
SIGH. I JUST PROPOSED A LITTLE WHILE AGO...
...AND WE'RE TALKING ABOUT GARBAGE AND BREAKFAST.
ONE MESSAGE FROM AUGUST 19TH.
REI... IT'S YOUR FATHER.

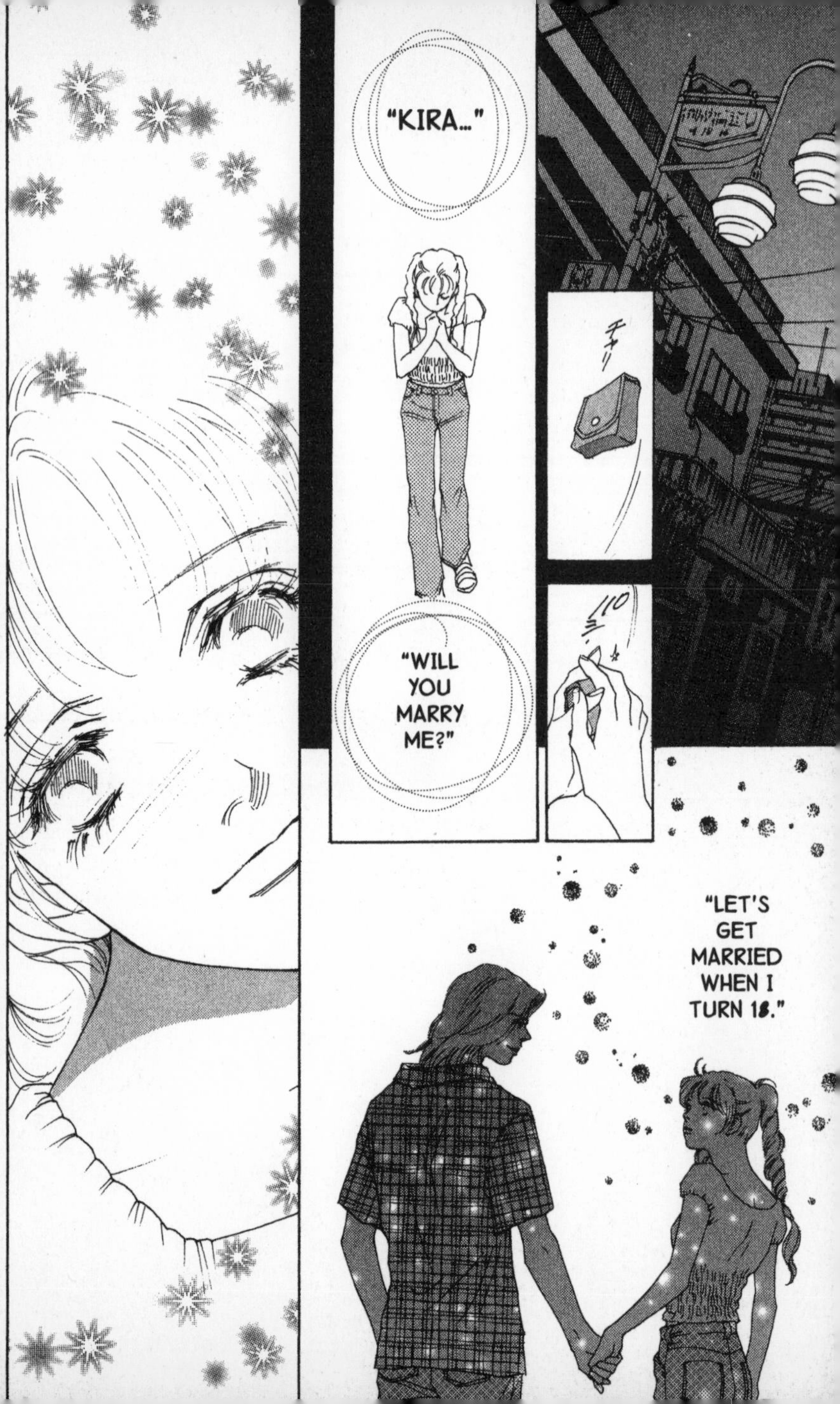
"KIRA..."
"WILL YOU MARRY ME?"
"LET'S GET MARRIED WHEN I TURN 18."

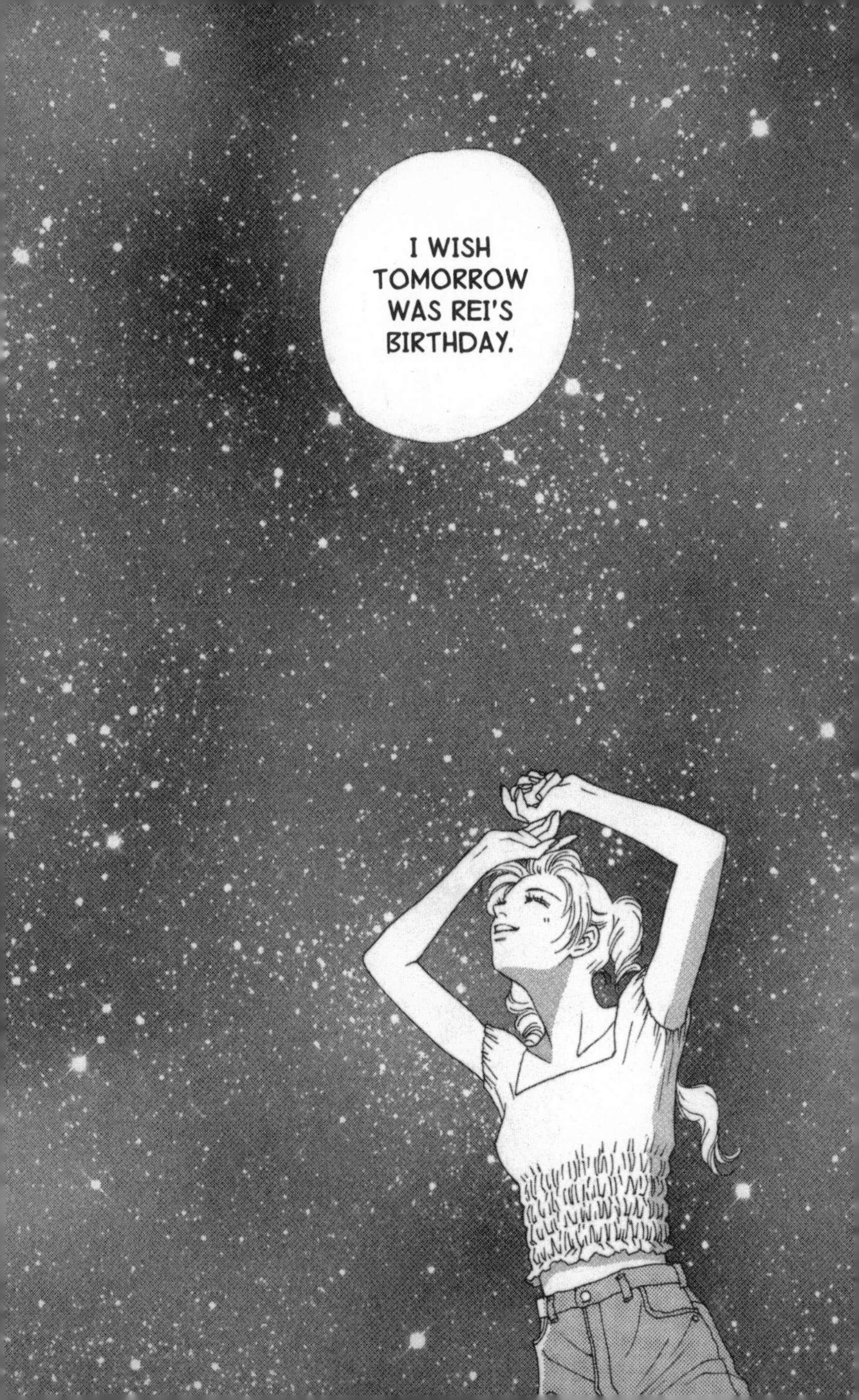
I WISH TOMORROW WAS REI'S BIRTHDAY.

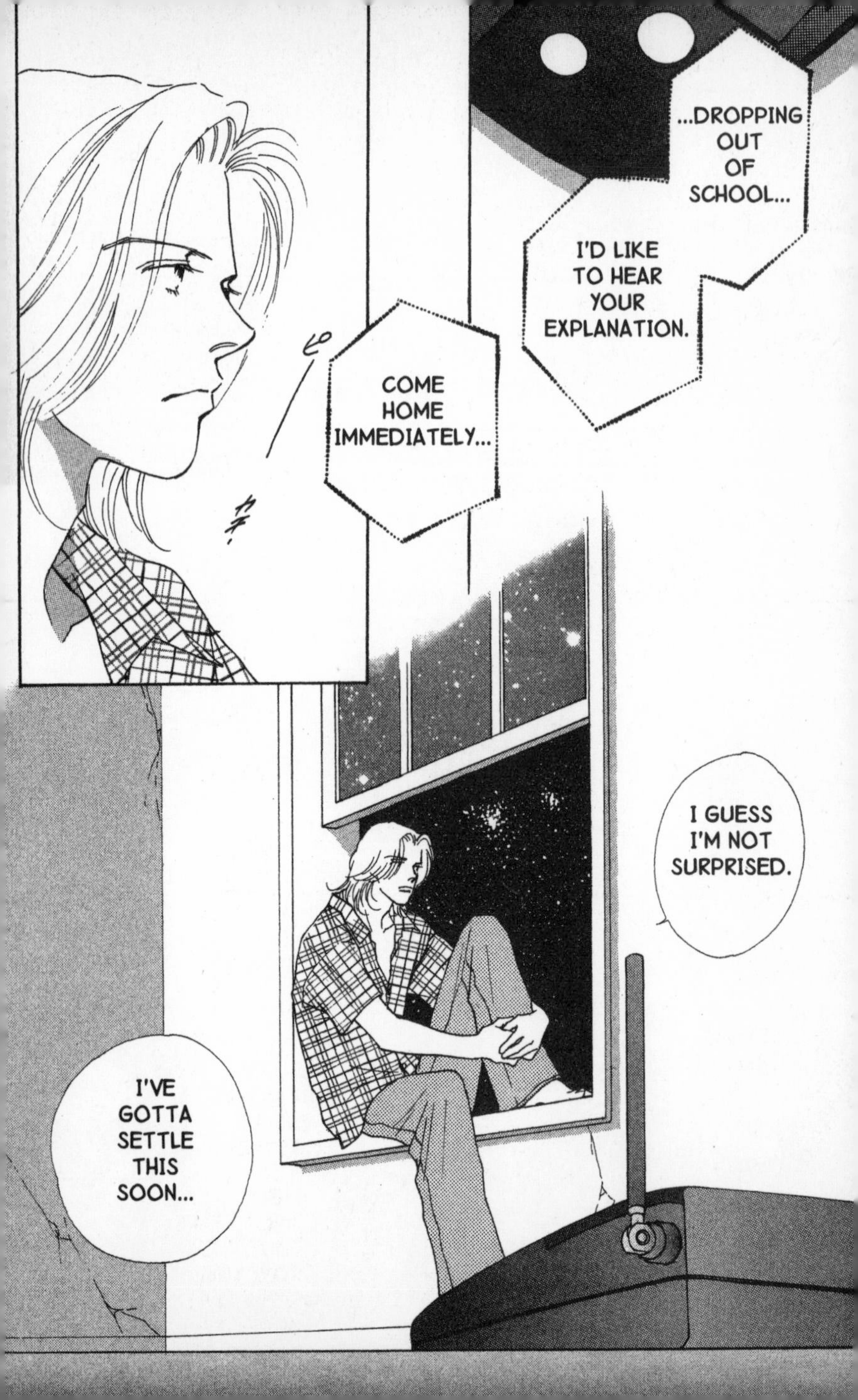
...DROPPING OUT OF SCHOOL...
I'D LIKE TO HEAR YOUR EXPLANATION.
COME HOME IMMEDIATELY...
I GUESS I'M NOT SURPRISED.
I'VE GOTTA SETTLE THIS SOON...

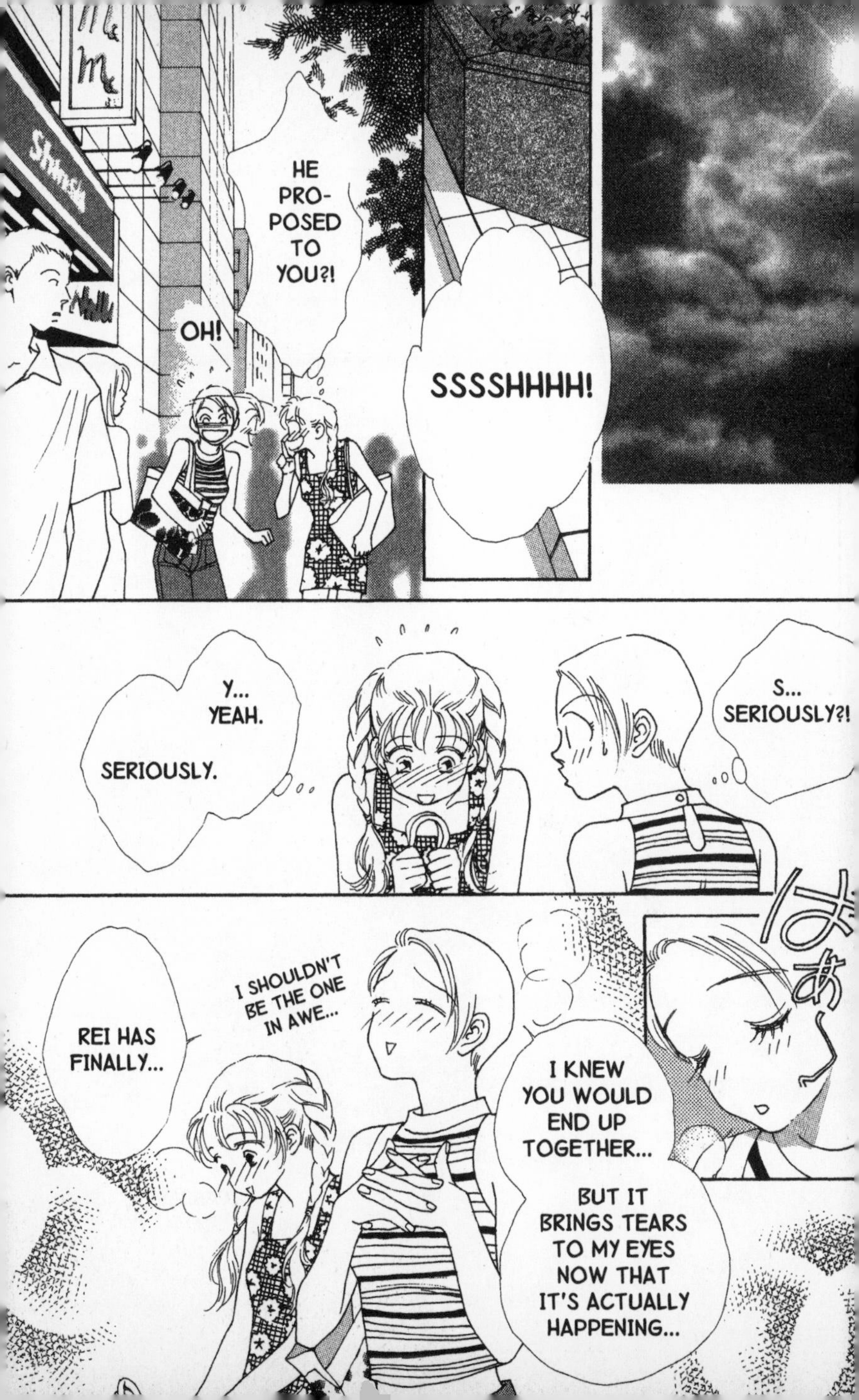
HE PRO-POSED TO YOU?!
SSSSHHHH!
OH!
S... SERIOUSLY?!
Y... YEAH.
SERIOUSLY.
はぁ
I KNEW YOU WOULD END UP TOGETHER...
BUT IT BRINGS TEARS TO MY EYES NOW THAT IT'S ACTUALLY HAPPENING...
I SHOULDN'T BE THE ONE IN AWE...
REI HAS FINALLY...

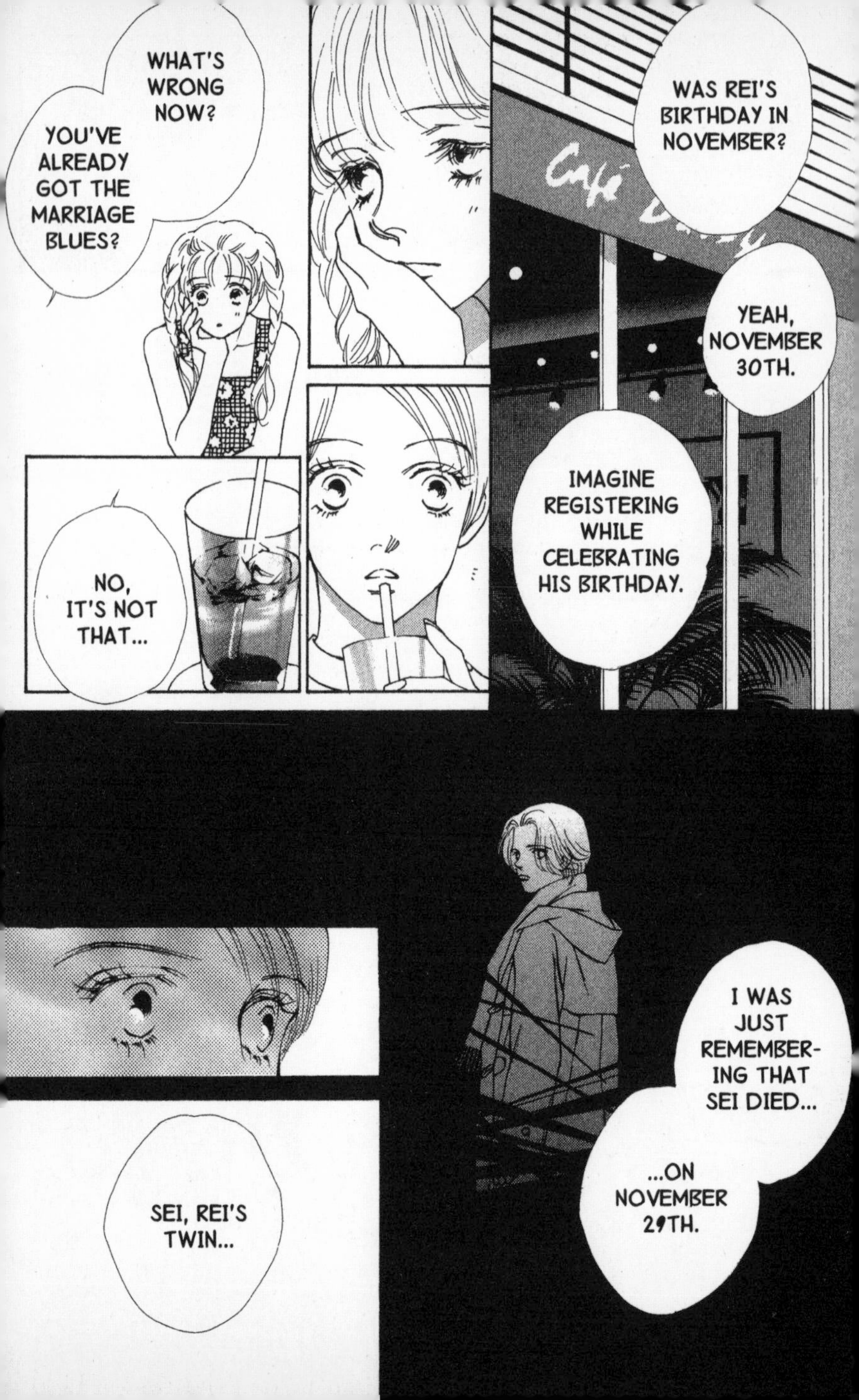
WAS REI'S BIRTHDAY IN NOVEMBER?
YEAH, NOVEMBER 30TH.
IMAGINE REGISTERING WHILE CELEBRATING HIS BIRTHDAY.
WHAT'S WRONG NOW?
YOU'VE ALREADY GOT THE MARRIAGE BLUES?
NO, IT'S NOT THAT...
I WAS JUST REMEMBER-ING THAT SEI DIED...
...ON NOVEMBER 29TH.
SEI, REI'S TWIN...

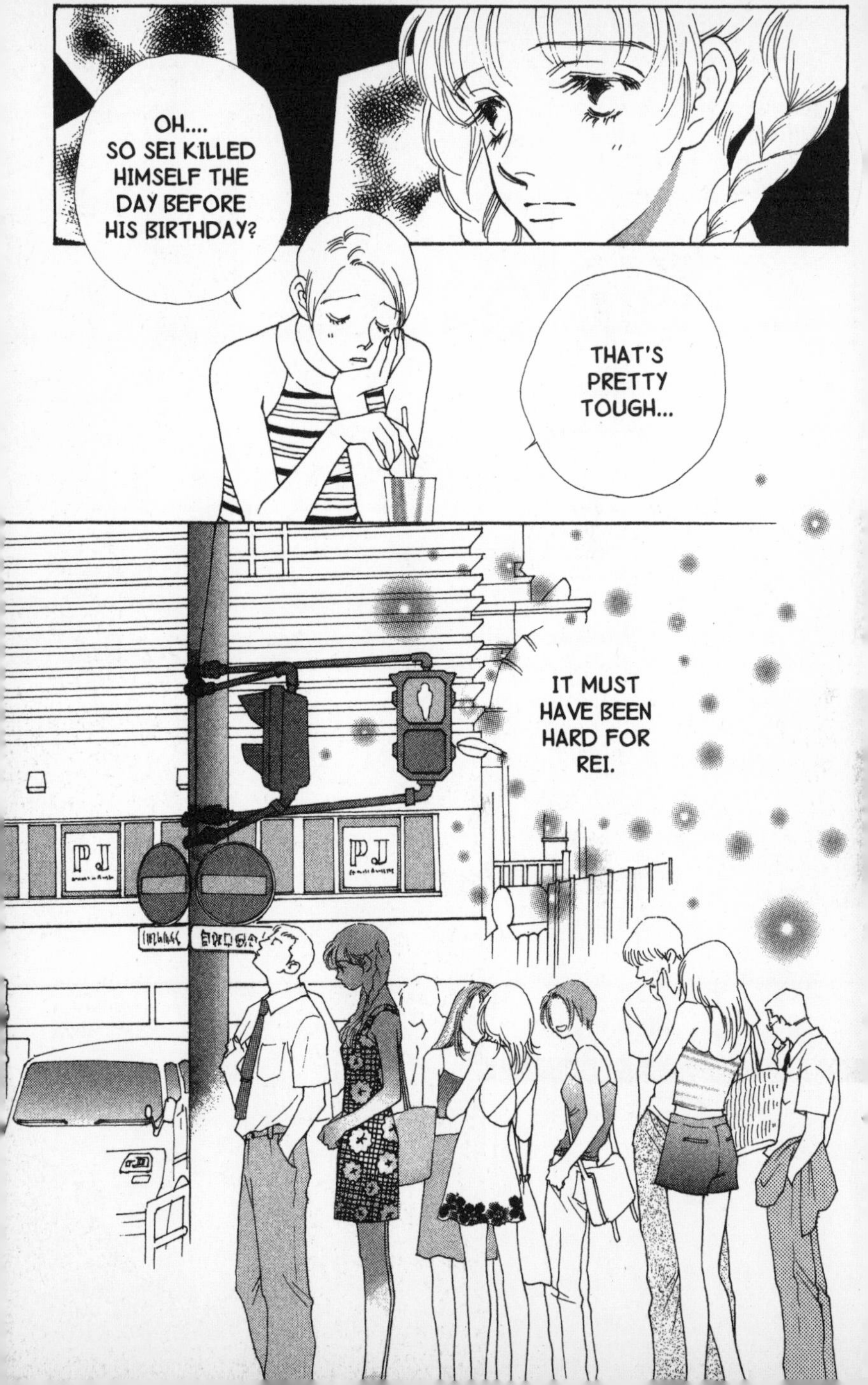
OH.... SO SEI KILLED HIMSELF THE DAY BEFORE HIS BIRTHDAY?
THAT'S PRETTY TOUGH...
IT MUST HAVE BEEN HARD FOR REI.

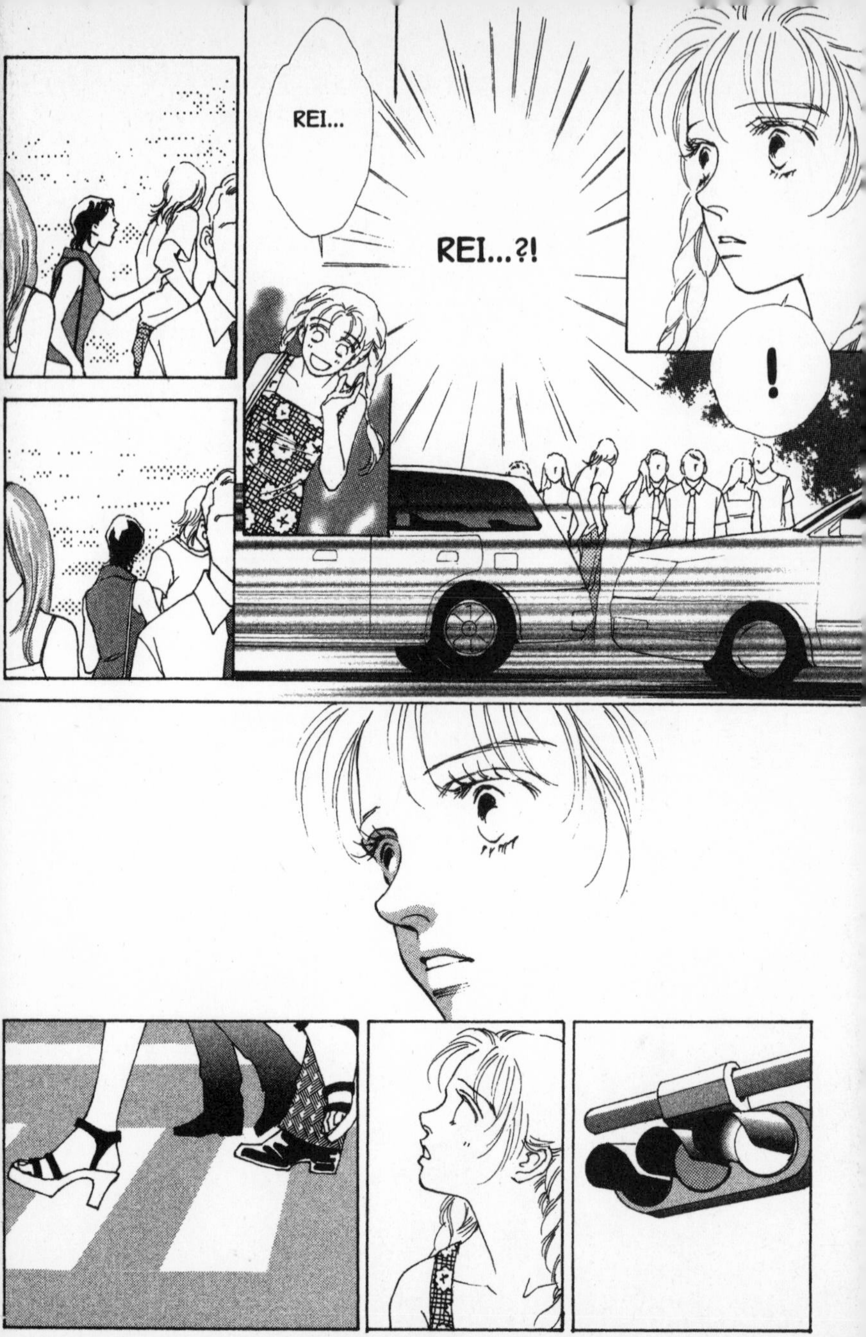
!
REI...?!
REI...

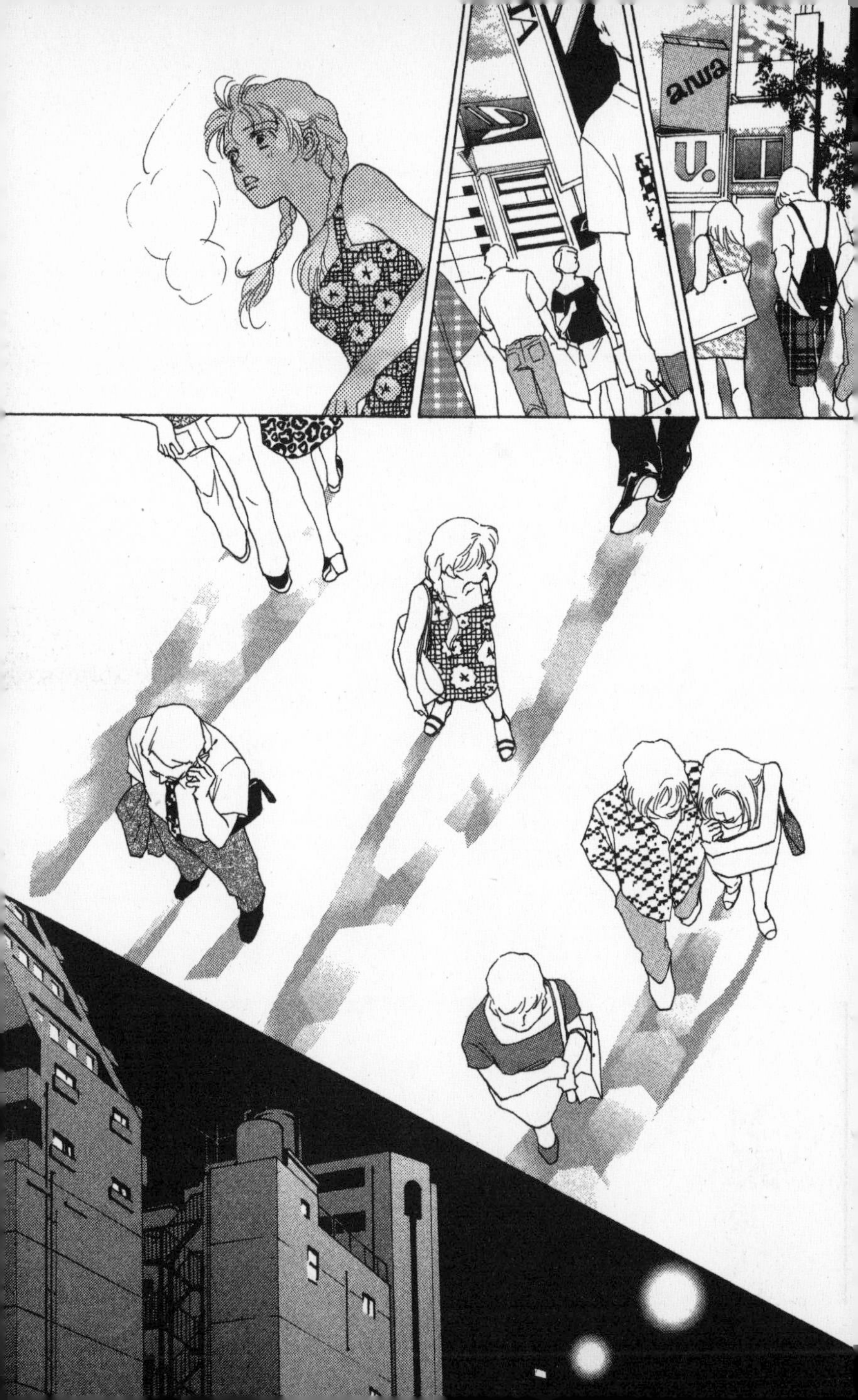

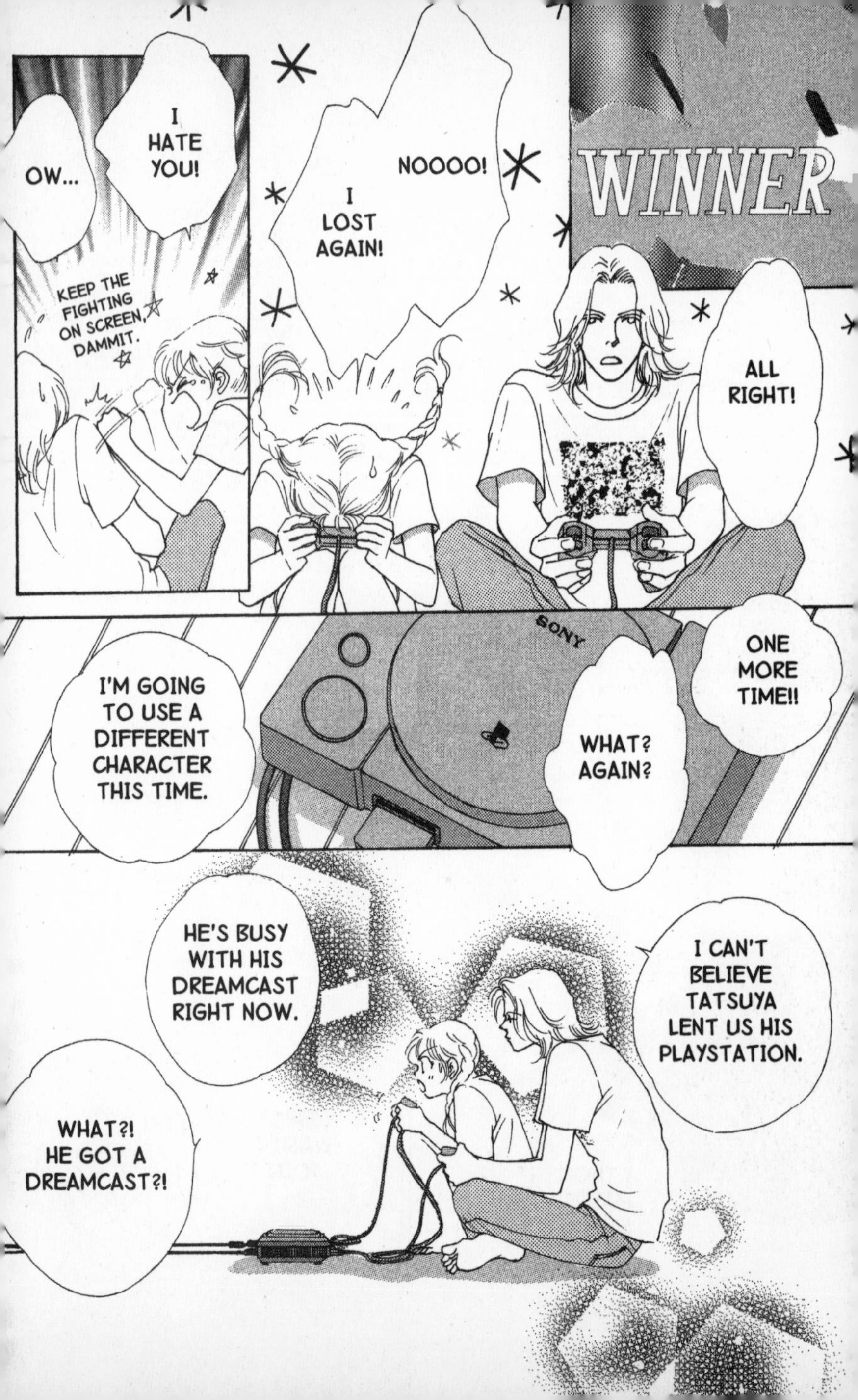
WINNER
ALL RIGHT!
NOOOO!
I LOST AGAIN!
I HATE YOU!
OW...
KEEP THE FIGHTING ON SCREEN, DAMMIT.
ONE MORE TIME!!
WHAT? AGAIN?
SONY
I'M GOING TO USE A DIFFERENT CHARACTER THIS TIME.
I CAN'T BELIEVE TATSUYA LENT US HIS PLAYSTATION.
HE'S BUSY WITH HIS DREAMCAST RIGHT NOW.
WHAT?! HE GOT A DREAMCAST?!

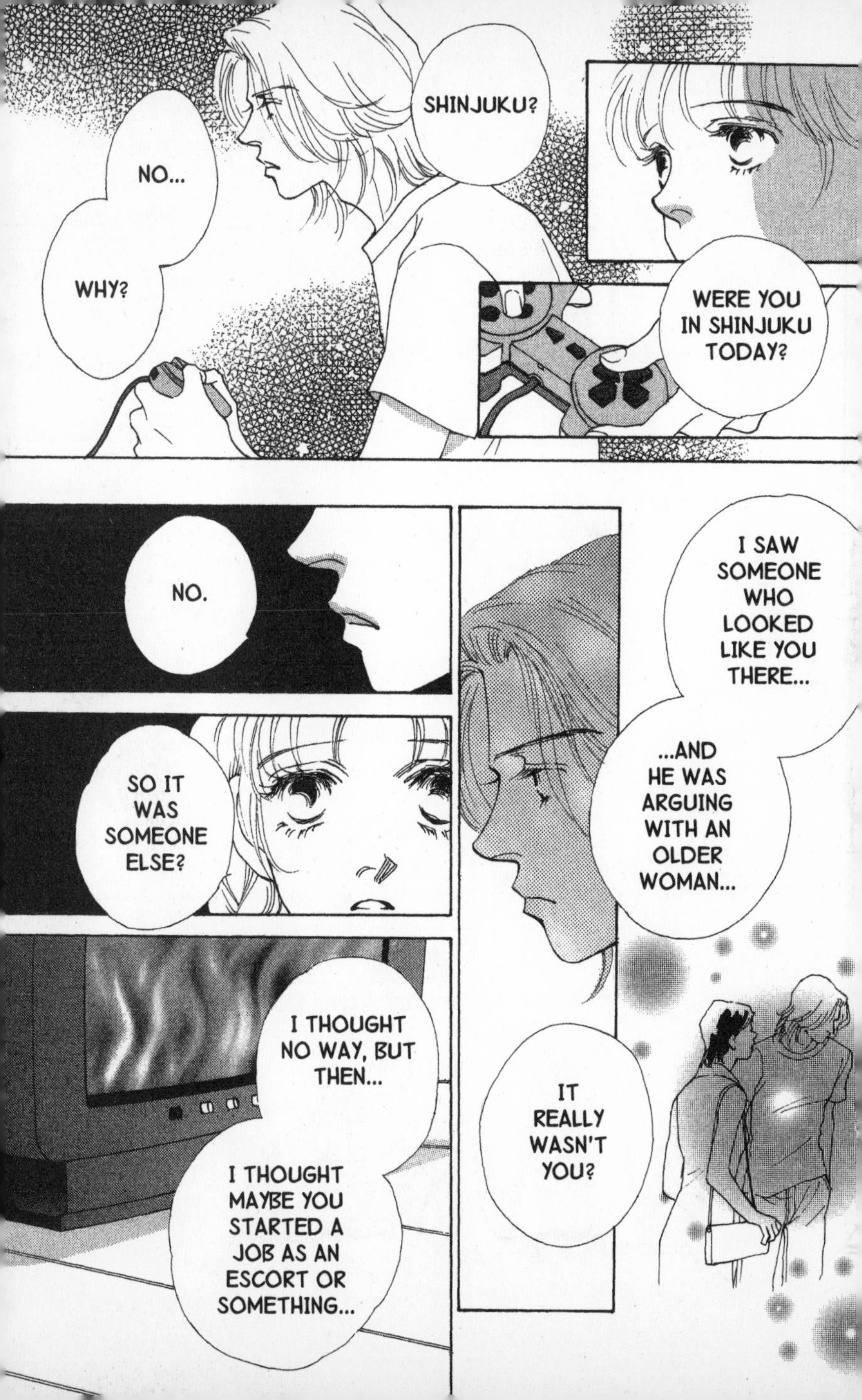
WERE YOU IN SHINJUKU TODAY?
SHINJUKU?
NO...
WHY?
I SAW SOMEONE WHO LOOKED LIKE YOU THERE...
...AND HE WAS ARGUING WITH AN OLDER WOMAN...
IT REALLY WASN'T YOU?
NO.
SO IT WAS SOMEONE ELSE?
I THOUGHT NO WAY, BUT THEN...
I THOUGHT MAYBE YOU STARTED A JOB AS AN ESCORT OR SOMETHING...

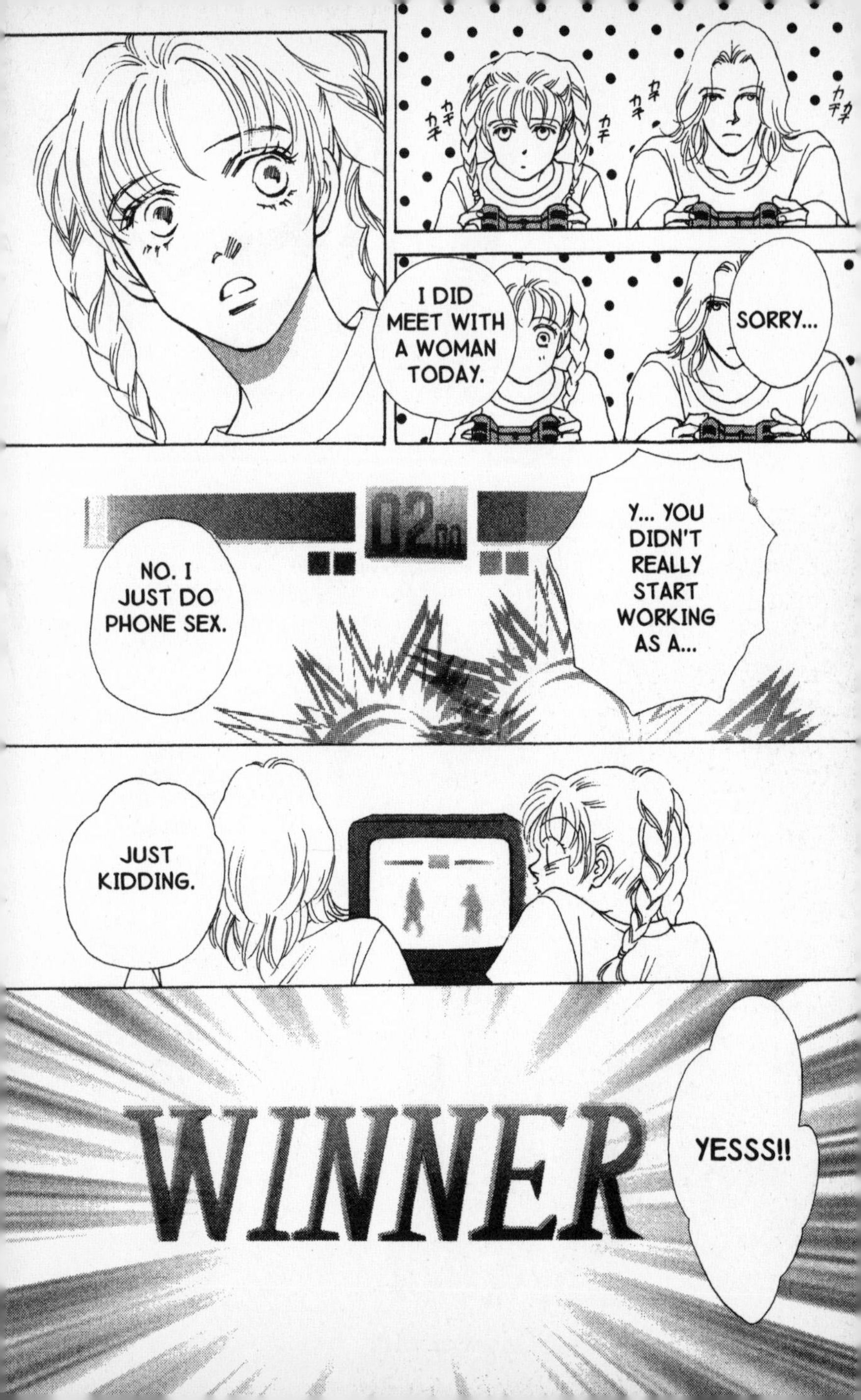
SORRY...
I DID MEET WITH A WOMAN TODAY.
Y... YOU DIDN'T REALLY START WORKING AS A...
NO. I JUST DO PHONE SEX.
JUST KIDDING.
YESSS!!
WINNER

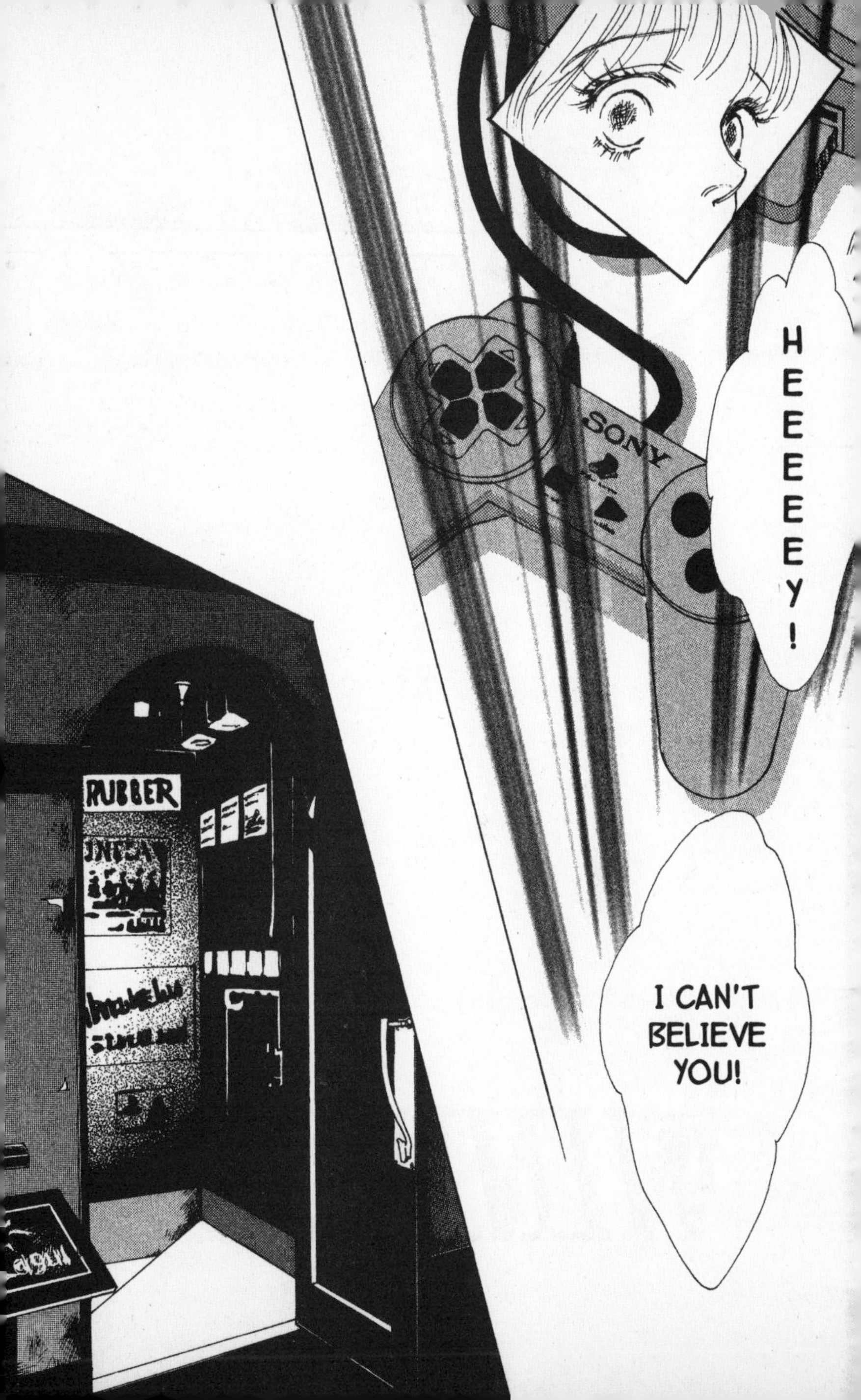
HEEEEEY!
I CAN'T BELIEVE YOU!
SONY
RUBBER

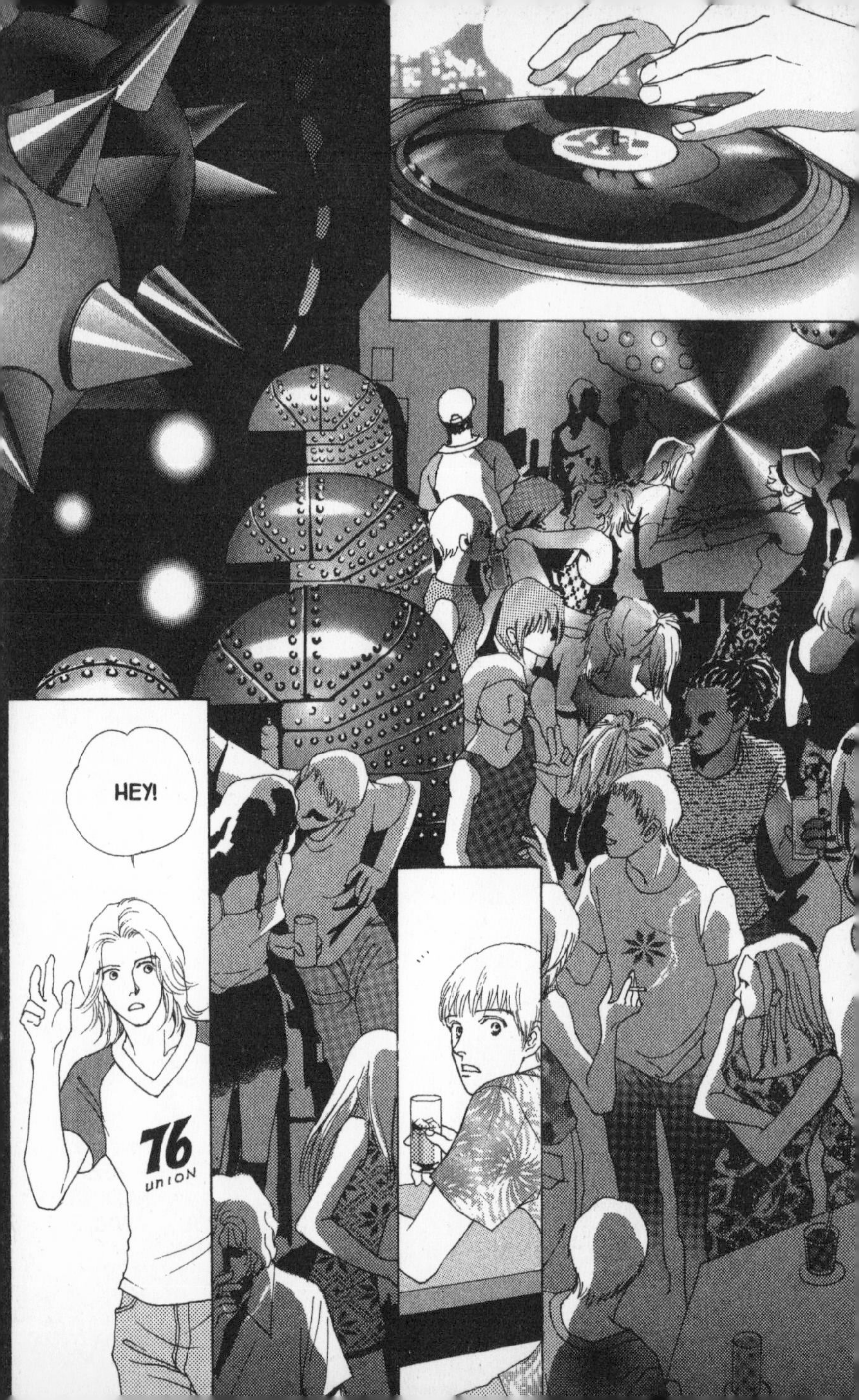
HEY!
...
76
union

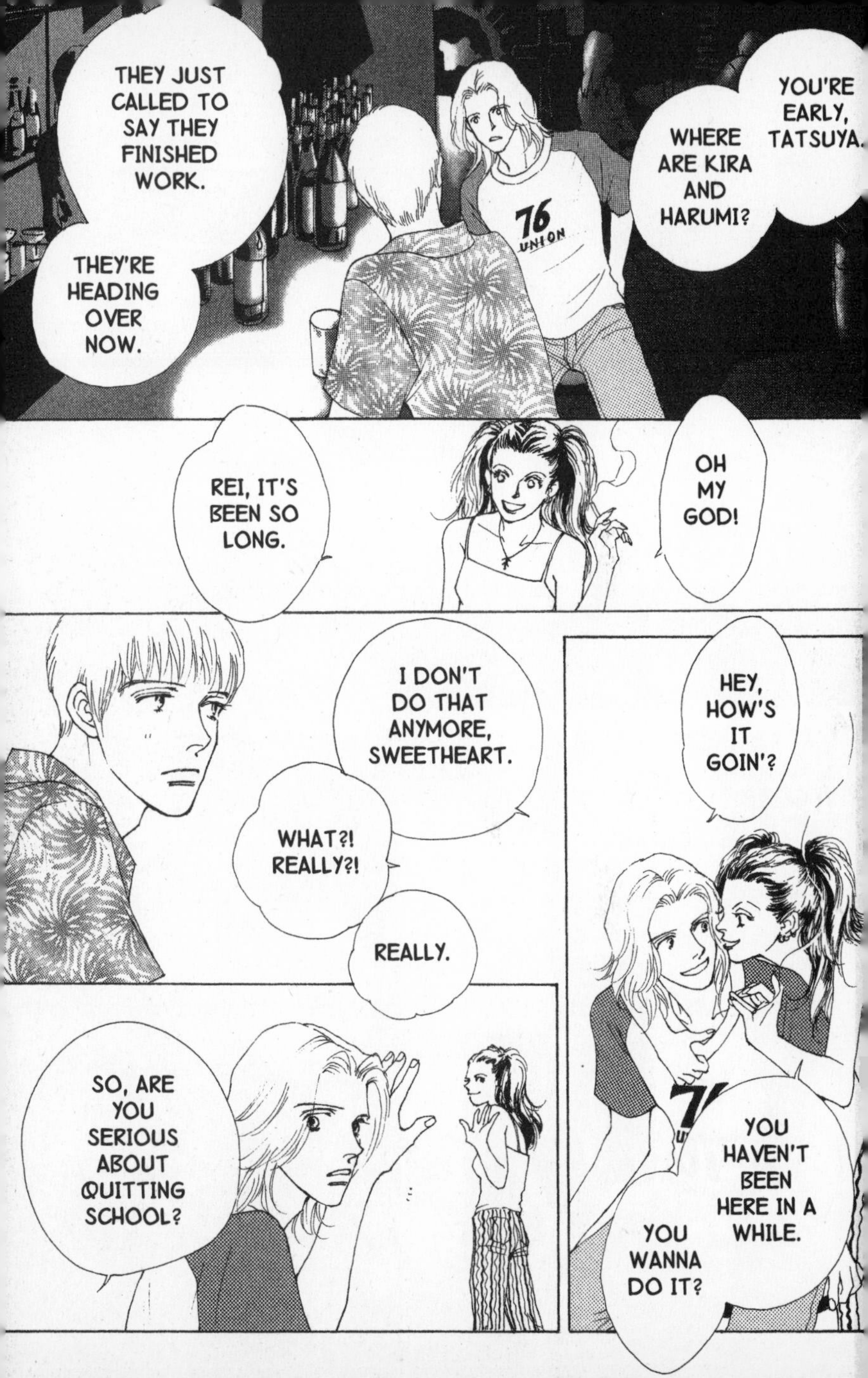
YOU'RE EARLY, TATSUYA.
WHERE ARE KIRA AND HARUMI?
THEY JUST CALLED TO SAY THEY FINISHED WORK.
THEY'RE HEADING OVER NOW.
76 UNION
OH MY GOD!
REI, IT'S BEEN SO LONG.
HEY, HOW'S IT GOIN'?
YOU HAVEN'T BEEN HERE IN A WHILE.
YOU WANNA DO IT?
I DON'T DO THAT ANYMORE, SWEETHEART.
WHAT?! REALLY?!
REALLY.
SO, ARE YOU SERIOUS ABOUT QUITTING SCHOOL?

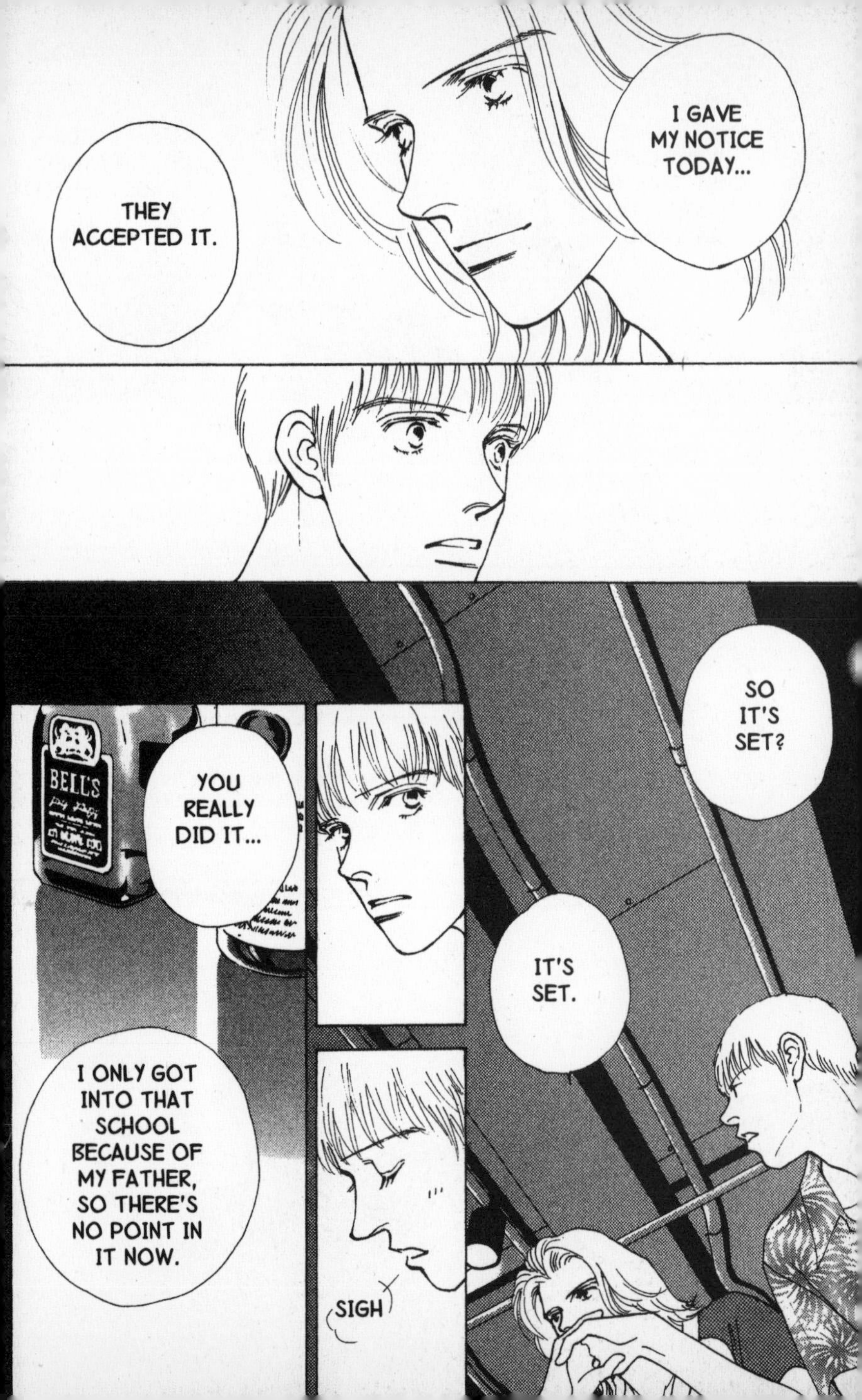
I GAVE MY NOTICE TODAY...
THEY ACCEPTED IT.
SO IT'S SET?
IT'S SET.
YOU REALLY DID IT...
I ONLY GOT INTO THAT SCHOOL BECAUSE OF MY FATHER, SO THERE'S NO POINT IN IT NOW.
SIGH

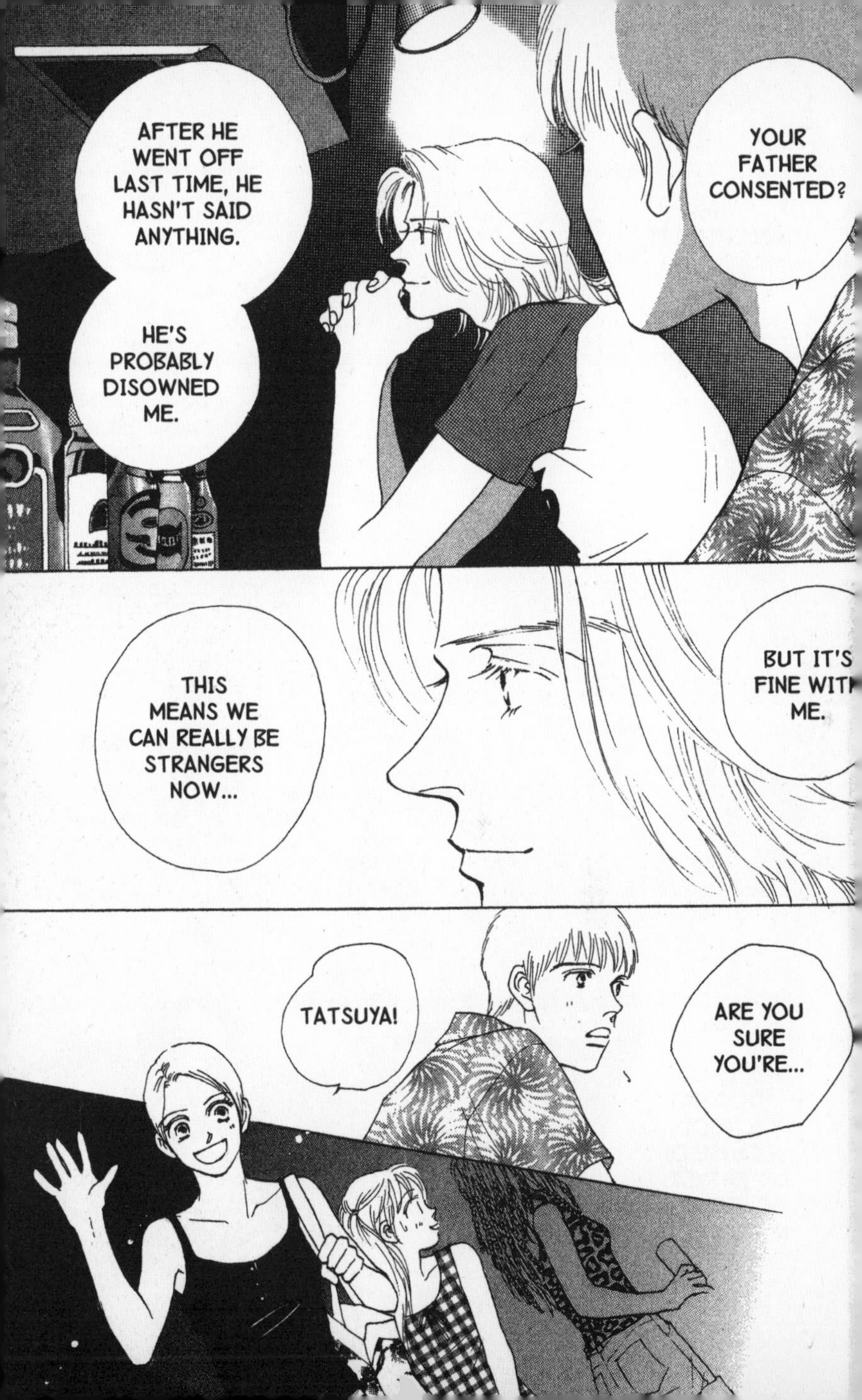
YOUR FATHER CONSENTED?
AFTER HE WENT OFF LAST TIME, HE HASN'T SAID ANYTHING.
HE'S PROBABLY DISOWNED ME.
BUT IT'S FINE WITH ME.
THIS MEANS WE CAN REALLY BE STRANGERS NOW...
ARE YOU SURE YOU'RE...
TATSUYA!

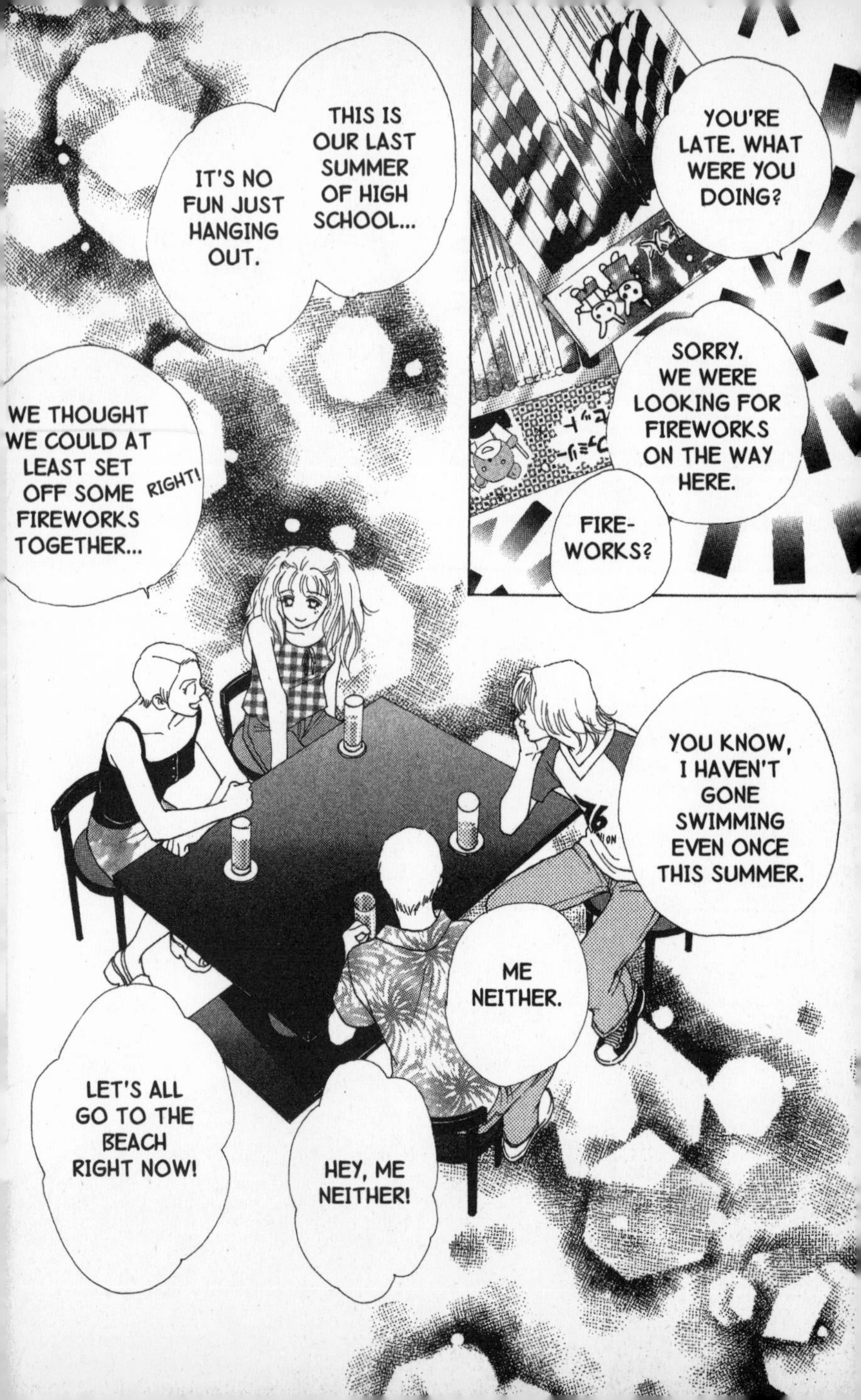
YOU'RE LATE. WHAT WERE YOU DOING?
SORRY. WE WERE LOOKING FOR FIREWORKS ON THE WAY HERE.
FIRE-WORKS?
THIS IS OUR LAST SUMMER OF HIGH SCHOOL...
IT'S NO FUN JUST HANGING OUT.
WE THOUGHT WE COULD AT LEAST SET OFF SOME FIREWORKS TOGETHER...
RIGHT!
YOU KNOW, I HAVEN'T GONE SWIMMING EVEN ONCE THIS SUMMER.
ME NEITHER.
HEY, ME NEITHER!
LET'S ALL GO TO THE BEACH RIGHT NOW!

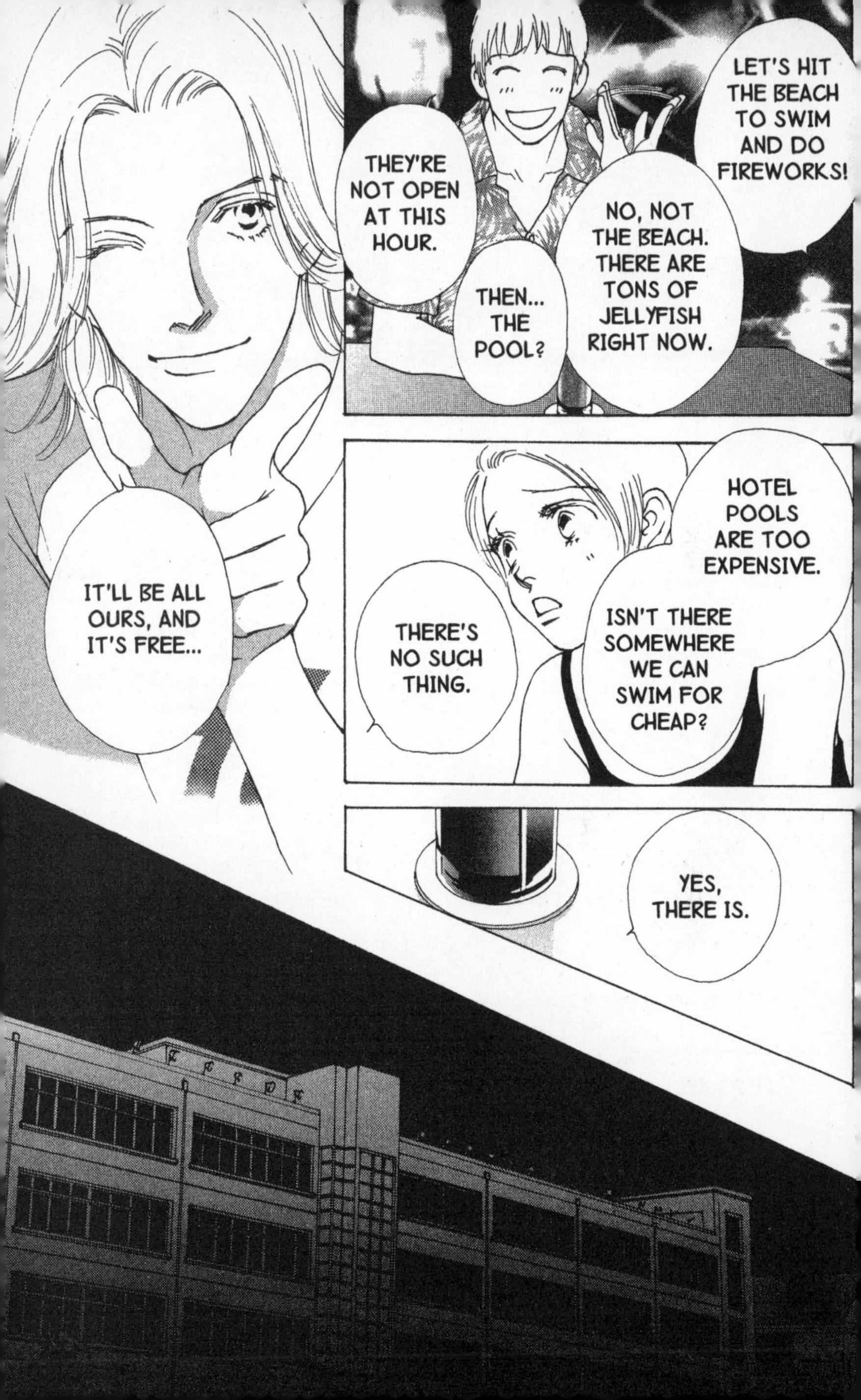
LET'S HIT THE BEACH TO SWIM AND DO FIREWORKS!
NO, NOT THE BEACH. THERE ARE TONS OF JELLYFISH RIGHT NOW.
THEN... THE POOL?
THEY'RE NOT OPEN AT THIS HOUR.
HOTEL POOLS ARE TOO EXPENSIVE.
ISN'T THERE SOMEWHERE WE CAN SWIM FOR CHEAP?
THERE'S NO SUCH THING.
YES, THERE IS.
IT'LL BE ALL OURS, AND IT'S FREE...

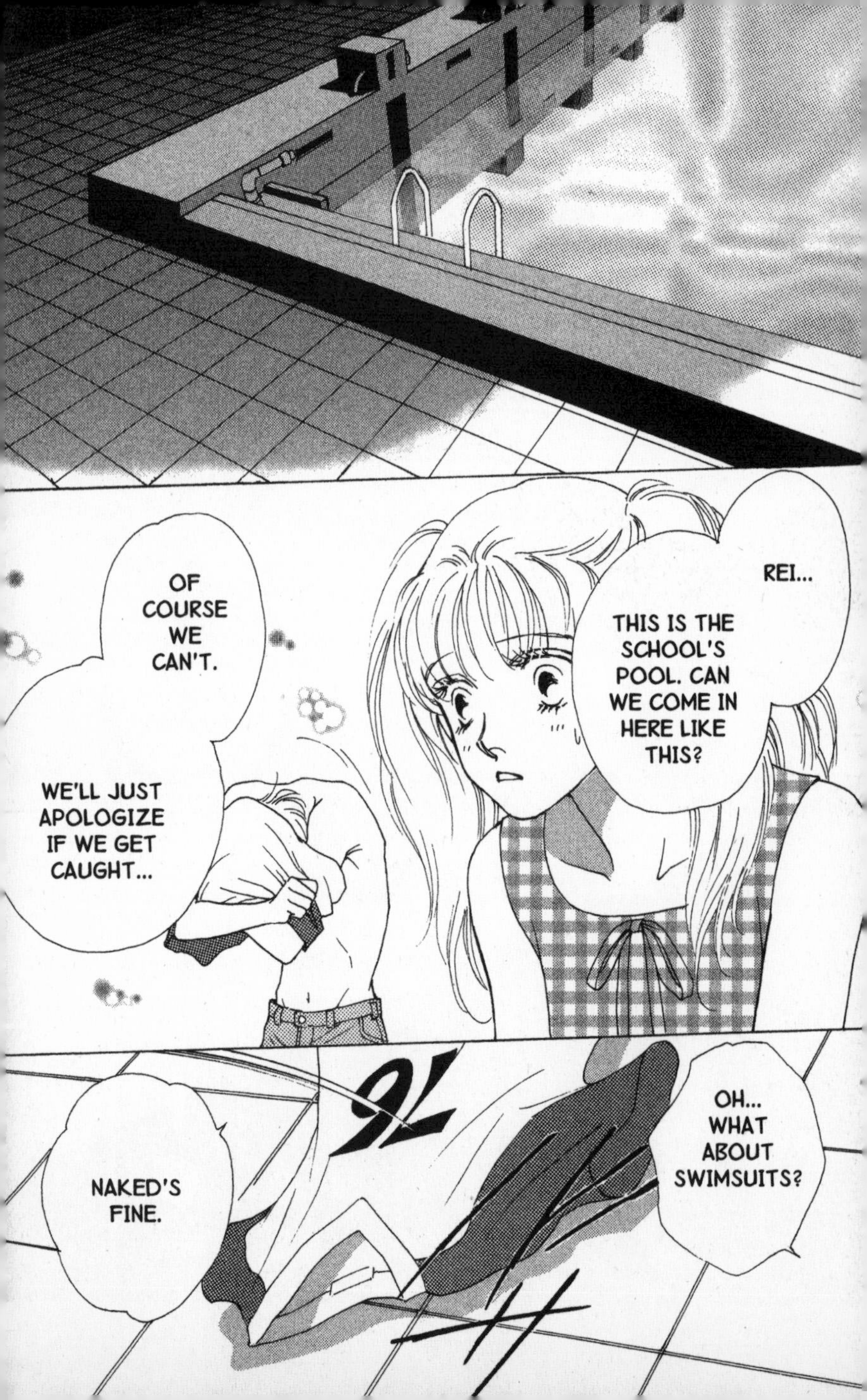
REI...
THIS IS THE SCHOOL'S POOL. CAN WE COME IN HERE LIKE THIS?
OF COURSE WE CAN'T.
WE'LL JUST APOLOGIZE IF WE GET CAUGHT...
OH... WHAT ABOUT SWIMSUITS?
NAKED'S FINE.

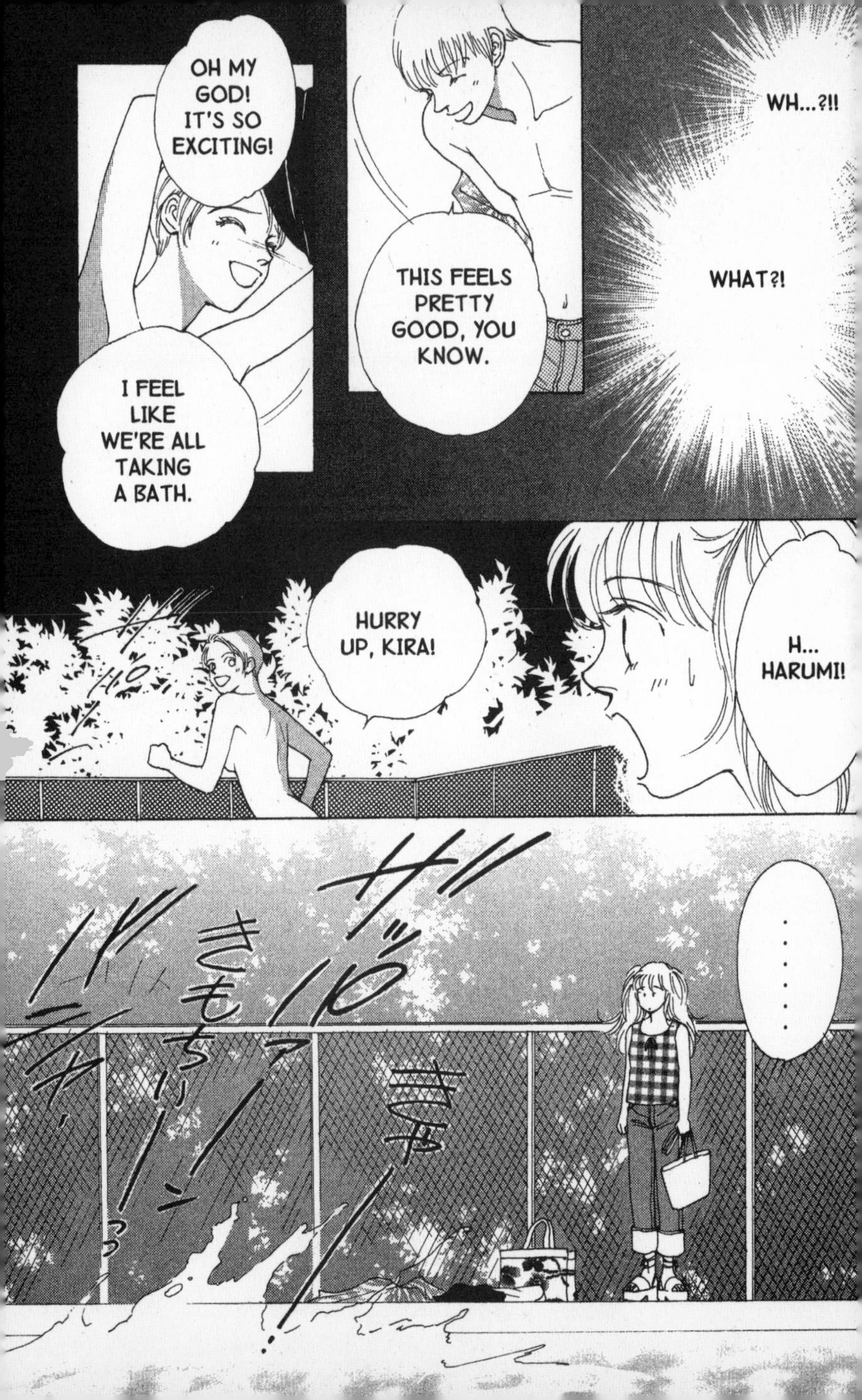
WH...?!!
WHAT?!
THIS FEELS PRETTY GOOD, YOU KNOW.
OH MY GOD! IT'S SO EXCITING!
I FEEL LIKE WE'RE ALL TAKING A BATH.
H... HARUMI!
HURRY UP, KIRA!
......

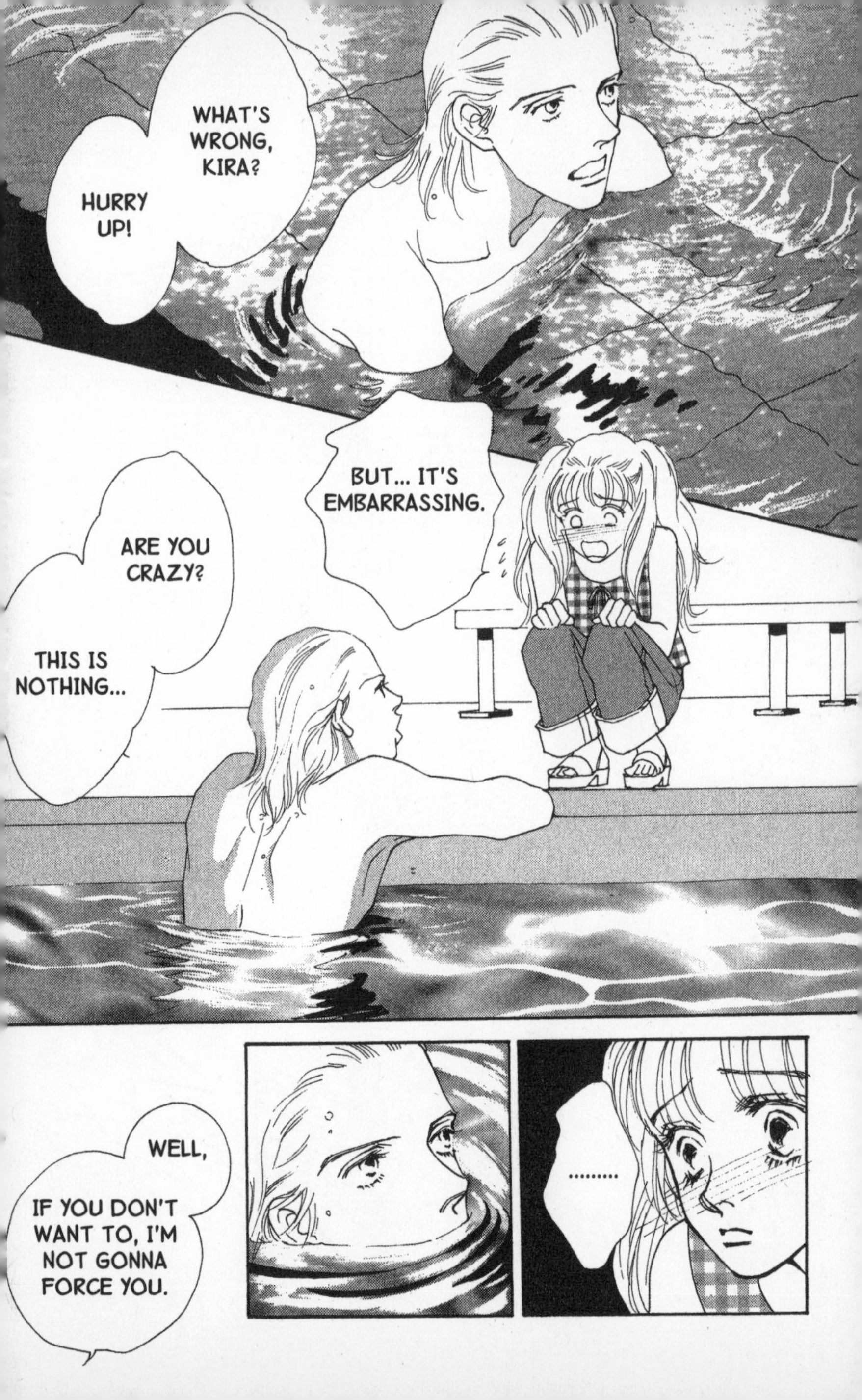
WHAT'S WRONG, KIRA?
HURRY UP!
BUT... IT'S EMBARRASSING.
ARE YOU CRAZY?
THIS IS NOTHING...
....
WELL,
IF YOU DON'T WANT TO, I'M NOT GONNA FORCE YOU.

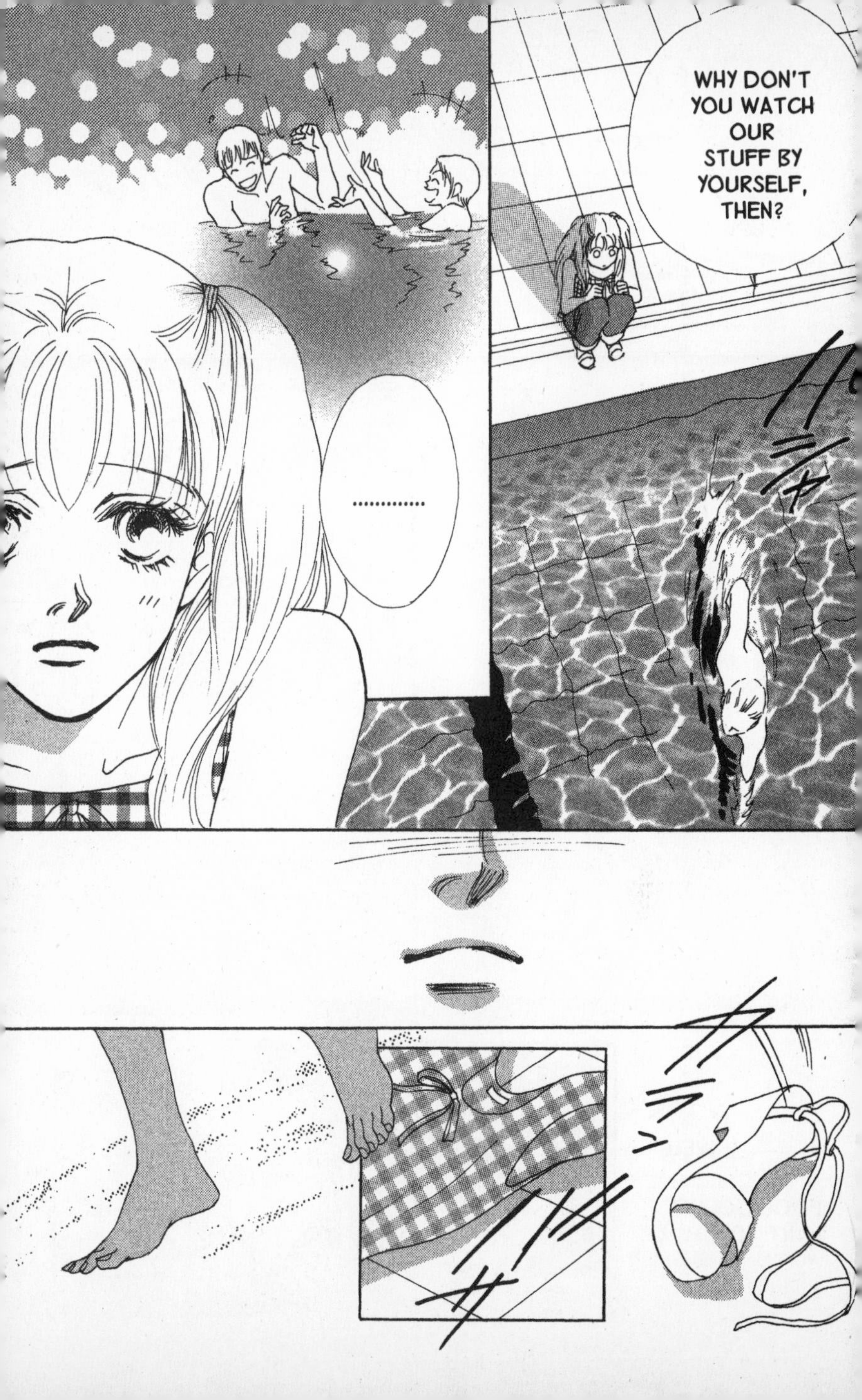
WHY DON'T YOU WATCH OUR STUFF BY YOURSELF, THEN?
....

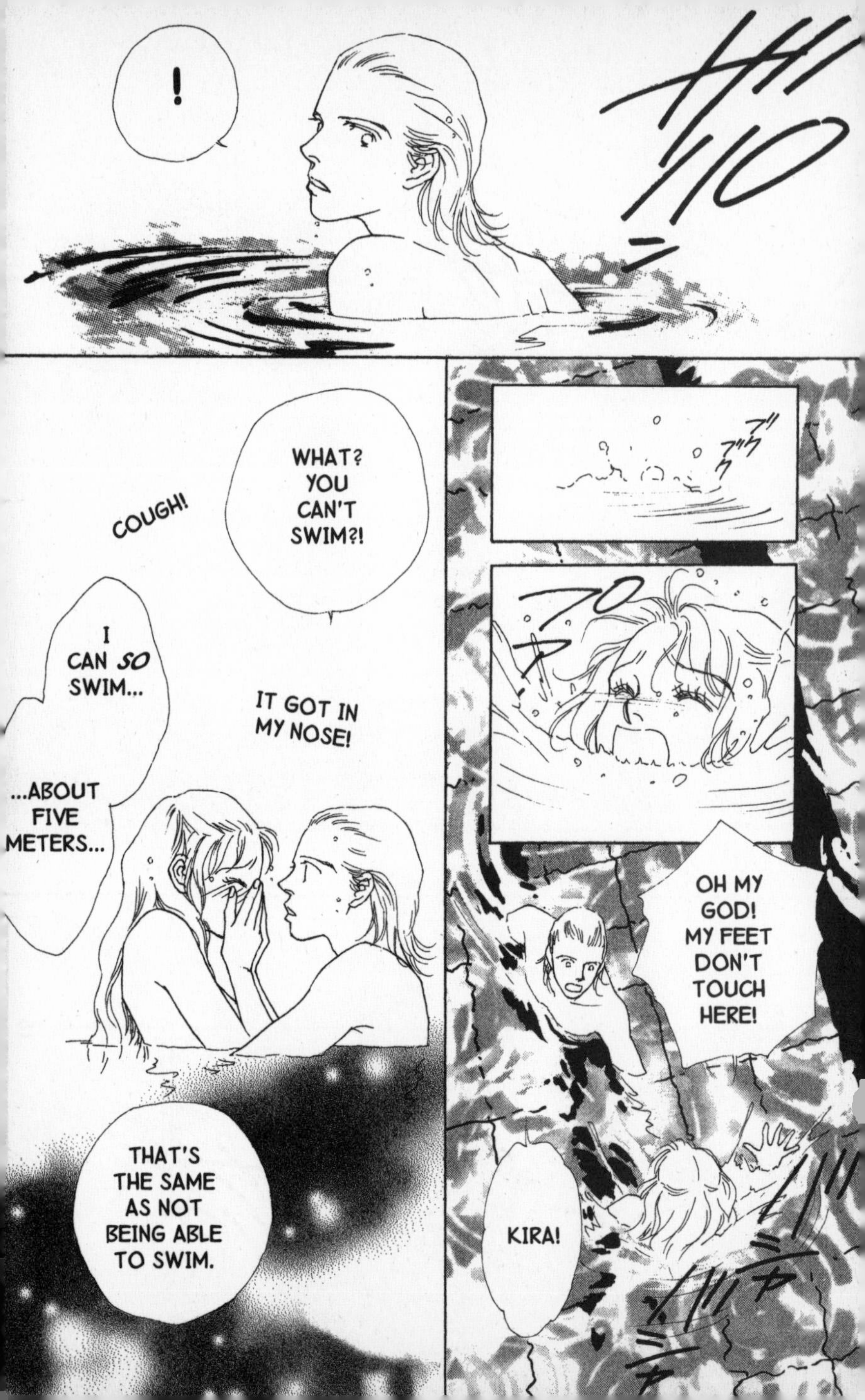
!
OH MY GOD! MY FEET DON'T TOUCH HERE!
KIRA!
WHAT? YOU CAN'T SWIM?!
COUGH!
IT GOT IN MY NOSE!
I CAN SO SWIM...
...ABOUT FIVE METERS...
THAT'S THE SAME AS NOT BEING ABLE TO SWIM.

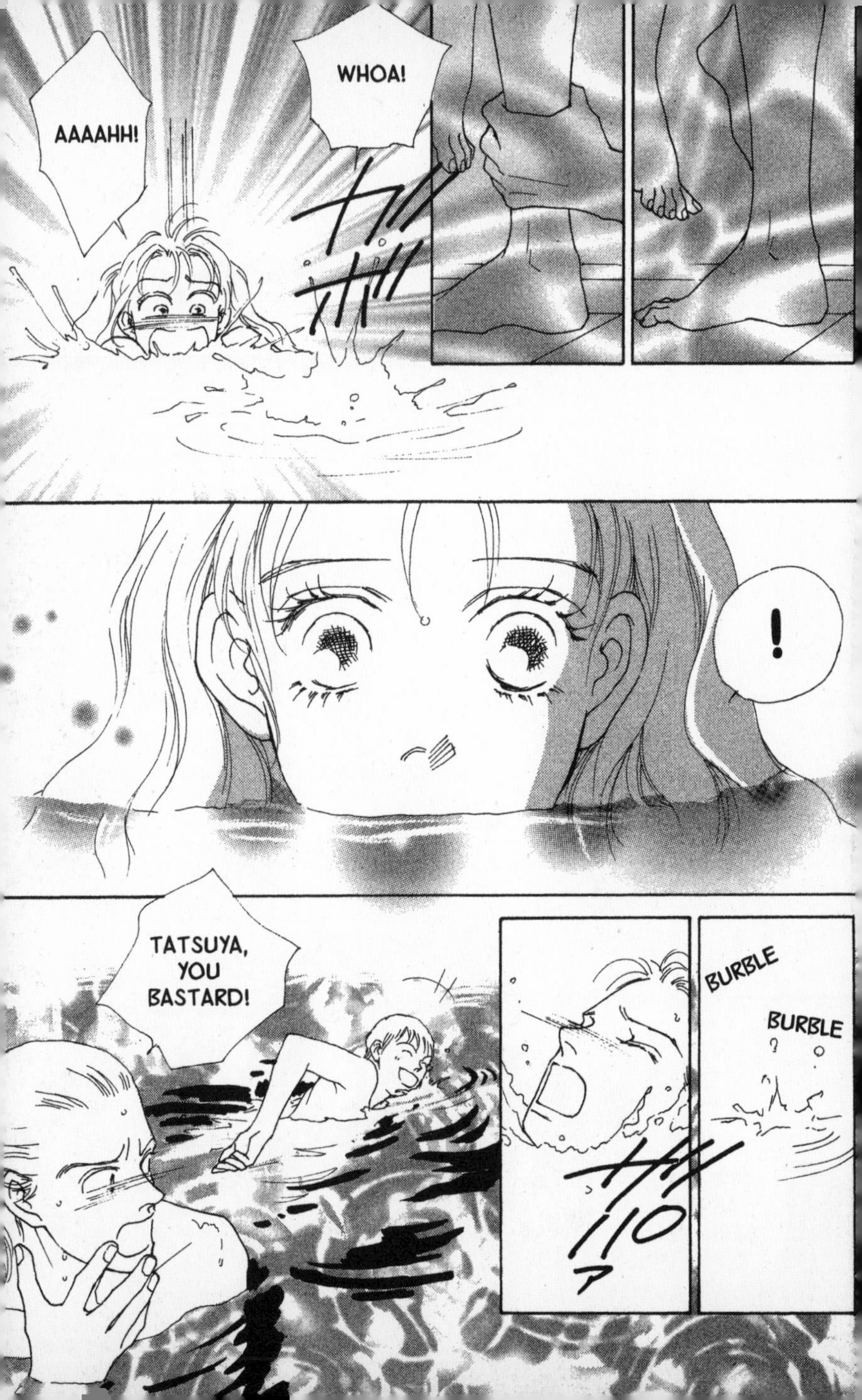
WHOA!
AAAAHH!
!
BURBLE
BURBLE
TATSUYA, YOU BASTARD!

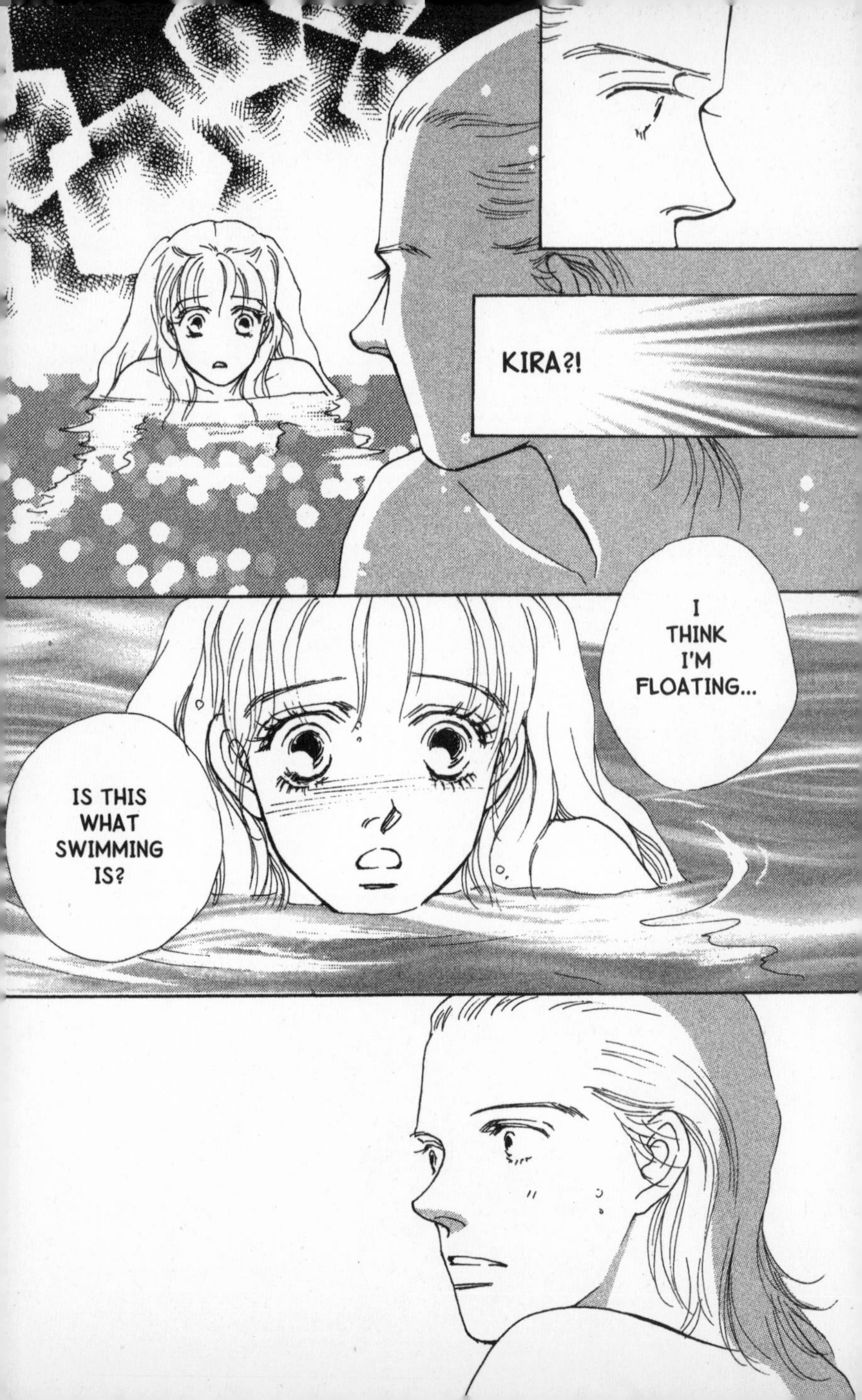
KIRA?!
I THINK I'M FLOATING...
IS THIS WHAT SWIMMING IS?

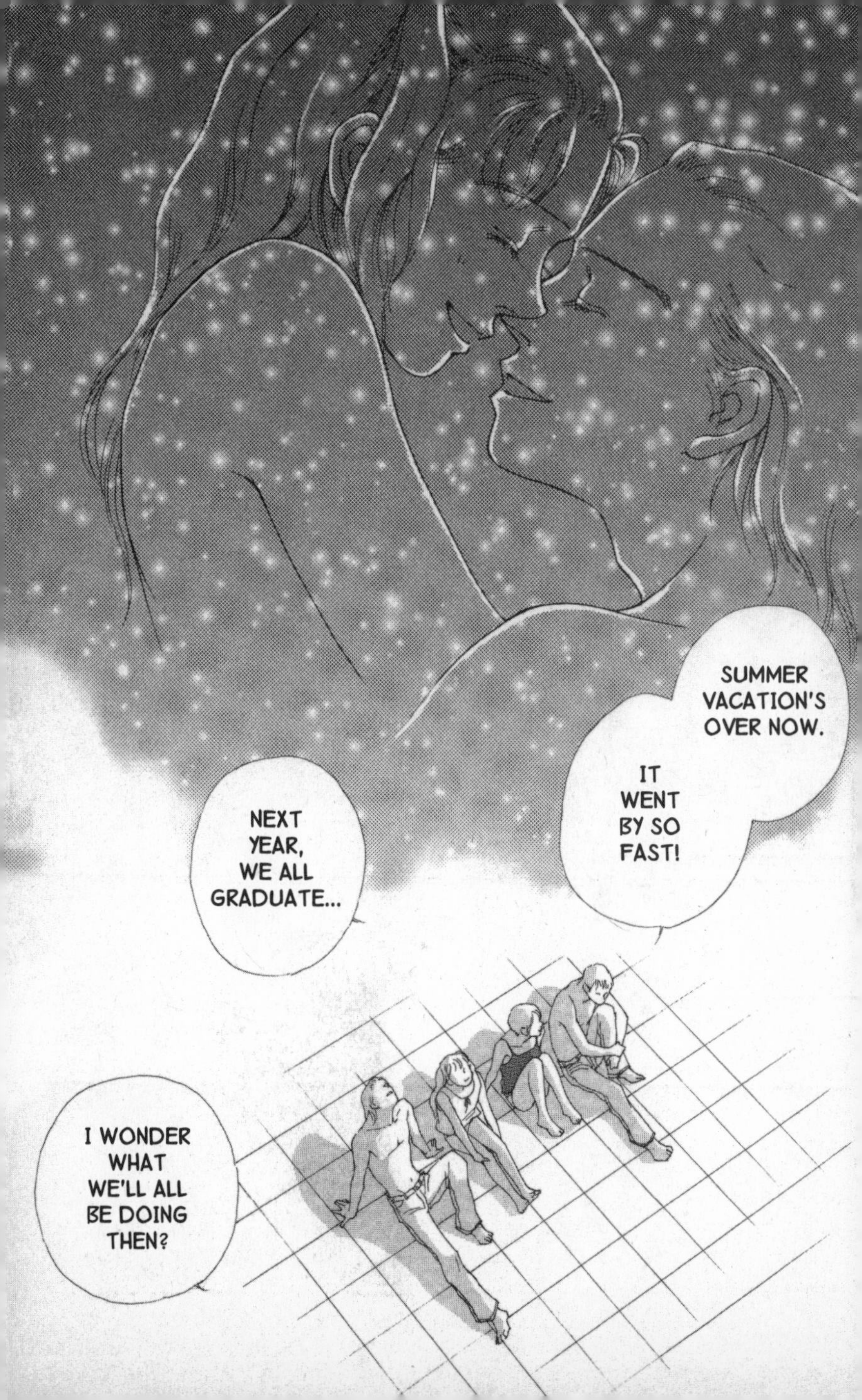
SUMMER VACATION'S OVER NOW.
IT WENT BY SO FAST!
NEXT YEAR, WE ALL GRADUATE...
I WONDER WHAT WE'LL ALL BE DOING THEN?

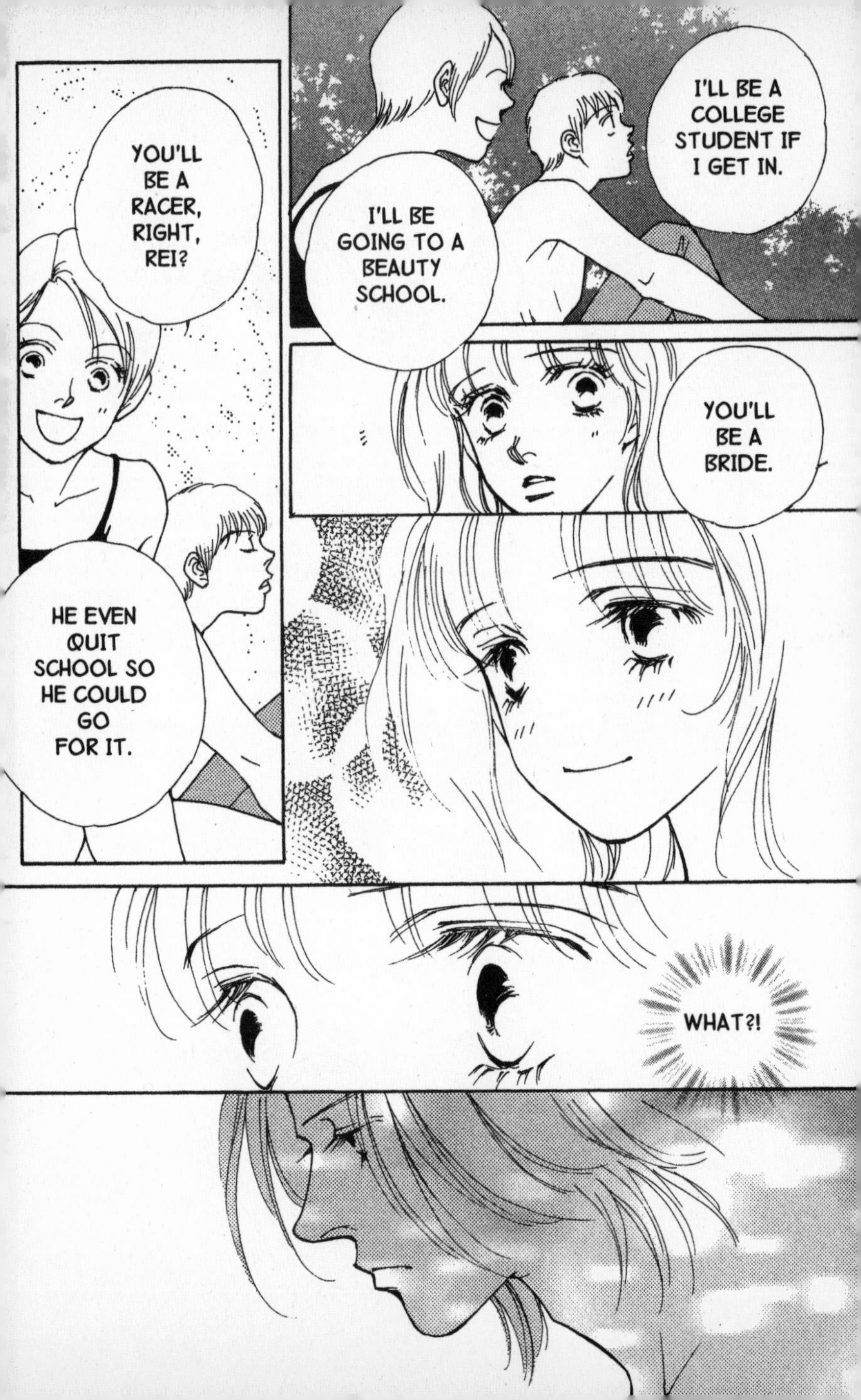
I'LL BE A COLLEGE STUDENT IF I GET IN.
I'LL BE GOING TO A BEAUTY SCHOOL.
YOU'LL BE A BRIDE.
YOU'LL BE A RACER, RIGHT, REI?
HE EVEN QUIT SCHOOL SO HE COULD GO FOR IT.
WHAT?!

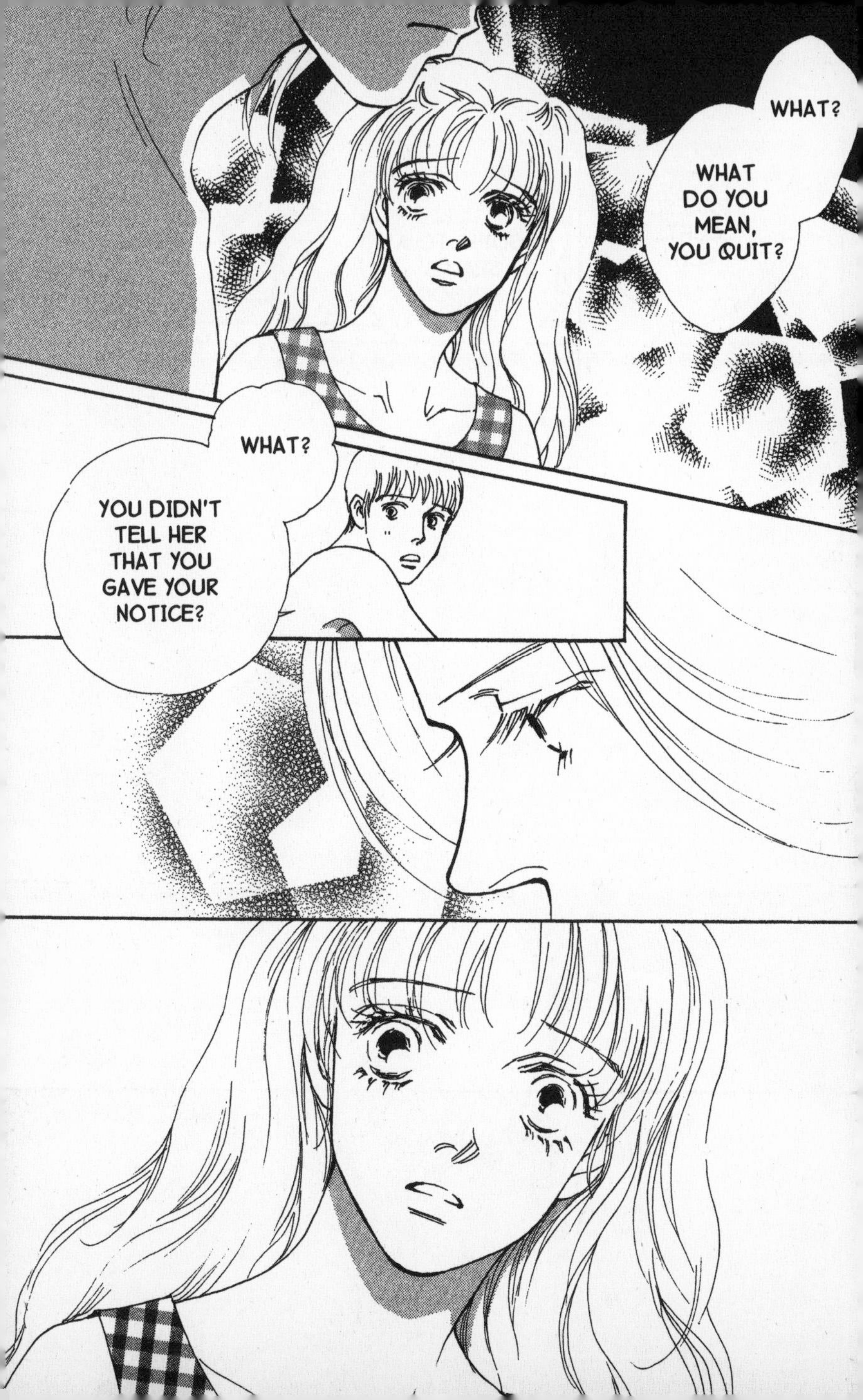
WHAT?
WHAT DO YOU MEAN, YOU QUIT?
WHAT?
YOU DIDN'T TELL HER THAT YOU GAVE YOUR NOTICE?

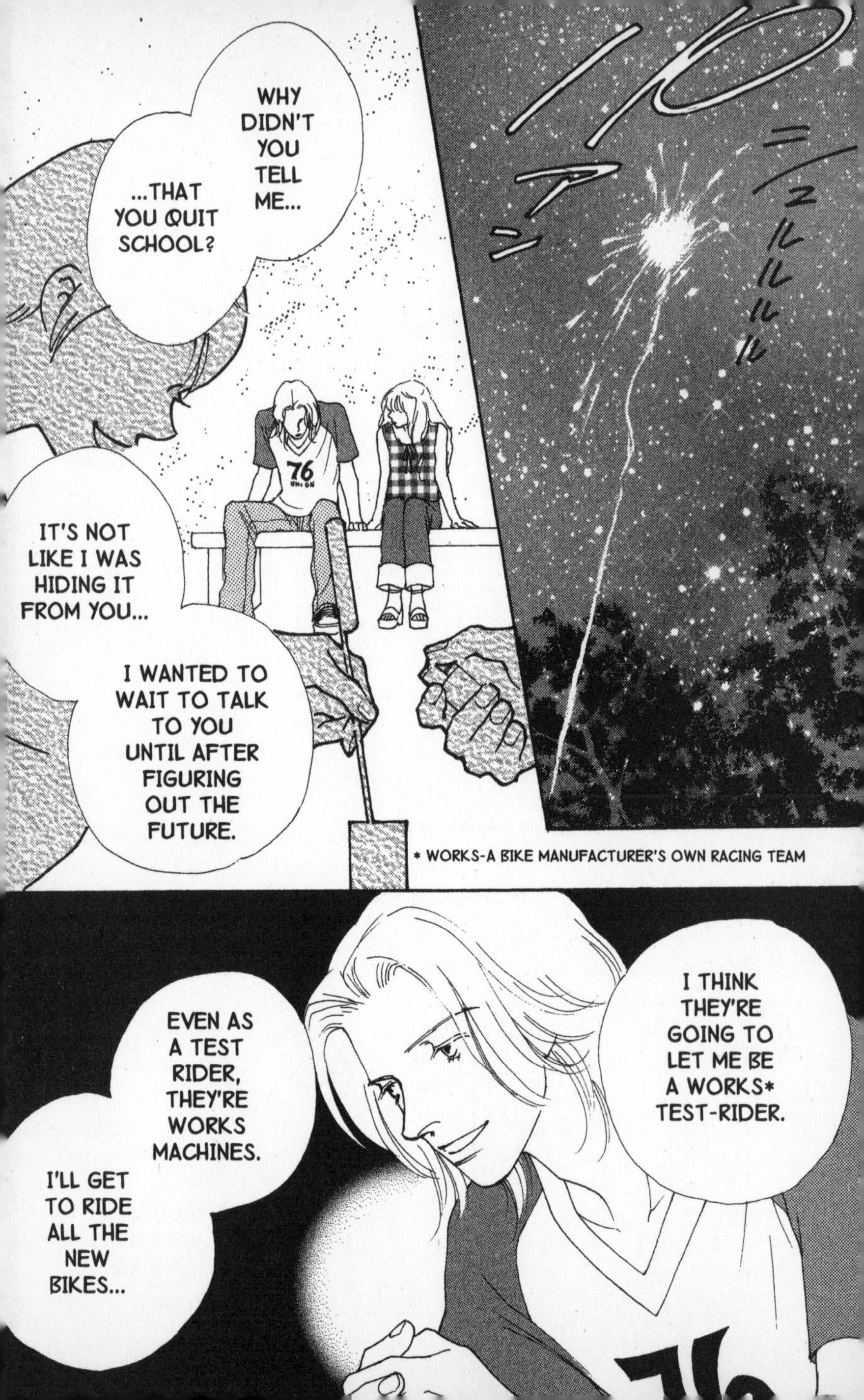
WHY DIDN'T YOU TELL ME...
...THAT YOU QUIT SCHOOL?
IT'S NOT LIKE I WAS HIDING IT FROM YOU...
I WANTED TO WAIT TO TALK TO YOU UNTIL AFTER FIGURING OUT THE FUTURE.
* WORKS-A BIKE MANUFACTURER'S OWN RACING TEAM
I THINK THEY'RE GOING TO LET ME BE A WORKS* TEST-RIDER.
EVEN AS A TEST RIDER, THEY'RE WORKS MACHINES.
I'LL GET TO RIDE ALL THE NEW BIKES...

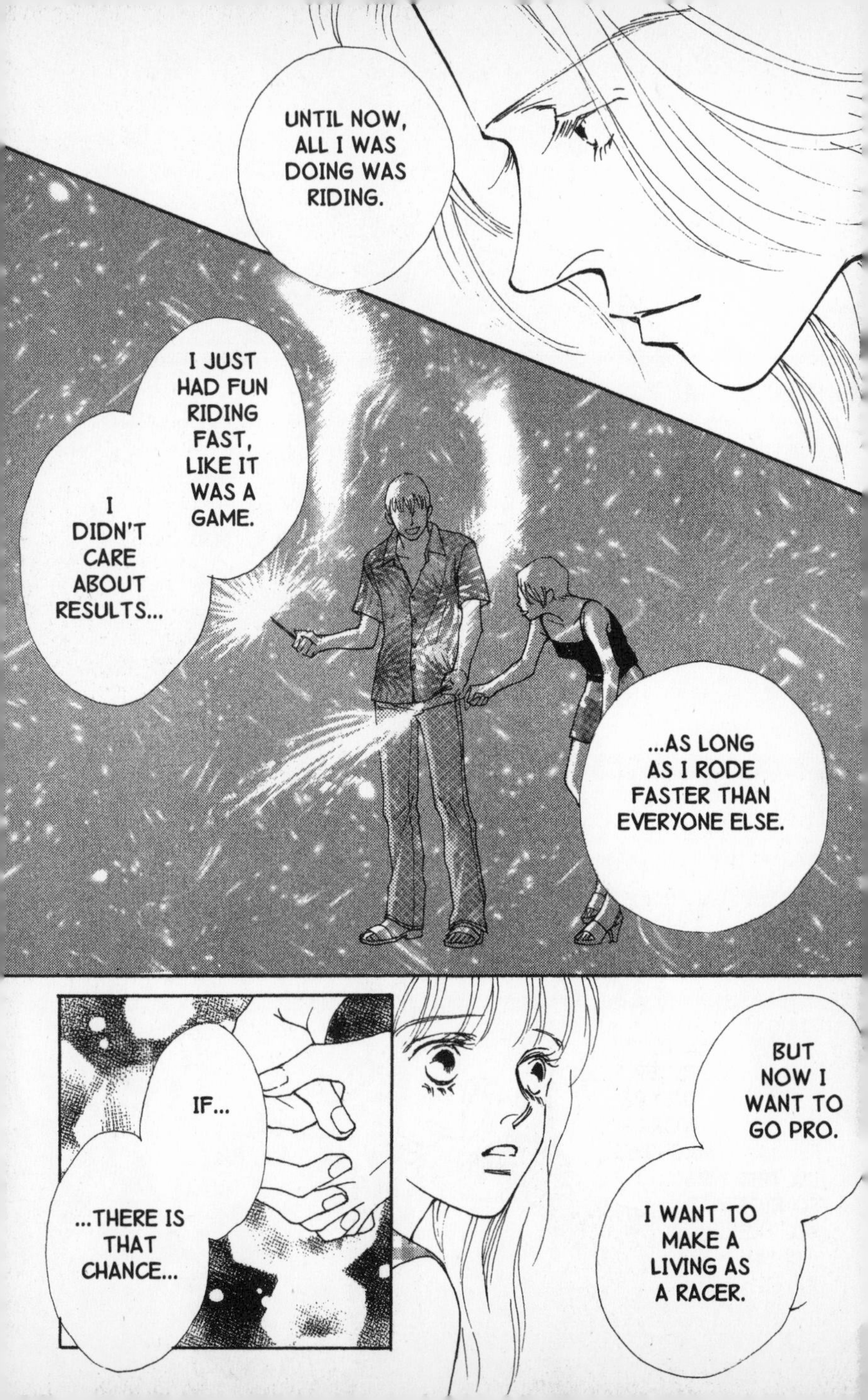
UNTIL NOW, ALL I WAS DOING WAS RIDING.
I JUST HAD FUN RIDING FAST, LIKE IT WAS A GAME.
I DIDN'T CARE ABOUT RESULTS...
...AS LONG AS I RODE FASTER THAN EVERYONE ELSE.
BUT NOW I WANT TO GO PRO.
I WANT TO MAKE A LIVING AS A RACER.
IF...
...THERE IS THAT CHANCE...

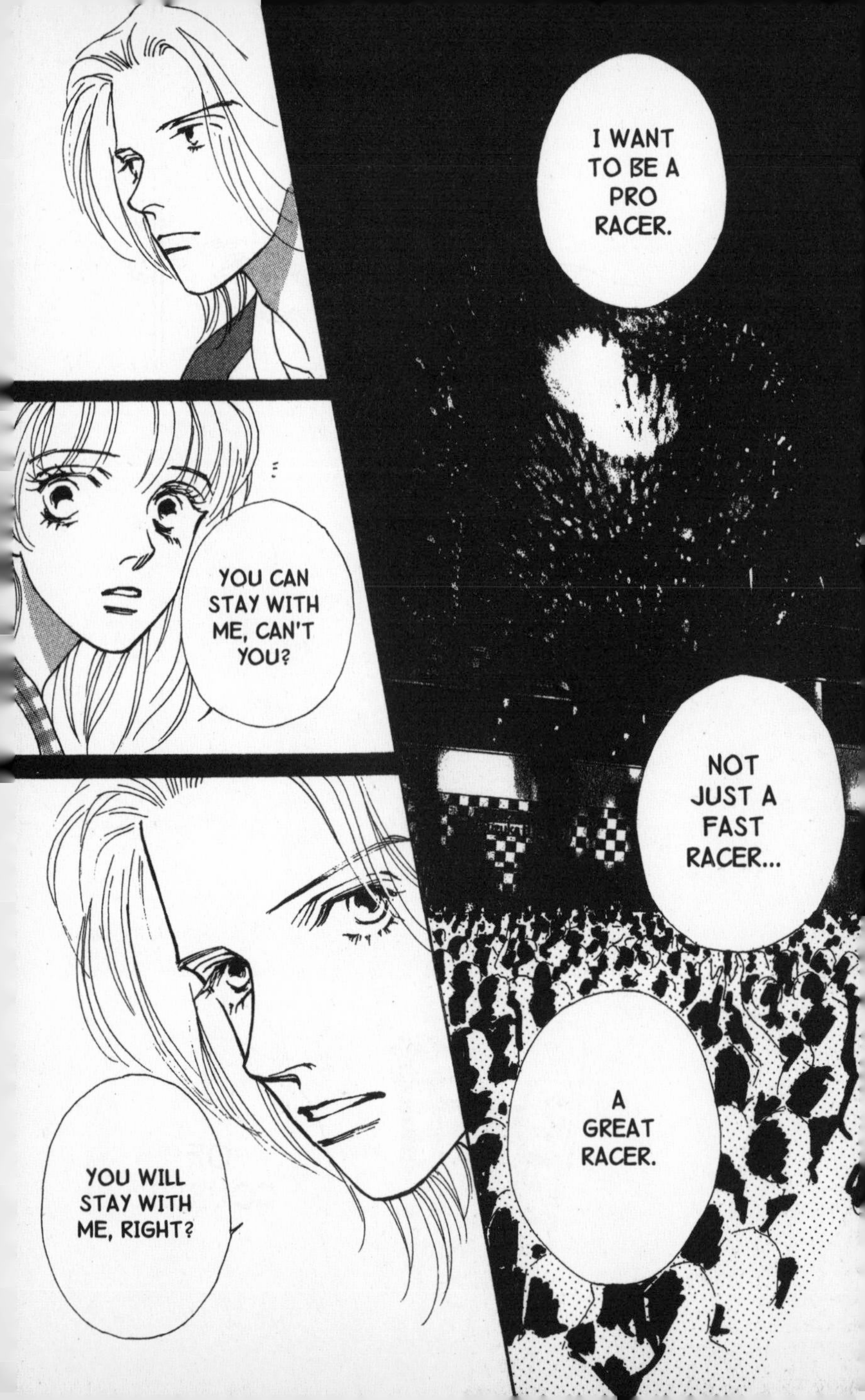
I WANT TO BE A PRO RACER.
NOT JUST A FAST RACER...
A GREAT RACER.
YOU CAN STAY WITH ME, CAN'T YOU?
YOU WILL STAY WITH ME, RIGHT?

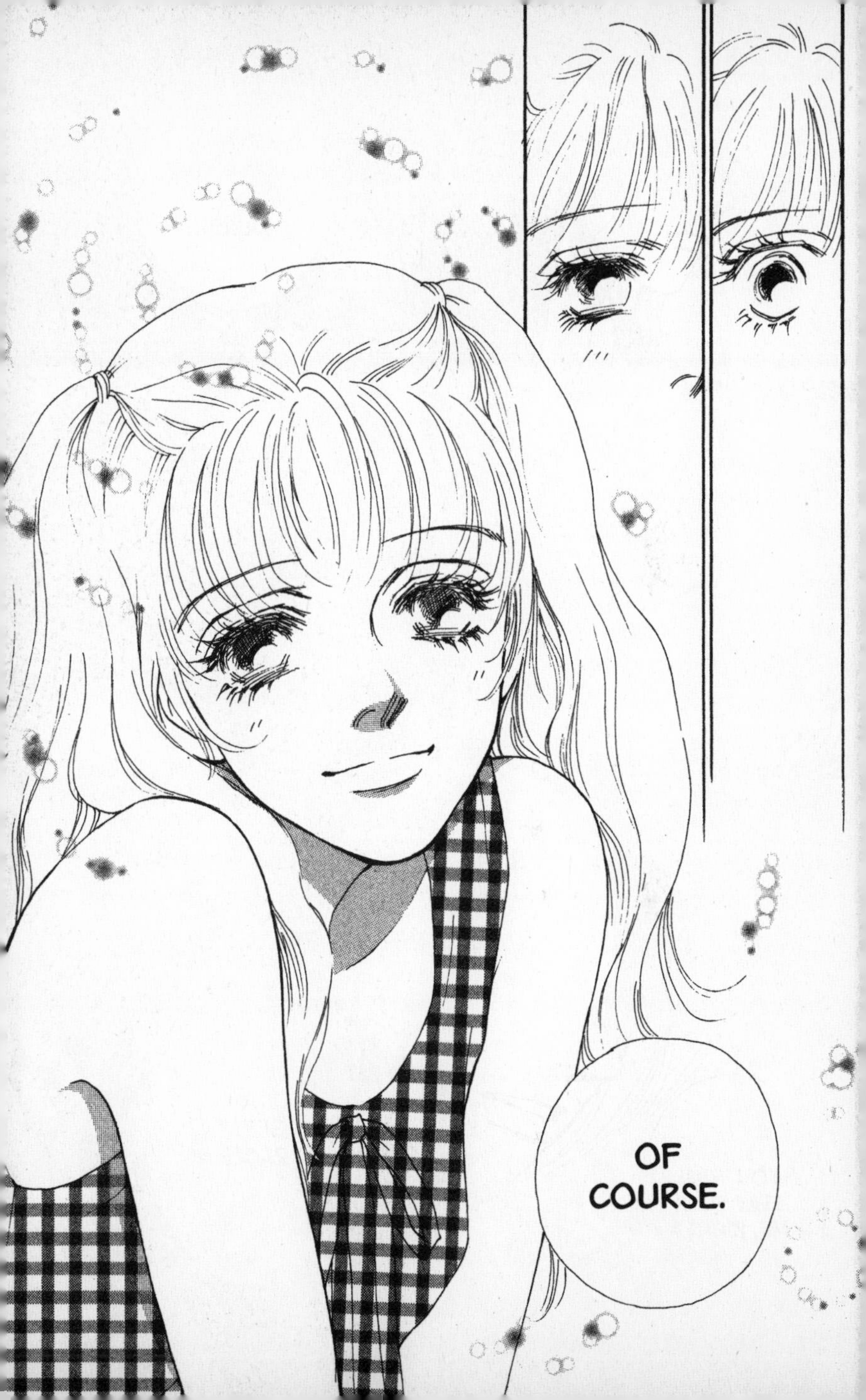
OF COURSE.

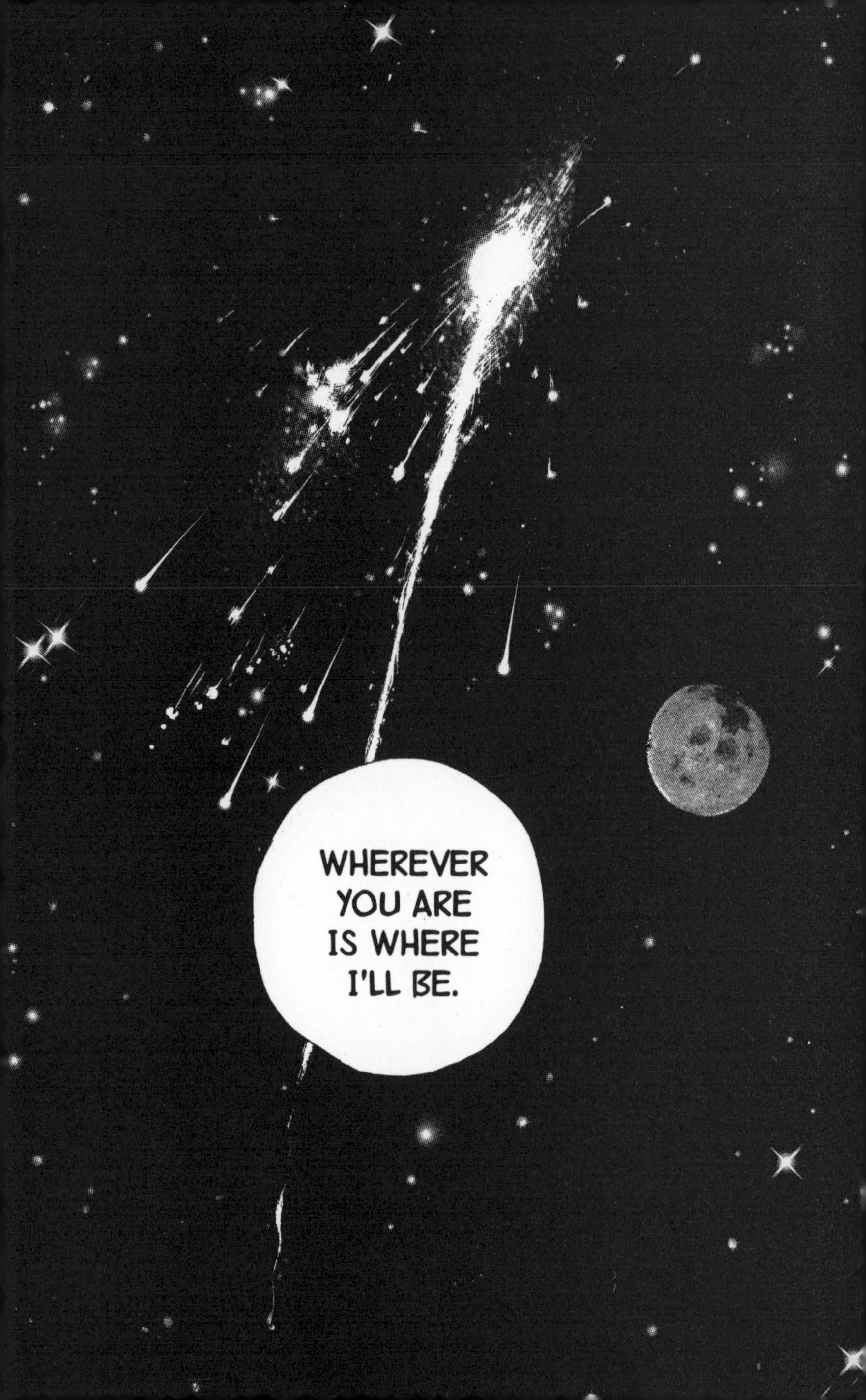
WHEREVER YOU ARE IS WHERE I'LL BE.

MARS

Coming Soon...

Volume Eleven

Rei and Kira's love for each other couldn't be stronger. But in the world they live in, love isn't always enough. When Rei drops out of school, he focuses on his dreams of becoming a professional motorcycle racer. However, those dreams are threatened when Kira's creepy stepfather re-enters the picture and attempts to sabotage Kira and Rei's serious plans for a future together. When Kira's stepfather relentlessly campaigns for Kira's acceptance, Rei is forced to turn to the last person in the world he would ever ask for help: his father. Can Kira and Rei's love overcome these obstacles?

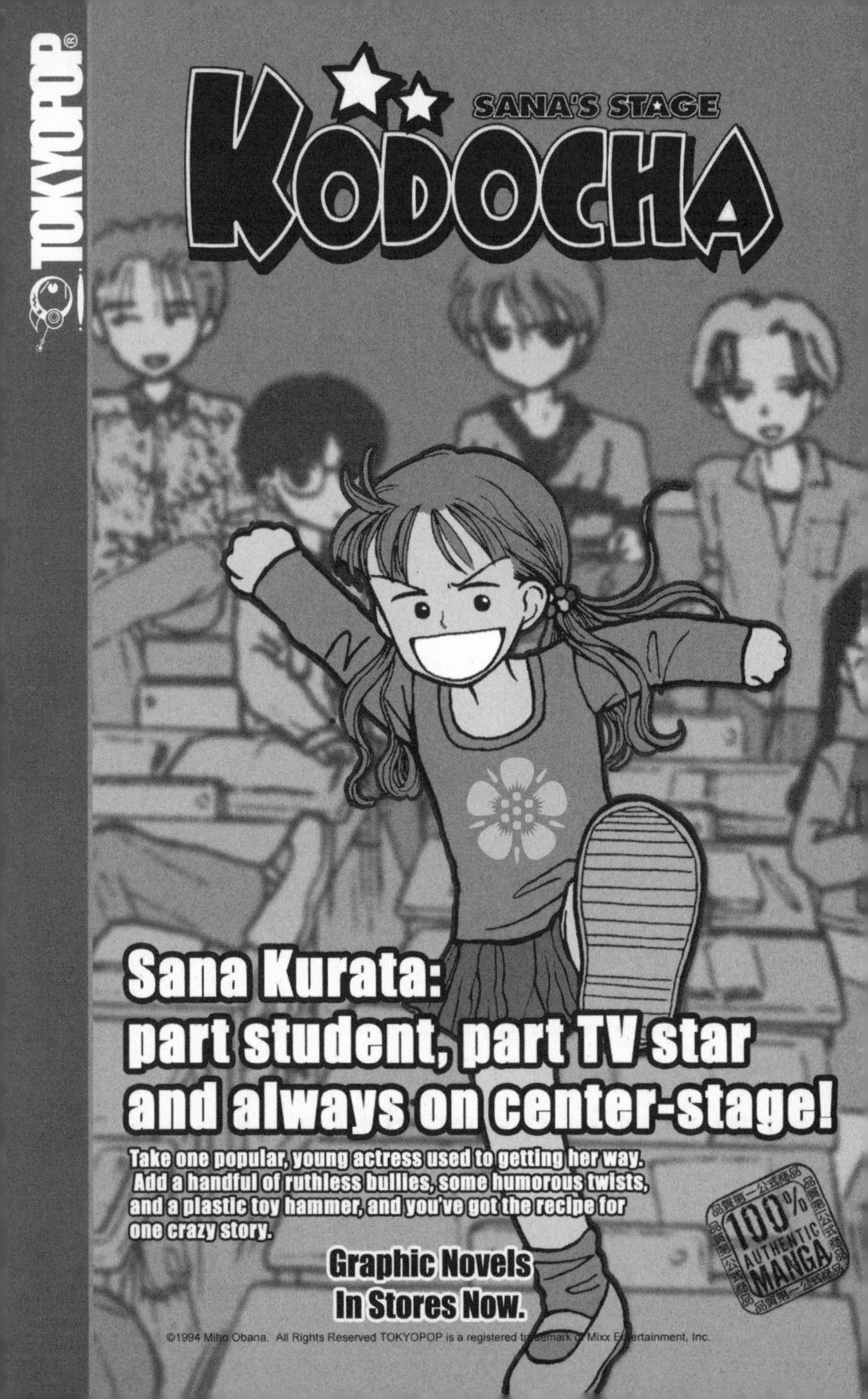
TOKYOPOP®
KODOCHA
SANA'S STAGE
Sana Kurata:
part student, part TV star
and always on center-stage!
Take one popular, young actress used to getting her way.
Add a handful of ruthless bullies, some humorous twists,
and a plastic toy hammer, and you've got the recipe for
one crazy story.
100% AUTHENTIC MANGA
Graphic Novels
In Stores Now.
©1994 Miho Obana. All Rights Reserved TOKYOPOP is a registered trademark of Mixx Entertainment, Inc.

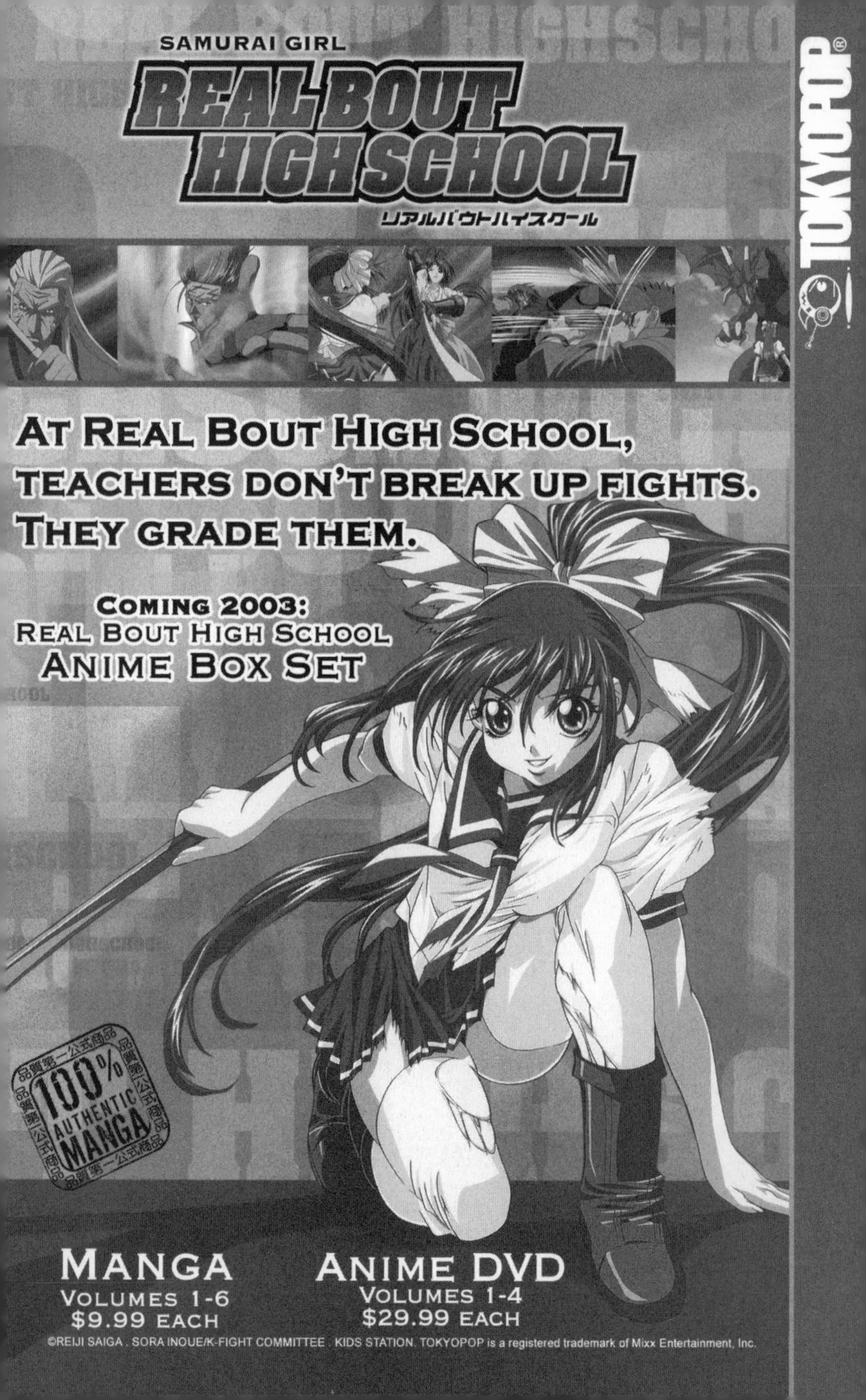
SAMURAI GIRL
REAL BOUT HIGH SCHOOL
リアルバウトハイスクール
TOKYOPOP®
AT REAL BOUT HIGH SCHOOL, TEACHERS DON'T BREAK UP FIGHTS. THEY GRADE THEM.
COMING 2003:
REAL BOUT HIGH SCHOOL ANIME BOX SET
100% AUTHENTIC MANGA
MANGA
VOLUMES 1-6
$9.99 EACH
ANIME DVD
VOLUMES 1-4
$29.99 EACH
©REIJI SAIGA . SORA INOUE/K-FIGHT COMMITTEE . KIDS STATION. TOKYOPOP is a registered trademark of Mixx Entertainment, Inc.

STOP!

This is the back of the book.
You wouldn't want to spoil a great ending!

This book is printed "manga-style," in the authentic Japanese right-to-left format. Since none of the artwork has been flipped or altered, readers get to experience the story just as the creator intended. You've been asking for it, so TOKYOPOP® delivered: authentic, hot-off-the-press, and far more fun!

DIRECTIONS

If this is your first time reading manga-style, here's a quick guide to help you understand how it works.

It's easy... just start in the top right panel and follow the numbers. Have fun, and look for more 100% authentic manga from TOKYOPOP®!